MURDER *On Tape*

A Comprehensive Guide to Murder and Mystery on Video

Ted Sennett

BillboardBooks
An imprint of Watson-Guptill Publications
New York

For my granddaughter, Katie, the newest blessing in my life

Senior Editor: Bob Nirkind
Editor: Amy Handy
Book and cover design: Jay Anning
Cover illustration: Owen Smith
Production manager: Hector Campbell

Copyright © 1997 by Ted Sennett
First published in 1997 by Billboard Books,
an imprint of Watson-Guptill Publications,
a division of BPI Communications, Inc.
1515 Broadway, New York, NY 10036

Library of Congress Cataloging-in-Publication Data

Sennett, Ted
     Murder on tape / Ted Sennett.
       p.   cm.
     ISBN 0-8230-8335-7
     1. Murder in motion pictures.   2. Detective and mystery films—
Catalogs.   3. Gangster films—Catalogs.   4. Video recordings—
Catalogs. I. Title.
PN1995.9.D4S42   1997
791.43'655—dc21
                                    97-15711
                                        CIP

INTRODUCTION

On a moonless evening in San Francisco, without a soul in sight, a car careens recklessly over the fabled hills, another car in hot pursuit. In a sleazy hotel room, with the hotel's neon sign flickering in the background, a no-good dame pumps bullets into her wayward lover. In a deserted warehouse, two rival gangs engage in a blood-drenched shootout, and the blood almost seeps through the walls.

Welcome to the movie world of crime and punishment, featuring murder, mayhem, and skulduggery. A world populated with flashy mobsters, cops both corrupt and straight-arrow, calculating killers from every walk of life, debonair thieves, and many others who are devious, despicable, or deranged. Nor should we forget the alluring, tough-as-nails ladies who exude danger and trouble in everything they say or do.

It's a grim world, certainly, a disturbing view deep within the darkest side of human endeavor. Its inhabitants will kill you for a bankroll, a jewel-encrusted statue, a perceived insult, or a chance at revenge. It's a world in which the violence quotient has increased measurably over the years, so that every heinous crime can be shown on screen, in sordid detail. (More about that in a moment.)

From the early days of film to the present, audiences have been fascinated by movies that deal with crime and punishment. From D. W. Griffith's *Musketeers of Pig Alley* (1912), which showed gangsters at large in the streets of New York City, to recent films such as *Donnie Brasco* (1997), the workings of the criminal underworld have been grist for the movie mill. In every decade of motion pictures, there has been no shortage of mystery tales, revenge thrillers, prison and courtroom dramas, crime-based comedies, and, of course, the film noir, past and present.* Those who are repelled by

such dark doings can always turn them off or turn to Shirley Temple or Doris Day. For most moviegoers and videotape watchers, however, viewing films on crime and punishment—especially everybody's favorite crime of murder—can be an enthralling experience.

My book is intended as a guide to this experience, a critical overview of more than one thousand films, from the early years of sound to the present, that deal with such all-too-human activities as thievery, retribution, treachery, lust, and murder. All available on videotape, these movies range widely across every subgenre: gangster films from *Scarface* to *GoodFellas*, noir thrillers from *Double Indemnity* to *Blood and Wine*, prison dramas from *The Last Mile* to *The Shawshank Redemption*, and many others. In these pages, from the safe distance of a theater or your living room, you will meet an assortment of killers, thieves, convicts, police officers, detectives, and other law-and-disorder types of whom the moviegoing public never tires.

After a steady diet of these films, both old and new, viewed over many months, it is not difficult to conclude that the level of graphic violence has accelerated in recent years. There seems to be no murderous act, no form of human brutality, that cannot be shown on the screen in gory detail. Inevitably the question arises: when can the level of violence in any film be considered excessive or intolerable? Many articles have been written in response to that question, and generally the answer is that the level of acceptable violence depends on its absolute relevance to the story.

In fact, this response is rather glib, and watching many recent films has led me to the conclusion that other factors must be considered in determining the acceptable level of violence. The brutal acts depicted in any movie might well be essential to the story (after

---

Film noir refers loosely to a body of film that emerged in the postwar years, characterized by dark views of human corruption and depravity in a mostly urban setting. Peopled by, among others, vicious gangsters, frightened losers, guilty men, and seductive women, noir films have never been entirely off the screen, and they have emerged stronger than ever in recent years.

all, they come with the territory), but the way they are depicted—the combination of elements that make up any film—must be considered as well. An artful or original blending of screenplay, direction, acting, photography, musical score, and editing can make the violence acceptable to many viewers. Conversely, an absence of these qualities can make the violence intolerable.

In the long run, every viewer must make his or her own decision on this matter. This writer, for example, found David Fincher's *Seven*, however gruesome in many of its details, a riveting and skillfully made journey into the darkest areas of the human condition. On the other hand, Gary Fleder's equally horrific *Things to Do in Denver When You're Dead*—with an inept screenplay and pretentious production

that its decent cast could not surmount—made the violence repellent. These days, unfortunately, there are far more films of the latter sort than those in which the violence is acceptable.

Of course those who would scrupulously avoid *both* movies are not reading this book. But for those who are forever intrigued by the depiction of crime and punishment in the movies, I hope that this book will serve as a useful reference. As you walk down the dark streets, remember a few rules. *Stay out of empty parking garages. Never enter a warehouse filled with mannequins. Don't go anywhere near the back room of a sleazy bar. And if you hear wind chimes, run for cover.*

Above all, have a terrifying, dangerous— and exhilarating—good time.

TED SENNETT

KEY TO SYMBOLS

For each entry, the title of the film is followed by a block of information:

- Star rating (see below)

- Name of the producing or releasing company

- The letter "c" (indicating that the film was made in color) or the letters "b/w" (for black-and-white films)

- Running time of the film

- Name of the director

- Name of the screenplay author(s), indicated with "SP"

- Principal cast members

STAR RATINGS

★★★★   Excellent

★★★☆   Very Good

★★★   Good

★★☆   Average

★★   Fair

★☆   Poor

★   The Worst

MURDER
On Tape

ABOVE THE LAW

★★ Warner Bros., 1988, c, 99 min. Dir: Andrew Davis. SP: Steven Pressfield, Ronald Shusett, Andrew Davis, b/o story by Andrew Davis, Steven Seagal. Cast: Steven Seagal, Pam Grier, Sharon Stone, Henry Silva, Daniel Faraldo, Ron Dean, Jack Wallace, Thalmus Rasulala.

Noisy, mindless mayhem from Steven Seagal in his film debut. Pony-tailed and stone-faced, Seagal plays a loose-cannon cop who makes his own rules. ("You think you're above the law. But you're not above mine!") He gets into big trouble by taking on corrupt government agents and big-shot drug dealers, and naturally he gets to display his skill at martial arts. There are at least three separate climaxes. Director Davis fared much better five years later with *The Fugitive*.

ABSOLUTE POWER

★★ Castle Rock, 1997, c, 121 min. Dir: Clint Eastwood. SP: William Goldman, b/o novel by David Baldacci. Cast: Clint Eastwood, Gene Hackman, Ed Harris, Laura Linney, Judy Davis, Scott Glenn, E. G. Marshall, Dennis Haysbert.

It begins brilliantly. Breaking into a mansion outside Washington, master thief Luther Whitney (Eastwood) is shocked to witness a scene that escalates from rough sex to murder. The victim is an elderly senator's young wife; the man involved is no less than the nation's president (Hackman). The scene is startling and suspenseful, but from this point, despite an expert cast and competent direction by Eastwood, the movie plummets into absurdity, mostly due to a far-fetched screenplay. Among the bewildered players, veteran actor E. G. Marshall comes off best as the old senator and Judy Davis fares most poorly as the president's ruthless, witch-like chief of staff. But nobody wins here.

ACROSS 110TH STREET

★ United Artists, 1972, c, 102 min. Dir: Barry Shear. SP: Luther Davis, b/o novel by Wally Ferris. Cast: Anthony Quinn, Yaphet Kotto, Harry Guardino, Paul Benjamin, Ed Bernard, Richard Ward, Antonio Fargas.

When three black thugs rob a Mafia-controlled numbers bank in Harlem and kill six people, the consequences are deadly. Although they despise each other, the Mafia and the black syndicate join together to exact revenge, with the police nipping at their heels. Quinn is the veteran cop on the case—brutal, racist, and long on the take—and Kotto is the reasonable black officer who wants his job. There's gore galore in this hectic and exceedingly ugly movie that spews its contempt at virtually everyone.

ACCUSED, THE

★★☆ Paramount, 1948, b/w, 101 min. Dir: William Dieterle. SP: Ketti Frings, b/o story by June Truesdell. Cast: Loretta Young, Robert Cummings, Wendell Corey, Sam Jaffe, Douglas Dick, Suzanne Dalbert, Henry Travers, Mickey Knox.

Young gives a persuasive performance as a prim professor of psychology who accidentally kills an amorous student (Dick). She covers up the crime, then spends most of the movie trying to keep from becoming unglued as the net tightens. There are some large gaps in logic, much late-forties "psychobabble," and a silly denouement, but it's mildly enjoyable nonetheless.

ACCUSED, THE

★★★☆ Paramount, 1988, c, 110 min. Dir: Jonathan Kaplan. SP: Tom Topor. Cast: Jodie Foster, Kelly McGillis, Bernie Coulsen, Leo Rossi, Ann Hearn, Carmen Argenziano, Steve Antin.

Foster deserved her Best Actress Oscar for her fierce, honest performance as a rape victim in this engrossing film. She plays Sarah Tobias, a coarse, provocative woman who was repeatedly raped in a bar as others watched and cheered the rapists on. Now she demands justice for the assault. Her lawyer (McGillis) finally rallies to her cause and insists on bringing the bystanders to trial. There was controversy over whether it was necessary to show the rape in graphic detail late into the film, but it's a devastating sequence. The movie was based on an actual notorious incident that was widely covered in the news.

ADVENTURES OF SHERLOCK HOLMES, THE

★★★ Fox, 1939, b/w, 85 min. Dir: Alfred Werker. SP: Edwin Blum, William Drake, b/o play by William Gillette. Cast: Basil Rathbone, Nigel Bruce, Ida Lupino, Alan Marshal, George Zucco, Terry Kilburn.

SHERLOCK HOLMES

Sir Arthur Conan Doyle's eccentric, amazingly deductive sleuth has a long history on film—too long and complicated to be covered in these pages. In early years he was played by such actors as John Barrymore (in a 1922 silent film), Raymond Massey, Clive Brook, Reginald Owen, and Arthur Wontner. In recent years he has been portrayed by British actors Christopher Lee and Peter Cushing. Over the last few decades he has also been virtually "reconstructed" for more sophisticated audiences. His drug addiction, his sexual behavior, and other aspects of his character have been examined in such movies as *The Private Life of Sherlock Holmes* (1970), *Murder by Decree* (1970), and *The Seven-Per-Cent Solution* (1976). He has even been spoofed in *The Adventure of Sherlock Holmes's Smarter Brother* (1975) and *Without a Clue* (1988).

The best-remembered portrayal of Sherlock Holmes is indisputably that of Basil Rathbone in a series of films that began at Fox in 1939 with an adroit adaptation of *The Hound of the Baskervilles*. Its success prompted a follow-up, *The Adventures of Sherlock Holmes*, that same year. Rathbone was an ideal Holmes—suave, unflappable, astute, and a perfect foil to Nigel Bruce's bumbling Dr. Watson. Three years later Rathbone and Bruce moved to Universal Studios to begin a series of twelve Holmes films that brought the detective into the modern era. Though modestly made and somewhat incongruous, they were very popular with movie audiences. Among the best were *Sherlock Holmes and the Secret Weapon* (1942) and *Sherlock Holmes Faces Death* (1943).

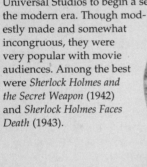
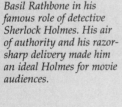

Basil Rathbone in his famous role of detective Sherlock Holmes. His air of authority and his razor-sharp delivery made him an ideal Holmes for movie audiences.

After the success of *The Hound of the Baskervilles*, Fox decided to cash in on the renewed popularity of detective Sherlock Holmes with this tidy mystery movie. Here Holmes (Rathbone) is pitted against his long-time adversary, Professor Moriarty (Zucco), who is attempting to steal the Crown jewels. Bumbling Dr. Watson (Bruce) is on hand, of course, to marvel at Holmes's powers of deduction. Three years later, Rathbone and Bruce would move to Universal, to begin their long-running series of Holmes mysteries.

AFFAIR IN TRINIDAD

★★☆ Columbia, 1952, b/w, 98 min. Dir: Vincent Sherman. SP: Oscar Saul, James Gunn, b/o story by Virginia Van Upp, Berne Giller. Cast: Rita Hayworth, Glenn Ford, Alexander Scourby, Torin Thatcher, Valerie Bettis, Juanita Moore, Steven Geray.

Returning to films after a failed marriage to Aly Khan, Hayworth reunited with Ford, her *Gilda* costar, for this hard-breathing but tired melodrama. Still displaying on-screen glamour, as well as limited acting ability, she plays a nightclub dancer who helps the police uncover the international spy ring that killed her husband. She must pretend to be a member of the ring, thus infuriating brother-in-law Ford. You will not be surprised when hatred turns eventually to love.

AFTER DARK, MY SWEET

★★ Avenue Films, 1990, c, 114 min. Dir: James Foley. SP: Robert Redlin, James Foley, b/o novel by Jim Thompson. Cast: Jason Patric, Rachel Ward, Bruce Dern, George Dickerson.

The title is pure noir, but it has no relevance whatever to this tedious, talky melodrama. Patric is a drifter—an ex-boxer and an escapee from a mental institution—who becomes the pawn in a kidnapping scheme hatched by a sexy young widow (Ward) and her criminally inclined friend (Dern). Patric and Ward become lovers, but the kidnapping maneuver goes seriously awry, and it all ends inevitably in death. The movie is based on a novel by Jim Thompson, who also wrote *The Grifters*, but this time the characters and situations hold little interest.

AFTER HOURS

★★★ Warner Bros., 1985, c, 97 min. Dir: Martin Scorsese. SP: Joseph Minion. Cast: Griffin Dunne, Rosanna Arquette, Teri Garr, John Heard, Verna Bloom, Thomas Chong, Cheech Marin, Catherine O'Hara, Bronson Pinchot, Dick Miller.

A curious entry in Scorsese's filmography, this nightmare, jet-black comedy is certainly not for everyone's taste, but some may find it fascinating. A young word-processor (Dunne) goes to New York's SoHo district for a date and becomes immersed in a terrifying, inexplicable series of events. He meets a number of very odd people and ends up fleeing from a crowd who believes he is a neighborhood thief. There are signs that the makers intended a whiff or two of Kafkaesque disorientation, but the movie emphasizes the black humor.

AFTER THE THIN MAN

★★★ MGM, 1936, b/w, 113 min. Dir: W. S. Van Dyke II. SP: Frances Goodrich, Albert Hackett, b/o story by Dashiell Hammett. Cast: William Powell, Myrna Loy, Jesse Ralph, Sam Levene, Joseph Calleia, Elissa Landi, James Stewart, Dorothy McNulty (Penny Singleton).

The unexpected success of *The Thin Man* prompted MGM to make a sequel, using the same writers and director. Surprisingly, the result was somewhat better than the original, with a nicely convoluted plot, an able cast, and a tidy batch of Nick-and-Nora quips. The plot, involving the murder of the shiftless husband of Nora's cousin (Landi), brings in the usual collection of colorful suspects, one of whom is a very young Jimmy Stewart. Once again, Nick and Nora Charles provide the main pleasure as they temper their obvious love for each other with the slightest edge of malice and mockery. At one point in the midst of the mayhem, Nick asks her, "Having a good time, Mrs. Charles?" "Couldn't be better," she replies. And who could blame her?

AGAINST ALL ODDS

★★☆ Columbia, 1984, c, 128 min. Dir: Taylor Hackford. SP: Eric Hughes, b/o screenplay and novel by Daniel Mainwaring. Cast: Jeff Bridges, Rachel Ward, James Woods, Alex Karras, Jane Greer, Richard Widmark, Dorian Harewood, Swoosie Kurtz, Saul Rubinek.

A loose remake of the highly regarded film noir *Out of the Past* (1947), this movie keeps the basic plot and adds some torrid modern sex

Rachel Ward and Jeff Bridges are lovers in trouble in Against All Odds *(1984). The background is Chichén Itzá, Mexico's historic ruin.*

scenes to spark audience interest. Bridges is a down-on-his-luck football player who is sent to Mexico by shady friend Woods to find treacherous Ward, who has run off with scads of his money. Many complications later, some cast members are dead, some alive and rich. The original had plenty of style and noirish wit; this version has not much of either.

AL CAPONE

★★ Allied Artists, 1959, b/w, 104 min. Dir: Richard Wilson. SP: Malvin Ward, Henry Greenberg. Cast: Rod Steiger, Fay Spain, Martin Balsam, Nehemiah Persoff, James Gregory, Murvyn Vye, Joe De Santis.

Steiger has never been known as a restrained actor, and here he pulls out all the stops in a flamboyant, overbaked performance as the notorious kingpin gangster Al ("Scarface")

Capone. The movie depicts Capone's blood-soaked rise to the top and his inevitable fall, covering all the familiar bases, including the St. Valentine's Day massacre and the flower shop assassination of rival Dion O'Banion. The staging throughout is rather crude and heavy-handed, and Steiger's hammy Capone is not on a par with other depictions of the mobster.

ALL THROUGH THE NIGHT

★★★ Warner Bros., 1942, b/w, 107 min. Dir: Vincent Sherman. SP: Leonard Spigelgass, Edwin Gilbert, b/o story by Leonard Q. Ross (Leo Rosten), Leonard Spigelgass. Cast: Humphrey Bogart, Conrad Veidt, Peter Lorre, Karen Verne, Jackie Gleason, Phil Silvers, Judith Anderson, Jane Darwell, Frank McHugh, William Demarest.

An interesting cast (Gleason and Lorre!) helps

this odd mixture of gangster comedy and spy melodrama. Bogart plays a Runyonesque tough guy named "Gloves" Donahue who rallies his cronies to find the murderer of a friendly baker and then becomes embroiled with a nest of Nazi spies. Very silly and improbable most of the time, but entertaining nonetheless.

ALPHABET CITY

★★ Atlantic, 1984, c, 98 min. Dir: Amos Poe. SP: Gregory Heller, Amos Poe. Cast: Vincent Spano, Kate Vernon, Michael Winslow, Zohra Lampert, Jami Gertz, Laura Carrington, Raymond Serra.

The criminal life on New York City's Lower East Side (Avenues A, B, C—hence the title). Young Spano is deeply involved in organized crime, but balks at burning down the apartment house in which his mother and sister live. His boss isn't happy. That's the plot, but the director overwhelms the simple story with too many arty barnacles, especially the overfancy and distracting camerawork.

AMBITION

★ Miramax, 1991, c, 100 min. Dir: Scott D. Goldstein. SP: Lou Diamond Phillips. Cast: Lou Diamond Phillips, Clancy Brown, Cecilia Peck, Haing S. Ngor, Richard Bradford, Willard Pugh, Grace Zabriskie.

An aspiring novelist (Phillips) becomes obsessed with a recently paroled mass killer (Brown) and hires him to work in the bookstore he manages. But when Phillips's own troubled life takes over, his agenda changes, and Brown becomes the manipulated tool of his deadly intentions. A truly dreadful movie, poorly written by Phillips and without a single believable moment.

AMERICAN BUFFALO

★★☆ Goldwyn, 1996, c, 88 min. Dir: Michael Corrente. SP: David Mamet, b/o his play. Cast: Dustin Hoffman, Dennis Franz, Sean Nelson.

Mamet's often-produced play is here transcribed onto the screen, and unless you are a Mamet fan, you may well wonder why. In a junk-filled antiques shop, the melancholy owner Don (Franz) and a garrulous, self-deceiving lowlife named Teach (Hoffman) talk about their shabby lives and other matters. Often present is a young black man named Bobby (Nelson), who is Don's surrogate son.

The action revolves around the possible theft of a coin collection, but Mamet is more concerned with using his stylized dialogue to expose three lost souls. Hoffman chatters on relentlessly, but Franz takes the acting prize with his portrait of a man who has given up on everything.

AMERICAN GIGOLO

★★ Paramount, 1980, c, 117 min. Dir and SP: Paul Schrader. Cast: Richard Gere, Lauren Hutton, Hector Elizondo, Nina Van Pallandt, Bill Duke, Frances Bergen.

Here's positive proof that posh settings and fancy duds are not enough to make a good movie. Julian Kaye (Gere) is a smugly confident fashion plate who provides high-priced sex and other services for wealthy California women. His latest conquest is a senator's beautiful wife (Hutton), who dotes on him despite the danger involved. Then his world comes apart when he becomes the prime suspect in the murder of one of his clients. Who is trying to frame Julian? And who cares? This glitzy would-be thriller is tedious going and it isn't helped by Gere's enervated performance.

AMERICAN ME

★★ Universal, 1992, c, 125 min. Dir: Edward James Olmos. SP: Floyd Mutrux, Desmond Nakano, b/o story by Floyd Mutrux. Cast: Edward James Olmos, William Forsythe, Pepe Serna, Danny de la Paz, Evelina Fernandez, Cary Hiroyuki Tagawa.

Based on a true story, this ambitious drama records life in the mean streets of the Mexican barrio in East Los Angeles. Olmos directs and also stars as Santana, who achieves power and "respect" as head of the Mexican Mafia in Folsom Prison and then finds even greater brutality and violence when he returns to the barrio. By the time he learns to change his perspective, it is too late. Long, solemn, and well intentioned, the movie is also extremely tedious.

AMONGST FRIENDS

★★☆ New Line, 1993, c, 86 min. Dir and SP: Rob Weiss. Cast: Steve Parlavecchio, Joseph Lindsey, Patrick McGaw, Mira Sorvino, Brett Lambson, Michael Artura, David Stepkin.

Three young friends (Parlavecchio, Lindsay, McGaw) grow up together in a wealthy area of suburban Long Island, but their aimless lives cause them to drift into crime, with ultimately tragic consequences. The movie at least offers a change from the mean streets of the inner city, but the story is still overly familiar, and it's sometimes difficult to sort out the characters. A not-bad try, however.

ANATOMY OF A MURDER

★★★★ Columbia, 1959, b/w, 160 min. Dir: Otto Preminger. SP: Wendell Mayes, b/o novel by Robert Traver. Cast: James Stewart, Lee Remick, Ben Gazzara, George C. Scott, Eve Arden, Arthur O'Connell, Joseph N. Welch, Kathryn Grant, Orson Bean, Murray Hamilton.

A totally absorbing courtroom drama, adapted from Robert Traver's best-selling novel, *Anatomy of a Murder* puts a first-rate cast through its paces under Preminger's assured direction. In a Michigan town, an army

lieutenant (Gazzara) has been accused of killing a local resident, allegedly after the man raped his wife (Remick). But what really happened—and why? A local attorney (Stewart) takes the case as the trial reveals layers of lies, deceptions, and half-truths. Real-life judge Welch plays the presiding judge with an engaging slyness and wit.

ANDERSON TAPES, THE

★★★ Columbia, 1971, c, 98 min. Dir: Sidney Lumet. SP: Frank R. Pierson, b/o novel by Lawrence Sanders. Cast: Sean Connery, Dyan Cannon, Martin Balsam, Christopher Walken, Ralph Meeker, Alan King, Val Avery, Garrett Morris, Margaret Hamilton.

A caper comedy-melodrama for the age of surveillance, this film has a clever gimmick: newly released from prison, safecracker Duke Anderson (Connery) organizes a group of

A tense courtroom moment in Anatomy of a Murder *(1959), with (left to right) James Stewart, Joseph Welch, Lee Remick, and George C. Scott.*

confederates to rob an entire Manhattan luxury building of its valuables. Unbeknownst to him, however, various independent groups (the FBI, the Treasury Department, the Narcotics Commission, and others) are monitoring the house with their own agenda. Chaos takes over, and Duke's elaborate caper becomes a violent comedy of errors. An entertaining movie with some bright dialogue and a good cast.

. . . AND JUSTICE FOR ALL

★★☆ Columbia, 1979, c, 117 min. Dir: Norman Jewison. SP: Valerie Curtin, Barry Levinson. Cast: Al Pacino, Christine Lahti, John Forsythe, Jack Warden, Lee Strasberg, Jeffrey Tambor, Sam Levene, Craig T. Nelson, Robert Christian, Thomas Waites.

Arthur Kirkland (Pacino) is a fiercely committed lawyer, but an out-of-control judicial system is wrecking his life. He must deal with, among others, a judge (Warden) who is clearly nuts, another judge (Forsythe) who is indescribably evil, and clients who are treated with callous indifference by the courts. Arthur's life is a mess, but so is this movie: a mixture of jet-black comedy, stark drama, and scathing satire. Pacino works hard, giving the role his usual intensity, but he is defeated by a screenplay that splinters into too many pieces. Lahti makes her movie debut as his lover, a lawyer who disagrees with him on almost every legal position. Pacino and the screenplay were nominated for Oscars.

AND THEN THERE WERE NONE

★★☆ Fox, 1945, b/w, 98 min. Dir: Rene Clair. SP: Dudley Nichols, b/o novel by Agatha Christie. Cast: Barry Fitzgerald, Walter Huston, Louis Hayward, Roland Young, June Duprez, Judith Anderson, C. Aubrey Smith, Richard Haydn, Mischa Auer.

A superb cast is the principal (and only) virtue of this first version of the Agatha Christie novel *Ten Little Indians*. You know the premise: ten people are summoned to a remote island where, one by one, they are murdered in ingenious ways. Who is the culprit and why? Considering the movie's credits, it should have been better, but, despite the determinedly light touch, it's performed with very little style or suspense. The story was remade three times (1966, 1975, 1989) under the title of Christie's novel, and Neil Simon spoofed it to some

degree in *Murder by Death* (1976).

ANGEL FACE

★★ RKO, 1953, b/w, 90 min. Dir: Otto Preminger. SP: Frank Nugent, Oscar Millard, b/o story by Chester Erskine. Cast: Robert Mitchum, Jean Simmons, Herbert Marshall, Mona Freeman, Leon Ames, Barbara O'Neil, Jim Backus, Kenneth Tobey.

On the surface, *Angel Face* has all the components of classic film noir: a beautiful woman with the propensities of a black widow spider; an unwary antihero who is caught in her web; shadowy photography, and even a few Freudian overtones. Unfortunately, the film is slow, heavy-handed, and unconvincing. Simmons, in a black wig, plays the angel of death who murders her much-hated stepmother (O'Neil) and, inadvertently, her beloved father (Marshall) as well. Chauffeur Mitchum becomes entangled in her crime, with fatal results. The fact that he is snared by this clearly deranged woman seems especially improbable in light of Mona Freeman's presence as the pretty, bright-eyed nurse he tosses aside.

ANGEL HEART

★★☆ Carolco, 1987, c, 113 min. Dir and SP: Alan Parker, b/o novel by William Hjortsberg. Cast: Mickey Rourke, Robert De Niro, Lisa Bonet, Charlotte Rampling, Stocker Fountelieu, Brownie McGhee.

Director Parker's style, charged with drive and energy, can sometimes produce striking results, as in *Midnight Express* (1978) and *Mississippi Burning* (1988). But in the case of *Angel Heart*, the sheer nastiness of the material overwhelms his style and causes unease. Rourke, once again displaying terminal grunginess, plays a seedy private detective who is asked by a mysterious De Niro to locate a long-missing person. His investigation takes him to Harlem and New Orleans and to a nightmarish world of violence and black magic. The final revelation is intended to shock, but no more than the gory sequences that precede it. The videotape includes the controversial love scene between Rourke and Bonet.

ANGELS WITH DIRTY FACES

★★★☆ Warner Bros., 1938, b/w, 97 min. Dir: Michael Curtiz. SP: John Wexley, Warren Duff, b/o story by Rowland Brown. Cast: James Cagney, Pat

Hoodlum James Cagney gives advice to the Dead End Kids in Angels with Dirty Faces *(1938), as Father Pat O'Brien (far right) watches disapprovingly.*

O'Brien, Ann Sheridan, Humphrey Bogart, George Bancroft, Billy Halop, Leo Gorcey, Huntz Hall, Bobby Jordan, Gabriel Dell.

Perhaps the best-known version of what might be called the "good boy/bad boy" plot, *Angels with Dirty Faces* has the vigor and drive of the best Warner melodramas of the thirties. Cagney and O'Brien are boyhood pals who grow up to be, respectively, a gangster and a priest. Killer Cagney is a bad influence on the neighborhood boys (the Dead End Kids in full bloom), and Father O'Brien tries to change that in a famous (and ambiguous) final sequence. Corny, yes, but also vintage Warner fare.

ANOTHER 48 HRS

★★ Paramount, 1990, c, 95 min. Dir: Walter Hill. SP: John Fasano, Jeb Stuart, Larry Gross, b/o story by Fred Braughton. Cast: Eddie Murphy, Nick Nolte, Brian James, Kevin Tighe, Ed O'Ross, David Anthony Marshall, Andrew Divoff, Bernie Casey.

A virtual duplication of the original 1982 movie (same director), but without much of the energy or sparkle. Once again Murphy, newly released from prison, is called on by rumpled cop Nolte to help him nail a drug lord called the "Iceman," who would like to see them dead. As before, there is a mix of violence and comedy, but it comes across as mechanical now, and neither Murphy nor Nolte seems particularly interested.

ANOTHER THIN MAN

★★☆ MGM, 1939, b/w, 105 min. Dir: W. S. Van Dyke III. SP: Dashiell Hammett. Cast: William Powell, Myrna Loy, C. Aubrey Smith, Otto Kruger, Nat Pendleton, Virginia Grey, Marjorie Main, Ruth Hussey, Tom Neal.

This third entry in the Thin Man series was written by Dashiell Hammett himself, author of the original novel on which the series was based. This time debonair detective Nick Charles (Powell), with the aid of his loving wife, Nora (Loy), concentrates on a fairly dull and nearly incomprehensible murder case on a Long Island estate. There's an addition to the Charles family—Nick, Jr.—which allows for a number of cutesy jokes.

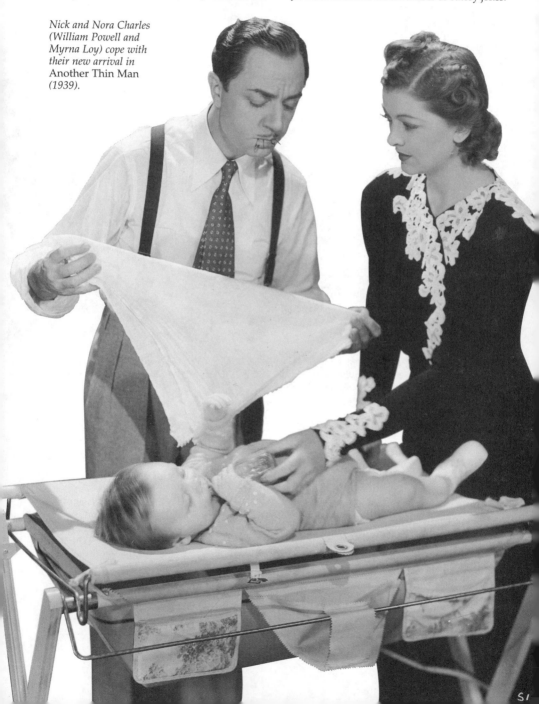

Nick and Nora Charles (William Powell and Myrna Loy) cope with their new arrival in Another Thin Man *(1939).*

APPOINTMENT WITH DEATH

★★ Cannon (British), 1988, c, 108 min. Dir: Michael Winner. SP: Anthony Shaffer, Peter Buckman, Michael Winner, b/o novel by Agatha Christie. Cast: Peter Ustinov, Lauren Bacall, Piper Laurie, Carrie Fisher, John Gielgud, David Soul, Hayley Mills, Jenny Seagrove.

The bloom is definitely off the rose in this most recent and weakest adaptation of an Agatha Christie mystery. Ustinov returns as detective Hercule Poirot, who assembles the suspects to uncover the killer of a wealthy and extremely odious dowager (Laurie, overacting badly). The setting is 1937 Palestine, which allows for some colorful scenery, but the movie is surprisingly dull and inept.

ARMED AND DANGEROUS

★★ Columbia, 1986, c, 88 min. Dir: Mark L. Lester. SP: Harold Ramis, Peter Torokvei, b/o story by Brian Grazer, Harold Ramis, James Keach. Cast: John Candy, Eugene Levy, Robert Loggia, Kenneth McMillan, Meg Ryan.

Helter-skelter comedy with John Candy and Eugene Levy as security guards who try to catch or evade the corrupt cops and union goons working for big-time gangster Robert Loggia. The bumbling duo seem to get trapped wherever they go, includung a steam room, a toxic waste dump, and that old reliable, an empty warehouse policed by vicious dogs. Ryan, in her prestardom days, provides some romantic interest.

ARSENIC AND OLD LACE

★★★ Warner Bros., 1944, b/w, 118 min. Dir: Frank Capra. SP: Julius J. Epstein, Philip G. Epstein, b/o play by Joseph Kesselring. Cast: Cary Grant, Priscilla Lane, Raymond Massey, Peter Lorre, Josephine Hull, Jean Adair, Jack Carson, Edward Everett Horton.

Filmed in 1941 but unreleased until 1944, *Arsenic and Old Lace* takes the long-running Broadway comedy and turns it into a shrill, heavy-handed farce. Still, there are enough genuine chuckles to warrant a viewing. Cary Grant is way over the top as apparently the only sane member of a Brooklyn family. His adorable aunts (Hull and Adair) are given to poisoning elderly strangers and burying their bodies in the cellar. Their long-lost brother (Massey) is a grotesque serial killer. Sounds grim, but it's all played for laughs more than thrills. An odd entry in director Capra's body of film.

ASPHALT JUNGLE, THE

★★★★ MGM, 1950, b/w, 112 min. Dir: John Huston. SP: Ben Maddow, John Huston, b/o novel by W. R. Burnett. Cast: Sterling Hayden, Louis Calhern, Sam Jaffe, Jean Hagen, James Whitmore, Marc Lawrence, John McIntire, Anthony Caruso, Marilyn Monroe.

One of the best caper melodramas ever filmed, and a model of its kind. A group of crooks come together for a bank heist, and as their plan is prepared and carried out, we come to know each of the members as they exchange accusations and recriminations. Among others, there's small-time hood Dix Handley (Hayden), lustful Doc Reidenschneider (Jaffe), and suave but corrupt lawyer Emmerich (Calhern), each of them pursuing his futile dream. The sequence of the jewel heist is justly famous, but it is the movie's emphasis on character that makes it outstanding. Monroe has one of her early roles, as Emmerich's blonde "niece" Angela. Remade three times, as *The Badlanders*, *Cairo*, and *Cool Breeze*.

ASSASSINATION

★ Cannon, 1987, c, 88 min. Dir: Peter Hunt. SP: Richard Sale. Cast: Charles Bronson, Jill Ireland, Stephen Elliott, Jan Gan Boyd, Randy Brooks, Erik Stein, Michael Ansara, William Prince.

A dreadful movie, extremely far-fetched and woefully inept. Charles Bronson is a Secret Service agent charged with guarding the obnoxious new first lady (Ireland). Repeated attempts to kill her finally convince the lady that something is amiss, and soon the two are in deperate flight from the assassins. Chases, explosions, and yards of ludicrous dialogue.

ASSAULT ON A QUEEN

★★☆ Paramount, 1966, c, 106 min. Dir: Jack Donohue. SP: Rod Serling, b/o novel by Jack Finney. Cast: Frank Sinatra, Virna Lisi, Anthony Francisoa, Richard Conte, Alf Kjellin, Errol John, Reginald Denny.

Fishing boat owner Sinatra joins five other conspirators (including blonde Lisi) in a bold caper: they salvage a small submarine that's been submerged for twenty years and use it to steal a million dollars from the bank of the docked *Queen Mary*. Despite much bickering, they manage to carry it off. That's the premise of this less-than-plausible melodrama. Swedish actor Kjellin plays one of the group: a former German U-boat commander with his own secret agenda.

Thieves gather in The Asphalt Jungle *(1950): Sam Jaffe, Sterling Hayden, Anthony Caruso, and James Whitmore (left to right).*

ASSAULT ON PRECINCT 13

★★☆ CKK, 1976, c, 94 min. Dir and SP: John Carpenter. Cast: Austin Stoker, Darwin Joston, Laurie Zimmer, Martin West, Tony Burton, Kim Richards.

It's difficult to figure out why this film has achieved cult status. A sort of urban, modern-day version of Howard Hawks's Western *Rio Bravo*, the movie has a simple premise: bent on revenge for the killing of some of their members, a violent street gang lays siege to a nearly abandoned police station where only a few helpless people remain. There are some harrowing moments, but also inadequate acting and much dumb dialogue. Director Carpenter would later fare better with *Halloween, Star Man*, and other movies.

AT CLOSE RANGE

★★★ Hemdale, 1986, c, 115 min. Dir: James Foley. SP: Nicholas Kazan. Cast: Sean Penn, Christopher Walken, Mary Stuart Masterson, Millie Perkins, Eileen Ryan, Alan Autry, Candy Clark, Kiefer Sutherland, David Strathairn, Tracey Walter.

An utterly depressing drama concerning a wayward son and his criminal father. Based on a true story, the movie stars Penn as a tough misfit in 1978 Pennsylvania who at first admires his father (Walken), a professional thief and killer, and begins to emulate him. When he learns how truly nasty and dangerous his father really is, he agrees to testify against him, leading to further carnage. Despite good acting, this oppressively ugly and brutal film leaves a strongly unpleasant aftertaste.

ATLANTIC CITY

★★★☆ Paramount (Canadian/French), 1980, c, 104 min. Dir: Louis Malle. SP: John Guare. Cast: Burt Lancaster, Susan Sarandon, Kate Reid, Robert Joy, Michel Piccoli, Hollis McLaren, Al Waxman, Wally Shawn.

Lancaster gives one of his best performances in Louis Malle's intriguing if not totally satisfactory film. He plays Lou, an aging small-time former mafioso, living in a decrepit area of Atlantic City and remembering a glorious time that never existed, at least for him. Sarandon is Sally, an ambitious young woman Lou secretly adores, whose disreputable husband (Joy) involves Lou with drugs and the mob. The movie captures the dank, decaying look of Atlantic City before its "renaissance," but it loses its footing toward the end. Lancaster and Sarandon, however, are excellent.

BACKFIRE

★★ ITC, 1987, c, 92 min. Dir: Gilbert Cates. SP: Larry Brand, Rebecca Reynolds. Cast: Karen Allen, Keith Carradine, Jeff Fahey, Bernie Casey, Dean Paul Martin, Dinah Manoff, Virginia Capers, Philip Sterling.

A twisty thriller with some unexpected turns, but the material covers familiar ground, and after a while the plot doesn't thicken—it curdles. Wealthy Fahey is tormented by memories of his experience in Vietnam. His wrong-side-of-the-tracks wife (Allen) plots his demise with her lover (Martin), but the attempt backfires, and Fahey is left catatonic. Enter mysterious stranger Carradine, with his own agenda. The actors try too hard to breathe some life into their foolish roles, and the effort shows.

BACKTRACK

★ Vestron, 1989, c, 98 min. Dir: Dennis Hopper. SP: Rachel Kronstadt Mann, Ann Louise Bardach, b/o story by Rachel Kronstadt Mann. Cast: Dennis Hopper, Jodie Foster, Dean Stockwell, John Turturro, Vincent Price, Fred Ward, Julie Adams, Bob Dylan, Charlie Sheen, Joe Pesci (unbilled).

A cast with so many notable actors deserves better material than this stupefyingly awful thriller. Foster plays an artist who witnesses a mob murder. Hit man Hopper is sent to kill her, and when he falls for her instead, the two flee from the Mafia and the police. The situations and the dialogue are relentlessly dumb, and the inane climax defies description. Pesci appears as yet another of his ferocious gangsters. Hopper disowned the original version, which was called *Catchfire*, then later had it restored to his cut for release on video and cable. The question is, why?

BAD BOYS

★★★ EMI, 1983, c, 123 min. Dir: Rick Rosenthal. SP: Richard Dilello. Cast: Sean Penn, Esai Morales, Reni Santoni, Clancy Brown, Eric Gurry, Ally Sheedy, Jim Moody.

Strong performances by its young cast, especially Penn, galvanize this urban melodrama. When tough, street-wise Mick (Penn) kills the brother of a Latino hood named Paco (Morales), he is caught and sent to prison. In revenge, Paco rapes Mick's girlfriend (Sheedy in her film debut), and he is also caught and sent to the same prison. Inevitably the feud of honor must be resolved in a bloody clash between the two adversaries. The movie looks on prison as a harsh and relentless purgatory, and it manages to work up some emotional force.

BAD COMPANY

★★☆ Touchstone, 1995, c, 106 min. Dir: Damian Harris. SP: Ross Thomas. Cast: Ellen Barkin, Laurence Fishburne, Frank Langella, Michael Beach, Gia Carides, David Ogden Stiers, Daniel Hugh Kelly, Spalding Gray, James Hong.

Now that the cold war is over, where can filmmakers go to depict covert operations carried out by sexy sneaks? Why, to the heady worlds of high-level business and government. Here, Fishburne, a former CIA operative, joins a secret agency specializing in corporate espionage and other forms of hanky-panky, including blackmail and murder. Barkin is a nasty sort who also works for the agency, and soon the two are not only engaging in sexual athletics but plotting to take over. Or are they? Double crosses and double dealings prevail in this complicated, fairly stylish but ultimately tedious melodrama.

BAD DAY AT BLACK ROCK

★★★☆ MGM, 1955, c, 81 min. Dir: John Sturges. SP: Millard Kaufman, b/o story by Howard Breslin. Cast: Spencer Tracy, Robert Ryan, Anne Francis, Walter Brennan, Dean Jagger, Ernest Borgnine, Lee Marvin, John Ericson.

A one-armed man named MacReady (Tracy) arrives in a bleak little Western town. His mission: to award a posthumous medal to the father of a fallen Japanese-American hero. Instead, he finds hostility and danger as he uncovers a long-buried secret about the father's grim fate. Eventually he faces a deadly confrontation with the town's vicious tyrant (Ryan) and his bullying hoods. There's not a wasted moment in Kaufman's lean, taut screenplay, and for once the widescreen CinemaScope process is used intelligently, to suggest a vast, pitiless Western wasteland. Tracy is on the mark, as always, and Ryan is chillingly effective as the town's meanest resident. The movie won Oscar nominations for Best Actor (Tracy), Screenplay, and Direction.

BADGE 373

★★ Paramount, 1973, c, 116 min. Dir: Howard W. Koch. SP: Pete Hamill. Cast: Robert Duvall, Verna Bloom, Henry Darrow, Eddie Egan, Felipe Luciano, Tina Christiana, Marina Durell.

In this heavy-handed police melodrama, Duvall is a hard-headed, bigoted cop who will stoop to anything to break up a crime syndicate. During the course of the movie, he conducts illegal drug raids, terrorizes a hood into a fatal rootop fall, endangers the lives of bus passengers, and commits assorted other subversive actions. Newspaper columnist Hamill claims that his screenplay was "inspired by the exploits of Eddie Egan," the New York City detective who also inspired *The French Connection*. Does he consider this a compliment?

BAD INFLUENCE

★★☆ Epic/Sarlui/Diamant, 1990, c, 99 min. Dir: Curtis Hanson. SP: David Koepp. Cast: Rob Lowe, James Spader, Lisa Zane, Christian Clemenson, Kathleen Wilhoite.

Another, and largely unconvincing, variation on the acquaintance-from-hell theme. Michael (Spader) is an unhappy computer whiz who meets the dangerously disturbed Alex (Lowe). Alex insinuates himself into Michael's life and soon involves him in robbery and murder. Somewhere at midpoint the movie goes out of control and becomes increasingly preposterous. Ultimately Michael seems less of a victim than a dim bulb. A few fleeting moments of suspense, but that's all.

BADLANDS

★★★ Warner Bros., 1972, c, 95 min. Dir and SP: Terrence Malick. Cast: Martin Sheen, Sissy Spacek, Warren Oates, Ramon Bieri, Alan Vint.

Based on a true case, in which teenagers Charlie Starkweather and Caril Fugate cut a wide swath of murder and mayhem across Nebraska and Wyoming, *Badlands* is an artful if somewhat overstudied drama in the Bonnie-and-Clyde tradition. Sheen plays an amoral drifter who teams up with Spacek, a girl whose life and dreams are shaped by what she reads in fan magazines or hears on soap operas. Together the deadly duo begin a wave of killings, showing no remorse or guilt whatever. The movie suggests that the emptiness of the couple's lives led to fantasies that became more real than reality and ultimately triggered their mindless violence. This, at least, is a change from the society-is-to-blame attitude of thirties films, or the rebels-without-a-cause approach in movies of the fifties and sixties.

BAD LIEUTENANT

★★★ LT Productions, 1992, c, 96 min. Dir: Abel Ferrara. SP: Zoe Lund, Abel Ferrara. Cast: Harvey Keitel, Victor Argo, Paul Calderone, Leonard Thomas, Robin Burrows, Frankie Thorn, Victoria Bastel.

In this corrosive, lurid, and relentlessly bleak film, Keitel is a depraved, drug-addicted criminal on a one-way road to disaster. He's also a police detective. When a nun is brutally raped in his district and refuses to identify her attackers, his long-submerged Catholic past surfaces, and he is sent reeling into an almost unendurable torment. Parts of this movie are so ugly they are difficult if not impossible to watch, but Keitel's performance is a bold tour de force that very few actors would ever attempt. Warning: this movie is rated NC-17, and for good reason.

BAD SEED, THE

★★☆ Warner Bros., 1956, c, 129 min. Dir: Mervyn LeRoy. SP: John Lee Mahin, b/o play by Maxwell Anderson and novel by William March. Cast: Nancy Kelly, Patty McCormack, Henry Jones, Eileen Heckart, Evelyn Varden, William Hopper.

The stage origins show all too plainly in this adaptation of Maxwell Anderson's Broadway play and the novel by William March. Kelly is the doting mother of little McCormack, but there's a problem. McCormack turns out to be a pint-sized demon who murders blithely whomever she dislikes or stands in her way. Mother is not too pleased when she learns the truth. Kelly, McCormack, Heckart, and Jones (memorable as a nasty house superintendant) all repeat their stage roles. The ending, dictated by the Production Code of the time, is ridiculous, but it's often cut.

BANK ROBBER

★ I.R.S. Media, 1993, c, 94 min. Dir and SP: Nick Mead. Cast: Patrick Dempsey, Lisa Bonet, Olivia D'Abo, Forest Whitaker, Judge Reinhold, Michael Jeter, Mariska Hargitay.

A truly dumb black comedy about a dim-witted fellow (Dempsey) who robs a bank to impress his cheating girlfriend (D'Abo). He holes up in a flophouse called the Heart-break Hotel, where everyone from the bellboy to the pizza delivery boy recognizes him and extorts money from him. Bonet is a good-hearted hooker, and Whitaker and Reinhold are wasted in cameo roles as sympathetic cops.

BANK SHOT

★★★ United Artists, 1974, c, 83 min. Dir: Gower Champion. SP: Wendell Mayes, b/o novel by Donald E. Westlake. Cast: George C. Scott, Joanna Cassidy, Sorrell Booke, G. Wood, Clifton James, Bob Balaban, Bibi Osterwald.

Famed dancer-Broadway director Champion directed this amusing caper movie. Scott stars as a bad-tempered bank robber with a novel idea: when a branch of a Los Angeles bank is temporarily relocated to a house trailer, he decides to put wheels under the trailer and carry off the entire bank. Naturally, nothing happens quite as planned. Booke is hilarious as a bank robber with no gift for disguises.

BARTON FINK

★★★ Fox, 1991, c, 117 min. Dir: Joel Coen. SP: Ethan Cohen, Joel Coen. Cast: John Turturro, John Goodman, Judy Davis, Michael Lerner, John Mahoney, Tony Shalhoub, Jon Polito.

Fascinating, bizarre, but not always successful, *Barton Fink* is another off-center entry from the Coen brothers. Fine actor Turturro plays the title role, a self-important Broadway playwright who comes to Hollywood in the thirties and discovers a living hell instead of fame and fortune. Among the people he meets are a seemingly genial next-door hotel neighbor (Goodman), an alcoholic writer (Mahoney), and the writer's mistress (Davis). Somewhere at midpoint the razor-sharp satire veers into inexplicable violence, and the movie collapses. Wonderfully seedy Art Deco sets and good performances, but still, many viewers will be puzzled and irritated.

BASIC INSTINCT

★ TriStar, 1992, c, 127 min. Dir: Paul Verhoeven. SP: Joe Eszterhas. Cast: Michael Douglas, Sharon Stone, George Dzunda, Jeanne Tripplehorn, Denis Arndt, Leilani Sarelle, Dorothy Malone, Wayne Knight, Stephen Tobolowsky.

A lurid and trashy thriller, with some highly explicit sex scenes and a plot that barely makes sense. When an ex-rock star is brutally murdered, two detectives (Douglas and Dzunda) encounter the chief suspect (Stone), an icy blonde beauty who turns out to be writing a novel in which . . . well, you get it. Is she the killer, or is she being framed? Although recognizing the danger, angry, burned-out Douglas falls hard for the foul-mouthed lady. Muddy plot, dumb dialogue, grisly scenes—they are all here in abundance.

BATMAN

★★★☆ Warner Bros., 1989, c, 126 min. Dir: Tim Burton. SP: Sam Hamm, Warren Skaaren, b/o characters created by Bob Kane. Cast: Michael Keaton, Jack Nicholson, Kim Basinger, Robert Wuhl, Michael Gough, Pat Hingle, Jack Palance, Billy Dee Williams.

Viewers expecting to see their comic-book hero doing brave deeds, or the campy character of the television series, are in for a big surprise. Imaginatively designed by Anton Furst, this movie is set in a bleak Gotham City in which debonair Bruce Wayne (Keaton) turns into a brooding, revenge-minded Batman bent on routing evil. His main adversary is the demonic Joker (Nicholson, having a field day), whose goal is to subvert Gotham City citizens with poisoned toiletries. Basinger is the photojournalist Vicky Vale, who is determined to expose Bruce Wayne's alter ego. A gloomy but fascinating film.

BATMAN FOREVER

★★☆ Warner Bros., 1995, c, 121 min. Dir: Joel Schumacher. SP: Lee Batchler, Janet Scott Batchler, Akiva Goldsman, b/o story by Lee Batchler, Janet Scott Batchler. Cast: Val Kilmer, Tommy Lee Jones, Jim Carrey, Nicole Kidman, Chris O'Donnell, Michael Gough, Pat Hingle, Drew Barrymore, Joe Grifasi.

Elaborate gimmickry and gadgetry take the place of the dark, nightmarish aura of the first *Batman* movie, and the result is a lot more cheerful and colorful but not much fun, at least for adult viewers. This time Batman and his alter ego Bruce Wayne (Kilmer), still brooding and glum, must face two adversaries: the grotesque Harvey Two-Face (Jones) and the Riddler (Carrey, twenty miles over the top). Nicole Kidman is the sexy psychologist attracted to Batman/Wayne, and Chris O'Donnell is the Boy Who Becomes Robin. Eye-popping sets may keep you watching, even while your brain is numbed.

Humphrey Bogart and Peter Lorre are a pair of crooks in John Huston's Beat the Devil *(1954).*

BATMAN RETURNS

★★★ Warner Bros., 1992, c, 126 min. Dir: Tim Burton. SP: Daniel Waters, b/o story by Daniel Waters, Sam Hamm, and on characters created by Bob Kane. Cast: Michael Keaton, Danny DeVito, Michelle Pfeiffer, Christopher Walken, Michael Gough, Michael Murphy, Cristi Conaway, Pat Hingle.

Less dark-hued and apocalyptic than the first *Batman* feature and less gadget-oriented than the third (*Batman Forever*), this second film in the series pits the Caped Crusader against some formidable misfit villains: the grotesque, fiendish Penguin (DeVito), the arrogant industrialist Max Shreck (Walken), and, best of all, the slinky, seductive Catwoman (Pfeiffer). Too often the story becomes incoherent and mean-spirited, but the stunning production design by Bo Welch provides something to look at and admire.

BEAT THE DEVIL

★★★ United Artists, 1954, b/w, 89 min. Dir: John Huston. SP: John Huston, Truman Capote, b/o novel by James Helvick. Cast: Humphrey Bogart, Jennifer Jones, Gina Lollobrigida, Robert Morley, Peter Lorre, Edward Underdown, Ivor Barnard, Marco Tulli, Bernard Lee.

A cult favorite for many years, *Beat the Devil* may not deserve its reputation, but it is an entertaining offbeat movie nevertheless. A satire on the "den-of-thieves" subgenre pioneered by *The Maltese Falcon*, the movie centers on an ill-assorted band of thieves involved in an illegal deal to buy uranium-rich property in Africa. Also present is an ersatz British aristocrat (Underdown) and his habitually lying wife (Jones). Some curious plot twists and much whimsical dialogue keep the cast from floundering. A zesty Robert Morley fares best in his Sydney Greenstreet-like role.

BEDROOM WINDOW, THE

★★☆ De Laurentiis, 1987, c, 112 min. Dir and SP: Curtis Hanson, b/o novel by Anne Holden. Cast: Steve Guttenberg, Isabelle Huppert, Elizabeth McGovern, Paul Shenar, Frederick Coffin, Carl Lumbly, Wallace Shawn.

Terry Lambert (Guttenberg) is in deep trouble. During a tryst with his boss's wife (Huppert) in his apartment, the lady witnesses a brutal assault from his bedroom window. She asks him to tell the police that *he* witnessed the attack. His gallant gesture sends him spinning into a terrifying vortex involving deception and murder by a serial killer on the loose. The movie would like to emulate Hitchcock, but about halfway through the story, it all falls apart and becomes mostly preposterous.

BEFORE AND AFTER

★★★ Hollywood, 1996, c, 107 min. Dir: Barbet Schroeder. SP: Ted Talley, b/o novel by Rosellen Brown. Cast: Meryl Streep, Liam Neeson, Edward Furlong, Alfred Molina, John Heard, Julia Weldon, Daniel von Bargen, Ann Magnuson.

A small-town family is torn apart when their teenage son (Furlong) becomes the prime suspect in a girl's murder and then flees. The father (Neeson) wants to save his son at all cost, even concealing evidence; the mother (Streep) wants to tell the unvarnished truth. This grim tale raises a serious moral issue, but the telling leaves something to be desired. The acting is capable, except for Furlong's monotonous performance, but there are too many awkward patches and a few scenes that strain credulity. Still, worth a look.

BEST SELLER

★★ Orion, 1987, c, 110 min. Dir: John Flynn. SP: Larry Cohen. Cast: Brian Dennehy, James Woods, Victoria Tennant, Paul Shenar, Allison Balson, George Coe, Anne Pitoniak.

An unconvincing melodrama in which Woods (at his most reptilian) plays a vicious hit man for hire with explosive—and dangerous—information about a leading citizen (Shenar) who happens to be one of his biggest clients. He wants cop and best-selling author Dennehy to put it all into a book. Dennehy is both repelled and fascinated as the body count keeps increasing around him. Woods and Dennehy are two of the best actors in films, but this is nasty stuff they cannot redeem.

BETRAYED

★ MGM/UA, 1988, c, 128 min. Dir: Costa-Gavras. SP: Joe Eszterhas. Cast: Debra Winger, Tom Berenger, John Heard, John Mahoney, Betsy Blair, Ted Levine, Jeffrey DeMunn, David Clennon.

A surprisingly poor film—dreary and exasperating—from director Costa-Gavras. After an abrasive radio personality is murdered, FBI agent Winger is sent to America's heartland to investigate a suspect, seemingly homespun farmer Tom Berenger. Instead, she uncovers a massive and dangerous conspiracy by rabid extremists to destroy minority groups across the country. The theme is sadly still relevant today, but *Betrayed* has yards of clumsy dialogue, situations that strain belief, and a heroine who seems amazingly dumb.

BEVERLY HILLS COP

★★★ Paramount, 1984, c, 105 min. Dir: Martin Brest. SP: Daniel Petrie, Jr., b/o story by Danilo Bach, Daniel Petrie, Jr. Cast: Eddie Murphy, Lisa Eilbacher, Steven Berkoff, Judge Reinhold, Ronny Cox, Stephen Elliott, Paul Reiser.

Murphy's sassy, streetwise persona works well in this mixture of rapid action and rude comedy. He plays Alex Foley, a Detroit cop who arrives in Beverly Hills to find the killer of his friend and stays to uncover a drug-smuggling ring. Naturally, this loose cannon is smarter and more resourceful than the police in upscale Los Angeles. Using mere bluster as his best weapon, he barrels into posh locations, including a fancy hotel and an exclusive club. Even when he barely escapes with his life, he remains unflappable and irreverent. The movie is fast, funny, and mindless. It was also popular enough to spawn two less successful sequels.

BEVERLY HILLS COP II

★★ Paramount, 1987, c, 102 min. Dir: Tony Scott. SP: Larry Ferguson, Warren Skaaren. Cast: Eddie Murphy, Judge Reinhold, Jurgen Prochnow, Ronny Cox, John Ashton, Brigitte Nielsen, Allen Garfield, Dean Stockwell, Paul Reiser.

Virtually all of the wicked fun Murphy brought to his role of Axel Foley in *Beverly Hills Cop* has disappeared in this lame sequel. Once again Detroit cop Foley is back in Los Angeles, investigating a series of violent robberies and dragging reluctant cops Ashton and Reinhold into the fray. The villains are dull and the action sequences are monotonous.

BEVERLY HILLS COP III

★ Paramount, 1994, c, 105 min. Dir: John Landis. SP: Steven E. de Souza. Cast: Eddie Murphy, Judge Reinhold, Bronson Pinchot, Hector Elizondo, Timothy Carhart.

The third and, hopefully, last of the *Beverly Hills Cop* series, and simply a mess. Cop Axel Foley (Murphy) should have stayed in Detroit, but no, he's back, this time pursuing a gang of counterfeiters into a popular theme park called WonderWorld. Murphy's stunt double works overtime as he is flung about the rides while bullets fly in all directions. Axel, go home.

Eddie Murphy is on the case with Judge Reinhold (center) and John Ashton (right) in Beverly Hills Cop *(1984).*

BEWARE, MY LOVELY

★★☆ RKO, 1952, b/w, 76 min. Dir: Harry Horner. SP: Mel Dinelli, b/o his play and short story. Cast: Ida Lupino, Robert Ryan, Taylor Holmes, Barbara Whiting, James Williams, O. Z. Whitehead.

Tense but standard lady-in-distress melodrama, with Ryan as a psychopathic killer who finds work in the home of teacher and war widow Lupino. Eventually she becomes his desperate prisoner and very nearly his next victim. Lupino and Ryan are expert actors, but the material shows its stage origins and is frayed around the edges.

BEYOND THE FOREST

★ Warner Bros., 1949, b/w, 96 min. Dir: King Vidor. SP: Lenore Coffee, b/o novel by Stuart Engstrand. Cast: Bette Davis, Joseph Cotten, David Brian, Ruth Roman, Dona Drake, Minor Watson, Regis Toomey.

This preposterous melodrama marked the end of Davis's career at Warners. Wearing a fright wig and garish makeup, she plays Rosa Moline, the restless, promiscuous wife of a small-town doctor (Cotten). She starts a torrid affair with a local rich man (Brian), and when an old hunter (Watson) discovers her guilty secret, she murders him. This being 1949, she pays the price. "What a dump!" Davis proclaims at the film's beginning, as she looks over her house. What a picture!

BIG BAD MAMA

★★☆ New Line, 1974, c, 83 min. Dir: Steve Carver. SP: William Norton, Frances Doel. Cast: Angie Dickinson, William Shatner, Tom Skerritt, Susan Sennett, Robbie Lee, Noble Willingham, Royal Dano, Joan Prather.

Proof positive that Bonnie and Clyde continued to live into the seventies. This time the Depression baddie is Wilma McClatchie (Dickinson), a Texas widow who, during the course of the movie, tries her hand as a bank robber, a rum runner, a jewel thief, and a kidnapper. She's also a mother and a lover. Skerritt and Shatner are the men in her life, and the sex scenes are quite steamy. A sequel, also with Angie Dickinson, was made thirteen years later.

BIG COMBO, THE

★★★ Allied Artists, 1955, b/w, 89 min. Dir: Joseph (H.) Lewis. SP: Philip Yordan. Cast: Cornel Wilde, Richard Conte, Jean Wallace, Brian Donlevy, Robert Middleton, Lee Van Cleef, Earl Holliman, Helen Walker, Ted De Corsia.

An exceptionally brutal crime melodrama, *The Big Combo* has all the basic ingredients of the genre, but they are well-handled. Wilde is an honest cop dedicated to bringing down vicious gangster Conte. True to form, both men are infatuated with the same woman (Wallace). In one especially nasty sequence, Wilde is tortured by having a hearing aid plugged into his ear while the receiver is held to a radio going full blast. He is also forced to drink a large bottle of hair tonic. Just everyday fun among the bad guys.

BIG EASY, THE

★★★ Kings Road, 1987, c, 108 min. Dir: Jim McBride. SP: Daniel Petrie, Jr. Cast: Dennis Quaid, Ellen Barkin, Ned Beatty, John Goodman, Ebbe Roe Smith, Lisa Jane Persky, Charles Ludlum, Grace Zabriskie.

This crime melodrama may be short on originality but it more than compensates with a bright screenplay, colorful atmosphere, and good performances. Quaid plays an easygoing New Orleans cop who clashes with an assistant district attorney (Barkin) bent on exposing police corruption. Not surprisingly, a steamy romance develops, interrupted only by a rival gang war that threatens to raise the city's body count. When something much more sinister seems to be behind the killings, the two join forces in dangerous pursuit of the culprits. As the Cajun cop Quaid offers charm to spare, and Barkin makes an attractive foil. In the midst of all the mayhem, there are some nice comic touches and a goodly amount of lively Cajun music.

BIG FIX, THE

★★★ Universal, 1978, c, 108 min. Dir: Jeremy Paul Kagan. SP: Roger L. Simon, b/o his novel. Cast: Richard Dreyfuss, Susan Anspach, John Lithgow, Bonnie Bedelia, F. Murray Abraham, Fritz Weaver, Ofelia Medina.

This nicely flavored movie has Dreyfuss as Moses Wine, a wisecracking Jewish private detective, once a sixties activist, who decides to work in the campaign of a liberal candidate for governor of California. When someone tries to sabotage the election by smearing the candidate as a radical, Wine investigates. His investigation leads him all over Los Angeles, and to various forms of skulduggery. Dreyfuss is fully in his "frisky puppy" mode, but the movie is fairly enjoyable.

BIG HEAT, THE

★★★☆ Columbia, 1953, b/w, 90 min. Dir: Fritz Lang. SP: Sydney Boehm, b/o novel by William McGivern. Cast: Glenn Ford, Gloria Grahame, Lee Marvin, Alexander Scourby, Jocelyn Brando, Jeanette Nolan, Adam Williams, Carolyn Jones.

Most viewers remember this film for the jolting scene in which vicious hoodlum Marvin tosses scalding coffee into the face of his girl (Grahame). But there are many other compelling moments in Lang's harsh, stinging melodrama.

Ford plays a grimly implaccable cop bent on exacting revenge on those who murdered his wife (Brando). His mission leads him to a nest of vipers headed by Scourby, and to Grahame, whose attempt to help him has deadly consequences for her. Time may have taken the edge off the movie's boldness, but it's still one of the best crime dramas of the fifties.

BIG HOUSE, THE

★★★ MGM, 1930, b/w, 86 min. Dir: George Hill. SP: Frances Marion, b/o story by Joe Farnham, Martin Flavin. Cast: Chester Morris, Wallace Beery, Lewis Stone, Robert Montgomery, Leila Hyams, George F. Marion, J. C. Nugent, Karl Dane, De Witt Jennings.

A pioneer prison film, primitive to be sure, but it still retains some of its original power. The

Alexander Scourby confronts Gloria Grahame, as Adam Williams (left) and Glenn Ford (right) look on, in The Big Heat *(1953).*

movie traces the fates of three convicts: forger Morris, who escapes and falls for Montgomery's sister (Hyams); killer and prison kingpin Beery, who engineers an ill-fated breakout; and a weak-willed young Montgomery, who was convicted of manslaughter. The action is surprisingly brutal and the film pulls no punches in exposing a corrupt, ineffectual prison system. Oscars for screenplay and sound recording.

BIG SCORE, THE

★★ Almi, 1983, c, 85 min. Dir: Fred Williamson. SP: Gail Morgan Hickman. Cast: Fred Williamson, Nancy Wilson, John Saxon, Richard Roundtree, Ed Lauter, D'Urville Martin, Michael Dante, Joe Spinell.

Williamson directed and starred in this strictly routine police story. He plays a dedicated Chicago cop who is suspected of taking a million dollars in drug money confiscated during a big drug raid. Nobody believes him, not even the drug dealers, and he becomes their main target for harrassment. Naturally he takes matters into his own hands, armed with an arsenal of weapons.

BIG SLEEP, THE

★★★★ Warner Bros., 1946, b/w, 114 min. Dir: Howard Hawks. SP: William Faulkner, Leigh Brackett, Jules Furthman, b/o novel by Raymond Chandler. Cast: Humphrey Bogart, Lauren Bacall, Martha Vickers, John Ridgely, Louis Jean Heydt, Elisha Cook, Jr., Dorothy Malone.

Reams of paper—as well as many hours of arguments among film buffs—have been expended in trying to unravel the tangled plot of this classic mystery thriller. Never mind. It's a perennially fascinating film, with quotable dialogue and offbeat characters. Bogart is detective Philip Marlowe, knee-deep in such matters as extortion, pornography, blackmail, and, of course, murder. Bacall is the rich, alluring Sternwood girl whose nymphomanical sister (Vickers) is one source of all the trouble. Watch for Bogart's bookstore scene with Malone, and cheers for Cook's performance as a pathetic grifter. The 1978 remake was small potatoes.

BIG SLEEP, THE

★★☆ United Artists, 1978, c, 100 min. Dir and SP: Michael Winner, b/o novel by Raymond Chandler.

Cast: Robert Mitchum, Sarah Miles, Richard Boone, Candy Clark, Joan Collins, Edward Fox, John Mills, James Stewart, Oliver Reed, Harry Andrews, Richard Todd.

A remake of Howard Hawks's 1946 Bogart-Bacall movie, this mystery thriller inexplicably transplants the story from Los Angeles to London. Once again private eye Philip Marlowe (Mitchum, repeating his role in *Farewell, My Lovely*, 1975), finds himself caught up in a complex plot involving blackmail and murder. The film may be more faithful to Chandler's novel than the Hawks version, but it's also duller and much less intriguing. The mostly British cast, however, is excellent.

BIG STEAL, THE

★★☆ RKO, 1949, b/w, 71 min. Dir: Don Siegel. SP: Geoffrey Homes, Gerald Drayson Adams, b/o story by Richard Wormser. Cast: Robert Mitchum, Jane Greer, William Bendix, Patric Knowles, Ramon Novarro, John Qualen, Don Alvarado.

Beautiful scenic views of Mexico, where the film was made, are the main attraction of this routine but lively mystery melodrama. Everybody seems to be chasing someone else: army finance officer Mitchum is after Knowles, who has stolen a huge wad of government money; government agent Bendix is trailing Mitchum; and police inspector Ramon Novarro is pursuing them all. At the same time, Mitchum enjoys a romance with the alluring Greer. The motives may not be clear, but the vistas sparkle.

BIG TROUBLE

★ Warner Bros., 1985, c, 93 min. Dir: John Cassavetes. SP: Warren Bogle (Andrew Bergman). Cast: Alan Arkin, Peter Falk, Beverly D'Angelo, Charles Durning, Robert Stack, Valerie Curtin, Richard Libertini, Paul Dooley.

When insurance salesman Arkin needs money to send his triplet sons to Yale, he makes a desperate move: he conspires with Beverly D'Angelo to kill her crackpot husband (Falk) and collect the money on the insurance policy Falk signed unwittingly. Sound familiar? This awful movie begins as a spoof of the classic *Double Indemnity*, then nosedives into frantic and unfunny farce. A bad mistake from director Cassavetes, barely released to theaters.

BILLY BATHGATE

★★☆ Touchstone, 1991, c, 108 min. Dir: Robert Benton. SP: Tom Stoppard, b/o novel by E. L. Doctorow. Cast: Dustin Hoffman, Nicole Kidman, Loren Dean, Bruce Willis, Steven Hill, Steve Buscemi, Katharine Houghton.

This movie should have worked, but it doesn't. Adapted by a noted playwright from a best-selling novel, and guided by a director with solid credentials, it had a major star (Hoffman) in the leading role. Yet somehow the movie never catches fire. Dean plays Billy, a Bronx teenager who, in 1935, becomes the protégé of mobster Dutch Schultz (Hoffman). Eventually he learns that his mentor is a cold-blooded killer undeserving of respect. Billy also comes to care for Schultz's mistress (Kidman)—a dangerous mistake. Somehow the characters arouse little interest, despite a lavish and attractive production.

BIRDMAN OF ALCATRAZ

★★★ United Artists, 1962, b/w, 143 min. Dir: John Frankenheimer. SP: Guy Trosper, b/o book by Thomas E. Gaddis. Cast: Burt Lancaster, Karl Malden, Thelma Ritter, Betty Field, Edmond O'Brien, Telly Savalas, Neville Brand, Whit Bissell, Hugh Marlowe.

A long, rambling, fairly interesting account of the life of Robert Stroud (Lancaster), the convict who became an authority on ornithology. Apparently Stroud was a bitter man who was imprisoned on a murder charge and placed in solitary confinement, and who built a makeshift haven for his feathered friends and a simple laboratory to study their diseases. Malden plays the warden who alternates between sympathy for Stroud and resentment of his criticism of the prison system. Lancaster received an Oscar nomination.

Convict Robert Stroud (Burt Lancaster) tends his precious charges in Birdman of Alcatraz *(1962).*

BIRD ON A WIRE

★★ Universal, 1990, c, 110 min. Dir: John Badham. SP: David Seltzer, Louis Venosta, Eric Lerner. Cast: Mel Gibson, Goldie Hawn, David Carradine, Bill Duke, Joan Severance, Stephen Tobolowsky.

Gibson and Hawn make an attractive team, but the material lets them down. Gibson is a gas station attendant who has been in the witness relocation program for years. By coincidence, his old girfriend (Hawn) recognizes him just when the drug thugs he fingered have caught up with him at last. Now Gibson and Hawn are in full flight from the gangsters, while their romance is rekindled. Flat and silly stuff, not worth your attention.

BLACK BIRD, THE

★★ Columbia, 1975, c, 98 min. Dir and SP: David Giler. Cast: George Segal, Stephane Audran, Lionel Stander, Lee Patrick, Elisha Cook, Jr., Felix Silla, Signe Hasso.

Proof positive that poking fun at a beloved old movie is hazardous business. A lame takeoff on John Huston's classic *The Maltese Falcon*, the film stars George Segal as Sam Spade, Jr., a pale shadow of his famous-detective father. Somehow the old falcon statue is still around, and the rivals for seizing the black bird include a midget Nazi and four Hawaiian gangsters. Virtually the only laughs are supplied by Stander as Spade's eccentric, green-suited sidekick. It's nice, however, to see Patrick and Cook reprising their old familiar roles from the original.

BLACK CAESAR

★★☆ American International, 1973, c, 96 min. Dir and SP: Larry Cohen. Cast: Fred Williamson, D'Urville Martin, Gloria Hendry, Art Lund, Val Avery, Minnie Gentry, Julius W. Harris.

One of the black exploitation movies that surfaced in the early seventies, *Black Caesar* is clearly meant to echo the gangland melodramas of the thirties (*Little Caesar*, etc.) Williamson is the bloodthirsty hood who rises to the top and then loses it all when he becomes too greedy and corrupt. Lots of action and some good Harlem locations.

BLACK EYE

★★ Warner Bros., 1974, c, 98 min. Dir: Jack Arnold. SP: Mark Haggard, Jim Martin, b/o novel by Jeff Jacks. Cast: Fred Williamson, Rosemary Forsyth, Teresa Graves, Bret Morrison, Richard X. Slattery, Larry Mann, Cyril Delevanti.

Routine action film with Williamson as a detective investigating a drug ring in Venice, California. Soon he is knee-deep in danger, tangling with a sinister pornographer (Morrison, radio's original "Shadow"), the head (Mann) of a flock of Jesus freaks, and assorted drug dealers. Graves plays his bisexual girlfriend.

BLACK HAND

★★★ MGM, 1950, b/w, 93 min. Dir: Richard Thorpe. SP: Luther Davis, b/o story by Leo Townsend. Cast: Gene Kelly, J. Carrol Naish, Teresa Celli, Marc Lawrence, Frank Puglia, Barry Kelley, Peter Brocco, Mario Siletti.

One of Kelly's few dramatic roles in the early part of his career, *Black Hand* has him playing a man bent on revenge against the notorious Black Hand Society for the murder of his father in turn-of-the-century New York City. The movie succeeds in conveying the dark, menacing atmosphere of Italian immigrant life in these years, and Kelly is surprisingly effective as an angry man who is willing to kill to get satisfaction.

BLACK RAIN

★★★ Paramount, 1989, c, 125 min. Dir: Ridley Scott. SP: Craig Bolotin and Warren Lewis. Cast: Michael Douglas, Andy Garcia, Kate Capshaw, Ken Takakura, Yusaku Matsuda, John Spencer.

An atmospheric, extremely violent thriller set largely in Japan. When a Japanese mobster escapes from the custody of cops Douglas and Garcia, they fly to that country to find him. Instead they come up against vicious Japanese gangsters and inscrutable Japanese bureacracy. When Garcia is brutally murdered, Douglas, playing a corrupt and nasty sort, goes all out for revenge and it turns him into a hero. The film goes in for quite a bit of Japan-bashing, but it certainly keeps moving.

BLACK SUNDAY

★★★☆ Paramount, 1977, c, 143 min. Dir: John Frankenheimer. SP: Ernest Lehman, Kenneth Ross, Ivan Moffet, b/o novel by Thomas Harris. Cast: Robert Shaw, Bruce Dern, Marthe Keller, Fritz Weaver, Steven Keats, Bekim Fehmiu, William Daniels.

A crackerjack "disaster" thriller, well-edited and featuring some stunning aerial photography. A group of terrorists plots to explode the Goodyear Blimp over the stadium in which the Super Bowl game is being held. Will they be thwarted? The outcome is inevitable (this is, after all, a movie), but the suspense is high. Shaw plays the heroic Israeli guerrilla who saves the day, and Dern is the nuttiest of the terrorists, an ex-pilot and former Vietnam prisoner of war.

BLACK WIDOW

★★★ Fox, 1987, c, 101 min. Dir: Bob Rafelson. SP: Ronald Bass. Cast: Debra Winger, Theresa Russell, Sami Frey, Nicol Williamson, Dennis Hopper, Terry O'Quinn, Leo Rossi, Lois Smith, James Hong, Diane Ladd.

The black widow spider "mates and kills," as the ads proclaimed, and so does Catharine (Russell), who seduces, marries, and then murders wealthy men. Enter Alex (Winger), agent for the Justice Department, who becomes intrigued, then obsessed, with catching Catharine before she kills again. But not before her own life becomes ensnared with Catharine's in unexpected ways. A moderately good thriller, with expert performances by Winger and Russell.

BLIND FURY

★★☆ TriStar, 1990, c, 96 min. Dir: Phillip Noyce. SP: Charles Robert Carner, b/o his novel. Cast: Rutger Hauer, Terrance (Terry) O'Quinn, Lisa Blount, Nick Cassavetes, Rick Overton, Meg Foster, Brandon Call, Noble Willingham.

Blinded in the war, Nick Parker (Hauer) has developed his other senses and fine-tuned his skills at the martial arts. Now he must use these skills to defend an old war buddy and his young son from the mob in Reno. The movie is ridiculous, but at least it *knows* that it's ridiculous and plays some of the material for laughs as well as action.

BLOOD AND WINE

★★★ Fox Searchlight, 1997, c, 100 min. Dir: Bob Rafelson. SP: Nick Villiers, Alison Cross, b/o story by Nick Villiers, Bob Rafelson. Cast: Jack Nicholson, Michael Caine, Stephen Dorff, Jennifer Lopez, Judy Davis.

Director Rafelson's long collaboration with Nicholson (*Five Easy Pieces*, *The Postman Always Rings Twice*, among others) continues with this twisty, cold-hearted film noir. The characters are pure noir: nasty, greedy, and often clueless about what they're doing or what's happening to them. Nicholson plays a Florida wine merchant who plots a jewel heist with tubercular thief Caine and gets much more than he expected when the jewel ends up in the possesion of his wretchedly unhappy, addicted wife (Davis) and hostile stepson (Dorff). Jennifer Lopez is the beautiful woman involved with both father and stepson. The ending is ironic but unconvincing.

BLOOD SIMPLE

★★★☆ Circle Films, 1985, c, 97 min. Dir: Joel Coen. SP: Joel Coen, Ethan Coen. Cast: John Getz, Frances McDormand, Dan Hedaya, M. Emmet Walsh, Samm-Art Williams.

The first movie of the Coen brothers, *Blood Simple* established their unique style of combining razor-sharp suspense and black comedy in surprising ways. Here the twisty plot involves a saloon owner (Hedaya) who hires a sleazy detective (Walsh) to kill his cheating wife (McDormand) and her lover (Getz). What happens is completely unexpected and sometimes grisly as the not overly bright characters blunder their way to a violent climax. The budget is low and the cast unfamiliar, but you won't be bored.

BLOODY MAMA

★ American International, 1970, c, 90 min. Dir: Roger Corman. SP: Robert Thom, b/o story by Robert Thom, Don Peters. Cast: Shelley Winters, Pat Hingle, Don Stroud, Diane Varsi, Robert De Niro, Clint Kimbrough, Robert Walden, Pamela Dunlap.

Winters is way over the top as "Ma" Barker, the notorious true-life mother of four vicious, moronic sons who cut a wide swath of murder and mayhem in Arkansas during the Depression years. Director Corman tries to add a smattering of documentary realism and a dab of psychology to the mix, but the result is still an awful film whose original warm reception now seems inexplicable. Appearing in his fourth movie, De Niro plays one of Ma's sons.

BLOWN AWAY

★★☆ MGM, 1994, c, 120 min. Dir: Stephen Hopkins. SP: Joe Batteer and John Rice, b/o story by Joe Batteer, John Rice, M. Jay Roach. Cast: Jeff Bridges, Tommy Lee Jones, Lloyd Bridges, Forest Whitaker, Suzy Amis, John Finn.

Explosions—huge and fiery—are the keynote of this contrived melodrama. Jeff Bridges is a Boston policeman assigned to the bomb squad. Jones is a cold-blooded Irish terrorist who knows about Bridges's secret past in Ireland, and who blames Bridges for an incident that killed their colleagues. A master bomber, Jones is now bent on taking revenge. Before the two finally meet in violent battle, there are threats, near-misses, and, of course, many large, impressive explosions. Too much flat-footed dialogue and too many plot holes tend to sink a basically workable premise.

BLOW OUT

★★☆ Orion, 1981, c, 107 min. Dir and SP: Brian De Palma. Cast: John Travolta, Nancy Allen, John Lithgow, Dennis Franz, John McMartin, John Aquino.

Jack Terry (Travolta) is a sound-effects wizard who finds himself involved in a dangerous mystery. One night in Philadelphia, he records what seems to be an accident in which a car plunges into a river. His close investigation shows that it was no accident but the political murder of a presidential aspirant. Naturally nobody believes him, and before it all ends, Jack and the girl (Allen) who was in the car with the victim are being stalked by a nasty serial killer (Lithgow). Still working Hitchcock territory, and with a nod to Antonioni's *Blow-Up*, director De Palma struggles to keep up the suspense, but the logic keeps disappearing, especially in a prolonged climax during a parade. The downbeat ending will leave many viewers baffled and depressed.

BLUE DAHLIA, THE

★★★ Paramount, 1946, b/w, 99 min. Dir: George Marshall. SP: Raymond Chandler. Cast: Alan Ladd, Veronica Lake, William Bendix, Howard Da Silva, Doris Dowling, Frank Faylen, Hugh Beaumont, Will Wright.

Novelist Raymond Chandler wrote the screenplay for this taut, typical film noir of the forties. Alan Ladd is a war veteran who comes home to find that his wife (Dowling) has become an easy-living tramp. When she's

murdered, he becomes the chief suspect. Veronica Lake is the ambiguous new woman in his life. Better than either the sleepwalking Ladd or Lake are the colorful side characters, especially a blackmailing house detective played by Wright.

BLUE STEEL

★ MGM/UA, 1990, c, 102 min. Dir: Kathryn Bigelow. SP: Kathryn Bigelow, Eric Red. Cast: Jamie Lee Curtis, Ron Silver, Clancy Brown, Elizabeth Peña, Philip Bosco, Louise Fletcher.

Meg Turner (Curtis) is a rookie cop. Eugene Hunt (Silver) is a commodities trader who also happens to be a deranged serial killer with a gun fetish. When he becomes obsessed with her (and her gun), the consequences are deadly. A lurid, ludicrous, and profoundly irritating movie, *Blue Steel* makes no sense at all, especially when the killer keeps escaping the clutches of the law time after time. This must surely mark the most embarrassing role of Silver's career to date.

BLUE THUNDER

★★ Columbia, 1983, c, 108 min. Dir: John Badham. SP: Dan O'Bannon, Don Jakoby. Cast: Roy Scheider, Malcolm McDowell, Candy Clark, Daniel Stern, Warren Oates, Paul Roebling, Joe Santos.

Can a high-tech thriller become more preposterous as it whirls along? Watch *Blue Thunder* and see. Roy Scheider is a troubled cop who works for L.A.'s police helicopter surveillance unit. When a murderous conspiracy surfaces regarding the unit's new state-of-the-art surveillance machine (called Blue Thunder), Scheider must expose it single-handedly. McDowell is the improbable British colonel who heads the conspiracy. Noisy, foolish, and also cold-blooded in its willingness to destroy innocent lives on land or in the air.

BLUE VELVET

★★ De Laurentiis, 1986, c, 120 min. Dir and SP: David Lynch. Cast: Kyle MacLachlan, Isabella Rossellini, Dennis Hopper, Laura Dern, Dean Stockwell, Hope Lange, Brad Dourif, Jack Nance.

In 1986 the National Society of Film Critics voted this the year's best film. You may wonder why. A fascinating but terminally weird, often repellent movie, *Blue Velvet* purports to find the depravity lurking just beneath the surface of a seemingly normal American town. A young man (MacLachlan) discovers a severed ear in the grass and his search for an explanation leads him into a nightmare world occupied by bizarre people, including a masochistic singer (Rossellini) and a sadistic drug dealer (Hopper). Original, certainly, but also ugly and off-putting.

BODY DOUBLE

★☆ Columbia, 1984, c, 109 min. Dir: Brian De Palma. SP: Robert H. Avrech, Brian De Palma, b/o story by De Palma. Cast: Craig Wasson, Melanie Griffith, Gregg Henry, Deborah Shelton, Dennis Franz, Guy Boyd.

Voyeurism. Fetishism. Violence with sexual overtones. All these turn up in Hitchcock movies, although in muted form. Working in a more permissive age, Hitchcock disciple De Palma could be as explicit as he chose to be, but in the case of *Body Double*, the result is disastrous. A slow-witted, claustrophobic actor (Wasson), spying on a sexy neighbor, cannot save her from being murdered. But what is really going on? A porno actress (Griffith) helps him to find the answer. More will not be revealed here, but the movie is far-fetched, lurid, and worthless, except for one Hitchcockian sequence in a Rodeo Drive shopping mall (the reason for the half-star above).

BODYGUARD, THE

★★☆ Warner Bros., 1992, c, 129 min. Dir: Mick Jackson. SP: Lawrence Kasdan. Cast: Kevin Costner, Whitney Houston, Gary Kemp, Bill Cobbs, Ralph Waite.

Kasdan, coauthor and director of *The Big Chill*, *Grand Canyon*, and other notable films, wrote this romantic thriller but left the direction to

THE LADIES OF NOIR

Alluring, wicked, and probably dangerous, the actresses who frequently inhabited the world of film noir were a special breed that intrigued movie audiences in the forties and fifties. At one time or another most of them played more benign, noble, or even comic women, but they are remembered for the aura of fatalism and forbidden desire that surrounded them like perfume in scores of noir melodramas.

BARBARA STANWYCK (1907–1990)

A talented actress well loved by her coworkers (she was known affectionately as Missy), Barbara Stanwyck entered films in 1929 and brought her professionalism and her hard-edged, straightforward style to a great many films from the thirties to the midsixties, when she moved for a while to television. In 1944 she starred as scheming, rotten-to-the-core Phyllis Dietrichson in Billy Wilder's *Double Indemnity* and established herself as the Queen of Noir. Victim or victimizer, she was memorable in such thrillers as *The Strange Love of Martha Ivers* (1946), *Sorry, Wrong Number* (1948), and *The File on Thelma Jordon* (1949).

CLAIRE TREVOR (b. 1912)

In 1948 Claire Trevor won an Academy Award as Best Supporting Actress for her role as Edward G. Robinson's pathetic, tippling moll Gay Dawn in John Huston's *Key Largo* (1948). It was a peak moment for a skillful, reliable actress who made her film debut in 1933. Trevor won John Wayne's heart as a true-blue prostitute in *Stagecoach* (1939), but she was especially adept at playing tough, no-nonsense dames with murder, larceny, or a mink coat on their minds in such movies as *Murder, My Sweet* (1944), *Born to Kill* (1947), and *Raw Deal* (1948).

GLORIA GRAHAME (1925–1981)

Gloria Grahame's insinuating voice and pouty mouth made her an ideal choice to play vixens, molls, and mistresses in films from the forties to the sixties. She was hard to forget as the ambiguous bargirl in *Crossfire* (1947), Humphrey Bogart's sultry neighbor in *In a Lonely Place* (1950), or Jack Palance's co-conspirator in *Sudden Fear* (1950). She won a Supporting Oscar in

Jackson. Glamorous and hugely popular singer Houston is Rachel Marron, a glamorous and hugely popular singer who is receiving death threats. Enter troubled bodyguard Frank Farmer (Costner, with a bad haircut) who protects her and falls for her. *The Bodyguard* generates a few suspenseful sequences, but it's basically a shiny property for a singing star's movie debut, rather than a fully realized movie.

BODY OF EVIDENCE

★ MGM/UA, 1993, c, 99 min. Dir: Uli Edel. SP: Brad Mirman. Cast: Madonna, Willem Dafoe, Joe Mantegna, Anne Archer, Julianne Moore, Jurgen Prochnow, Frank Langella, Stan Shaw, Charles Hallahan, Lillian Lehman.

The real mystery about this dreadful thriller is how so many good actors were persuaded to appear in it. The premise is ridiculous: alluring Madonna is brought to trial, accused of killing her older lover with too much rough sex. (She inherits his fortune.) Dafoe is her married lawyer who falls under her spell and is soon engaging in steamy sex acts with his client. Is she a victim of circumstance or a scheming, cold-blooded vixen? The violent climax provides the answer. Madonna is adequate in her noirish role, and the others try not to look too embarrassed.

BOILING POINT

★☆ Warner Bros., 1993, c, 92 min. Dir and SP: James B. Harris, b/o novel by Gerald Petievich. Cast: Wesley Snipes, Dennis Hopper, Lolita Davidovich, Viggo Mortensen, Jonathan Banks, Valerie Perrine, Dan Hedaya, Tony LoBianco, Seymour Cassel.

Cliché-ridden and (for all the action) dull melodrama starring Wesley Snipes as a brooding

1952 for playing Dick Powell's Southern-belle wife in *The Bad and the Beautiful*. And yes, she was the hapless moll who had scalding-hot coffee thrown in her face by Lee Marvin in *The Big Heat* (1953).

JOAN BENNETT (1910–1990)

The daughter of actor Richard Bennett and the sister of actresses Constance and Barbara Bennett, this beautiful actress began her career in 1928 as a demure or spirited blonde ingenue. In the late thirties she turned brunette and took on a somewhat harder edge. By the midforties, she was a full-fledged noir woman, playing treacherous trollops in two Fritz Lang melodramas, *The Woman in the Window* (1945) and *Scarlet Street* (1946). There were other noir roles, but in 1950 she turned benign and domesticated as Elizabeth Taylor's level-headed mother in *Father of the Bride* (1950) and its sequel, *Father's Little Dividend* (1951).

VERONICA LAKE (1919–1973)

Diminutive and flat-voiced, Veronica Lake never was, or claimed to be, much of an actress, but in 1941 she attracted viewer attention with her blonde "peek-a-boo" bangs in an aviation movie called *I Wanted Wings*. (Actually, she had played bit roles in a few earlier movies under the name of Constance Keane.) Her star rose when she costarred with equally diminutive Alan Ladd in the tense melodrama *This Gun For Hire* (1942), and they were reteamed in *The Glass Key* (1942), *The Blue Dahlia* (1946), and *Saigon* (1948). Most of her subsequent roles were disappointing.

JANE GREER (b. 1924)

If for nothing else, Jane Greer will be remembered as the very essence of noir wickedness in Jacques Tourneur's *Out of the Past* (1947). Seductive and treacherous, she gave both Robert Mitchum and Kirk Douglas a difficult time indeed. In a loose 1984 remake of that movie, called *Against All Odds*, she played the mother of the same character. She reteamed with Robert Mitchum for *The Big Steal* (1949), but most of her other roles were routine.

Faye Dunaway and Warren Beatty soared to stardom as thirties outlaws Bonnie
Parker and Clyde Barrow in Bonnie and Clyde (1967).

federal agent out to apprehend the person who
killed his partner during a stakeout. There is no
character that hasn't been done better else-
where, from the strutting ex-con (Hooper)
looking for his next big score to the sympathetic hooker (Davidovich). At least Hopper isn't
playing his usual out-of-control fruitcake.

BONNIE AND CLYDE

★★★★ Warner Bros., 1967, c, 111 min. Dir: Arthur
Penn. SP: David Newman, Robert Benton. Cast:
Warren Beatty, Faye Dunaway, Gene Hackman,
Estelle Parsons, Michael J. Pollard, Gene Wilder, Dub
Taylor, Denver Pyle.

One of the most controversial and outstanding
films of the sixties, Bonnie and Clyde is a superb
achievement in which all the elements—
screenplay, direction, performances, music,
settings—cohere into an effective unit. The
movie shows how Clyde Barrow (Beatty) and
Bonnie Parker (Dunaway), two small-time
thieves and murderers of the Depression
years, turn into folk heroes who come to
believe fatally in their self-created myth. Bois-
terous comedy and explicit violence combine
to unsettle the viewer, right up to the blood-
soaked ending. Oscars went to Parsons, marvelous as Clyde's sister-in-law, and to Burnett
Guffey for his stunning cinematography.

BOOMERANG!

★★★☆ Fox, 1947, b/w, 88 min. Dir: Elia Kazan. SP:
Richard Murphy, b/o article by Anthony Abbott. Cast:
Dana Andrews, Jane Wyatt, Lee J. Cobb, Arthur
Kennedy, Sam Levene, Robert Keith, Taylor Holmes,

Ed Begley, Karl Malden, Cara Williams.

An adroit, compelling drama from director Kazan, made in the semidocumentary style pioneered by the film's producer, Louis de Rochemont. Based on a factual incident, the story revolves around the murder of a popular priest. A young drifter (Kennedy) is arrested, but the prosecuting attorney (Andrews) is not convinced that they are holding the guilty party, and he launches an investigation that proves Kennedy's innocence. Fine acting by a good cast, especially by Kennedy in a grueling third-degree scene.

BORDER, THE

★★☆ Columbia, 1982, c, 107 min. Dir: Tony Richardson. SP: Deric Washburn, Walon Green, David Freeman. Cast: Jack Nicholson, Harvey Keitel, Valerie Perrine, Warren Oates, Elpidia Carrillo, Shannon Wilcox, Manuel Viescas.

British director Richardson's first American film in seventeen years, *The Border* is a harsh melodrama dealing with a topic still sadly timely: illegal immigration. Nicholson stars as a border guard in El Paso, who, spurred on by his money-hungry wife (Perrine), begins accepting payoffs from exploiters of Mexican "wetbacks." Soon he is enmeshed in a violent world of bribes, beatings, and murder. He also begins an affair with a young Mexican woman (Carrillo). Nicholson brings some conviction to his role, but the movie is only fair.

BORDERLINE

★★☆ Universal-International, 1950, b/w, 88 min. Dir: William A. Seiter. SP: Devery Freeman, b/o his story. Cast: Fred MacMurray, Claire Trevor, Raymond Burr, Roy Roberts, Jose Torvay, Morris Ankrum, Charles Lane.

A standard melodrama, with MacMurray as a Narcotics Bureau agent and Trevor as a police-woman posing as a brassy chorine. They are both out to demolish a drug syndicate headed

Prosecuting attorney Dana Andrews questions the guilt of the man he is trying for murder in Boomerang! *(1947).*

by Burr, but each is unaware of the other's true intentions. Of course they complicate matters by falling in love. It all comes to a head in a gun battle at the syndicate's headquarters. Okay, but nothing new.

BORN LOSERS, THE

★ American International, 1967, c, 112 min. Dir: T. C. Frank (Tom Laughlin). SP: James Lloyd (Tom Laughlin). Cast: Tom Laughlin, Elizabeth James, Jane Russell, Jeremy Slate, William Wellman, Jr.

Notable only as being the movie that introduced Billy Jack, the taciturn but forceful Vietnam veteran and half-breed who enjoyed brief popularity in several early seventies features. Here he deals in his own strong-arm way with a gang of raping, marauding motocyclists and, to put it succinctly, the movie is excrutiatingly awful. Russell turns up as the blowsy mother of one of the gang's teenage victims.

BORN TO KILL

★★★ RKO, 1947, b/w, 92 min. Dir: Robert Wise. SP: Eve Green, Richard Macauley, b/o novel by James Gunn. Cast: Lawrence Tierney, Claire Trevor, Walter Slezak, Audrey Long, Philip Terry, Elisha Cook, Jr.

This tough-minded little film noir was directed by Wise during his RKO years, and it's light-years away from his later movies (*The Sound of Music*, for instance). The central character is a psychotic murderer (Tierney) who is married to a naive young woman (Long) but can't keep away from her older, tougher divorced sister (Trevor), with deadly results. The movie is now considered a cult item, but at the time of its release, the *New York Times* condemned it as "not only morally disgusting but an offense to a normal intellect." Judge for yourself.

BOSTON STRANGLER, THE

★★★ Fox, 1968, c, 116 min. Dir: Richard Fleischer. SP: Edward Anhalt, b/o book by Gerold Frank. Cast: Tony Curtis, Henry Fonda, George Kennedy, Mike

Henry Fonda interrogates Tony Curtis, playing true-life serial killer Albert De Salvo in The Boston Strangler *(1968).*

THE BOYS NEXT DOOR

Kellin, Murray Hamilton, Hurd Hatfield, Sally Kellerman, Jeff Corey, George Voskovec.

Sporting a prosthetic nose, Tony Curtis gives a riveting performance as Albert De Salvo, the true-life serial killer who preyed on many women between 1962 and 1964. The semi-documentary film shows how the police pursued, captured, and prosecuted him, as well as how he operated in the Boston area. Fonda is also quietly effective as Massachusetts's dogged assistant attorney general. At times the movie makes use of multiscreens, but the device really doesn't help much.

BOUND

★★★☆ Gramercy, 1996, c, 107 min. Dir and SP: Larry Wachowski, Andy Wachowski. Cast: Jennifer Tilly, Gina Gershon, Joe Pantoliano, John P. Ryan, Christopher Meloni, Richard Sarafian, Barry Kivel.

How much does stylishness and originality weigh against the depiction of raw and sometimes unwatchable violence? You may have to answer this question for yourself if you view this startlingly original, often powerful film noir. Corky (Gershon) is a tough lesbian recently out of prison. She meets and begins a sizzling affair with Violet (Tilly), the girlfriend of a low-level hood (Pantoliano) who is much smarter than she seems to be. Together the lovers plot to steal a fortune in laundered money from the mob. Naturally everything goes awry, and there is much graphic bloodletting. There are twists, turns, and surprises along the way, and the young writer-directors display a genuine talent for this sort of thriller. Gershon is fine as Corky, and Tilly, who seems to play every role in the same breathless, baby-doll way, is aptly cast as Violet. *Bound* may turn you off, but then again, it may not. Your pick.

BOUND BY HONOR

★★☆ Hollywood, 1993, c, 180 min. Dir: Taylor Hackford. SP: Jimmy Santiago Baca, Jeremy Ioacone, Floyd Mutrux, b/o story by Ross Thomas. Cast: Damian Chapa, Jesse Borrego, Benjamin Bratt, Enrique J. Castillo, Victor Rivers, Delroy Lindo, Tom Towles, Carlos Carrasco, Teddy Wilson, Raymond Cruz, Billy Bob Thornton, Ving Rhames.

A very long, ambitious, but failed attempt to record the Chicano experience in America, *Bound by Honor* covers twenty brutal years in the lives of three young men from East Los Angeles. Related by blood and by gang membership, they meet various fates. One (Chapa) becomes a San Quentin kingpin; another (Borrego) has artistic ability but almost destroys himself with drugs, and the third (Bratt), the most violent of the three, becomes a tough, honest cop. Baca, one of the authors, wrote award-winning poetry while in prison. The movie tries to cover too much territory, and ultimately the clichés seriously weaken the intended impact. Retitled *Blood In, Blood Out*.

BOXCAR BERTHA

★★★ American International, 1972, c, 97 min. Dir: Martin Scorsese. SP: Joyce H. Corrington, John William Corrington, b/o characters in autobiography of "Boxcar Bertha" Thompson, as told to Dr. Ben L. Reitman. Cast: Barbara Hershey, David Carradine, Barry Primus, Bernie Casey, John Carradine.

Scorsese's first studio film shows some glimmers of the skill he would develop later in his career, but it is essentially just another variation of the highly influential *Bonnie and Clyde* (1967). Hershey plays the true-life "Boxcar Bertha" Thompson who, in the Depression years, joined up with a trio of robbers and apparently lived to tell the tale. Predictably her romance with one of the robbers, "Big Bill" Shelly (David Carradine), a labor organizer and reluctant thief, ends in a furious burst of violence. Not at all bad, but not memorable either.

BOYS NEXT DOOR, THE

★ New World/Republic, 1985, c, 90 min. Dir: Penelope Spheeris. SP: Alan Morgan, James Wong. Cast: Maxwell Caulfield, Charlie Sheen, Patti D'Arbanville, Christopher McDonald, Hank Garrett, Moon Zappa.

Teenagers Roy Alston (Caulfield) and Bo Richards (Sheen) may seem like the boys next door, but watch out. Choking with unfocused rage at the world (Roy, in particular), they move in one terrible day from mischief to murder, leaving a trail of bodies behind them. Their end is inevitable. A gratuitously brutal and awkwardly made movie, guaranteed to leave viewers depressed and unenlightened. Not to be confused with the play and television movie about mentally challenged men who live together.

BOYZ N THE HOOD
★★★ Columbia, 1991, c, 107 min. Dir and SP: John Singleton. Cast: Cuba Gooding, Jr., Larry Fishburne, Ice Cube, Morris Chestnut, Angela Bassett, Nia Long, Tyra Ferrell, Whitman Mayo.

With this flawed but honest film about young blacks in the inner city, twenty-three-year-old John Singleton became the first black director to be nominated for an Academy Award. He doesn't flinch from violence or despair, but he also offers some rays of hope as well. The central character is Tre (Gooding), a basically decent young man who, along with his friends, is swept up in a maelstrom of murder and revenge. Singleton pauses too often to deliver a message, but the cast plays out his story with conviction.

BRANNIGAN
★★☆ United Artists, 1975, c, 111 min. Dir: Douglas Hickox. SP: Christopher Trumbo, Michael Butler, William P. McGivern, William Norton, b/o story by Christopher Trumbo, Michael Butler. Cast: John Wayne, Richard Attenborough, Judy Geeson, Mel Ferrer, John Vernon, Lesley-Anne Down.

Wayne forgoes his usual chaps and buckskin for modern-day garb in this routine melodrama set in London. He's a Chicago detective who is sent to England's capital city to track down a fugitive mobster (Vernon). Inevitably he comes up against some unsavory types who draw him into the usual gun battles, car chases, and one outsize brawl in a pub. Interesting change of pace for the Duke, but the movie's best feature is its tour of London landmarks.

BREAKDOWN
★★★☆ Paramount, 1997, c, 105 min. Dir: Jonathan Mostow. SP: Jonathan Mostow, Sam Montgomery, b/o story by Jonathan Mostow. Cast: Kurt Russell, J. T. Walsh, Kathleen Quinlan, M. C. Gainey, Jack Noseworthy, Rex Linn.

This taut nail-biter may begin by reminding you of other movies, particularly *Duel* and *The Vanishing* (both American and Dutch-French versions), but it succeeds in generating its very own suspense. Massachusetts couple Jeff and Amy Taylor (Russell and Quinlan) are traveling across vast, deserted Western vistas when their Jeep breaks down. Hitching a ride for help with a trucker (Walsh), Amy suddenly vanishes, and of course nobody has seen her. Soon Jeff plunges into a waking nightmare that pits him against some very nasty types, turning him (rather improbably) into an action hero, bent on rescuing his wife. First-time director Mostow knows how to use the Western terrain for maximum sinister effect, and he works up to a wingding of a climax. *Breakdown* gives a fresh new spin to a familiar theme.

BREAKING IN
★★☆ Goldwyn, 1989, c, 91 min. Dir: Bill Forsyth. SP: John Sayles. Cast: Burt Reynolds, Casey Siemaszko, Sheila Kelley, Lorraine Toussaint, Albert Salmi, Harry Carey.

Burt Reynolds takes on a character role in this amiable, lightweight film. He plays an aging, slightly pot-bellied professional thief who takes an apprentice (Siemaszko)—a garage hand who enjoys breaking into houses to raid the refrigerator and read the mail. The two become partners, resulting in comic capers and a surprise or two along the way.

BREAKOUT
★★ Columbia, 1975, c, 96 min. Dir: Tom Gries. SP: Howard B. Kreitsek, Frank Kowalski, b/o their novel. Cast: Charles Bronson, Robert Duvall, Jill Ireland, John Huston, Randy Quaid, Sheree North, Alejandro Rey.

Standard Bronson heroics, with the actor as a carefree aviator who rescues Duvall—framed for murder by father-in-law John Huston—from a Mexican prison. Ireland is Duvall's loyal wife. A few good action sequences, but nothing more.

BREATHLESS
★★ Orion, 1983, c, 100 min. Dir: Jim McBride. SP: L. M. Kit Carson, Jim McBride, b/o screenplay by Jean-Luc Godard of story by François Truffaut. Cast: Richard Gere, Valerie Kaprisky, Art Metrano, John P. Ryan, William Tepper.

Fans of Gere may enjoy this close remake of Truffaut's influential 1959 French film of the same name; others beware. In the Jean-Paul Belmondo role, Gere plays an amoral punk who accidentally kills a policeman. He attempts to elude the law with the help of a French UCLA student (Kaprisky) he claims to love. Her ambivalent feelings for him spark the melodramatic climax. Gere gives the role his all, but much of the material is surprisingly dull, even when it duplicates the original film.

BRINK'S JOB, THE

★★☆ Universal, 1978, c, 103 min. Dir: William Friedkin. SP: Walon Green, b/o book by Noel Behn. Cast: Peter Falk, Warren Oates, Peter Boyle, Allen Goorwitz (Garfield), Gena Rowlands, Paul Sorvino, Sheldon Leonard.

In Boston, in 1950, a group of amateur criminals broke into the vaults of Brink's security company and made off with several million dollars. The media labeled it "the crime of the century." This movie takes a mostly comic spin on the story, with Falk leading his bumbling friends (Boyle, Sorvino, Goorwitz, and others) in the robbery that succeeds, at least temporarily, in spite of their ineptitude. The cast is good (with an outstanding performance by Oates), but the movie is somewhat diminished by an uncertain tone and underdeveloped characters.

BRONX TALE, A

★★★ Savoy, 1993, c, 122 min. Dir: Robert De Niro. SP: Chazz Palminteri, b/o his play. Cast: Robert De Niro, Chazz Palminteri, Lillo Brancato, Francis Capra, Taral Hicks, Joe Pesci.

De Niro makes a respectable directorial debut in this flavorful coming-of-age story set in the Bronx of the sixties. He also stars as a decent, hard-working bus driver whose young son (Brancato) idolizes the neighborhood's top hood (Palminteri). The struggle between father and gangster for the son's loyalty constitutes the heart of the movie. Also triggering complications is the son's involvement with a black girl (Hicks). Since Palminteri wrote the screenplay, it comes as no surprise that the most interesting and many-faceted character in the film is the one that he plays.

BROTHERHOOD, THE

★★★ Paramount, 1968, c, 98 min. Dir: Martin Ritt. SP: Lewis John Carlino. Cast: Kirk Douglas, Alex Cord,

Kirk Douglas plays aging mafioso Frank in The Brotherhood *(1968).*

Irene Papas, Luther Adler, Susan Strasberg, Murray Hamilton, Eduardo Ciannelli, Joe De Santis, Val Avery, Val Bosoglio.

The idea that the Mafia organization is big business unfettered to ethnic ties and traditions received pre-*Godfather* treatment in this melodrama. Douglas stars as Frank Ginetta, a Mafia godfather concerned with family honor and the well-being of his community. When his organization decides to become more in tune with the times, Frank's refusal to change makes him a dangerous liability. Cord is his younger brother, compelled to deal with the situation. Douglas's intense performance helps to hoist this film out of the ordinary.

BROTHER ORCHID

★★★ Warner Bros., 1940, b/w, 91 min. Dir: Lloyd Bacon. SP: Earl Baldwin, b/o story by Richard Connell. Cast: Edward G. Robinson, Ann Sothern, Humphrey Bogart, Ralph Bellamy, Donald Crisp, Allen Jenkins, Cecil Kellaway, Morgan Conway.

An enjoyable, if improbable, gangster comedy, with Robinson as Little John Sarto, a racketeer with a yen for "culture." When he finds his life in jeopardy after a jaunt to Europe, he hides out in a monastery. The monks have no idea of his identity and as time passes, Little John finds that he enjoys the life of quiet contemplation. He finishes off his rival (Bogart) and returns to the monastery—for good. Sothern gives a typically pleasing performance as Little John's moll.

BRUBAKER

★★★ Fox, 1980, c, 131 min. Dir: Stuart Rosenberg. SP: W. D. Richter, b/o story by W. D. Richter, Arthur Ross. Cast: Robert Redford, Yaphet Kotto, Jane Alexander, Murray Hamilton, David Keith, Tim McIntyre, Morgan Freeman, John McMartin, Wilford Brimley.

Based on a true story, this fairly engrossing prison drama stars Redford as Henry Brubaker, newly appointed warden at a prison farm overrun by decay and corruption, and even hiding deadly secrets. His determined efforts to reform this hellish place meet with hostility and resentment from prison board members, politicians, and even the convicts themselves. The movie is certainly well-intentioned but sometimes plodding, although it gains some momentum toward the end. Good, earnest performance by Redford.

BRUTE FORCE

★★★ Universal, 1947, b/w, 98 min. Dir: Jules Dassin. SP: Richard Brooks, b/o story by Robert Patterson. Cast: Burt Lancaster, Hume Cronyn, Charles Bickford, Yvonne De Carlo, Ann Blyth, Ella Raines, Sam Levene, Howard Duff, Jeff Corey.

This blistering, high-decibel prison drama may have been overshadowed in recent years by more graphic displays of behind-the-walls violence, but it still manages to shock. Lancaster stars as the leader of a group of convicts bent on breaking out of prison. Their efforts lead to a pitched battle that nobody can win. A few sequences are exceptionally vivid, notably the climactic moment in which the sadistic warden (Cronyn) is hurled to his death by the convicts from a high guard tower. Another scene, in which an informer is crushed in a huge printing press by vindictive convicts, should freeze your blood. The women in the cast are all peripheral to the central story.

BUGSY

★★★☆ TriStar, 1991, c, 135 min. Dir: Barry Levinson. SP: James Toback. Cast: Warren Beatty, Annette Bening, Harvey Keitel, Ben Kingsley, Elliott Gould, Joe Mantegna, Bebe Neuwirth.

Warren Beatty gives his best performance since *Bonnie and Clyde* in this gripping and well-made movie concerning the true-life big-time gangster Benjamin ("Bugsy") Siegel. Beatty depicts Siegel as a vicious, cold-blooded killer with a hair-trigger temper but also as a visionary who dreamed of turning the Las Vegas desert into a golden mecca for gamblers and tourists. Siegel's tempestuous romance with Virginia Hill (Bening) is emphasized. The movie also does an Oscar-winning job of reconstructing California in the forties.

BULLET

★☆ New Line, 1996, c, 96 min. Dir: Julien Temple. SP: Bruce Rubenstein, Sir Eddie Cook. Cast: Mickey Rourke, Tupac Shakur, Ted Levine, Adrien Brody, John Enos III, Suzanne Shepherd.

Any hope that once-promising actor Rourke might resuscitate his floundering career dims even further with this tiresome crime drama. Rourke plays a Jewish (!) hoodlum who is released from prison and returns to his old Brooklyn world of drugs and violence. His two brothers are not much better, and one

(Levine) has been wrecked by his experiences in Vietnam. Rourke's principal nemesis is a black drug lord (Shakur). The ending for this depressing movie is inevitable.

BULLET IS WAITING, A

★★☆ Columbia, 1954, c, 82 min. Dir: John Farrow. SP: Thames Williamson, Casey Robinson, b/o story by Thames Williamson. Cast: Jean Simmons, Rory Calhoun, Stephen McNally, Brian Aherne.

Ruggedly beautiful backgrounds, photographed in color, are the most inviting feature of this fairly verbose melodrama. On a sprawling ranch in the California desert, an escaped prisoner (Calhoun) and a beautiful rancher's daughter (Simmons) fall in love, while a vindictive sheriff (McMally) pursues his quarry to the ranch. (The prisoner killed his brother in self-defense.) Much talk, some fighting, and that gorgeous scenery.

BULLETPROOF HEART

★★ Keystone/Republic, 1994, c, 96 min. Dir: Mark Malone. SP: Gordon Melbourne, b/o story by Mark Malone. Cast: Anthony LaPaglia, Mimi Rogers, Peter Boyle, Matt Craven, Monika Schnarre, Joseph Maher.

Different is not necessarily good, as demonstrated by this extremely odd erotic thriller. LaPaglia is a cold-blooded but burned-out hit man assigned to kill Rogers, a beautiful woman who has incriminating knowledge about a number of high-ranking men. The trouble is, she *wants* to die, for her own reasons. Inevitably LaPaglia falls for her (they share a very steamy sex scene), and their relationship is meant to be poignant and suspenseful. The movie, however, is merely unsettling in all the wrong ways, despite expert performances.

BULLETS OR BALLOTS

★★★ Warner Bros., 1936, b/w, 81 min. Dir: William Keighley. Sp; Seton I. Miller, b/o story by Seton I. Miller, Martin Mooney. Cast: Edward G. Robinson, Joan Blondell, Barton MacLane, Humphrey Bogart, Frank McHugh.

Robinson plays a cop who pretends to quit the force in order to infiltrate and expose a powerful gang led by MacLane. He succeeds, but at a terrible cost. That's the gist of the story, but Robinson invests the role (based on a real New York cop) with his characteristic energy;

the pace is lively in the best Warners style; and the studio's stock company is in there pitching along with Robinson. Blondell is his staunch girlfriend, and Bogart is a nasty gangster.

BULLITT

★★★☆ Warner Bros., 1968, c, 113 min. Dir: Peter Yates. SP: Alan R. Trustman and Barry Kleiner, b/o novel by Robert Pike. Cast: Steve McQueen, Jacqueline Bisset, Robert Vaughn, Don Gordon, Robert Duvall, Simon Oakland, Norman Fell.

For decades, the cops-versus-culprits chase sequence has been a standard part of many police dramas. *Bullitt* has one of the best: a hair-raising winging over the hills of San Francisco, complete with hairpin turns and screeching tires. The rest is a superior example of the genre, with McQueen in the title role of a loose-cannon detective who starts his own investigation after a key witness he is assigned to protect is critically wounded. One especially tense sequence takes place at San Francisco's airport, where Bullitt and the police pursue a suspect. Frank Keller's editing won an Oscar.

BURGLAR

★☆ Warner Bros., 1987, c, 102 min. Dir: Hugh Wilson. SP: Joseph Loeb III, Matthew Weisman, Hugh Wilson, b/o books by Lawrence Block. Cast: Whoopi Goldberg, Bob (Bobcat) Goldthwait, G. W. Bailey, Lesley Ann Warren, James Handy, John Goodman, Anne DeSalvo, Elizabeth Ruscio.

Bernice Rhodenbarr (Goldberg) is in deep trouble. An ex-convict and skilled cat burglar, she is blackmailed into committing one last heist and finds herself witness to—and then chief suspect in—a murder. What can she do but track down the killer herself? One in a series of career mistakes made by Goldberg in the late eighties, *Burglar* is a wildly incoherent and unfunny comedy-melodrama. Goldberg knows how to draw laughs, but here she is burdened with comedian Goldthwait, who may have you racing for the "off" button.

BUSTING

★★★ United Artists, 1974, c, 92 min. Dir and SP: Peter Hymans. Cast: Elliott Gould, Robert Blake, Allen Garfield, Antonio Fargas, Michael Lerner, John Lawrence, Cornelia Sharpe.

A better-than-average cop movie in which Gould and Blake play eccentric Los Angeles vice detectives. When they decide to go after the big-shot (Garfield) who controls the city's multimillion-dollar rackets, they get clobbered by the gangsters and their own department superiors. Nothing new here, but director Hyams, in his first theatrical film, knows how to stage a convincing action scene. (Wait for the gun battle in a late-night market.)

CALL ME

★ Vestron, 1988, c, 98 min. Dir: Sollace Mitchell. SP: Karyn Kay, b/o story by Karyn Kay, Sollace Mitchell. Cast: Patricia Charbonneau, Patti D'Arbanville, Steve McHattie, Boyd Gaines, Sam Freed, Steve Buscemi.

This appalling erotic thriller has a heroine whose stupidity appears to have no bounds. Charbonneau plays a girl who responds to an obscene caller she thinks is her boyfriend, then plunges into a nightmare world inhabited by murderous drug dealers and corrupt cops. The obscene calls continue and, despite the obvious danger, the girl is really fascinated. Dumb from improbable first to ridiculous last.

CALL NORTHSIDE 777

★★★ Fox, 1948, b/w, 111 min. Dir: Henry Hathaway. SP: James Cady and Jay Dratler, adapted by Leonard Hoffman, Quentin Reynolds from article by James P. McGuire. Cast: James Stewart, Richard Conte, Lee J. Cobb, Helen Walker, Betty Garde, Howard Smith.

Another competent entry in Fox's late-forties series of semidocumentary dramas. Based on a true story, this one has Chicago reporter Stewart bent on proving a man (Conte) innocent of committing a long-ago murder. He spends years stubbornly raking up and sifting evidence, until a key photograph proves his case. Hathaway, Fox's resident director for films of this sort, handles the material efficiently.

CAPE FEAR

★★★ Universal, 1962, b/w, 105 min. Dir: J. Lee Thompson. SP: James R. Webb, b/o novel by John D. MacDonald. Cast: Gregory Peck, Robert Mitchum, Polly Bergen, Lori Martin, Martin Balsam.

This original version of the story remade in 1991 has a number of visceral thrills but is not as gruesomely explicit or as ambiguously motivated as the later film. The plot is basically the same: vicious Max Cady (Mitchum), newly released from prison, is out to exact revenge from lawyer Sam Bowden (Peck) by targeting Sam's wife (Bergen) and young daughter (Nelson). His plan of terror leads to a violent climax that is much more credible than the one in the remake. Acting honors go to Mitchum as the evil Cady.

CAPE FEAR

★★☆ Universal, 1991, c, 123 min. Dir: Martin Scorsese. SP: Wesley Strick, b/o novel by John D. MacDonald. Cast: Robert De Niro, Nick Nolte, Jessica Lange, Juliette Lewis, Joe Don Baker, Illeana Douglas, Robert Mitchum, Gregory Peck, Martin Balsam.

A remake of J. Lee Thompson's 1962 thriller, this movie takes the brutal tale of the original and projects it into the 1990s. Once again lawyer Sam Bowden (Nolte) and his family (wife Lange, daughter Lewis) are being being tormented by Max Cady (De Niro), a nasty ex-convict bent on revenge against Bowden for a perceived betrayal that sent him to prison for fourteen years. In this version, however, Bowden is morally ambiguous—he did betray the lawyer-client trust in this case. What's more, his marriage to Lange is on shaky ground. Director Scorsese and writer Strick use these nineties perceptions to disguise the fact that their intent is to create one visceral shock after another by increasing the violence quotient. In the long run, viewers are left unsettled and depressed rather than exhilarated.

CARLITO'S WAY

★★★☆ Universal, 1993, c, 144 min. Dir: Brian De Palma. SP: David Koepp, b/o novels by Edwin Torres. Cast: Al Pacino, Sean Penn, Penelope Ann Miller, Luis Guzman, James Rebhorn, Viggo Mortensen, John Leguizano, Richard Foronjy, Ingrid Rogers.

Released from prison after five years, former drug lord Carlito Brigante (Pacino) wants only

Robert De Niro is gambler "Ace" Rothstein and Joe Pesci is his enforcer, Nicky Santoro, in Casino *(1995).*

to leave the criminal life forever. But events conspire to bring him back to the old ways, and he is forced to deal with treachery from rivals, friends, and even his corrupt, drug-addled lawyer (Penn). He tries to retain his code of honor, but in the end there is no escape. De Palma's film is too long but is vividly staged and acted, particularly by Penn, one of the best young actors. De Palma knows how to build tension and excitement, and his climactic sequence in a subway and Grand Central Station recalls his breathtaking sequence in Chicago's Union Station in *The Untouchables* (1987).

CASINO

★★★☆ Universal, 1995, c, 177 min. Dir: Martin Scorsese. SP: Nicholas Pileggi, b/o his book. Cast: Robert De Niro, Sharon Stone, Joe Pesci, James Woods, Don Rickles, Alan King, Kevin Pollak, I. Q. Jones, Dick Smothers.

Director Scorsese (*GoodFellas*) returns to the world of gangsterdom with this long, ambitious, and extraordinarily graphic melodrama. His intention is to record no less than the rise and fall of the big-time Las Vegas mobsters of the seventies, as seen largely through the eyes of top gambler and casino manager Sam ("Ace") Rothstein (De Niro). Also figuring prominently in the story are Nicky Santoro (Pesci), Ace's longtime friend and violent enforcer, and Ginger (Stone), Ace's desperately unstable wife. Scorsese's ample filmmaking talents are in full display here, but the characters are all so off-putting that watching the movie becomes an emotionally barren rather than an emotionally draining experience. The acting, however, is good, most notably in the surprising case of Stone, who gives a top-notch performance as the hapless Ginger.

CAUSE FOR ALARM

★★★ MGM, 1951, b/w, 74 min. Dir: Tay Garnett. SP: Mel Dinelli, Tom Lewis, b/o story by Larry Marcus. Cast: Loretta Young, Barry Sullivan, Bruce Cowling, Margalo Gillmore, Bradley Mora, Irving Bacon.

A low-budget, surprisingly effective thriller. Filmed in only fourteen days, it stars Young as a suburban housewife whose psychotically jealous husband (Sullivan) devises a fiendish plot to commit suicide and have her and her alleged lover (Cowling) accused of his murder. Young searches desperately for the letter to the district attorney in which he makes his accusation against her. The end features a clever plot twist.

CHAMBER, THE

★★☆ Universal, 1996, c, 110 min. Dir: James Foley. SP: William Goldman, Chris Reese, b/o novel by John Grisham. Cast: Chris O'Donnell, Gene Hackman, Faye Dunaway, Lela Rochon, Bo Jackson, Millie Perkins.

Time seems to be running out for Sam Cayhall (Hackman). Convicted of a Mississippi bombing that killed two small boys, the unregenerate bigot has been on Death Row for many years. Now his young lawyer-grandson (O'Donnell) is working desperately for a stay of execution. This latest installment in adaptations of John Grisham's novels is also morally ambiguous and dramatically muddled. Coming down on both sides of the death-penalty ledger, it portrays Cayhall first as an unredeemable racist worthy of execution, then attempts to sentimentalize him and nearly excuse him as someone doomed by his background.

CHARADE

★★★★ Universal-International, 1963, c, 114 min. Dir: Stanley Donen. SP: Peter Stone, b/o story by Peter Stone, Marc Behm. Cast: Cary Grant, Audrey Hepburn, Walter Matthau, George Kennedy, James Coburn, Ned Glass, Jacques Marin.

Take Grant and Hepburn, two of the screen's most attractive stars. Add Stone's clever, suspenseful screenplay and a stylish production directed artfully by Donen, and you have first-rate entertainment. The Hitchcockian tale revolves around a young wife (Hepburn) in Paris whose husband is brutally murdered. Soon she is being pursued by the killers and helped (or stalked?) by a smooth-talking but mysterious man (Grant) who takes on various identities. Some scenes are surprisingly violent, but you are bound to be swept along by the leads, the setting, and Henry Mancini's lilting score.

CHARLEY VARRICK

★★★☆ Universal, 1973, c, 111 min. Dir: Don Siegel. SP: Howard Rodman, Dean Riesner, b/o novel by John Reese. Cast: Walter Matthau, Joe Don Baker, Felicia Farr, Andy Robinson, John Vernon, Sheree North, Norman Fell, Jacqueline Scott, Woodrow Parfrey.

The plot is by no means new, but Siegel's sharp direction, a quirky, interesting screenplay, and Matthau's low-key performance make this movie highly satisfactory entertainment. Matthau is Charley Varrick, a resourceful, confident, small-time thief who robs a New Mexico bank, only to learn that he has stolen three-quarters of a million dollars belonging to the Mafia. Soon the bad guys and the good guys are hot on his trail. The story takes some clever turns, and there's a great climactic sequence in the desert.

CHARLIE CHAN AT THE OPERA

★★★ Fox, 1936, b/w, 66 min. Dir: H. Bruce Humberstone. SP: Scott Darling, Charles P. Beldon, b/o story by Bess Meredyth. Cast: Warner Oland, Boris Karloff, Keye Luke, Charlotte Henry, Thomas Beck, Margaret Irving, Gregory Gaye.

Generally regarded as the best of the Charlie Chan movies, *Charlie Chan at the Opera* has the canny detective on the trail of a mysterious figure who is committing murders backstage at an opera house. The pace is swift, the story is suspenseful, and Boris Karloff plays the leading suspect at full melodramatic throttle. Keye Luke is again on hand as Chan's Number One Son and assistant. The movie's bogus opera was written by Oscar Levant.

CHASE, THE

★★ United Artists, 1946, b/w, 86 min. Dir: Arthur D. Ripley. SP: Philip Yordan, b/o novel by Cornell Woolrich. Cast: Robert Cummings, Michele Morgan, Steve Cochran, Peter Lorre, Lloyd Corrigan, Jack Holt, Don Wilson, Nina Koshetz.

CHARLIE CHAN

Wily, imperturbable, and spouting aphorisms as he followed clues, novelist Earl Derr Biggers's Asian detective Charlie Chan found favor with movie audiences in the thirties and early forties. Actually, Chan had turned up in a 1926 silent movie, but he first made an impression in 1931 when Swedish actor Warner Oland took the role in *Charlie Chan Carries On*. (He played Al Jolson's father in *The Jazz Singer*.) The series of popular films that followed received a boost in 1935 when Keye Luke joined the cast as Chan's eager-beaver Number One Son. Sidney Toler replaced Warner Oland in 1937 in a group of lesser mysteries, with (Victor) Sen Yung often turning up as Jimmy Chan, the detective's Number Two Son. After Toler's death, Roland Winters took over the role in the last few movies, and the series ended in 1949. The Oland series is the best, modestly but trimly made and fun to watch.

Over a dozen of the Chan movies are available on tape, including *Charlie Chan in Paris* (1935), *Charlie Chan's Secret* (1936), *Charlie Chan at the Opera* (1936) with Boris Karloff, *Charlie Chan at the Wax Museum* (1940), *Charlie Chan in Rio* (1941), and *Charlie Chan in the Secret Service* (1944).

RIVALS TO CHAN

Triggered by audience reception of the Charlie Chan movies, several studios tried to emulate the cagy Honolulu sleuth with their own Asian detectives.

Mr. Moto: In 1937 Twentieth Century-Fox introduced J. P. Marquand's Japanese sleuth, Mr. Moto, with *Think Fast, Mr. Moto*. Played by Peter Lorre, the diminutive detective seemed mild-mannered and obsequious, but he proved to be adept at ferreting out thieves and murderers. Like Chan he was also given to aphorisms, such as "Much information can be obtained by tongues loosened in anger." Obviously made on a shoestring, the movies, eight in all, were acceptable time killers. *Thank You, Mr. Moto* (1938) is generally considered the best of the series, but only *Mr. Moto's Last Warning* (1939) appears to be on tape.

Mr. Wong: Bargain-basement studio Monogram decided to make its own contribution to the Asian-detective sweepstakes with Mr. Wong, created by author Hugh Wiley. Played by horror-film star Boris Karloff, Wong was gentlemanly and rather austere but no less skilled at solving crimes. Other running characters included a gruff police captain (Grant Withers) and a pushy reporter (Marjorie Reynolds). In the last Wong movie, *Phantom of Chinatown* (1941), the role was played by Keye Luke, Charlie Chan's former Number One Son. Titles available on tape include *Mr. Wong, Detective* (1938), *Mr. Wong in Chinatown* (1938), and *Fatal Hour* (1940).

An offbeat, muddled melodrama, starring Cummings as a war-shocked veteran who takes a job as chauffeur to wealthy, sadistic gangster Cochran. Cummings and Cochran's unhappy wife (Morgan) fall for each other and they flee together, only to come to a bad end. But wait: there's a trick ending. Lorre stands out as Cochran's cynical bodyguard. Based on a Woolrich novel with a much better title, *The Black Path of Fear*.

CHASE, THE

★ Columbia, 1966, c, 135 min. Dir: Arthur Penn. SP: Lillian Hellman, b/o novel and play by Horton Foote.

Cast: Marlon Brando, Jane Fonda, Robert Redford, Angie Dickinson, Janice Rule, James Fox, E. G. Marshall, Miriam Hopkins, Martha Hyer, Robert Duvall, Henry Hull.

Welcome to a Texas town where rich men are decadent, their women either promiscuous or alcoholic, the young are wild, and ordinary citizens are both stupid and helpless. This is the unsavory terrain of *The Chase*, and despite the truly impressive credits, the movie is an appalling mess from beginning to apocalyptic end. When Bubber Reeves (Redford) escapes from prison, many lives are affected and soon not even honorable Sheriff Calder (Brando) can keep events under control. It all ends tragically, but not a moment too soon. Reportedly there were many fights among the participants during the filming. Small wonder.

CHEAP DETECTIVE, THE

★★★ Columbia, 1978, c, 92 min. Dir: Robert Moore. SP: Neil Simon. Cast: Peter Falk, John Houseman, Nicol Williamson, Fernando Lamas, Madeline Kahn, Dom DeLuise, Marsha Mason, Ann-Margret, Eileen Brennan, Louise Fletcher, Sid Caesar, Stockard Channing.

Movie buffs will find some pleasure in identifying the movies being spoofed in this occasionally amusing but rather slapdash comedy. Falk is the Bogart-like private eye who comes up against characters drawn from *The Maltese Falcon, Casablanca, The Big Sleep,* and many other movies of the past. Some of the parodies are on target—the *Casablanca* take-off, for one, in which the Nazis and the Free French sing opposing tunes (the French choose "Deep Purple")—but others are fairly lame.

CHICAGO JOE AND THE SHOWGIRL

★★☆ Polygram/Working Title (British), 1990, c, 103 min. Dir: Bernard Rose. SP: David Yallop. Cast: Keifer Sutherland, Emily Lloyd, Patsy Kensit, Keith Allen, Liz Fraser, Alexandra Pigg.

London, 1944. Sutherland is an American serviceman who claims to be a big-time mobster called "Chicago Joe." Lloyd is a none-too-bright, amoral girl who fantasizes about being a film star. When they meet, she goads him into a crime spree that ends in murder. After they are arrested, the pathetic truth about them emerges. Based on a sensational true British murder case, the movie has a chillingly effective performance by Lloyd, but the cheap production and awkward direction ultimately make it less than satisfactory.

CHICAGO SYNDICATE

★★ Columbia, 1955, b/w, 83 min. Dir: Fred F. Sears. SP: Joseph Hoffman, b/o story by William Sackheim. Cast: Dennis O'Keefe, Abbe Lane, Paul Stewart, Xavier Cugat, Allison Hayes, Dick Cutting.

How many crime movies can claim to have a certified public accountant as their hero? Or contain characters played by bandleader Cugat and his singer-wife Lane? This cheap little melodrama scores on both counts. Otherwise it's just another racket-busting tale from an era when racket-busting was Big News, as CPA Dennis O'Keefe brings down kingpin crook Paul Stewart.

CHINA MOON

★★★ Orion, 1994, c, 99 min. Dir: John Bailey. SP: Roy Carlson. Cast: Ed Harris, Madeleine Stowe, Benicio Del Toro, Charles Dance, Pruitt Taylor Vance, Roger Aaron Brown.

A classic noir plot, very much like that of *Body Heat* (1981), gets yet another spin in this tricky, absorbing melodrama. Apparently detective Harris has never been to the movies—he is seduced by beautiful Stowe into a labyrinthine plot involving her nasty, faithless husband (Dance), with predictably deadly results. Some looseness in plot details keeps the movie from being top-drawer, but the atmosphere is appropriately steamy and threatening.

CHINATOWN

★★★★ Paramount, 1974, c, 131 min. Dir: Roman Polanski. SP: Robert Towne. Cast: Jack Nicholson, Faye Dunaway, John Huston, Perry Lopez, Joe Mantell, John Hillerman, Darrell Zwerling, Diane Ladd, Burt Young.

An intricate, tantalizing thriller, *Chinatown* has all the ingredients of classic noir: a private eye (Nicholson) with his own code of behavior, an alluring femme fatale hiding a dark secret, and a tangled plot involving skulduggery and murder in high and low places. Set in Los Angeles in the thirties, beautifully evoked by John A. Alonso's camera, the movie gives Nicholson one of his best roles, as Jake Gittes, a man who finds he cannot escape the elusive power of Chinatown. Note Jerry Goldsmith's haunting musical score. The film won an Oscar for its screenplay, as well as many nominations, including one for Best Picture. A sequel, *The Two Jakes* turned up in 1990.

CHOIRBOYS, THE

★ Lorimar, 1977, c, 119 min. Dir: Robert Aldrich. SP: Christopher Knopf, b/o novel by Joseph Wambaugh. Cast: Charles Durning, Louis Gossett, Jr., Perry King, Clyde Kusatsu, Stephen Macht, Randy Quaid, James Woods, Burt Young, Robert Webber, Blair Brown.

Adapted from Joseph Wambaugh's novel, this dreadful movie involves a group of unsavory

Jack Nicholson gives one of his most memorable performances as detective Jake Gittes in Roman Polanski's Chinatown *(1974).*

cops who, when they are not covering up their misdeeds, find pleasure in playing asinine jokes on each other or their superior officers. Some of their private pain seeps through, and there is one shocking suicide, but the movie seems to be intended mainly as black comedy. Best advice: pass it by.

CITY HALL

★★★ Castle Rock, 1996, c, 110 min. Dir: Harold Becker. SP: Ken Lipper, Paul Schrader, Nicholas Pileggi, Bo Goldman. Cast: Al Pacino, John Cusack, Bridget Fonda, Danny Aiello, David Paymer, Martin Landau, Tony Franciosa, Lindsay Duncan.

In Brooklyn, a shootout between a cop and a drug dealer leaves both dead and also kills a six-year-old boy. The incident unleashes a firestorm that threatens to engulf major New York City figures, including a judge (Landau), a political boss (Aiello), and even the impassioned mayor (Pacino). Leading the investigation of past corruption and expediency is the mayor's idealistic deputy (Cusack). The movie is dense with good,

authentic-sounding dialogue, but it somehow fails to cohere as drama. Pacino is intense, as always, but acting honors go to Aiello, superb as an outwardly genial, astute politician who sees his life gradually crashing around him. Look for opera star Roberta Peters as his wife.

CITY HEAT

★★☆ Warner Bros., 1983, c, 97 min. Dir: Richard Benjamin. SP: Sam O. Brown (Blake Edwards), Joseph C. Stinson, b/o story by Sam O. Brown. Cast: Clint Eastwood, Burt Reynolds, Madeline Kahn, Tony LoBianco, Jane Alexander, Rip Torn, Richard Roundtree.

Nice cast in a routine crime caper set in the thirties. The two leads play off their usual personalities: Eastwood is a laconic, hard-nosed cop and Reynolds is a carefree private eye and former cop. They pretend to despise each other, but when Reynolds's partner (Roundtree) is killed, they join forces reluctantly to wipe out rival crime bosses. The screenplay is laced with feeble attempts at comedy, and the thirties ambiance is not very convincing. At least the stars seem to be having a good time. Author "Sam O. Brown" is a pseudonym for Blake Edwards.

CITY THAT NEVER SLEEPS

★★☆ Republic, 1953, b/w, 90 min. Dir: John H. Auer. SP: Steve Fisher. Cast: Gig Young, Mala Powers, William Talman, Edward Arnold, Chill Wills, Marie Windsor, Paula Raymond.

Chicago is the insomniac city in this humdrum melodrama. The story centers on policeman Young and his experiences on the night he plans to leave his job and his wife (Raymond) for a honky-tonk performer (Powers). On this night, however, he tangles with a fugitive killer (Talman), whom he captures single-handedly. Clichéd characters abound, including a corrupt lawyer (Arnold) and a cop whimsically named Joe Chicago (Wills).

CLASS ACTION

★★★ Fox, 1991, c, 109 min. Dir: Michael Apted. SP: Carolyn Shelby, Christopher Ames, Samantha Shad. Cast: Gene Hackman, Mary Elizabeth Mastrantonio, Colin Friels, Joanna Merlin, Larry Fishburne, Jonathan Silverman, Donald Moffat, Jan Rubes, Fred Dalton Thompson.

Exemplary performances by Hackman and Mastrantonio bolster this reasonably engrossing drama. They play father and daughter, both lawyers, who, after years of estrangement, find themselves on opposite sides of a case involving a major car company. Questions of corporate corruption and the violation of legal ethics are raised, deeply affecting their relationship. The outcome is never in doubt but the film is well made and interesting.

CLIENT, THE

★★★ Warner Bros., 1994, c, 121 min. Dir: Joel Schumacher. SP: Akiva Goldsman, Robert Getchell, b/o novel by John Grisham. Cast: Susan Sarandon, Tommy Lee Jones, Brad Renfro, Mary Louise Parker, Anthony LaPaglia, J. T. Walsh, Anthony Edwards, Ossie Davis, Will Patton.

Solid, no-frills suspense from John Grisham. In Memphis, a young boy (Renfro) witnesses the suicide of a mob lawyer who, before he dies, reveals information about a senator's dead body that the mob would rather keep secret. Suddenly the boy becomes a target for hit men

as well as a key figure in the investigation of a politically ambitious FBI agent (Jones). For help he turns to Reggie Love (Sarandon), a lawyer with a checkered past. Soon the two are running for their lives. Sarandon is on target, as usual, and the rest of the cast keeps things moving at a fast clip.

CLOCKERS

★★★☆ Universal, 1995, c, 129 min. Dir: Spike Lee. SP: Richard Price, Spike Lee, b/o novel by Richard Price. Cast: Harvey Keitel, Mekhi Phifer, Delroy Lindo, John Turturro, Isaiah Washington, Keith David, Regina Taylor.

Trapped in an inner city plagued by violence and despair, young Strike Durham (Phifer) seems to have no future. Trouble erupts when his hard-working brother Victor (Washington) confesses to a murder that he, Strike, was ordered to commit by his drug-dealing mentor, Rodney (Lindo). A jaded white cop (Keitel) is determined to learn the truth. A superficial "whodunit" on the surface, Lee's movie becomes a powerful, complex drama that skewers the drug-ridden culture in today's cities. This time Lee's anger is tempered with a deep melancholy for lost lives. Best performance: Lindo as the outwardly genial but malevolent Rodney.

CLUE

★★☆ Paramount, 1985, c, 87 min. Dir and SP: Jonathan Lynn. Cast: Tim Curry, Eileen Brennan, Christopher Lloyd, Madeline Kahn, Michael McKean, Martin Mull, Lesley Ann Warren, Colleen Camp.

A mildly amusing conceit, based on the popular board game of the same name. In a Gothic mansion in New England in 1954, an eccentric man (Curry) assembles a group of people to play a game of murder. Soon the game becomes all too real. The characters are assigned pseudoynyms drawn from the game: Colonel Mustard (Mull), Mrs. Peacock (Brennan), Mr. Green (McKean), Miss Scarlet (Warren), and so on. For theatrical release, the audience was shown one of three alternate endings. On video, all three endings are shown in a row.

COBRA

★ Warner Bros., 1986, c, 87 min. Dir: George P. Cosmatos. SP: Sylvester Stallone, b/o novel by Paula

Gosling. Cast: Sylvester Stallone, Brigitte Nielsen, Rene Santoni, Andrew Robinson, Lee Garlington.

Here we go again: Sylvester Stallone is a tough cop known as the Cobra, who believes in bending and even subverting the law to rid the streets of criminal vermin. In this dreadful movie he takes on a band of serial killers who call themselves the Night Slashers. "This is where the law stops, and I start!" he shouts at the chief villain, just before burning him to a crisp. The preposterous climax has him single-handedly destroying a virtual army of Slashers.

CODE OF SILENCE

★★☆ Orion, 1985, c, 101 min. Dir: Andy Davis. SP: Michael Butler, Dennis Shryack, Mike Gray, b/o story by Michael Butler, Dennis Shryack. Cast: Chuck Norris, Henry Silva, Bert Remsen, Molly Hagan.

A notch or two above the usual Chuck Norris item of martial-arts mayhem, Code of Silence has Norris as a laconic undercover cop who investigates a drug war between rival underworld gangs. A subplot involves a police coverup. Less karate than usual, but Norris gets in his kicks.

COFFY

★★☆ American International, 1973, c, 91 min. Dir and SP: Jack Hill. Cast: Pam Grier, Booker Bradshaw, Robert Doqui, William Elliott, Alan Arbus, Sid Haig.

This brash, body-strewn vehicle for Grier has her playing a nurse who goes after the mobsters and drug pushers who hooked her kid sister and killed her boyfriend. The actress continued her vendetta against evil in *Foxy Brown* (1974) and *Friday Foster* (1975).

COLLECTOR, THE

★★★ Columbia, 1965, c, 119 min. Dir: William Wyler. SP: Stanley Mann, John Kohn, b/o novel by John Fowles. Cast: Terence Stamp, Samantha Eggar, Maurice Dallimore, Mona Washbourne.

This psychological thriller generates some suspense with basically two characters. Stamp plays a British sociopath who has won a huge sum of money in a football pool. He kidnaps Eggar, the young woman with whom he is sexually obsessed, and keeps her a prisoner in his remote farmhouse. Most of the movie concerns her desperate efforts to escape while

Terence Stamp is mesmerized by his beautiful prisoner, Samantha Eggar, in William Wyler's virtually two-character drama, The Collector *(1965).*

enduring the moods and whims of her strange captor. There are holes in the story that make it less than believable, but Stamp is fine as a man who collects butterflies (and Eggar is the jewel in his collection).

COLORS

★★★ Orion, 1988, c, 120 min. Dir: Dennis Hopper. SP: Michael Schiffer, b/o story by Michael Schiffer, Richard Dilello. Cast: Sean Penn, Robert Duvall, Mari Conchita Alonso, Randy Brooks, Grand Bush, Trinidad Silva, Rudy Ramos, Don Cheadle.

A harsh, uncompromising view of street gangs, *Colors* takes the audience deep into the mean streets and alleys of Los Angeles. When a gang member is murdered, police partners Penn and Duvall are assigned to the force charged with containing the resulting explosion. The contrasting characters of the two cops—Penn as an out-of-control hothead, Duvall as a more temperate veteran—is a cliché of police melodramas, and a subplot involving Penn with "home girl" Alonso is hardly credible. But actor-director Hopper gets good mileage out of his setting, and in the end, *Colors* comes through.

COMA

★★★ United Artists, 1978, c, 113 min. Dir and SP: Michael Crichton, b/o novel by Robin Cook. Cast: Genevieve Bujold, Michael Douglas, Richard Widmark, Elizabeth Ashley, Rip Torn, Lois Chiles, Harry Rhodes, Lance Le Gault.

Forget about plausibility, and you'll probably have a good time with this medical thriller, adapted from the best-selling novel. When her best friend suffers irreparable brain damage after a minor operation, Dr. Susan Wheeler (Bujold) becomes suspicious and begins an investigation. Her life is threatened when she uncovers a massive conspiracy in which healthy patients are killed and their bodies stolen from the hospital. Douglas is her doctor-lover and Widmark is the seemingly benign hospital head. Not much style or sense, but some suspense.

COME BACK, CHARLESTON BLUE

★★ Warner Bros., 1972, c, 100 min. Dir: Mark Warren. SP: Bontche Schweig, Peggy Elliott, b/o novel by Chester Himes. Cast: Godfrey Cambridge, Raymond St. Jacques, Peter DeAnda, Jonelle Allen, Maxwell Glanville, Minnie Gentry.

A sequel to *Cotton Comes to Harlem* (1970), this action-comedy is frenetic but only sporadically funny. Cambridge and St. Jacques return as Digger Jones and Coffin Ed Johnson, two loose-cannon detectives who use their own offbeat methods to bring down big-time drug operations in Harlem. Side note: presumably, co-author "Bontsche Schweig" is a pseudonym, since the name is that of a character in a famous tale by Sholem Aleichem.

COMPROMISING POSITIONS

★★★ Paramount, 1985, c, 98 min. Dir: Frank Perry. SP: Susan Isaacs, b/o her novel. Cast: Susan Sarandon, Raul Julia, Edward Hermann, Judith Ivey, Mary Beth Hurt, Joe Mantegna, Josh Mostel, Anne De Salvo.

The first half of this comedy-mystery is enjoyable, but then it goes astray with unconvincing romance. Still, it's good fun, with Sarandon as a Long Island housewife and former reporter who sets about investigating the murder of a local womanizing dentist (Mantegna). Many of her neighbors become suspects. Julia is the policeman with whom she starts an extramarital affair. The movie's best role goes to Ivey as Sarandon's wisecracking friend.

COMPULSION

★★★☆ Fox, 1959, b/w, 103 min. Dir: Richard Fleischer. SP: Richard Murphy, b/o novel by Meyer Levin. Cast: Orson Welles, Diane Varsi, Dean Stockwell, Bradford Dillman, E. G. Marshall, Martin Milner.

Compulsion draws on one of the most shocking events of the 1920s, in which Nathan Leopold and Richard Loeb, two young scions of wealthy Chicago families, kidnapped and murdered a neighbor's young son in cold blood. The fictionalized story, from Levin's novel, covers the mental state of the killers, the crime itself, the police investigation, and the trial. Orson Welles turns up at the trial, playing the defense lawyer (actully a surrogate for Clarence Darrow) who orates at length against capital punishment. Dillman and Stockwell are impressive as the deadly duo, and Fleischer directs skillfully.

Lawyer Orson Welles defends his clients eloquently in Compulsion *(1959). At left is E. G. Marshall.*

CONFLICT

★★☆ Warner Bros., 1945, b/w, 86 min. Dir: Curtis Reinhardt. SP: Arthur T. Horman, Dwight Taylor, b/o story by Robert Siodmak, Alfred Neumann. Cast: Humphrey Bogart, Sydney Greenstreet, Alexis Smith, Rose Hobart, Charles Drake, Grant Mitchell.

A scarcely credible thriller, with Bogart as an unhappily married man who plots his wife's demise. He carries out the dire deed, then finds himself trapped by a clever psychologist (Greenstreet) who has planted evidence and staged illusions to make Bogart believe that his

Humphrey Bogart, Sydney Greenstreet, and George Carleton ponder the fate of Bogart's wife in Conflict *(1945).*

wife (Hobart) is still alive. Smith plays the woman who unwittingly inspires the murder plot.

CONSENTING ADULTS

★★★ Hollywood, 1992, c, 95 min. Dir: Alan J. Pakula. SP: Matthew Chapman. Cast: Kevin Kline, Mary Elizabeth Mastrantonio, Kevin Spacey, Rebecca Miller, Forest Whitaker, E. G. Marshall, Kimberly McCullogh.

Talk about neighbors from hell. Richard and Priscilla Parker (Kline and Mastrantonio) get chummy with their new next-door neighbors, the Otises (Spacey and Miller). Then Richard is plunged into a waking nightmare when he is accused of killing Kay Otis. Before long he realizes that he is the victim of an elaborate and nasty scheme involving insurance fraud and murder. There are serious gaps in logic and credibility, but the movie maintains suspense, and the acting is good.

CONVERSATION, THE

★★★★ Paramount, 1974, c, 113 min. Dir and SP: Francis Ford Coppola. Cast: Gene Hackman, John Cazale, Teri Garr, Allen Garfield, Frederick Forrest, Cindy Williams, Michael Higgins, Harrison Ford, Elizabeth MacRae, Robert Duvall (unbilled).

A brilliant film, possibly director Coppola's finest to date, *The Conversation* works as both an intriguing, labyrinthine thriller and as a commentary on personal responsibility in an age of sophisticated, modern-day surveillance. Hackman is superb as Harry Caul, "the best bugger on the West Coast," who is drawn inexorably into a sinister plot involving murder and deception. Caul finds his life falling apart when he violates his own rules, and the ending is shattering, for him and for the audience. One of the very best film actors, Hackman seems to discover the dark heart of his tormented character.

CONVICTS 4

★★☆ Allied Artists, 1962, b/w, 105 min. Dir and SP: Millard Kaufman, b/o book by John Resko. Cast: Ben Gazzara, Stuart Whitman, Rod Steiger, Broderick Crawford, Vincent Price, Ray Walston, Sammy Davis, Jr., Dodie Stevens, Jack Kruschen.

A good cast cannot cope with the rather muddled, oddly uninvolving screenplay in this prison drama. Based on the principal character's autobiography, it focuses on a murderer (Gazzara) who is saved from execution, rehabilitated, and freed because of his artistic gift. Resko is convicted of killing a storekeeper to get a toy for his infant daughter, but his talents and sensitive nature ultimately win his release. There are glimpses of old-time prison movies in the tough performances of Broderick Crawford, Rod Steiger, and others, but the movie lacks excitement.

COOGAN'S BLUFF

★★☆ Universal, 1968, c, 100 min. Dir: Don Siegel. SP: Herman Miller, Dean Riesner, Howard Rodman, b/o story by Herman Miller. Cast: Clint Eastwood, Lee J. Cobb, Susan Clark, Tisha Sterling, Don Stroud, Betty Field, Tom Tully.

This efficient but predictable police drama stars Eastwood as an Arizona sheriff who is sent to New York to retrieve a prisoner (Stroud). Tough, blunt, and laconic in the Eastwood manner, he clashes with New Yorkers who mock his "cowboy" style, especially with gruff lieutenant Cobb, but he gets his man. He also starts a tentative romance with parole officer Clark. Nice turn by Field as the prisoner's mother. The movie was the basis for the TV series *McCloud*.

COOL HAND LUKE

★★★☆ Warner Bros., 1967, c, 126 min. Dir: Stuart Rosenberg. SP: Donn Pearce, Frank R. Pierson, b/o novel by Donn Pearce. Cast: Paul Newman, George Kennedy, J. D. Cannon, Lou Antonio, Robert Drivas, Strother Martin, Jo Van Fleet, Dennis Hopper, Wayne Rogers.

Chain-gang convict Paul Newman takes some "lip" from fellow inmate George Kennedy in Cool Hand Luke *(1967). Kennedy won a Supporting Oscar.*

"What we've got here is a failure to communicate." These words, uttered by a prison guard (Martin), to a brutalized member of a chain gang, entered permanent movie lore after the release of this strong and stirring film. Newman gives one of his best performances as Luke, a lonely convict whose stubborn refusal to capitulate to authority or to concede defeat under any circumstances earns him the respect and admiration of his fellow inmates. (They also admire his ability to eat fifty hard-boiled eggs in an hour.) Kennedy won a Supporting Oscar as Luke's opponent who becomes his friend.

COP

★★☆ Paramount, 1987, c, 110 min. Dir: James B. Harris. SP: James B. Harris, b/o novel by James Ellroy. Cast: James Woods, Lesley Ann Warren, Charles Durning, Randi Brooks, Charles Haid, Raymond J. Barry.

Woods's intensity raises this movie a notch or two above the average, but not far enough to make it essential viewing. He plays a dedicated cop who becomes so obsessed with catching a serial killer that it costs him his job and his marriage. His investigation into the suspected killer uncovers long-buried secrets involving feminist poet Warren and others. The ending is something of a shocker.

COP AND A HALF

★☆ Universal, 1993, c, 93 min. Dir: Henry Winkler. SP: Lawrence Konner, Mark Rosenthal, Arne Olsen. Cast: Burt Reynolds, Norman D. Golden II, Ruby Dee, Holland Taylor, Ray Sharkey, Sammy Hernandez.

A really lamentable action comedy, starring Reynolds as a cop who is assigned to watch over a murder witness. The witness (Golden) happens to be an unruly eight-year-old (Golden) who worships the cops he sees on television. He refuses to talk about the killing unless he is made an honorary cop for a day. Naturally the little nuisance eventually leads Reynolds to the guilty party, a Miami mobster (Sharkey). Nothing objectionable here but no fun either.

COPS AND ROBBERS

★★★ United Artists, 1973, c, 89 min. Dir: Aram Avakian. SP: Donald E. Westlake. Cast: Cliff Gorman, Joseph Bologna, Dick Ward, Shepperd Strudwick, Ellen Holly, John Ryan, Dolph Sweet, Joe Spinell.

A diverting caper movie, *Cops and Robbers* centers on two hard-working cops (Gorman and Bologna) who would like to do more with their lives. So "doing more" becomes committing the perfect crime: on a day when New York City is enjoying a ticker-tape parade for astronauts, they carry out a million-dollar robbery against a Wall Street firm. Naturally, the caper doesn't run smoothly, but the two manage to muddle through. For once, a chase sequence is really amusing, and the New York City locations are well used.

COPS AND ROBBERSONS

★ TriStar, 1994, c, 93 min. Dir: Michael Ritchie. SP: Bernie Somers. Cast: Chevy Chase, Jack Palance, Dianne Wiest, Robert Davi, David Barry Gray, Jason James Richter, Fay Masterson.

A dreadful comedy starring Chase as a stupid suburban father who is addicted to television police dramas. When his house is used as a stakeout by veteran cop Palance to catch some crooks, Chase generates chaos by his eagerness to "help." Meanwhile, grumpy Jack learns to be part of a family. Chase's character is so obnoxious that he single-handedly destroys every vestige of humor, and almost every gag falls flat. Gifted actress Wiest must grapple with the thankless role of his wife.

COPYCAT

★★★ Warner Bros., 1995, c, 123 min. Dir: Jon Amiel. SP: Ann Biderman, Jay Presson Allen, b/o story by David Madsen. Cast: Sigourney Weaver, Holly Hunter, Dermot Mulroney, William McNamara, Will Patton, John Rothman, Harry Connick, Jr.

Weaver and Hunter, two exceptionally able actors, costar in this suspenseful and grisly thriller. Weaver is a noted psychologist specializing in serial killers, who becomes agoraphobic after being viciously attacked by one. Hunter is the feisty cop assigned to find and capture a serial killer at large, who turns out to be copying in exact detail the most notorious members of that monstrous brood. There are some well-handled fright scenes, mostly involving Weaver alone, but the movie is plotted too loosely and cluttered with too many half-formed ideas. The climactic sequence is shocking but also a cheat.

CORNERED

★★★ RKO, 1945, b/w, 102 min. Dir: Edward Dmytryk. SP: John Paxton, b/o story and adaptation by John Wexley. Cast: Dick Powell, Walter Slezak, Micheline Cheirel, Morris Carnovsky, Nina Vale, Edgar Barrier, Luther Adler, Steven Geray.

In his first film after launching his new tough-guy screen image with *Murder, My Sweet,* Powell plays a revenge-driven man who comes to Buenos Aires to seek out and kill the man who betrayed his French bride during World War II. Apparently the city is a hotbed of escaped Fascists, and they are soon giving Powell much trouble. Slezak stands out as a sleazy sort who is at the center of most of the intrigue. And Powell proves that his hard-boiled stance was not a one-picture fluke.

COTTON CLUB, THE

★★★ Orion, 1984, c, 127 min. Dir: Francis Coppola. SP: William Kennedy, Francis Coppola, b/o story by William Kennedy, Francis Coppola, Mario Puzo. Cast: Richard Gere, Gregory Hines, Diane Lane, Bob Hoskins, Lonette McKee, Nicolas Cage, James Remar, Fred Gwynne, Maurice Hines, Gwen Verdon, Allen Garfield, Lisa Jane Persky.

This musical drama about the famed Harlem nightclub certainly *looks* good: the production design and cinematography capture the razzle-dazzle and excitement of a time in the twenties when the club launched some of the best black entertainers. (Ironically, no blacks were allowed as patrons, only slumming whites.) But there's also a cliché-ridden story—something about two sets of brothers (Gere and Cage, Hines and his true brother, Maurice), and their involvement with women and with the gangsters who run the club. There are some vividly staged scenes of violent action, some top-notch dances, and the cast is game, but this trouble-plagued production never really coheres.

CRACKERS

★★ Universal, 1984, c, 92 min. Dir: Louis Malle. SP: Jeffrey Fiskin. Cast: Donald Sutherland, Jack Warden, Sean Penn, Wallace Shawn, Larry Riley, Trinidad Silva, Christine Baranski, Charlaine Woodard, Irwin Corey.

In this ill-advised remake of Mario Monicelli's 1958 Italian comedy *Big Deal on Madonna Street,* a gang of clumsy safecrackers gets together for a big score, and sure enough just about everything goes wrong. Not very funny, but the cast works hard: Donald Sutherland as the gang's leader, Shawn as his forever-hungry sidekick, Penn as a none-too-bright electrician. Best: Baranski as a meter maid.

CRACK-UP

★★★ RKO, 1946, b/w, 93 min. Dir: Irving Reis. SP: John Paxton, Ben Bengal, Ray Spencer. Cast: Pat O'Brien, Claire Trevor, Herbert Marshall, Wallace Ford, Ray Collins, Dean Harens.

Art critic George Steele (O'Brien) survives a train crash with a nasty crack on the head and partial amnesia. He also believes that great paintings are being stolen from a museum and replaced with forgeries by an international ring of art thieves. Is he on target or out of his mind? And which of his friends and colleagues is behind it all? Suspense heightens when the museum's art curator is murdered. A neatly turned out minor thriller.

CRASHOUT

★★☆ Filmmakers, 1955, b/w, 90 min. Dir: Lewis R. Foster. SP: Hal E. Chester, Lewis R. Foster. Cast: Arthur Kennedy, William Bendix, Luther Adler, Marshall Thompson, Gene Evans, Beverly Michaels, William Talman, Gloria Talbot, Adam Williams.

A good cast helps this modest, unsurprising, but competent prison-break melodrama. Sadistic Bendix heads a band of convicts who "crash out" of prison and find everything from doom to a touch of romance in their desperate flight to freedom and some buried treasure. Kennedy comes off best, as a sympathetic gang member.

CRAZY JOE

★★☆ Columbia (Italian-U.S.), 1973, c, 100 min. Dir: Carlo Lizzani. SP: Lewis John Carlino, b/o story by Nicholas Gage. Cast: Peter Boyle, Paula Prentiss, Fred Williamson, Charles Cioffi, Rip Torn, Luther Adler, Fausto Tozzi.

This Italian-American coproduction purports to relate the true story of Brooklyn mobster Joey Gallo (Boyle), from his rise in the criminal ranks to his execution in Umberto's Clam House in New York City in 1972. The movie traces his alliance with black criminals while in prison, his violent rivalry with another ambitious mobster (Cioffi), and the inexorable steps that lead to his demise. Routine crime melodrama.

CRIME AND PUNISHMENT

★★★ Columbia, 1935, b/w, 88 min. Dir: Josef von Sternberg. SP: S. K. Lauren, Joseph Anthony, b/o novel by Fyodor Dostoyevski. Cast: Peter Lorre, Edward Arnold, Marian Marsh, Tala Birell, Elisabeth Risdon, Mrs. Patrick Campbell.

A respectable low-budget adaptation of the classic novel. Lorre plays Raskolnikov, the impoverished student who murders an old pawnbroker (famed actress Mrs. Patrick Campbell), then engages in a cat-and-mouse game with the prosecutor (Arnold) who suspects him of the crime. The movie omits most of the psychological underpinnings of the novel, but director Sternberg provides some artful touches, and Lorre is striking (if much too old) in his tormented role.

CRIME IN THE STREETS

★★☆ Allied Artists, 1956, b/w, 91 min. Dir: Donald Siegel. SP: Reginald Rose, b/o his television play. Cast: John Cassavetes, James Whitmore, Sal Mineo, Mark Rydell, Denise Alexander, Virginia Gregg, Will Kulava, Peter Votrian.

In the midfifties, some filmmakers decided that the Dead End Kids, the Bowery Boys, and their ilk were no longer clowns but a serious national problem. Writer Reginald Rose contributed to this cycle on juvenile delinquency by adapting his television play about three young punks (Cassavetes, Mineo, Rydell) who conspire to commit murder. Whitmore is the preachy social worker who wants to talk them out of it. Four decades later, it all seems banal and overwrought. Cassavetes and Rydell later turned to directing.

CRIME OF PASSION

★★ United Artists, 1957, b/w, 84 min. Dir: Gerd Oswald. SP: Jo Eisinger. Cast: Barbara Stanwyck, Sterling Hayden, Raymond Burr, Fay Wray, Royal Dano, Virginia Grey, Dennis Cross, Jay Adler.

Stanwyck's professionalism can carry a turgid screenplay only so far, and this one is heavy going. She plays a wretchedly unhappy wife so anxious to advance her dull husband (Hayden) in his job as detective that she tries to seduce the only man (Burr) who can promote him. Instead she ends up killing Burr—not the best road to career advancement. There are glimpses of what the movie might have been, but only glimpses.

CRIMES AND MISDEMEANORS

★★★★ Orion, 1989, c, 104 min. Dir and SP: Woody Allen. Cast: Martin Landau, Alan Alda, Mia Farrow, Woody Allen, Anjelica Huston, Claire Bloom, Sam Waterston, Joanna Gleason, Jerry Orbach, Caroline Aaron.

Allen's brilliant film mixes drama and comedy, with emphasis on the former. A bleak view of the perversity and shaky moral structure of our times, the movie revolves around a prominent ophthalmologist (Oscar-nominated Landau) who agrees to having his unstable mistress (Huston) murdered. Afterward he overcomes his pangs of conscience, while the basically decent people in his orbit of friends suffer for their minor sins or their innocence. A somber movie, but there is no shortage of funny Allen quips. Beautifully acted by all.

CRIMES OF PASSION

★ New World, 1984, c, 101 min. Dir: Ken Russell. SP: Barry Sandler. Cast: Kathleen Turner, Anthony Perkins, John Laughlin, Annie Potts, Bruce Davison.

Utter rot from director Russell. Turner has a double personality: by day an uptight fashion designer named Joanna, by night a ludicrous, blonde-wigged hooker named China Blue. Perkins is the deranged, sexually obsessed self-styled "preacher" who stalks her and taunts her. No good can come of their bizarre relationship, and it doesn't. Both actors should have been embarrassed to play their roles.

CRIMINAL CODE, THE

★★★ Columbia, 1931, b/w, 95 min. Dir: Howard Hawks. SP: Seton I. Miller, Fred Niblo, Jr., b/o play by Martin Flavin. Cast: Walter Huston, Phillips Holmes, Constance Cummings, Boris Karloff, Mary Doran, DeWitt Jennings.

This antique prison melodrama still holds interest due to its director and star. One of the best American actors, Huston plays a compassionate district attorney who becomes warden of a prison. When his daughter (Cummings) falls for an inmate (Holmes), there's plenty of trouble. Compounding his dilemma is the fact that he prosecuted the young man and knew at the time that he had an inadequate defense. Karloff repeats his stage role as a treacherous convict. Remade in 1938 and 1950.

CRIMINAL LAW

★★ Hemdale, 1989, c, 118 min. Dir: Martin Campbell. SP: Mark Kasdan. Cast: Gary Oldman, Kevin Bacon, Karen Young, Tess Harper, Joe Don Baker, Elizabeth Shepherd, Ron Lea.

Boston defense lawyer Ben Cross (Oldman) wins an acquittal for wealthy young Martin (Bacon) in a hideous rape-and-murder case. Then, to his horror, after new victims turn up, he comes to realize that Martin is, in fact, a serial killer. Disregarding the law, and with the help of the friend (Young) of one of the victims, he contrives to prove Martin guilty. Long, lurid, and unconvincing, *Criminal Law* plays more like a horror movie than a crime drama, with long tracking shots, ominous music, and the like. It ends with one climax following another to diminishing returns. As the tormented lawyer, Oldman gives another of his over-the-top performances.

CRISS CROSS

★★★ Universal, 1949, b/w, 87 min. Dir: Robert Siodmak. SP: Daniel Fuchs, b/o novel by Don Tracy. Cast: Burt Lancaster, Yvonne De Carlo, Dan Duryea, Stephen McNally, Richard Long, Tom Pedi, Alan Napier.

A sense of inexorable fate hangs over this dark melodrama from director Siodmak. Here the usually forceful Lancaster plays a weak sort, lured into crime and dangerous passion when he connects again with his ex-wife (De Carlo). Now she's married to nasty Duryea, and there's plenty of trouble and violence in store. McNally plays a cop who functions as Lancaster's voice of doom. ("They used you. They took you. The prize sucker of all time.") Sometimes the dialogue sounds like a parody of film noir, but the movie is never dull. Remade in 1995 as *The Underneath*.

Yvonne De Carlo and ex-husband Burt Lancaster face plenty of trouble in Criss Cross *(1949).*

CROSSFIRE

★★★☆ RKO, 1947, b/w, 86 min. Dir: Edward
Dmytryk. SP: John Paxton, b/o novel by Richard
Brooks. Cast: Robert Young, Robert Ryan, Robert
Mitchum, Gloria Grahame, Paul Kelly, Sam Levene,
Steve Brodie, George Cooper, Jacqueline White.

At first glance, *Crossfire* seems like standard
material. A man has been murdered in a hotel
room, and the police are investigating. But the
victim was an unassuming Jew (Levene), and
his killing appears to have been committed by
an out-of-control bigot. The movie combines
noir atmosphere with a message about prejudice, and it scores quite well in both areas. Ryan
is scary as the vicious ex-soldier whose anti-
Semitic rage explodes in violence, and Young is
the police captain who delivers the message
about hate. Creating some interest on the side-
lines are Grahame as a surly bargirl and Kelly
as a man who may or may not be her husband.
The movie won five Oscar nominations.

CROSSING GUARD, THE

★★ Miramax, 1995, c, 114 min. Dir and SP: Sean
Penn. Cast: Jack Nicholson, David Morse, Anjelica
Huston, Robin Wright, Piper Laurie, Richard
Bradford, Priscilla Barnes, David Baerwald, Robbie
Robertson, John Savage.

Written and directed by actor Penn
(*Dead Man Walking*), this somber drama is,
unfortunately, static, pretentious, and rather
dreary. Nicholson is a jeweler consumed
with rage against the drunken driver
(Morse) who killed his daughter five years
earlier. Now, with the man released from
prison, Nicholson is determined to kill him.
Morse, for his part, is overwhelmed by
guilt and sorrow. A collison course is
inevitable and when the climax comes, it's
meant to be affecting but instead it's absurd.
Huston has several good scenes as
Nicholson's ex-wife.

*Crossfire (1947):
Detective Robert Young
(left) investigates a
murder in which bigoted
soldier Robert Ryan is a
chief suspect.*

CRUISING

★ Lorimar, 1980, c, 106 min. Dir and SP: William Friedkin. Cast: Al Pacino, Paul Sorvino, Karen Allen, Richard Cox, Don Scardino, Joe Spinell.

A series of brutal murders committed against gay men has rocked New York City's West Village, and cop Steve Burns (Pacino) is assigned to go undercover in the homosexual community and find the killer. He becomes so deeply affected by this world that the consequences are devastating, and his life is changed forever. This is the central premise of Friedkin's grim, ugly thriller, a film that seems to wallow in its repellent detail. An initial disclaimer asserts that the movie is "not intended as an indictment of the homosexual world," and yet it depicts this world as violent, dangerous, and devoid of feeling. A serious mistake from the director of *The French Connection*.

CRUSH, THE

★ Warner Bros., 1993, c, 89 min. Dir and SP: Alan Shapiro. Cast: Cary Elwes, Alicia Silverstone, Jennifer Rubin, Amber Benson, Kurtwood Smith, Gwynyth Walsh.

We've had crazy women who were editors, secretaries, and nannies. Why not a delectable teenager? *The Crush* stars Silverstone as a fourteen-year-old girl whose obsession with a none-too-bright journalist (Elwes) turns deadly. Hopelessly silly business.

CRY DANGER

★★★ RKO, 1951, b/w, 79 min. Dir: Robert Parrish. SP: William Bowers, b/o story by Jerome Cady. Cast: Dick Powell, Rhonda Fleming, Richard Erdman, William Conrad, Regis Toomey, Jean Porter.

This lively revenge melodrama stars Powell as an ex-convict bent on finding out who framed him for a robbery he did not commit, and on retrieving the robbery loot for himself. His quest allows him to meet some amusingly devious types, including the inevitable beautiful dame (Fleming), an unscrupulous ex-marine (Erdman), and a treacherous big shot (Conrad). He also survives bullets, fists, and careening cars without a scratch.

CRY OF THE CITY

★★★ Fox, 1948, b/w, 95 min. Dir: Robert Siodmak. SP: Richard Murphy, b/o novel by Henry Edward Helseth. Cast: Victor Mature, Richard Conte, Debra Paget, Shelley Winters, Hope Emerson, Berry Kroeger, Fred Clark, Betty Garde.

Have you heard the one about childhood friends who end up on opposite sides of the law? Here it is again, competently handled, with Mature as the stalwart cop and Conte as the criminal who can't seem to go straight. Many of the characters are clichés— like the sweet girl (Paget) who loves Conte in spite of everything—but there are a few striking supporting performances, notably Emerson as a sinister masseuse and Kroeger as a corrupt lawyer.

CRY WOLF

★★ Warner Bros, 1947, b/w, 83 min. Dir: Peter Godfrey. SP: Catherine Turney, b/o novel by Marjorie Carleton. Cast: Barbara Stanwyck, Errol Flynn, Geraldine Brooks, Richard Basehart, Jerome Cowan, John Ridgely, Patricia White, Helene Thimig, Rory Mallinson.

Stanwyck plays a lady-in-peril in this Warners misfire. She's a recent widow who comes to her late husband's gloomy estate, where she is menaced at every turn. In her terrified state the actress was required to race through dark woods, find her way across high rooftops, and generally behave like an aging Nancy Drew. Flynn was grievously miscast as the mysterious head of the dysfunctional family.

CUTTER'S WAY

★★☆ United Artists, 1981, c, 105 min. Dir: Ivan Passer. SP: Jeffrey Alan Fiskin, b/o novel by Newton Thornburg. Cast: Jeff Bridges, John Heard, Lisa Eichhorn, Arthur Rosenberg, Stephen Elliott, Nina Van Pallandt, Ann Dusenberry.

When rootless, drifting Richard Bone (Bridges) sees a prominent citizen who may well be a murderer, his friend Alex Cutter (Heard), a crippled, rage-filled Vietnam veteran, goads him into taking action. Their curious plan: to blackmail the suspected killer, then return the money. The consequences in the end are tragic for everyone. A bleak, rather tedious drama of troubled lives, with a fine, ferocious performance by Heard. Originally released as *Cutter and Bone*, the title of the novel on which the film is based.

DAMNED DON'T CRY, THE

★★☆ Warner Bros., 1950, b/w, 103 min. Dir: Vincent Sherman. SP: Harold Medford, Jerome Weidman, b/o story by Gertrude Walker. Cast: Joan Crawford, David Brian, Steve Cochran, Kent Smith, Selena Royle, Richard Egan.

A tawdry melodrama, Joan Crawford style. Once again she's a poor, drab housewife hungering for wealth and position. Unfortunately she finds them by way of nasty crime lord Brian and learns the hard way that you cannot get to the top without a price. Lots of florid dialogue and many costume changes for the leading lady.

DANCE WITH A STRANGER

★★★☆ Goldwyn (British), 1989, c, 101 min. Dir: Mike Newell. SP: Shelagh Delaney. Cast: Miranda Richardson, Rupert Everett, Ian Holm, Matthew Carroll, Tom Chadbon, Joanne Whalley.

On July 13, 1955, Ruth Ellis, the former hostess of a rather sleazy London nightclub, and the mother of two young children, became the last woman in Britain to be sent to the gallows, convicted of murdering her abusive young lover (Everett). *Dance with a Stranger* speculates on the events leading up to the murder, clearly suggesting that Ellis was hanged more for her way of life than for her crime. Richardson makes a brilliant film debut as Ellis, and she gets excellent support in this darkly compelling and powerful film.

DANGEROUS MISSION

★★ RKO, 1954, c, 75 min. Dir: Louis King. SP: Horace McCoy, James Edmiston. Cast: Victor Mature, Piper Laurie, Vincent Price, William Bendix, Betta St. John, Steve Darrell, Dennis Weaver.

Scenic but strictly routine melodrama. Laurie witnesses a gang murder and flees New York City to Glacier National Park. Mature tracks her down and falls for her. Price plays a villainous sort and Bendix is a park cop. An avalanche and a forest fire do not help much.

DANGEROUSLY CLOSE

★★ Cannon, 1986, c, 95 min. Dir: Albert Pyun. SP: Scott Fields, John Stockwell, Marty Ross, b/o story by Marty Ross. Cast: John Stockwell, J. Eddie Peck, Carey Lowell, Bradford Bancroft, Don Michael Paul, Thom Matthews.

To "clean up" a southern California suburban school overrun with rebels and troublemakers, a group of rich young fascists called the Sentinels take over and systematically terrorize, torture, and finally murder their fellow students. The cops are invisible, and the adults are too frightened, indifferent, or stupid to interfere. A fairly smooth production wrecked by dumb material.

DANIEL

★★★ Paramount, 1983, c, 130 min. Dir: Sidney Lumet. SP: E. L. Doctorow, b/o his novel. Cast: Timothy Hutton, Mandy Patinkin, Lindsay Crouse, Edward Asner, Amanda Plummer, John Rubenstein, Ellen Barkin, Tovah Feldshuh, Julie Bovasso, Carmen Matthews.

This flawed but often compelling movie, derived by Doctorow from his novel, is patterned on the famous (and, to many, notorious) case of Julius and Ethel Rosenberg, who were executed for espionage in 1953. Hutton plays the title role, a young man anguished by the execution of his Communist parents (Patinkin and Crouse). The film moves back and forth in time, from the days of revolutionary idealism to the explosive period of the trial to the anti-Vietnam protest. The story never fully jells, but there are powerfully effective moments.

DARK CORNER, THE

★★☆ Fox, 1946, b/w, 99 min. Dir: Henry Hathaway. SP: Jay Dratler, Bernard Schoenfeld, b/o story by Leo Rosten. Cast: Lucille Ball, Clifton Webb, William Bendix, Mark Stevens, Kurt Kreuger, Cathy Downs, Reed Hadley.

Despite some attempts at snappy noir dialogue ("I can be framed easier than Whistler's mother"), this is a routine melodrama. Private eye Stevens becomes the prime suspect in the murder of his ex-partner (Kreuger), who framed him into prison. The real culprit is art dealer Webb, doing virtually a repeat of his sensationl role in *Laura* as a sexually obsessed, acerbic snob. Ball plays Stevens's adoring and helpful secretary, and Bendix is the thug in cahoots with Webb.

DARK MIRROR, THE

★★ Universal-International, 1946, b/w, 85 min. Dir: Robert Siodmak. SP: Nunnally Johnson, b/o story by Vladimir Pozner. Cast: Olivia de Havilland, Lew Ayres, Thomas Mitchell, Richard Long, Charles Evans, Garry Owen.

Hollywood's postwar fascination with psychiatric problems is reflected in this rather absurd noir melodrama. Havilland plays twin sisters who come under police investigation when one of their suitors is found murdered. Would you be surprised to learn that one twin is sweet and loving, and the other is ruthless, cunning, and dangerous? Psychologist Ayres probes their states of mind and uncovers the killer before she can do her sister in. De Havilland works hard, but the movie's mumbo-jumbo psychiatry seems antiquated.

DARK PASSAGE

★★★ Warner Bros., 1947, b/w, 106 min. Dir and SP: Delmer Daves. Cast: Humphrey Bogart, Lauren Bacall, Agnes Moorehead, Bruce Bennett, Tom D'Andrea.

Dark Passage gets off to an interesting start: innocent but convicted wife-murderer Bogart escapes from prison, and for a while a subjective camera sees all events from his point of view. Then he undergoes plastic surgery and becomes the Bogie we know. He also hides out in Bacall's apartment until he can uncover the real murderer. Does a romance develop? Of course. This Warners melodrama is not one of the best Bogart-Bacall vehicles, but it has some suspense and an amusingly over-the-top performance by Moorehead as a bitchy "friend" of Bogart's.

DARK PAST, THE

★★★ Columbia, 1948, b/w, 75 min. Dir: Rudolph Mate. SP: Philip MacDonald, Michael Blankfort, Albert Duffy, adapted by Malvin Wald, Oscar Saul

Humphrey Bogart points an accusing finger at Agnes Moorehead in Dark Passage *(1947).*

from play by James Warwick. Cast: William Holden, Nina Foch, Lee J. Cobb, Adele Jergens, Stephen Dunne, Lois Maxwell, Berry Kroeger, Steven Geray.

A remake of *Blind Alley* (1939), which had started as a Broadway success in 1935, *The Dark Past* is a good example of Hollywood's burgeoning interest in psychiatry in the postwar years. Departing from his usual wholesome American heroes, Holden plays a psychotic killer, newly escaped from prison, who takes over the house of psychiatrist Cobb. The good doctor manages to psychoanalzye the killer and uncover the traumatic event in his past that led him to his vicious ways. The psychiatry may be simplistic, but the movie is taut and suspenseful.

DARK WATERS
★★☆ United Artists, 1944, b/w, 90 min. Dir: Andre de Toth. SP: Joan Harrison, Marian Cockrell, b/o story by Frank Cockrell, Marian Cockrell. Cast: Merle Oberon, Franchot Tone, Thomas Mitchell, Fay Bainter, John Qualen, Elisha Cook, Jr.

Some eerie atmospheric flourishes, courtesy of the murky Louisiana bayou country, are the main asset of this standard "damsel-in-distress" thriller. Oberon is the troubled lady who comes to a plantation to visit her aunt and confronts strange, terrifying occurences instead of hospitality. Tone, as her doctor, helps her to sort out the mystery before she can lose her mind.

DARKER THAN AMBER
★★☆ Cinema Center, 1970, c, 97 min. Dir: Robert Clouse. SP: Ed Waters, b/o novel by John D. McDonald. Cast: Rod Taylor, Suzy Kendall, Theodore Bikel, Ahna Capri, William Smith, Robert Phillips, Janet MacLachlan, Jane Russell.

Taylor plays McDonald's fictional detective Travis McGee in this fast-moving but run-of-the-mill crime drama. The settings are Florida and Nassau as McGee tracks down a girl's killers and tangles with a vicious psycho (Smith). It all ends in a shoot-'em-up climax on a cruise ship and the Miami pier.

DEAD AGAIN
★★★ Paramount, 1991, c, 108 min. Dir: Kenneth Branagh. SP: Scott Frank. Cast: Kenneth Branagh, Emma Thompson, Andy Garcia, Derek Jacobi, Hanna Schygulla, Robin Williams (unbilled).

Decidedly offbeat but not totally successful, *Dead Again* is actor-director Branagh's attempt at emulating classic film noir. The premise is tricky: a private eye (Branagh) meets an amnesiac (Thompson) haunted by nightmares of a famous murder forty years earlier. Somehow the two seem to be reincarnations of the killer and victim in that long-ago murder. So what's really going on? Watch and find out. Strangest character: Jacobi as a hypnotist with an interest in antiques. The cast is fine, and there are a few nifty plot twists, but some parts are off the mark.

DEAD-BANG
★★ Warner Bros., 1989, c, 103 min. Dir: John Frankenheimer. SP: Robert Foster. Cast: Don Johnson, Penelope Ann Miller, William Forsythe, Tim Reid, Bob Balaban, Frank Military, Tate Donovan.

This action film stars Johnson as a grungy Los Angeles cop with a cocky attitude, overdue taxes, and an ex-wife who has a restraining order against him. While investigating the murder of a policeman, he uncovers a virulent white supremacy group that is wreaking havoc across the country. Of course nobody believes him until it is almost too late. Director Frankenheimer has done good work in the past (*The Manchurian Candidate* and others), but here he is defeated by substandard material. Most ludicrous scene: Johnson and the department psychologist.

DEAD CALM
★★★ Warner Bros., 1989, c, 96 min. Dir: Phillip Noyce. SP: Terry Hayes, b/o novel by Charles Williams. Cast: Nicole Kidman, Sam Neill, Billy Zane.

A small-scale but quite effective Australian-made thriller, this film relies largely on tight closeups to get across its tale of terror. John and Ray (Neill and Kidman) are a married couple trying to deal with their young son's death by sailing their yacht through calm waters. But there's no calm in sight when killer Hughie (Zane) comes aboard. While John tries to survive in Hughie's rapidly sinking schooner, Ray must cope with the killer by herself. A stock situation, and an absurd climax, but not bad.

DEAD END
★★★☆ United Artists, 1937, b/w, 93 min. Dir: William Wyler. SP: Lillian Hellman, b/o play by Sidney

The Dead End Kids gather on a New York street in Dead End *(1937). The film duplicated the stage version's famous slum setting.*

Kingsley. Cast: Sylvia Sidney, Joel McCrea, Humphrey Bogart, Dead End Kids, Claire Trevor, Wendy Barrie, Allen Jenkins, Marjorie Main, Ward Bond.

In the famous opening, the camera swoops over New York City, then down to a grimy slum area where most of the film takes place. The rest is a commendable version of the hit Broadway play, now a trifle musty, about life in these mean streets. That favorite Depression heroine Sidney plays the slum girl who tries— and fails—to keep her kid brother from a life of crime, and McCrea is the struggling young architect she loves. Bogart is much more colorful than either as the vicious gangster returning to his old neighborhood. Great production design by Richard Day, and first-rate photography by Gregg Toland.

DEADLINE AT DAWN

★★☆ RKO, 1946, b/w, 83 min. Dir: Harold Clurman. SP: Clifford Odets, b/o novel by William Irish (Cornell Woolrich). Cast: Susan Hayward, Bill Williams, Paul Lukas, Joseph Calleia, Lola Lane, Osa Massen.

Considering this movie's credits, it should have been much better, but it's only fair. A sailor on leave (Williams) is implicated in the murder of a call girl (Lane) and enlists the help of a dancer (Hayward) and a philosophical cab driver (Lukas) in finding the killer by morning. A few odd suspects turn up, and the murder is eventually solved. The highfalutin dialogue of famed playwright Odets seems curiously out of place in this modest mystery.

DEADLY HERO

★★ Avco Embassy, 1976, c, 102 min. Dir: Ivan Nagy. SP: George Wislocki. Cast: Don Murray, Diahn Williams, James Earl Jones, Lilia Skala, Treat Williams, George S. Irving.

Murray plays a character familiar in many a police drama: the angry law-and-order cop with an itchy trigger finger. When he kills a black mugger-shakedown artist (Jones) who's been terrorizing a teacher (Diahn Williams), he should be a hero. But the teacher changes her testimony and implicates Murray as a cold-blooded killer. His life becomes a nightmare from which he cannot seem to waken. A decent premise, routinely handled.

DEAD MAN WALKING

★★★★ Gramercy, 1995, c, 120 min. Dir and SP: Tim Robbins, b/o book by Sister Helen Prejean. Cast: Susan Sarandon, Sean Penn, Robert Prosky, Raymond J. Barry, R. Lee Ermy, Roberta Maxwell.

Few films call for discussion after viewing, but this searing, intensely moving drama is one of them. Sarandon plays a compassionate Louisiana nun (the story is based on the true nun's experience) who becomes the spiritual adviser to a convicted killer (Penn) now on Death Row. Her troubled odyssey to the moment of his execution, and the relationship that grows between them, constitute the heart of the movie. The film strives to strike a balance in its point of view on capital punishment, but it is clearly against the death penalty. Under Robbins's assured direction, the two leading players give extraordinary performances that are certain to linger in your mind.

DEAD MEN DON'T WEAR PLAID

★★★ Universal, 1982, b/w, 89 min. Dir: Carl Reiner. SP: Carl Reiner, George Gipe, Steve Martin. Cast: Steve Martin, Rachel Ward, Reni Santoni, Carl Reiner, George Gaynes, Frank McCarthy.

A clever idea, although it wears thin by midpoint. The film is actually an extended sketch, a spoof of forties film noir, with Martin as a hard-boiled detective who interacts with many characters drawn from old clips. He gets to tangle with such tough guys as Humphrey Bogart, Kirk Douglas, and Burt Lancaster, and to exchange quips and kisses with such alluring dames as Barbara Stanwyck, Lana Turner, Joan Crawford, and Veronica Lake. Fun for movie buffs.

DEAD OF WINTER

★★★ MGM/UA, 1987, c, 100 min. Dir: Arthur Penn. SP: Marc Shmuger, Mark Malone. Cast: Mary Steenburgen, Roddy McDowell, Jan Rubes, William Russ, Ken Pogue.

A neatly turned out lady-in-distress thriller. Steenburgen plays an actress who travels to a spooky New England house in the dead of winter to audition for a role and finds herself a prisoner, trapped in a nefarious scheme involving blackmail and murder. A good wintry setting helps, although the story gets more far-fetched as it goes along. Inspired by the 1945 movie *My Name Is Julia Ross*.

DEAD POOL, THE

★★☆ Warner Bros., 1988, c, 91 min. Dir: Buddy Van Horn. SP: Steve Sharon, b/o story by Steve Sharon, Durk Pearson, Sandy Shaw. Cast: Clint Eastwood, Patricia Clarkson, Liam Neeson, Evan C. Kim, David Hunt, Michael Currie, James (Jim) Carrey.

Here we go again. This fifth entry in the "Dirty Harry" series has the loose-cannon cop (Eastwood) battling a secret satanic organization called the Dead Pool, in which people bet on certain celebrities dying within a specific time. A toy car loaded with real dynamite provides a suspenseful sequence, but the material is getting very tired. And so is Harry.

DEAD PRESIDENTS

★★★☆ Hollywood, 1995, c, 119 min. Dir: Allen Hughes, Albert Hughes. SP: Michael Henry Brown, b/o story by Allen Hughes, Albert Hughes, Michael Henry Brown. Cast: Larenz Tate, Keith David, Chris Tucker, Freddy Rodriguez, N'Bushe Wright, Rose Jackson, Bokeem Woodbine, Michael Imperioli, Jenifer Lewis.

An overlong, uneven, but frequently powerful drama, *Dead Presidents* (a reference to paper currency) should have received a much better reception. It relates the unrelievedly grim story of a young black man (Tate) and his six-year odyssey from the mean streets of the Bronx, through the war in Vietnam (a defining experience in his life), and back to the even bleaker streets of his old neighborhood. The feeling throughout is one of utter hopelessness. The film loses its footing toward the end, but much of it is haunting. Created by the makers of *Menace II Society*. Warning: the violence is exceptionally graphic but for once it seems justified.

DEAD RECKONING

★★☆ Columbia, 1947, b/w, 100 min. Dir: John Cromwell. SP: Oliver H. P. Garrett, Steve Fisher. Cast: Humphrey Bogart, Lizabeth Scott, Morris Carnovsky, Marvin Miller, Wallace Ford, William Prince.

A standard-issue film noir, *Dead Reckoning* stars Bogart as an ex-paratrooper bent on finding the killer of his best buddy. His investigation leads him to several sinister or devious figures in a long-ago murder trial, including a big-time mobster (Carnovsky), his sadistic henchman (Miller), and, most of all, a sultry blonde (Scott) with whom he falls in love. The dialogue often sounds like a parody of the genre ("Maybe she was all right. And maybe Christmas comes in July. But I didn't believe it"), and a climactic scene shamelessly rips off a similar scene from *The Maltese Falcon*. ("You're going to fry, Dusty.")

DEAD RINGER

★★ Warner Bros., 1964, b/w, 115 min. Dir: Paul Henreid. SP: Albert Beich, Oscar Millard, b/o story by Rian James. Cast: Bette Davis, Karl Malden, Peter Lawford, Philip Carey, Jean Hagen, George Macready, Estelle Winwood.

Two Bette Davises for the price of one in this creaky, overbaked melodrama. The actress plays twin sisters, one of whom kills the other in retaliation for stealing her fiancé. She then assumes the identity of her dead twin, making for additional complications. (One is that she inherits her sister's suspicious lover, played by Lawford.) Silly stuff, but the actress seems to be having fun. The director is Davis's forties costar Henreid.

DEATH HUNT

★★ Fox, 1981, c, 97 min. Dir: Peter R. Hunt. SP: Michael Grais, Mark Victor. Cast: Charles Bronson, Lee Marvin, Andrew Stevens, Angie Dickinson, Carl Weathers, Ed Lauter, Scott Hylands, Henry Beckman, William Sanderson.

A different sort of Charles Bronson movie, but not good. At least he's not a trigger-happy vigilante this time. He plays a taciturn fur trapper wrongly accused of murder, who is pursued through the Arctic Circle wilderness by a determined sergeant in the Royal Canadian Mounted Police. Dickinson wanders in for some reason, but the emphasis is on the chase.

DEATH ON THE NILE

★★★ EMI (British), 1978, c, 140 min. Dir: John Guillermin. SP: Anthony Shaffer, b/o novel by Agatha Christie. Cast: Peter Ustinov, Jane Birkin, Lois Chiles, Mia Farrow, Jon Finch, Bette Davis, David Niven, Angela Lansbury, Maggie Smith, Jack Warden, Olivia Hussey, Simon MacCorkindale.

Ustinov made his first appearance as Agatha Christie's wily Belgian detective Hercule Poirot in this atmospheric mystery, set in the thirties on a ship sailing down the Nile. Who murdered Lois Chiles, the arrogant millionairess who stole her best friend's fiancé? Was it haughty Washington hostess Bette Davis? Or eccentric novelist Angela Lansbury? Or Maggie Smith, caustic companion to the victim? There are other murders to come among the star-filled cast, but Poirot uses his "little gray cells" to unmask the killer.

DEATHTRAP

★★☆ Warner Bros., 1982, c, 115 min. Dir: Sidney Lumet. SP: Jay Presson Allen, b/o play by Ira Levin. Cast: Michael Caine, Christopher Reeve, Dyan Cannon, Irene Worth, Henry Jones, Joe Silver.

Caine is a once-successful playwright whose last few plays have been flops. Along comes Reeve, a novice playwright with a great manuscript. Using the pretext of a collaboration, Caine invites Reeve to his home, but his intention is to kill him and take credit for the play. Cannon is Caine's overwrought wife. *Deathtrap* may have seemed clever on the stage, but here the mechanics show, and the movie is little more than an exercise in twisty suspense.

DEATH WARRANT

★★ Pathe, 1990, c, 89 min. Dir: Deran Serafian. SP: David S. Goyer. Cast: Jean-Claude Van Damme, Robert Guillaume, Cynthia Gibb, George Dickerson, Art Le Fleur, Patrick Kilpatrick.

Van Damme, the Belgian-born karate champion, plays a veteran of the Royal Canadian Mounted Police who goes undercover to learn why so many inmates are being murdered in a California prison. He uncovers a dastardly plot involving the sale of human organs for transplants in South America. The plot is merely a peg on which to hang Van Damme's formidable skills in karate, which he demonstrates at every opportunity.

DEATH WISH II

★ Columbia/Cannon, 1982, c, 93 min. Dir: Michael Winner. SP: David Engelbach. Cast: Charles Bronson, Jill Ireland, Vincent Gardenia, J. D. Cannon, Anthony Franciosa, Ben Frank.

Same star, same director, same dreadful carnage. For this occasion, architect and self-styled vigilante Paul Kersey is back in business, killing thugs in Los Angeles after his Spanish cook is raped and murdered. His catatonic daughter is also raped (for the second time) and killed by vicious hoodlums. For those who may care, there were three more sequels in the *Death Wish* series, proving that the series never took its title seriously.

DECEIVED

★★ Touchstone, 1991, c, 103 min. Dir: Damian Harris. SP: Mary Alice Donoghue, Derek Saunders, b/o story by Mary Alice Donoghue. Cast: Goldie Hawn, John Heard, Ashley Peldon, Tom Irwin, Robin Bartlett, Amy Wright, Kate Reid.

Happily married for years, Adrian Saunders (Hawn) suddenly suspects that her husband, Jack (Heard), has been lying about his identity. To her horror, she also learns that he is a thief and a murderer. Soon her life is in jeopardy, and eventually she is being chased about a deserted loft. A standard-cut "lady-in-peril" thriller with not much credibility. Perky Goldie tries, to little avail.

DECEPTION

★★★ Warner Bros., 1946, b/w, 112 min. Dir: Irving Rapper. SP: John Collier, Joseph Than, b/o play by Louis Verneuil. Cast: Bette Davis, Paul Henreid, Claude Rains, John Abbott, Benson Fong, Richard Walsh, Richard Erdman, Russell Arms.

Vintage Bette Davis, ridiculous but also hugely entertaining. She's a concert pianist who is the mistress of overbearing conductor Rains.

When the husband (Henreid) she presumed dead—a cellist by profession—turns up alive, she strives desperately to keep her new life a secret from him. Her efforts end in murder. Rains steals the movie, although Davis battles him all the way through yards of overwrought or high-toned dialogue and much awful music. Fun, nevertheless. A remake of a 1929 movie called *Jealousy*.

DECEPTION

★★ Miramax, 1993, c, 90 min. Dir: Graeme Clifford. SP: Robert Dillon, Michael Thomas, b/o story by Robert Dillon. Cast: Liam Neeson, Andie MacDowell, Viggo Mortensen, Jack Thompson.

A highly scenic but dull melodrama, with MacDowell as a woman determined to solve the mystery of her husband's death. The search takes her around the world, and leads to the discovery that the man she loved and trusted lived a dangerous secret life. Neeson costars as a man who seems to be only peripherally involved in the action.

DEEP COVER

★★★ New Line, 1992, c, 112 min. Dir: Bill Duke. SP: Michael Tolkin, Henry Bean, b/o story by Michael Tolkin. Cast: Larry Fishburne, Jeff Goldblum, Victoria Dillard, Gregory Sierra, Clarence Williams III, Charles Martin Smith, Sydney Lassick.

Superficially, *Deep Cover* appears to be just another action movie, but it is actually more complex and interesting than that. Harsh and cynical, it focuses on a dedicated cop (Fishburne) who goes so deeply undercover to break up a top-level drug ring that he is trapped in a moral quagmire where he must behave like the icy killer he pretends to be. Ultimately he finds a kind of redemption. Fishburne is a compelling presence as the agonized cop, and Goldblum adds some dimension to his role as a corrupt lawyer who is involved in the drug scene.

DEFENSELESS

★★☆ New Visions, 1991, c, 106 min. Dir: Martin Campbell. SP: James Hicks, b/o story by James Hicks, Jeff Burkhart. Cast: Barbara Hershey, Sam Shepard, Mary Beth Hurt, J. T. Walsh, Kellie Overbey, Jay O. Sanders, Sheree North.

A rather muddled, occasionally suspenseful thriller, *Defenseless* stars Hershey as a lawyer whose client (Walsh) is also her lover. He also has a wife (Hurt) who turns out to be an old school friend of Hershey's. When he's murdered, Hershey becomes a suspect and another possible victim. Shepard is the suspicious cop on the case. One stalking scene in Hershey's apartment is a real nail-biter. Otherwise, not much.

DEFIANCE

★★☆ American International, 1980, c, 102 min. Dir: John Flynn. SP: Thomas Michael Donnelly, b/o story by Thomas Michael Donnelly, Mark Tulin. Cast: Jan-Michael Vincent, Theresa Saldana, Danny Aiello, Art Carney, Fernando Lopez, Rudy Ramos.

A not-bad variation on the basic young-hero-against-the-gang plot. Nice guy Vincent moves into a bad neighborhood where a group of nasty deliquents called the Souls has everyone terrorized. After many harrassments, he finally takes a stand and tames them. Aiello is the friendly barfly and ex-gang member and Saldana is that proverbial girl upstairs.

DEFIANT ONES, THE

★★★ United Artists, 1958, b/w, 97 min. Dir: Stanley Kramer. SP: Nathan E. Douglas, Harold Jacob Smith. Cast: Tony Curtis, Sidney Poitier, Theodore Bikel, Cara Williams, Lon Chaney, Jr., Charles McGraw, Claude Akins, Carl Switzer.

Once widely admired as a potent social melodrama, *The Defiant Ones* now seems to make its points with an anvil. Still, it has some effective moments and strong performances by Curtis and Poitier. They play chain-gang convicts who escape from their captors shackled to each other. Curtis is white and bigoted, Poitier black and seething with anger and resentment. During their desperate flight from the law, they arrive grudgingly at mutual respect and caring. The authors won an Oscar for their original screenplay, but years later it was revealed that "Nathan E. Douglas" was actually blacklisted writer Nedrick Young. Sam Leavitt also won an Oscar for his black-and-white photography.

DELIVERANCE

★★★★ Warner Bros., 1972, c, 109 min. Dir: John Boorman. SP: James Dickey, b/o his novel. Cast: Jon Voight, Burt Beynolds, Ned Beatty, Ronny Cox, Billy McKinney, Herbert "Cowboy" Coward.

You will have a difficult time forgetting this somber and unsettling drama. Four friends decide to go white-water canoeing in Georgia's Appalachian region. Big mistake. After one of them plunges into the river, the remaining trio are forced to deal with two deranged mountain men (McKinney and Coward) who attack one of the men sexually. Now the friends must

On a canoe trip that has turned harrowing, Ned Beatty, Burt Reynolds, and Jon Voight battle the forces of nature as they try to dispose of the body of mountain man Billy McKinney in Deliverance *(1972).*

resort to their most basic instincts to confront the evil and survive. James Dickey adapted his own novel and also plays a small role. One early memorable scene: Cox, the party's gentlest member, plays guitar in a duet with a retarded youngster and his banjo.

DELUSION

★★★ IRS Media, 1991, c, 100 min. Dir: Carl Colpaert. SP: Carl Colpaert, Kurt Voss. Cast: Jim Metzler, Jennifer Rubin, Kyle Secor, Jerry Orbach, Robert Costanzo.

By turns amusing, baffling, and irritating, *Delusion* won both admiring and hostile reviews for its offbeat variation on an old movie theme. When his computer company is taken over, angry George O'Brien (Metzler) flees with $450,000 in misappropriated funds. On the highway from Los Angeles to Reno, he is taken prisoner by Chevy (Secor), a bizarre sort who turns out to be a contract killer, and Chevy's dumb girlfriend Patti (Rubin). A few surprises follow, not all of them credible. Belgian-born filmmaker Colpaert may or may not be kidding, but his odd little movie holds your attention.

DESPERATE HOURS, THE

★★★ Paramount, 1955, b/w, 112 min. Dir: William Wyler. SP: Joseph Hayes, b/o his novel and play. Cast: Humphrey Bogart, Fredric March, Martha Scott, Arthur Kennedy, Dewey Martin, Mary Murphy, Gig Young, Robert Middleton, Richard Eyer.

There's a gaping hole at the center of *The Desperate Hours*, and it's hard to ignore. March, head of a nice American family, suddenly finds his home invaded by hoodlums on the run, with Bogart as the chief hoodlum. He must use all his courage and resourcefulness to triumph over the villains. The situation is tense, if familiar from other movies, but you are asked to believe that March would never contact the police, even when he is allowed to leave the house. No way. Both Bogart and March are much too old for their roles, but Bogart, at least, seems to relish returning one last time to his old gangster persona. The story was remade badly in 1990.

DESPERATE HOURS

★ Fox/de Laurentiis, 1990, c, 105 min. Dir: Michael Cimino. SP: Laurence Konner, Mark Rosenthal, Joseph Hayes, b/o novel and play by Joseph Hayes. Cast: Anthony Hopkins, Mickey Rourke, Mimi Rogers, Lindsay Crouse, Kelly Lynch, David Morse.

A remake of the 1955 film that's so bad it makes the original seem like a classic, which it never was. Once again a psychotic hoodlum (Rourke) and his dimwit cohorts hold a family hostage. Head of the family is Hopkins, who must have wished he were back tending to the Elephant Man a decade earlier. There's more bloodshed than in the original movie, but not a fraction of the suspense is retained.

DETECTIVE, THE

★★★ Fox, 1968, c, 114 min. Dir: Gordon Douglas. SP: Abby Mann, b/o novel by Roderick Thorp. Cast: Frank Sinatra, Lee Remick, Ralph Meeker, Jack Klugman, Horace McMahon, Jacqueline Bisset, Tony Musante, Robert Duvall, Al Freeman, Jr.

Sinatra followed his double stint as private eye Tony Rome (*Tony Rome*, 1967; *Lady in Cement*, 1968) with this much grittier crime story adapted from Thorp's best-selling novel. He plays a New York detective investigating the murder of a homosexual and who is very uneasy about the execution of the convicted killer (Musante). Ultimately he not only uncovers the sordid truth about the murder but also exposes a web of corruption among government officials and the police. Pulpish material, to be sure, but also some stinging dialogue and good performances.

DETECTIVE STORY

★★★☆ Paramount, 1951, b/w, 103 min. Dir: William Wyler. SP: Philip Yordan, Robert Wyler, b/o play by Sidney Kingsley. Cast: Kirk Douglas, Eleanor Parker, William Bendix, Horace McMahon, Lee Grant, Joseph Wiseman, Michael Strong, Cathy O'Donnell, Bert Freed, George Macready.

The single-set stage origins of *Detective Story* are very apparent, and yet the movie is so riveting you are not likely to notice. In a characteristically feverish performance, Douglas plays a cop whose moral rigidity and deeply rooted antipathy to lawbreakers have him paying a very stiff price. Eleanor Parker is the loving wife who causes him to finally unravel when her long-buried secret comes to light. Fine acting, especially by Oscar-nominated Grant, repeating her stage role as a shoplifter, and by Wiseman, also from the stage, as a dangerous felon.

DETOUR

★★☆ PRC, 1945, b/w, 68 min. Dir: Edgar G. Ulmer. SP and story: Martin Goldsmith. Cast: Tom Neal, Ann Savage, Claudia Drake, Edmund MacDonald, Tim Ryan, Esther Howard.

A minor cult classic of the forties, *Detour* hardly deserves its reputation. Made on an obviously frayed shoestring, it has all of the ingredients of film noir but none of the style or skill. A hitchhiker (Neal) panics when his driver dies, and he decides to assume the dead man's identity. Enter a femme fatale (Savage) and trouble, and our shaky hero is doomed. The acting and the dialogue are dreadful, but some of the noir lines are amusing: "That's life! Whatever way you turn, fate sticks out a foot to trip you!"

DEVIL IN A BLUE DRESS

★★★ TriStar, 1995, c, 102 min. Dir: Carl Franklin. SP: Carl Franklin, b/o novel by Walter Mosley. Cast: Denzel Washington, Tom Sizemore, Jennifer Beals, Don Cheadle, Maury Chaykin, Terry Kinney.

In 1948 Los Angeles, down-on-his-luck Easy Rawlins (Washington) takes a job locating the missing girlfriend of a politician. Soon he is up to his neck in big trouble, suspected of several murders and enmeshed in a labyrinthine plot at high and low levels. *Devil in a Blue Dress* trots out all the familiar noir characters, including dangerous women, corrupt politicians, and nasty policeman, but it's only a moderate example of the genre. Washington makes an acceptable noir hero, but Cheadle steals the show as his volatile friend. Director Franklin won critical attention with his 1992 movie, *One False Move.*

DEVIL'S OWN, THE

★★★ Columbia, 1997, c, 110 min. Dir: Alan J. Pakula. SP: David Aaron Cohen, Vincent Patrick, Kevin Jarre, b/o story by Kevin Jarre. Cast: Harrison Ford, Brad Pitt, Margaret Colin, Ruben Blades, Treat Williams, George Hearn, Mitchell Ryan, Natascha McElhone.

Ford and Pitt generate some authentic star power in this tense but ambivalent drama. Pitt is a revenge-driven, long-pursued IRA terrorist who comes to America to purchase weapons for his cause. Ford is the veteran Irish-American cop, decent and honorable, who brings Pitt into his home without knowing his identity. Their relationship, and their inevitable clash, not only makes for several suspenseful action sequences but also raises many questions about violence, the IRA, and other matters that the screenplay doesn't begin to answer. Ford is excellent in his usual dour fashion, and Pitt is surprisingly good, although some of his dialogue could use subtitles.

DEVIL THUMBS A RIDE, THE

★★☆ RKO, 1947, b/w, 62 min. Dir and SP: Felix Feist. Cast: Lawrence Tierney, Ted North, Nan Leslie, Betty Lawford, Andrew Tombes.

Pursued by the police, thief and murderer Tierney hitches a ride with tipsy North, then proceeds to almost ruin North's reputation before he is captured. Five decades ago, The *New York Times* remarked, "It is pictures like this which give the movies a black eye and give us a pain in the neck." Now it is regarded by many as a trim little "B" film of the period. See for yourself, if you can find it. Tierney played gangster John Dillinger in 1945.

DIABOLIQUE

★ Morgan Creek, 1996, c, 107 min. Dir: Jeremiah Chechik. SP: Don Roos. Cast: Sharon Stone, Isabelle Adjani, Chazz Palminteri, Kathy Bates, Spalding Gray, Shirley Knight, Allen Garfield, Adam Hann-Byrd.

Released in the United States in 1955, Henri-Georges Clouzot's French film *Diabolique* created something of a sensation with its perverse tale of murder and deception at a boys' school. Following the general lines of the original, this remake, now set in Pittsburgh, is more grotesque than macabre, a badly judged piece of cinematic lunacy. Once again, the wife (Adjani) and mistress (Stone) of a sadistic headmaster (Palminteri) plot to murder him, with unforeseen and unsettling consequences. (Yes, the shocking bathtub sequence is duplicated.) Hard and sluttish, Stone is nobody's idea of a teacher at a boys' school, and Palminteri is woefully miscast.

DIAL M FOR MURDER

★★★ Warner Bros, 1954, c, 105 min. Dir: Alfred Hitchcock. SP: Frederick Knott, b/o his play. Cast: Ray Milland, Grace Kelly, Robert Cummings, John Williams, Anthony Dawson.

A compact if stagebound mystery thriller from

Alfred Hitchcock, *Dial M for Murder* manages to keep viewers on their toes through all the plot's twists and turns. (The play was an enormous success in London and on Broadway.) Milland stars as a British bounder who is scheming to murder his rich and beautiful wife (Kelly). His scheme goes away when his hired assassin (Dawson) is killed instead, and the rest of the film involves the cat-and-mouse game between Milland and a Scotland Yard inspector (Williams). All hands perform admirably, with a special nod to Williams's cagey and imperturbable policeman. The movie was originally shot in the 3-D process.

DIARY OF A HITMAN

★★☆ Vision International, 1992, c, 91 min. Dir: Roy London. SP: Kenneth Pressman, b/o his play. Cast: Forest Whitaker, Sherilyn Fenn, James Belushi, Sharon Stone, Seymour Cassel, John Bedford-Lloyd, Lois Chiles.

Whitaker is an intense actor, but his perennial mood of pain and despair can wear you down. Here he plays a hit man with angst—he wants to give it all up after one last job. But this calls for his killing Fenn and her baby, and his misery is now total. Clearly adapted from a play, the movie deals mostly with the Whitaker-Fenn relationship: will he kill her or spare her? You may or may not care, but the acting is good. Stone appears briefly as Fenn's trampish sister.

DICK TRACY

★★★ Touchstone, 1990, c, 105 min. Dir: Warren Beatty. SP: Jim Cash, Jack Epps, Jr., b/o characters created by Chester Gould. Cast: Warren Beatty, Madonna, Al Pacino, Dustin Hoffman, Glenne Headly, Charlie Korsmo, James Caan, Charles Durning, Mandy Patinkin, Dick Van Dyke, William Forsythe.

A visually striking but curiously hollow film version of the long-running comic strip, *Dick Tracy* draws most of its fun from having the assorted villains played by leading actors in thick, disfiguring makeup (Pacino as Big Boy Caprice, Hoffman as Mumbles, and so on). However, Beatty is hardly riveting as the trenchcoated police detective. As Breathless Mahoney, Madonna gets to perform a few Stephen Sondheim songs. It's all Oscar-winning production design (courtesy of Richard Sylbert), but little else.

DIE! DIE! MY DARLING!

★★ Columbia/Hammer (British), 1965, c, 97 min. Dir: Silvio Narizzano. SP: Richard Matheson, b/o novel by Anne Blaisdell. Cast: Tallulah Bankhead, Stefanie Powers, Peter Vaughan, Yootha Joyce, Donald Sutherland, Maurice Kaufmann.

Many years after her brief film career had effectively ended, Bankhead joined the list of aging actresses turning to horror by making this absurd thriller in England. She goes way over the top as Mrs. Trefoile, a deranged dowager who imprisons the fiancée (Powers) of her dead son, believing that the hapless girl was responsible for his death. She is aided and abetted by several dimwitted retainers, who include a young Donald Sutherland. Until the crazy lady is dispatched, there is little in the movie except clichéd damsel-in-distress theatrics.

DIE HARD

★★★ Fox, 1988, c, 131 min. Dir: John McTiernan. SP: Jeb Stuart, Steven E. de Souza, b/o novel by Roderick Thorp. Cast: Bruce Willis, Alan Rickman, Bonnie Bedelia, Alexander Godunov, Reginald VelJohnson, De'voreaux White, William Atherton, Hart Bochner.

DICK TRACY

Chester Gould's comic-strip hero Dick Tracy first showed up on the screen in a quartet of Republic Pictures serials in the late thirties and early forties. Tracy was played by a minor actor named Ralph Byrd, who quickly became identified as the intrepid crime fighter. In 1945 RKO revived the character for four low-budget movies, the first two with Morgan Conway as Tracy and the last two with Byrd returning to the role.

None of these films was more than mediocre, but they made passable second features. Boris Karloff played the villain in the last of the four, *Dick Tracy Meets Gruesome* (1947). Ralph Byrd also starred in a television series in 1950–51. In 1990 Warren Beatty produced and starred in *Dick Tracy*, an elaborate, stylish, but not particularly entertaining version of the comic strip.

Hold on to your seat, and watch out for flying bodies. *Die Hard* doesn't make much sense, but you won't care as one breathtaking action sequence follows another. It seems that a group of terrorists, led by Hans Gruber (Rickman), have broken into a Los Angeles building and are holding people hostage on Christmas eve. Their price: millions in negotiable bonds. Enter New York cop John McClane (Willis), who is in the building and trying to let everyone know what is happening. Soon the battle is joined between tough, wisecracking McClane and the terrorists. The stunt men must have worked overtime and some of the effects are quite spectacular. The movie was hugely successful, and, to date, spawned two sequels.

DIE HARD 2

★★★ Fox, 1990, c, 124 min. Dir: Renny Harlin. SP: Steven E. de Souza, Doug Richardson, b/o novel by Walter Wager. Cast: Bruce Willis, Bonnie Bedelia, William Atherton, Reginald Vel Johnson, Franco Nero, William Sadler, John Amos, Dennis Franz.

More of the same, and as mindlessly enjoyable as the first *Die Hard* feature. This time cop John McClane (Willis), while waiting for his wife (Bedelia) at Washington's Dulles Airport, finds himself in the middle of a terrorist plot. Terrorists seize control of the airport to free a foreign dictator (Nero) being transported to the U.S. The stage is set for outsize action scenes that defy credibility but are fun to watch. Wherever McClane goes, trouble follows.

DIE HARD WITH A VENGEANCE

★★ Fox, 1995, c, 131 min. Dir: John McTiernan. SP: Jonathan Hensleigh. Cast: Bruce Willis, Jeremy Irons, Samuel L. Jackson, Graham Greene, Colleen Camp, Larry Bryggman, Anthony Peck, Nick Wyman.

The third and hopefully the last of the *Die Hard* series, this movie is more of a nonstop action machine than a film. Once again cop John McClane (Willis) is caught up in a desperate, dangerous situation. This time he's the target of a diabolically clever terrorist (Irons) apparently out for revenge. McClane, joined by reluctant new friend Jackson, must defuse a series of bombs planted throughout New York City. There are countless explosions, chases, and shootouts, but the movie is almost totally mindless. It's time to retire, McClane.

DILLINGER

★★★ Monogram, 1945, b/w, 70 min. Dir: Max Nosseck. SP: Phil Yordan. Cast: Lawrence Tierney, Anne Jeffreys, Edmund Lowe, Eduardo Ciannelli, Elisha Cook, Jr., Marc Lawrence, Ludwig Stossel, Elsa Janssen.

One of the first films to deal with a notorious gangster by name, this low-budget movie is compactly made and surprisingly effective. Tierney plays a fictionalized version of the vicious John Dillinger, whose death in front of a movie theater in 1934 became part of America's criminal lore. Other versions of Dillinger's sordid story turned up in 1973 and in 1991 (for television).

DILLINGER

★★★ American International, 1973, c, 96 min. Dir and SP: John Milius. Cast: Warren Oates, Ben Johnson, Michelle Phillips, Richard Dreyfuss, Cloris Leachman, Harry Dean Stanton.

Another version of the short life and violent death of gangster John Dillinger, who dominated the world of crime in 1933-34. This version adds some blood and gore and also extracts a good performance from Oates as Dillinger. Much footage is given to Melvin Purvis (Johnson), the FBI man responsible for killing Dillinger in Chicago.

DILLINGER AND CAPONE

★ Paramount, 1995, c, 94 min. Dir: Jon Purdy. SP: Michael B. Druxman. Cast: Martin Sheen, F. Murray Abraham, Catherine Hicks, Stephen Davies, Sasha Jenson, Jeffrey Combs, Michael C. Gwynne, Anthony Crivello, Don Stroud.

A wildly outlandish premise gets the screenplay it deserves: it supposes that public enemy John Dillinger (Sheen) was not killed in 1934 but survived to take up a new life with wife and son. Released from prison in 1939, kingpin gangster Al Capone (Abraham), now deranged by syphilis, kidnaps Dillinger's family and holds them hostage until Dillinger can steal the fortune he (Capone) has hidden in Chicago. Violent gunplay ensues, as one absurd sequence follows another. Most ludicrous character: Capone's genteel, proper English butler (Davies).

DIRTY HARRY

★★★ Warner Bros., 1972, c, 102 min. Dir: Don Siegel. SP: Harry Julian Fink, R. M. Fink, Dean Riesner, b/o story by Harry Julian Fink, R. M. Fink. Cast: Clint Eastwood, Harry Guardino, Reni Santoni, Andy Robinson, John Larch, John Vernon, John Mitchum.

This tough police melodrama introduced "Dirty Harry" Callahan (Eastwood) to movie audiences. He's the uncompromising cop who is willing to bend the law to achieve his end of ridding San Francisco of bad guys. Harry has his own code of justice and retribution, and he applies it to his search for a nasty serial killer (Robinson). The movie's vigilante attitude was embraced by a large number of viewers, and the movie's success led to four "Dirty Harry" sequels. The movie also triggered a number of cops-above-the-law variations in the early seventies (for example, *The Seven-Ups,* 1973), Apart from its dubious and possibly dangerous premise, the film is well made, crisply edited and vividly photographed.

DIRTY MARY, CRAZY LARRY

★★☆ Fox, 1974, c, 93 min. Dir: John Hough. SP: Leigh Chapman, Antonio Santean, b/o novel by Richard Unekis. Cast: Peter Fonda, Susan George, Adam Roarke, Vic Morrow, Roddy McDowall.

A race car driver (Fonda) and a mechanic (Roarke) extort money from a supermarket

"Make my day!" Clint Eastwood in his famous role of detective Harry Callahan in Dirty Harry *(1972).*

and spend the rest of the time trying to elude and outwit the police. They are accompanied by a dull-witted parolee named Mary (George). The movie is one long chase, with spectacular examples of multivehicle smashups. Lively stuff for action fans.

DISORGANIZED CRIME
★★ Touchstone, 1989, c, 101 min. Dir and SP: Jim Kouf. Cast: Corbin Bernsen, Ruben Blades, Fred Gwynne, Ed O'Neill, Lou Diamond Phillips, Hoyt Axton, Daniel Roebuck, William Russ.

A feeble crime comedy, with Bernsen as a thief who invites four accomplices to help him rob a small Montana bank. But he is arrested by two dim-witted New Jersey detectives, and the gang decides to proceed without him. Bernsen escapes, the bank is robbed, and everyone is chasing everyone else. A ride on a manure truck is the funniest gag the screenplay can muster.

D.O.A.
★★★ United Artists, 1950, b/w, 83 min. Dir: Rudolph Mate. SP: Russel Rouse, Clarence Greene, b/o their story. Cast: Edmond O'Brien, Pamela Britton, Luther Adler, Beverly Campbell (Garland), Lynn Baggett, William Ching, Neville Brand.

A modestly made but unusual and suspenseful drama, with O'Brien as an unlucky accountant who is given a fatal dose of slow-acting poison. Now he must strive desperately to find his murderer before he expires, and when he does find him he pursues him through the atmospheric streets of San Francisco. Edmond O'Brien gives an intense performance as the doomed man. Remade as *Color Me Dead* in 1969 and under its original title in 1988.

D.O.A.
★★ Touchstone, 1988, c, 104 min. Dir: Rocky Morton, Annabel Jankel. SP: Charles Edward Pogue, b/o story by Charles Edward Pogue, Russell Rouse, Clarence Greene. Cast: Dennis Quaid, Meg Ryan, Daniel Stern, Charlotte Rampling, Jane Kaczmarek, Christopher Keane, Robin Johnson.

A loose—and very feeble—remake of the well-remembered 1950 film, *D.O.A.* retains the basic premise and little else. This time the unlucky hero (Quaid) is a burned-out college teacher who is fatally poisoned and has only twenty-four hours to learn who murdered him. With

the aid of an infatuated student (Ryan), he races about looking for answers and uncovers some deadly secrets. The identity of the killer may be something of a surprise, but it just doesn't wash. Better to rent the original version.

DOG DAY AFTERNOON
★★★☆ Warner Bros., 1975, c, 130 min. Dir: Sidney Lumet. SP: Frank Pierson, b/o article by P. F. Kluge and Thomas Moore. Cast: Al Pacino, Charles Durning, James Broderick, John Cazale, Chris Sarandon, Sully Boyar, Penny Allen, Carol Kane, Lance Henriksen.

A colorful, offbeat melodrama based on an actual incident, *Dog Day Afternoon* relates what happens when a born loser named Sonny (Pacino) holds up a Brooklyn bank to obtain money for his lover's sex-change operation. The holdup becomes a media event that brings together the bank's employees, the police, and a mob of cheering bystanders. Oscar-nominated Pacino is outstanding as Sonny, both funny and pathetic (only listen to him dictate his last will and testament to a bank employee), and so are Cazale as his slow-witted confederate and Sarandon as Sonny's bewildered lover Leon. Leon's phone conversation with Sonny is the movie's high point.

DOLORES CLAIBORNE
★★★ Columbia, 1995, c, 130 min. Dir: Taylor Hackford. SP: Tony Gilroy, b/o novel by Stephen King. Cast: Kathy Bates, Jennifer Jason Leigh, Christopher Plummer, David Strathairn, Judy Parfitt, John C. Reilly, Bob Gunton, Eric Bogosian.

In this fascinating but uneven adaptation of a Stephen King novel, Bates gives a stunning performance as an eccentric, reclusive Maine woman who is suspected of killing her abusive husband (Strathairn). Years later she is again suspected of murder, this time of her rich, now-senile employer (Parfitt). Her embittered, alcoholic daughter (Leigh) returns reluctantly for the investigation, which uncovers some terrible, long-buried secrets. Bates's suffering, defiant Dolores overrides the movie's flaws to hold the viewer's interest.

DONNIE BRASCO
★★★☆ TriStar, 1997, c, 121 min. Dir: Mike Newell. SP: Paul Attanasio, b/o book by Joseph D. Pistone with Richard Woodley. Cast: Al Pacino, Johny Depp, Michael Madsen, Bruno Kirby, James Russo, Anne Heche.

A superior crime drama in which character is as important as violent action, *Donnie Brasco* stars Pacino as Lefty, a weary, low-level wiseguy who mistakenly gives his trust and friendship to one Donnie Brasco (Depp) and brings him into the mob. Donnie is really a federal agent who comes to like Lefty, and to understand that he is not only risking his own life but Lefty's as well. The movie's suspense is made achingly real by this terrible realization, and a sad, hopeless ending is inevitable. Pacino gives a wonderfully assured, quietly measured performance (no grandstanding here), and Depp is equally fine. The film may not have the bravura style of *GoodFellas* or *The Untouchables*, but it has more emotional heat. Based on a true story.

DON IS DEAD, THE

★★☆ Universal, 1973, c, 115 min. Dir: Richard Fleischer. SP: Marvin H. Albert, b/o his novel. Cast: Anthony Quinn, Frederic Forrest, Robert Forster, Al Lettieri, Angel Tompkins, Charles Cioffi, Ina Balin.

We're back in Mafialand, with Quinn as an aging don who unwittingly triggers an all-out war between rival mobs when he falls for Forster's dewy-eyed girlfriend (Tompkins). Forrest plays the intelligent hood who (shades of Michael Corleone and *The Godfather*) would like to escape the mob but ends up as a don. Quinn, at least, contributes some professional style to the familiar blood-letting.

DON'T BOTHER TO KNOCK

★★☆ Fox, 1952, b/w, 76 min. Dir: Roy Baker. SP: Daniel Taradash, b/o novel by Charlotte Armstrong. Cast: Marilyn Monroe, Richard Widmark, Anne Bancroft, Jeanne Cagney, Elisha Cook, Jr., Gloria Blondell.

One of Monroe's first starring vehicles, and not very good. She plays a seriously disturbed young woman who is hired to baby-sit at a New York hotel. Widmark is the tough guy who ultimately keeps her from killing herself and her young charge. Monroe's blank expression and baby-doll voice suggest an inexperienced actress rather than a mentally unbalanced person, but she manages a few effective moments toward the end. Bancroft makes her film debut as a singer who is Widmark's alienated girlfriend.

DOUBLE INDEMNITY

★★★★ Paramount, 1944, b/w, 107 min. Dir: Billy Wilder. SP: Billy Wilder, Raymond Chandler, b/o novel by James M. Cain. Cast: Barbara Stanwyck, Fred MacMurray, Edward G. Robinson, Tom Powers, Jean Heather, Porter Hall.

A scorching melodrama from director Wilder,

Lovers Barbara Stanwyck and Fred MacMurray plot their dastardly deed in Billy Wilder's classic Double Indemnity *(1944).*

Double Indemnity has many of the ingredients of classic film noir, served up piping hot: tough, insinuating dialogue, an air of bleak fatalism, and a wicked woman pulling all the strings. Stanwyck excels as the ice-cold, diamond-hard California housewife who seduces gullible insurance agent MacMurray (cast against his usual affable type) into murdering her husband (Powers). Robinson is the doggedly suspicious claims investigator for MacMurray's company. Sexual innuendos abound as the tension mounts, and the guilty parties begin to unravel. Most heartstopping moment: the getaway car stalls at the murder scene.

DOUBLE LIFE, A
★★★☆ Universal, 1947, b/w, 104 min. Dir: George Cukor. SP: Ruth Gordon, Garson Kanin. Cast: Ronald Colman, Signe Hasso, Edmond O'Brien, Shelley Winters, Ray Collins, Philip Loeb, Millard Mitchell.

Remembered for his mellifluous voice and aristocratic bearing, Colman gave one of his best—and most surprising—performances in this film. He plays Anthony John, a renowned actor whose most challenging role is Othello, Shakespeare's Moor of Venice. Unfortunately, he becomes so obsessed with this ferociously jealous character that it takes over his life, and a violent streak in his nature begins to surface. Coming to believe that he is Othello, he murders a waitress (Winters), then blanks out the crime in his mind. He is finally exposed by a suspicious publicity agent (O'Brien). Colman's Academy Award-winning performance is unlike any he had given to date, and he handles the role skillfully under Cukor's smooth direction. Miklos Rozsa's music score also won an Oscar.

DOWNTOWN
★★☆ Fox, 1990, c, 96 min. Dir: Richard Benjamin. SP: Nat Mauldin. Cast: Anthony Edwards, Forest Whitaker, Penelope Ann Miller, Joe Pantoliano, David Clennon, Art Evans, Rick Aiello.

Standard cop movie, with Edwards as a naive policeman who works in an upscale precinct of Philadelphia's Main Line. When he makes enemies in high places, he is transferred to a tough inner-city neighborhood, where his partner is street-smart Whitaker. Together they go after a stolen-car ring. Lots of action, and lots of noisy music on the soundtrack, but nothing special.

DRAGNET
★★☆ Warner Bros., 1954, c, 89 min. Dir: Jack Webb. SP: Richard I. Breen. Cast: Jack Webb, Ben Alexander, Richard Boone, Ann Robinson, Stacy Harris, Virginia Gregg.

This feature-length movie version of the popular TV program that ran through most of the fifties and also in the late sixties is a humdrum business. Webb repeats his role as Sgt. Joe Friday (and also directs), using that clipped monotone so often parodied. Friday also has the attitude toward wiretapping and the Fifth Amendment that is very much a part of his time and place. The 1987 movie version parodied the program.

DRAGNET
★★☆ Universal, 1987, c, 106 min. Dir: Tom Mankiewicz. SP: Dan Aykroyd, Alan Zweibel, Tom Mankiewicz. Cast: Dan Aykroyd, Tom Hanks, Christopher Plummer, Harry Morgan, Elizabeth Ashley, Alexandra Paul.

Essentially a parody of the popular television program of the fifties and sixties, *Dragnet* has Aykroyd as Police Sgt. Joe Friday, the straight-arrow, by-the-rules nephew and namesake of Jack Webb's original Friday. Partnered with free-wheeling Pep Streebek (Hanks), Friday sets out to rout the wild, destructive cult group who call themselves PAGANs (People Against Goodness and Normalcy). Aykroyd's flat-voiced, humorless routine starts out amusingly but quickly grows tiresome, and the whole movie is noisy and frenetic but not much fun.

DREAM LOVER
★★☆ Gramercy, 1994, c, 103 min. Dir and SP: Nicholas Kazan. Cast: James Spader, Madchen Amick, Bess Armstrong, Fredric Lehne, Larry Miller, Kathleen York, Blair Tefkin.

Screenwriter Nicholas Kazan, son of director Elia Kazan, made his directorial debut with this fairly intriguing mystery. Wealthy young architect Spader meets the girl of his dreams (Amick), and for a while their marriage is made in heaven. Then he becomes increasingly suspicious about her past identity and present activities until it is too late and he falls into her deadly trap. Despite some stylish touches, believability begins draining away at midpoint, and the ending does not make much sense.

DRESSED TO KILL

★★★ Filmways, 1980, c, 105 min. Dir and SP: Brian De Palma. Cast: Michael Caine, Angie Dickinson, Nancy Allen, Keith Gordon, Dennis Franz, David Margulies, Brandon Maggart.

Many moments in De Palma's movie will remind you of Alfred Hitchcock, and why not? At this time, the director was still paying homage to the master while falling short of his artistry. A clearly deranged killer savagely murders a woman in an elevator, then goes after another woman who is helping the victim's son to find the killer. That's all we will say, but there are several frightening sequences, some red herrings, and a bogus shock ending. Best Hitchcockian scene: Angie Dickinson in a museum. Most erotic scene: the first.

DRIFTER, THE

★★☆ Concorde, 1988, c, 90 min. Dir and SP: Larry Brand. Cast: Kim Delaney, Timothy Bottoms, Al Shannon, Miles O'Keeffe, Larry Brand.

If you're looking for a thriller with no less than *three* psychotics, look no further. Following in the tradition of *Fatal Attraction*, this twisty movie stars Delaney as a fashion designer who at least appears to be stalked by the drifter (O'Keeffe) she picked up on the highway. Ah, but wait. This sort of movie can hardly fail to work up some suspense, but it's highly contrived. As in so many movies of this kind, the lurid climax goes over the top.

DRIVER, THE

★★☆ Fox, 1978, c, 91 min. Dir and SP: Walter Hill. Cast: Ryan O'Neal, Bruce Dern, Isabelle Adjani, Ronee Blakley, Matt Clark, Felice Orlandi, Joseph Walsh, Andy Ramos.

Several flashy, noisy car chases are the mainstay of this adequate crime drama. O'Neal is the skilled getaway driver-for-hire, and Bruce Dern is the singularly nasty detective who is willing to bend the law to catch him. The movie has only two minor distinctions: the characters have no names, and the crook is more sympathetic than the cop. Writer-director Hill fared much better the following year with *The Warriors*.

DROWNING POOL, THE

★★★ Warner Bros., 1975, c, 108 min. Dir: Stuart Rosenberg. SP: Tracy Keenan Wynn, Lorenzo Semple, Walter Hill, b/o novel by Ross Macdonald. Cast: Paul Newman, Joanne Woodward, Tony Franciosa, Murray Hamilton, Gail Srickland, Melanie Griffith, Linda Haynes, Richard Jaeckel, Coral Browne, Richard Derr.

Private detective Lew Harper (*Harper*, 1966) returns in the person of Newman in this moderate mystery. This time he is summoned to New Orleans to help an old girlfriend (Woodward), now a society woman, who is being blackmailed anonymously. Inevitably Harper must deal with several corpses and an assortment of strange characters, including Woodward's homosexual husband (Derr), her nymphomaniacal daughter (Griffith), and an eccentric, greedy oil baron (Hamilton). Newman carries out his assignment with crisp authority, but the movie is not up to the original.

DRUGSTORE COWBOY

★★★☆ Avenue, 1989, c, 104 min. Dir: Gus Van Sant, Jr. SP: Gus Van Sant, Jr., Daniel Yost, b/o novel by James Fogle. Cast: Matt Dillon, Kelly Lynch, James Remar, James Le Gros, Heather Graham, Beah Richards, Grace Zabriskie, Max Perlich, William S. Burroughs.

Based on prison inmate Fogle's unpublished autobiographical novel, *Drugstore Cowboy* is an unflinching, utterly fascinating look at the world of the junkie. Dillon gives a sterling performance as an addict who, along with his wife (Lynch) and friends (Remar, Graham), robs pharmacies and hospitals for the drugs they need desperately. Set in the seventies, the film never judges, sentimentalizes, or excoriates their sordid, pathetic lives and, as such, is one of the most honest films on the drug culture. Novelist Burroughs appears as an elderly defrocked priest who is a longtime junkie.

EACH DAWN I DIE

★★★ Warner Bros., 1939, b/w, 92 min. Dir: William Keighley. SP: Norman Reilly Raine, Warren Duff, b/o novel by Jerome Odlum. Cast: James Cagney, George

Raft, Jane Bryan, George Bancroft, Maxie Rosenbloom, Stanley Ridges, Alan Baxter, Thurston Hall.

The corn is even higher than an elephant's eye in this typical Warners prison melodrama of the period. Cagney is in there pitching, and that makes all the difference. He plays a reporter who is framed into prison and who learns to cope with the violent life within its walls. He becomes involved in a breakout masterminded by fellow convict Raft. Pure hokum but fun for Cagney fans.

EDDIE MACON'S RUN

★★☆ Universal, 1983, c, 95 min. Dir and SP: Jeff Kanew, b/o novel by James McLendon. Cast: Kirk Douglas, John Schneider, Lee Purcell, Leah Ayres, Lisa Dunsheath, Tom Noonan, John Goodman.

A cut-and-dried chase melodrama, with relentless cop Douglas on the trail of wrongly convicted prison escapee Schneider (of television's *The Dukes of Hazard*). Schneider is determined to rejoin his family in Mexico, but Douglas is equally determined to stop him. Purcell is the bored rich girl who gets involved with Schneider's escape. Film debut of Goodman.

EIGHT MEN OUT

★★★ Orion, 1988, c, 119 min. Dir and SP: John Sayles, b/o book by Eliot Asinof. Cast: John Cusack, Charlie Sheen, John Mahoney, D. B. Sweeney, David Strathairn, Michael Lerner, Clifton James, Michael Rooker, Bill Irwin, Kevin Tighe, Studs Turkel, John Anderson, Perry Lang.

Flavorsome, interesting version of the infamous "Black Sox" baseball scandal of 1919,

In Each Dawn I Die *(1939), crusading reporter James Cagney is framed in an automobile accident that sends him to prison.*

in which eight members of the highly favored Chicago White Six team agreed to throw the World Series in return for money. In trying to cover the individual stories of the men, the film loses some of its forcefulness, but it is extremely well played, especially by Mahoney as the team's manager and Strathairn as the most contrite of the players. Cusack also scores as the one player who was not corrupted but who was caught up in the scandal.

8 MILLION WAYS TO DIE

★ TriStar, 1986, c, 115 min. Dir: Hal Ashby. SP: Oliver Stone, David Lee Henry, b/o novel by Lawrence Block. Cast: Jeff Bridges, Rosanna Arquette, Andy Garcia, Alexandra Paul, Randy Brooks, Christa Denton, Lisa Sloan.

Bridges is one of the best actors in films, but he would do well to eliminate this movie from his list of credits. Dreadful in almost every way, it casts Bridges as an alcoholic ex-detective who tries to turn his life around by nailing the sleek Latino drug dealer (Garcia) who murdered a prostitute (Paul). Bridges also falls for the dealer's girlfriend (Arquette). Big trouble, bad movie: foul-mouthed, dull, and incomprehensible. It's hard to believe that Stone coauthored the screenplay.

EL MARIACHI

★★★ Columbia, 1992, c, 81 min. Dir: Robert Rodriguez. SP: Robert Rodriguez, Carlos Gallardo. Cast: Carlos Gallardo, Consuelo Gomez, Reinol Martinez, Peter Marquardt, Jaime de Hoyos.

Young director Rodriguez also coproduced, coauthored, edited, and photographed this striking movie, an astonishing feat considering that he did it for just $7,000 in two weeks! The premise is simple: an aspiring young mariachi player (Gallardo) arrives in a small Mexican town and is instantly mistaken for a vicious hit man bent on retribution. Soon the town is littered with bodies and the mariachi has learned how to handle a gun in an amazingly short time. There are some stylish touches, but Rodriguez is determined to show off his skill, and almost every shot becomes overfancy. He later reworked the film as *Desperado* (1995).

ELECTRA GLIDE IN BLUE

★★★ United Artists, 1973, c, 114 min. Dir: James William Guercio. SP: Robert Boris, b/o story by Robert Boris, Rupert Hitzig. Cast: Robert Blake, Billy Green Bush, Mitchell Ryan, Jeannine Riley, Elisha Cook, Royal Dano.

A decidedly offbeat, rambling, but not uninteresting movie that clearly reveals the hand of a first-time director. John Wintergreen (Blake) is a short, plucky Arizona motoycycle cop who dreams of becoming a homicide detective. He gets the chance to investigate a murder, but disillusion sets in when his superior (Ryan) proves to be fascistic. Along the way to an ultimately grim fate, Wintergreen becomes involved with various people, many photographed in extreme closeup and all played with perhaps too much emphasis on their quirkiness.

ENFORCER, THE

★★★ Warner Bros., 1951, b/w, 87 min. Dir: Bretaigne Windust. SP: Martin Rackin. Cast: Humphrey Bogart, Everett Sloane, Zero Mostel, Ted de Corsia, Roy Roberts, Bob Steele, King Donovan.

In his last movie for Warners, Bogart plays a crusading district attorney dedicated to wiping out the vicious crime syndicate known as Murder, Inc. And murder is indeed the order of the day, as victims are dispatched with ice picks, razors, blunt instruments, and, of course, guns. De Corsia has the most memorable role as a remorseless killer who becomes a doomed and terrified "squealer." No relation to Clint Eastwood's 1976 movie.

ENFORCER, THE

★★★ Warner Bros., 1976, c, 96 min. Dir: James Fargo. SP: Stirling Silliphant, Dean Riesner. Cast: Clint Eastwood, Tyne Daly, Harry Guardino, Bradford Dillman, John Crawford, DeVeren Bookwalter, John Mitchum.

This third installment in the "Dirty Harry" series repeats the formula: tough, laconic, and a lone wolf, San Francisco Police Inspector Harry Callahan (Eastwood) is bent on destroying a band of vicious urban terrorists, even if he must do it by himself. This time, however, Harry has a new partner, Kate Moore (Daly), who must prove herself in the line of fire. As in the other Dirty Harry entries, the movie displays equal contempt for virtually everyone except Harry, but the action is fast and furious.

Detective Dirty Harry Callahan returns in The Enforcer *(1976), here with police sergeant Tom O'Neil.*

ESCAPE FROM ALCATRAZ

★★★ Paramount, 1979, c, 112 min. Dir: Don Siegel. SP: Richard Tuggle, b/o book by J. Campbell Bruce. Cast: Clint Eastwood, Patrick McGoohan, Roberts Blossom, Jack Thibeau, Fred Ward, Paul Benjamin, Larry Hankin.

A prison movie with some basis in truth. In 1960 three men, including bank robber Frank Morris (Eastwood), apparently became the only convicts ever to break out of the seemingly impregnable prison fortress called Alcatraz. The early part of the film is standard prison-movie material (is a course in sadism required of every movie warden and hardened convict?), but then the story concentrates on planning and carrying out the escape, and despite our knowledge of the outcome, it's still fairly gripping.

EVELYN PRENTICE

★★☆ MGM, 1934, b/w, 80 min. Dir: William K. Howard. SP: Lenore Coffee, b/o novel by W. E. Woodward. Cast: William Powell, Myrna Loy, Rosalind Russell, Una Merkel, Harvey Stephens, Isabel Jewell.

A typically glossy MGM melodrama reuniting the famous *Thin Man* stars, Powell and Loy. This time it's not a mystery-comedy, but a courtroom soap opera in which Loy plays the rich, neglected wife of attorney Powell. In a moment of weakness she dallies with bounder Stephens, and when he's murdered, she somehow believes that she's guilty. Is there a happy ending? Does Leo the Lion roar? Russell made her film debut here as a divorcée infatuated with Powell.

EVERYBODY WINS

★ Orion, 1990, c, 97 min. Dir: Karel Reisz. SP: Arthur Miller. Cast: Nick Nolte, Debra Winger, Jack Warden, Will Patton, Judith Ivey, Frank Converse, Kathleen Wilhoite, Frank Military.

It's hard to believe that distinguished playwright Miller authored this irritating, incoherent film. Nolte plays a private detective who is hired by a peculiar, probably schizoid woman (Winger) to investigate a murder for which a young man (Military) has already been convicted. Nolte's investigation leads to the revelation of corruption and skulduggery in high and low places, and to an unlikely romantic involvement with Winger. In this movie, nobody wins.

EVIL THAT MEN DO, THE

★☆ TriStar, 1984, c, 89 min. Dir: J. Lee Thompson. SP: David Lee Henry, John Crowther, b/o novel by R. Lance Hill. Cast: Charles Bronson, Theresa Saldana, Jose Ferrer, Joseph Maher, Rene Enriquez, Raymond St. Jacques, Antoinette Bower.

Only die-hard Bronson fans will want to see this entry in his series of violent action movies. Granite-hard and virtually expressionless, as always, he plays a retired professional hit man who is assigned to kill a notorious, sadistic doctor (Maher) in Latin America. Ferrer is the university professor who persuades a reluctant Bronson to come out of retirement.

EVIL UNDER THE SUN

★★☆ Universal, 1982, c, 102 min. Dir: Guy Hamilton. SP: Anthony Shaffer, b/o novel by Agatha Christie. Cast: Peter Ustinov, Jane Birkin, Colin Blakely, James Mason, Diana Rigg, Maggie Smith, Roddy McDowall, Sylvia Miles, Denis Quilley, Nicholas Clay.

Ustinov returns for the third time as Belgian detective Hercule Poirot in another loose spinoff of an Agatha Christie mystery. This time the band of familiar actors is gathered at a resort hotel on a remote island where a caustic actress (Rigg) is murdered. Smith stands out as the hotel proprietor who loves the victim's husband (Quilley). As usual, the sets and costumes (plus the Cole Porter music) outshine the story, but the movie is reasonably diverting.

EX-MRS. BRADFORD, THE

★★★ RKO, 1936, b/w, 80 min. Dir: Stephen Roberts. SP: Anthony Veiller, b/o story by James Edward Grant. Cast: William Powell, Jean Arthur, James Gleason, Eric Blore, Robert Armstrong.

Obviously inspired by the success of *The Thin Man* two years earlier, this sprightly comedy-mystery stars Powell as a prominent surgeon whose ex-wife (Arthur) is a prolific writer of mystery stories. Together they investigate a series of murders beginning with a jockey's mysterious death during a race. The two stars deliver their flippant lines in high style, but Blore steals the movie as another of his supercilious butlers.

EXCESSIVE FORCE

★★ New Line, 1993, c, 90 min. Dir: Jon Hess. SP: Thomas Ian Griffith. Cast: Thomas Ian Griffith, James Earl Jones, Charlotte Lewis, Lance Henriksen, Burt Young, Tony Todd, Tom Hodges.

There are no surprises (well, maybe one) in this exceptionally violent police drama. Martial arts expert Griffith, who also wrote the screenplay, stars as a loose-cannon cop obsessed with bringing down vicious ganglord Young. When several million dollars are missing from a police raid and Griffith's partners are murdered, he is suspected of corruption and collusion. Many blood-splattered shootouts for fans of this sort of mayhem. There was a sequel: *Excessive Force II: Force on Force*.

EXPERIMENT IN TERROR

★★★ Columbia, 1962, b/w, 123 min. Dir: Blake Edwards. SP: Mildred Gordon, Gordon Gordon, b/o their novel. Cast: Glenn Ford, Lee Remick, Stefanie Powers, Ross Martin, Roy Poole, Ned Glass.

Nothing in this workmanlike thriller can top the terrifying opening sequence: San Francisco bank teller Remick is trapped in her garage by an asthmatic madman (Martin) who swears to kill her or her younger sister (Powers) unless she helps him rob her bank. From this point on, it's a suspenseful cat-and-mouse game as Remick goes to the FBI for help. Ford is the FBI agent heading the case. There are a few exciting moments along the way, including a scary encounter in a ladies room, with all principals finally converging at Candlestick Park. San Francisco provides some good scenic flavor.

EXPERIMENT PERILOUS

★★☆ RKO, 1944, b/w, 91 min. Dir: Jacques Tourneur. SP: Warren Duff, b/o novel by Margaret

Carpenter. Cast: Hedy Lamarr, George Brent, Paul Lukas, Albert Dekker, Carl Esmond, Olive Blakeney, Margaret Wycherly, Stephanie Bachelor.

A moderate melodrama in the *Gaslight* tradition, this movie places Lamarr in peril from crazed husband Lukas in 1903 New York City. Insanely jealous, Lukas schemes to drive his wife out of her mind, until a doctor (Brent) appears on the scene to rescue the beleaguered lady. As an actor, Lukas is so far superior to virtually every other member of the cast that he almost makes the viewer believe this nonsense. Almost, but not quite.

EXTERMINATOR, THE

★ Interstar, 1980, c, 101 min. Dir and SP: James Glickenhaus. Cast: Robert Ginty, Christopher George, Samantha Eggar, Steve James, Tony Di Benedetto.

"Exterminator" Ginty must have seen *Death Wish* since he's taken a leaf from Paul Kersey's blood-stained book. When Ginty's war buddy is paralyzed permanently by a street gang attack, Ginty takes it on himself to wipe them out one by one. More gore galore, and there's even a sequel.

EXTREME MEASURES

★★★ Columbia/Castle Rock, 1996, c, 118 min. Dir: Michael Apted. SP: Tony Gilroy, b/o novel by Michael Palmer. Cast: Hugh Grant, Gene Hackman, Sarah Jessica Parker, David Morse, Bill Nunn, Debra Monk, Paul Guilfoyle, Shaun Austin-Olsen, Andre De Shields.

What's going on at New York City's Gramercy Hospital? Homeless men have been turning up at the hospital, displaying strange symptoms and begging for help. Before long, dedicated neurologist Guy Luthan (Grant) uncovers an ominous plot involving Nobel Prize-winning Dr. Lawrence Myrick (Hackman), who has his own dangerous view of medical ethics. The story takes a few surprising if far-fetched turns before all is resolved. At least Grant offers a refreshing change from his usual stammering, fluttering demeanor, and Hackman gives more to his role than it deserves.

EXTREME PREJUDICE

★★☆ TriStar, 1987, c, 104 min. Dir: Walter Hill. SP: Deric Washburn, Harry Kleiner, b/o story by John Milius, Fred Rexer. Cast: Nick Nolte, Powers Boothe, Maria Conchita Alonso, Michael Ironside, Rip Torn, Clancy Brown, William Forsythe.

Director Hill knows how to turn up the juice in action films, but over the past few years, the material has usually let him down. (His best film to date is probably *The Warriors*, 1979.) *Extreme Prejudice*, alas, is no exception: an ultra-violent riff on the hoary plot about childhood friends on opposite sides of the law. Nolte is a small-town Texas Ranger, and Boothe is a drug kingpin, and now the battle between them is joined on the U.S.-Mexican border. Hill gives the old story a few stylistic flourishes, but it's still rather worn.

EYE FOR AN EYE

★★☆ Paramount, 1996, c, 102 min. Dir: John Schlesinger. SP: Amanda Silver, Rick Jaffa, b/o novel by Erika Holzer. Cast: Sally Field, Kiefer Sutherland, Ed Harris, Beverly D'Angelo, Joe Mantegna, Charlayne Woodward, Olivia Burnette.

Disturbing questions about justice and morality are advanced in this provocative thriller, but the movie fails as drama. After a teenage girl (Burnette) is brutally raped and murdered, her anguished mother (Field) discovers that justice will *not* prevail, and that the repellent killer (Sutherland) is free to commit other crimes. In desperation she considers killing him herself, with the help of those who have already administered their own brand of "justice." The movie is heartfelt but unpersuasive, trying too hard to cover all sides of the issue and also stacking the cards against opposing players in the deadly game— the killer is evil incarnate and the "avengers" resemble secret hit men.

EYE FOR AN EYE, AN

★★ Avco Embassy, 1981, c, 106 min. Dir: Steve Carver. SP: William Gray, James Bruner, b/o story by James Bruner. Cast: Chuck Norris, Christopher Lee, Richard Roundtree, Matt Clark, Mako, Maggie Cooper, Rosalind Chao.

Routine martial-arts material. Norris is a cop who seeks revenge against the villains who murdered his partner and his partner's girlfriend. Soon he is dodging bullets and delivering well-placed kicks to the anatomy of various bad guys. Lee makes a formidable chief villain.

EYES OF LAURA MARS

★★☆ Columbia, 1978, c, 103 min. Dir: Irvin Kershner. SP: John Carpenter, David Zelag Goodman,

Faye Dunaway is terrified (with very good reason) in the thriller Eyes of Laura Mars *(1978).*

b/o story by John Carpenter. Cast: Faye Dunaway, Tommy Lee Jones, Rene Auberjonois, Brad Dourif, Rose Gregorio, Raul Julia, Michael Tucker, Frank Adonis, Darlanne Fluegel.

Famous fashion photographer Laura Mars (Dunaway) has a serious problem: suddenly, she has visions of a series of gory murders, and the victims are friends or colleagues. And the visions all come true! Why is this happening to her, and who is the deranged killer? Jones is the detective on the case who becomes her lover. This thriller may have seemed flashy and trendy in the seventies, but it now seens a little absurd, and the denouement is not believable. Best performance in a small role: Julia as Laura's creepy ex-husband.

EYEWITNESS

★★ Fox, 1981, c, 103 min. Dir: Peter Yates. SP: Steve Tesich. Cast: William Hurt, Sigourney Weaver, Christopher Plummer, James Woods, Irene Worth, Kenneth McMillan, Pamela Reed, Steven Hill, Morgan Freeman, Albert Paulsen.

An exceptionally good cast cannot overcome Tesich's contrived and cluttered screenplay. Hurt is a janitor who comes upon a murdered Chinese businessman in his building. To impress the television reporter (Weaver) with whom he is infatuated, he pretends to know more about the crime than he does. Soon his life is in danger. Many hard-to-swallow contrivances and far too many subsidiary characters sink the project long before the absurd climax in a stable.

FAIR GAME

★ Warner Bros., 1996, c, 90 min. Dir: Andrew Sipes. SP: Charlie Fletcher, b/o novel by Paula Gosling. Cast: William Baldwin, Cindy Crawford, Steven Berkoff, Christopher McDonald, Miguel Sandoval, Johann Carlo, Salma Hayek.

"Stupid" is the word for this action thriller. When former KGB operatives (remember them?) decide to kill lawyer Crawford for some obscure reason, cop Baldwin comes to her rescue, and together they sprint from one close call to another. This time the Russians use state-of-the-art computer technology to track their prey. Chases, explosions, and miles of dumb dialogue, plus many views of the beautiful Ms. Crawford.

FAITHFUL

★☆ New Line/Savoy, 1996, c, 91 min. Dir: Paul Mazursky. SP: Chazz Palminteri, b/o his play. Cast: Cher, Chazz Palminteri, Ryan O'Neal, Paul Mazursky, Amber Smith.

Cher made a misguided return to films with this slim and tiresome black comedy that clearly shows its origins as a play. She's a rich, unhappy wife whose faithless husband (O'Neal) hires a hit man (Palminteri) to kill her. Wife and hit man talk (and talk and talk), and a relationship evolves as they become more intimate. Husband returns, and after a few twists and turns, he gets his comeuppance. A boring misfire.

FALLEN SPARROW, THE

★★★ RKO, 1943, b/w, 94 min. Dir: Richard Wallace. SP: Warren Duff, b/o novel by Dorothy B. Hughes. Cast: John Garfield, Maureen O'Hara, Walter Slezak, Patricia Morison, Martha O'Driscoll, John Miljan, Bruce Edwards.

This atmospheric but difficult-to-follow melodrama stars Garfield as a troubled Spanish Civil War veteran who comes to New York to unravel the mystery surrounding a friend's death. He soon finds a corrupt world where former Nazis are posing as displaced aristocrats. Inevitably he also finds a mysterious woman (O'Hara) whose motives are suspect. Garfield plays his best scene alone in a hotel room, when he suspects that a relentless man with a limp is waiting to kill him.

FALLING DOWN

★★ Warner Bros, 1993, c, 115 min. Dir: Joel Schumacher. SP: Ebbe Roe Smith. Cast: Michael Douglas, Robert Duvall, Barbara Hershey, Frederic Forrest, Tuesday Weld, Rachel Ticotin, Lois Smith, Michael Paul Chan.

On the hottest day of the year, Douglas, a divorced, unemployed defense worker known only as "D-Fens" (his personalized license plate), is having a particularly bad day. Convinced that he is being badgered, humiliated, or ignored by everyone he encounters, he becomes increasingly violent, until a cop (Duvall) with his own personal hang-ups must track him down. This odd, heavy-handed cautionary tale about the perils of urban stress not only stacks the cards against its beleaguered "hero" but also panders reprehensibly to viewers who may also feel disenfranchised.

FAMILY BUSINESS

★★ TriStar, 1989, c, 110 min. Dir: Sidney Lumet. SP: Vincent Patrick, b/o his novel. Cast: Sean Connery, Dustin Hoffman, Matthew Broderick, Rosana DeSoto, Janet Carroll, Victoria Jackson, Bill McCutcheon.

"We are some family!" Hoffman exclaims in this movie, and he is certainly right, but the movie is a disappointment. Three generations of thieves—grandpa Connery, his son Hoffman, and grandson Broderick—come together for one final caper. Connery is joyously disreputable, Hoffman is conservative and worried, and Broderick is eager to learn from his beloved grandfather. But they botch the caper, with unhappy consequences. The movie is a wearisome comedy-drama, and despite the careful attempt to explain the genealogy, the three actors simply do not convince as a family. Connery comes off best with a lusty performance.

FAMILY PLOT

★★★ Universal, 1976, c, 120 min. Dir: Alfred Hitchcock. SP: Ernest Lehman, b/o novel by Victor Canning. Cast: Bruce Dern, Karen Black, Barbara Harris, William Devane, Ed Lauter, Cathleen Nesbitt, Katherine Helmond.

Hitchcock's fifty-fourth and final movie calls for complete suspension of disbelief, plus rapt attention to the plot's many twists and turns. Two dim bulbs, a fake psychic (Harris) and her cabdriver boyfriend (Dern), decide to make a bundle by finding the heir to dowager Nesbitt's fortune. The heir turns out to be Devane, a jewelry dealer who dabbles in kidnapping, thievery, and (long ago) murder. When Devane and his cohort (Black)

William Devane and Karen Black are a scheming pair in Alfred Hitchcock's fifty-fourth and last movie, Family Plot *(1976).*

misinterpret the sniffing about of the dumb duo, the consequences include various forms of mayhem. There's not a shred of believability in this comedy thriller—one strained coincidence follows another—but it's mildly amusing nonetheless. Hitchcock can be spotted in silhoutte standing behind a door marked "Registrar of Births and Deaths."

FAN, THE

★★ Paramount, 1981, c, 95 min. Dir: Edward Bianchi. SP: Priscilla Chapman, John Hartwell, b/o novel by Bob Randall. Cast: Lauren Bacall, James Garner, Michael Biehn, Maureen Stapleton, Hector Elizondo, Anna Maria Horsford.

A good cast, and a strong central performance by Bacall, cannot help this disappointingly clumsy and lurid melodrama. An obsessed young fan (Biehn) of stage star Sally Rogers (Bacall) turns dangerous when he is ignored, striking out at those around her, and becomes homicidal when his adoration changes to hatred. The suspense is pumped up in obvious ways, and the final confrontation between star and fan is scarcely believable.

FAN, THE

★☆ TriStar/Mandalay, 1996, c, 117 min. Dir: Tony Scott. SP: Phoeff Sutton, b/o novel by Peter Abrahams. Cast: Robert De Niro, Wesley Snipes, Ellen Barkin, John Leguizano, Benicio Del Toro, Patti D'Arbanville-Quinn, Andrew J. Ferchland, Brandon Hammond.

Quite possibly De Niro's worst major film to date, *The Fan* is a lamentable, clanky melodrama that grows increasingly hard to believe as it progresses. Playing in the crackpot mode of Travis Bickle (*Taxi Driver*) or Max Cady (*Cape Fear*), De Niro is Gil Renard, a baseball fan dangerously obsessed with star player Bobby Rayburn (Snipes). When Rayburn disappoints him on the ballfield, Gil's mind snaps and he topples over the edge into murder and kidnapping. The climactic sequence, set at a rain-soaked ball game in San Francisco's Candlestick Park, is laughable rather than suspenseful.

FAREWELL, MY LOVELY

★★☆ Avco Embassy/ITC (British), 1975, c, 97 min. Dir: Dick Richards. SP: David Zelag Goodman, b/o novel by Raymond Chandler. Cast: Robert Mitchum, Charlotte Rampling, John Ireland, Sylvia Miles, Jack O'Halloran, Anthony Zerbe.

A rather listless third version of the Chandler novel featuring his world-weary, cynical private eye Philip Marlowe. Once again Marlowe (Mitchum) is asked to locate the old girlfriend of an ex-con, and the search soon embroils him in various forms of skulduggery, including murder. The forties atmosphere is created well, but the material seems rather tired. Filmed previously as *The Falcon Takes Over* (1942) and *Murder, My Sweet* (1944). Sylvester Stallone appears briefly.

FARGO

★★★★ Gramercy, 1996, c, 95 min. Dir: Joel Coen. SP: Joel Coel, Ethan Coen. Cast: Frances McDormand, William H. Macy, Steve Buscemi, Harve Presnell, Peter Stormare, John Carroll Lynch.

The films of the Coen brothers (director Joel, writers Joel and Ethan) have often combined mirth and mayhem in original ways that can disconcert—or delight—the audience. *Fargo* simply tops them all to date. A marvelous murder mystery drenched in black humor, it revolves about a mild-mannered Minnesota used-car salesman (Macy) who plots to have his wife kidnapped for the desperately needed

Robert Mitchum stars as detective Philip Marlowe in Farewell, My Lovely *(1975), a remake of* The Falcon Takes Over *(1942) and* Murder, My Sweet *(1944).*

Frances McDormand is memorable as the smarter-than-she-looks police chief (here with husband John Carroll Lynch) in the Coen brothers' Fargo (1996).

ransom money. His plan goes hideously, hilariously wrong. Oscar winner McDormand is memorable as the dogged, genial, and very pregnant police chief who unravels the mystery. There's not a false or wasted moment in *Fargo*, and to this we can only say, "Thanks a bunch!"

FATAL ATTRACTION

★★★ Paramount, 1987, c, 119 min. Dir: Adrian Lyne. SP: James Dearden, b/o his short subject "Diversion." Cast: Michael Douglas, Glenn Close, Anne Archer, Fred Gwynne, Ellen Hamilton Latzen, Mike Nussbaum, Stuart Pankin, Ellen Foley, Meg Mundy.

What is this nerve-shattering thriller saying about straying husbands or sexually active women? You won't ponder its meaning while biting your nails, but you may think about it afterward. Douglas is a devoted husband and father whose one-night stand with a dangerously disturbed woman (Close) turns into a waking nightmare. When he tries to drop her, she turns into a revenge-minded virago, endangering him and his family. The movie rushes from one frightening situation to another, seldom pausing for logic or reason, and Close creates a convincing monster. But the Grand Guignol ending doesn't wash.

FATAL BEAUTY

★ MGM/UA, 1987, c, 104 min. Dir: Tom Holland. SP: Hilary Henkin, Dean Riesner, b/o story by Bill Svanoe. Cast: Whoopi Goldberg, Sam Elliott, Ruben Blades, Harris Yulin, John P. Ryan, Jennifer Warren, Brad Dourif, Mike Jolly.

This cop is tough, profane, and mockingly arrogant with snobbish Californians. No, it isn't Axel Foley of *Beverly Hills Cop* but Rita Rizzoli, played by Goldberg in yet another of her late eighties fiascos. Rita is gunning for a group of lowlifes who spread a deadly batch of tainted cocaine, and she is not about to stop until she gets them all. The body count is extremely high in this witless movie.

FBI STORY, THE

★★★ Warner Bros., 1959, c, 149 min. Dir: Mervyn LeRoy. SP: Richard L. Breen, John Twist, b/o book by Don Whitehead. Cast: James Stewart, Vera Miles, Murray Hamilton, Larry Pennell, Nick Adams, Diane Jergens, Jean Willes.

An earnest but overlong salute to the Federal Bureau of Investigation, as seen through the eyes of fictional agent Chip Hardesty (Stewart). The movie stirs in some documentary footage of the Bureau's operations, along with a series of episodes recounting Hardesty's own experiences over the years. His domestic life with wife Vera Miles is also given considerable footage. As unjudgmental as you would expect, but competently made.

FEAR

★★ Universal, 1996, c, 97 min. Dir: James Foley. SP: Christopher Crowe. Cast: Mark Wahlberg, Reese Witherspoon, William Petersen, Amy Brenneman, Alyssa Milano, Tracy Fraim, Jason Kristofer.

Sixteen-year-old Nicole (Witherspoon) falls for young David (Wahlberg), and teenage romance is in the air. *Wrong.* Nicole's father (Petersen) senses something is off with David. *Right.* David turns out to be a world-class psychotic, and when he is rejected, he turns vicious, and he and his nasty friends besiege Daddy's home. The movie generates suspense for a while, but it gets out of hand toward the end and turns ugly and sordid.

FEAR CITY

★ Zupnik/Curtis, 1985, c, 96 min. Dir: Abel Ferrara. SP: Nicholas St. John. Cast: Tom Berenger, Billy Dee Williams, Jack Scalia, Melanie Griffith, Rossano Brazzi, Rae Dawn Chong, Jan Murray, Michael V. Gazzo.

Early sleaze from director Ferrara, who later won some critical attention with *Bad Lieutenant, The Funeral,* and other films. Two men (Berenger and Scalia) run a "talent" agency that supplies women to work in strip clubs. Soon the girls are being viciously attacked by a martial-arts expert who is conducting his private war against smut. Williams plays a cop, and Brazzi is a Mafia bigshot.

FEDERAL HILL

★★★ Eagle Beach/Trimark, 1994, b/w, 100 min. Dir and SP: Michael Corrente. Cast: Nicholas Turturro, Anthony DeSando, Michael Raynor, Libby Langdon, Robert Turano, Jason Andrews.

Most reviewers of this film were quick to point out its resemblance to Martin Scorsese's *Mean Streets,* and it's true that they both concern raucous, reckless young urban men living on the edge of lawlessness and violence. *Federal Hill* is set in Providence's Little Italy, where Ralph (Turturro) and Nick (DeSando) are best buddies. Ralph is a thief and troublemaker, and Nick is a more decent sort, with aspirations. When Nick breaks their bond for a girl (Langdon), the outcome is tragic. The movie is unfocused and sometimes clumsy, but with affecting portions.

FIGHTING BACK

★★☆ De Laurentiis, 1982, c, 98 min. Dir: Lewis Teague. SP: Tom Hedley, David Z. Goodman. Cast: Tom Skerritt, Patti LuPone, Michael Sarrazin, Yaphet Kotto, David Rasche, Ted Ross, Pat Cooper.

Infuriated by a street incident that causes his pregnant wife to lose the baby, a Philadelphia storekeeper (Skerritt) forms a security patrol. But he is unprepared for the opposition, and for the violent complications that follow. The movie touches on such important matters as racism, vigilantism, and political expediency, but it comes down as merely an average urban melodrama.

FILE ON THELMA JORDON, THE

★★★ Paramount, 1949, b/w, 100 min. Dir: Robert Siodmak. SP: Ketti Frings, b/o story by Marty Holland. Cast: Barbara Stanwyck, Wendell Corey, Joan Tetzel, Paul Kelly, Richard Rober, Stanley Ridges.

Beautiful Thelma Jordon (Stanwyck) has been accused of murdering her elderly aunt for her money. But will the real Thelma please stand up? Is she the innocent victim of someone else's plot, or a wicked, scheming dame with homicide in her heart? Restless, unhappily married Assistant D.A. Cleve Marshall (Corey) would like to know, since he is passionately in love with Thelma and dangerously involved in circumstances surrounding the murder. When he's asked to prosecute Thelma in the courtroom, the plot thickens. Murky but oddly compelling, this film noir enjoys the benefits of Siodmak's atmospheric direction and Stanwyck's usual solid performance as the ambiguous Thelma.

FINAL ANALYSIS

★★ Warner Bros., 1992, c, 125 min. Dir: Phil Joanou. SP: Wesley Strick, b/o story by Robert Reiger, Wesley Strick. Cast: Richard Gere, Kim Basinger, Uma Thurman, Eric Roberts, Keith David, Paul Guilfoyle, Robert Harper.

Contrived and more than slightly absurd, this thriller stars Gere as a San Francisco psychiatrist who is treating the apparently disturbed Thurman. When Thurman's beautiful sister (Basinger) turns up, she and Gere become bedmates in no time flat. Then Basinger kills her nasty husband (Roberts), and Dr. Gere finds himself trapped in a web of seduction and deceit. It's all meant to be sexy and stylish, but despite a few clever twists you may find your-self laughing at the wrong moments. Gere is simply a blank as the ensnared shrink, and for some reason Basinger speaks most of her lines in a whisper.

FINGERS

★★★ Gala/Brut, 1978, c, 89 min. Dir and SP: James Toback. Cast: Harvey Keitel, Tisa Farrow, Jim Brown, Michael V. Gazzo, Marian Seldes, Danny Aiello, Anthony Sirico, Tanya Roberts.

Keitel's ability to depict existential despair received an early workout in this often striking downbeat drama. He plays a walking paradox named Jimmy Fingers: on one hand, he is a classical pianist who dreams of playing Carnegie Hall; on the other he is a brutal enforcer, "collecting" on debts for his father (Gazzo) in any way possible. His life begins to come apart when he becomes obsessed with a prostitute (Farrow). The final image of a naked, shattered Jimmy staring out of his bed-room window is haunting.

FIRM, THE

★★★ Fox, 1993, c, 154 min. Dir: Sydney Pollack. SP: David Rabe, Robert Towne, David Rayfiel, b/o novel by John Grisham. Cast: Tom Cruise, Gene Hackman, Jeanne Tripplehorn, Holly Hunter, Ed Harris, Wilford Brimley, Gary Busey.

There are some tense moments in this long, incoherent, and improbable melodrama from the best-selling novel by Grisham. Cruise is an ambitious young lawyer who joins a leading Memphis law firm, only to discover that it is at the center of a monstrous conspiracy with orga-nized crime. Suddenly his life is in terrible dan-ger. Tripplehorn is his anxious wife. Hackman (as usual) takes the acting honors as an out-wardly genial but devious member of the firm. Glossy hi-tech melodrama, no more and no less.

FIRST BLOOD

★★ Carolco, 1982, c, 97 min. Dir: Ted Kotcheff. SP: Michael Kozoll, William Sackheim, Sylvester Stallone, b/o novel by David Marell. Cast: Sylvester Stallone, Richard Crenna, Brian Dennehy, David Caruso, Jack Starrett.

Vietnam veteran John Rambo (Stallone), brutalized and psychologically damaged by the war, becomes the target of a massive manhunt when he defies the law in a small California community. Driven by rage and survival instincts, he becomes a primitive warrior, wreaking havoc at every turn. In the end, he offers an emotional (and incoherent) monologue on the plight of Vietnam veterans. Much action but a severely questionable point of view. Followed by *Rambo: First Blood: Part Two* (1985) and *Rambo III* (1988).

FIRST DEADLY SIN, THE

★★☆ Warner Bros., 1980, c, 112 min. Dir: Brian G. Hutton. SP: Mann Rubin, b/o novel by Lawrence Sanders. Cast: Frank Sinatra, Faye Dunaway, James Whitmore, David Dukes, Brenda Vaccaro, Martin Gabel, Anthony Zerbe, George Coe.

Everyone in this gloomy, offbeat drama, with the exception of Sinatra, appears to be overacting. While his wife (Dunaway) lies critically ill in the hospital, detective Ed Delaney (Sinatra) is on the trail of a serial killer (Dukes). Naturally he must work alone, since nobody believes him. His final confrontation with the killer is startling but not credible. The constant interaction between the activities of Delaney and the murderer seems to have no point, and the effect is grating. Sinatra's first film in ten years.

FIVE CORNERS

★★☆ Hand Made Films, 1988, c, 92 min. Dir: Tony Bill. SP: John Patrick Shanley. Cast: Jodie Foster, Tim Robbins, John Turturro, Elizabeth Berridge, Rose Gregorio, Gregory Rozakis.

Several skilled actors who would later play better roles in much better films star in this atmospheric but disappointing comedy-drama. The lives of a group of people in the Bronx converge in 1964, and one of them (Turturro) is a sad, demented soul with a penchant for violent behavior. Foster is the neighborhood girl he loves, and Robbins is a moody activist who figures in the wildly melodramatic and quite awful climax on a rooftop. Screenwriter Shanley did much better a year earlier with *Moonstruck*.

FIVE MILES TO MIDNIGHT

★★ United Artists (French-Italian), 1962, c, 110 min. Dir: Anatole Litvak. SP: Peter Viertel, Hugh Wheeler, b/o idea by Andre Versini. Cast: Sophia Loren, Anthony Perkins, Gig Young, Jean Pierre Aumont, Yolande Turner, Tommy Norden.

This glum, miscast thriller stars Loren as a woman trapped in a wretched marriage to Perkins. His plane crashes and he is presumed dead, but miraculously he has survived to force his wife into an insurance swindle. When she collects the $120,000 on his life, he promises to disappear forever. With Perkins hiding in her flat, her existence becomes an ordeal, and she gets little help from sympathetic friends Aumont and Young. Inevitably, the climax is violent. Loren strives gamely, but Perkins is not believable as her nasty husband.

FLASHPOINT

★★☆ TriStar, 1983, c, 93 min. Dir: William Tannen. SP: Dennis Shryack, Michael Butler, b/o book by George La Fountaine. Cast: Kris Kristofferson, Treat Williams, Rip Torn, Tess Harper, Jean Smart.

Two Texas border-patrol officers (Kristofferson and Williams) come upon a buried jeep containing a cache of money that figures in an old unsolved mystery. It turns out to be one crucial part of a deep conspiracy that reaches to Very High Places. A good cast and some flashy direction, but the movie is strictly routine.

FLED

★☆ MGM, 1996, c, 108 min. Dir: Kevin Hooks. SP: Preston A. Whitmore II. Cast: Laurence Fishburne, Stephen Baldwin, Salma Hayek, Will Patton, Robert John Burke, Robert Hooks, Victor Rivers, David Dukes.

Here, at last, is the bionic movie—made up of scraps from much better films. It begins with a rip-off of *The Defiant Ones*, then makes reference to such movies as *The Fugitive*, *The Godfather*, and others. Fishburne and Baldwin are Georgia convicts (or so it seems) who escape from a chain gang and are pursued all over a scenic Atlanta by the mob and by government officials. There's not a believable scene from first frame to last, and very little excitement. Best advice: flee *Fled*.

FLESH AND BONE

★★★ Paramount, 1993, c, 124 min. Dir and SP: Steve Kloves. Cast: Dennis Quaid, Meg Ryan, James Caan, Gwyneth Paltrow, Scott Wilson, Christopher Rydell.

This dark thriller begins stunningly: during a botched robbery in Texas, a cold-blooded thief (Caan) murders a farm family, with the exception of a crying infant. His small son watches in numb horror. Years later, the now-grown son (Quaid) meets the now-grown infant (Ryan), and they fall in love. Then daddy returns, as nasty as ever. Writer-director Kloves proved his talent with the likable *Fabulous Baker Boys* (1989), but here he never quite lives up to the promise of the opening sequence, despite some striking moments. Paltrow steals the movie as Caan's easy-virtue companion.

FLETCH

★★☆ Universal, 1985, c, 96 min. Dir: Michael Ritchie. SP: Andrew Bergman, b/o novel by Gregory McDonald. Cast: Chevy Chase, Joe Don Baker, Dana Wheeler-Nicholson, Richard Libertini, Tim Matheson, M. Emmet Walsh, George Wendt, Kenneth Mars, Geena Davis.

Fans of Chevy Chase may be amused by this mystery-comedy, but others will not be so inclined. In his usual smirky, oddly detached fashion, he plays an investigative reporter determined to find the connection between some Los Angeles cops and the drug business. He also has a penchant for assuming disguises, including a doctor, an insurance salesman, and a black basketball player. Some clever touches, and a good supporting cast, but you have to like Chevy.

FORCE OF EVIL

★★★ MGM, 1948, b/w, 78 min. Dir: Abraham Polonsky. SP: Abraham Polonsky, Ira Wolfert, b/o novel by Ira Wolfert. Cast: John Garfield, Beatrice Pearson, Thomas Gomez, Marie Windsor, Roy Roberts.

A cult following has developed over the years for this strong but somewhat self-conscious melodrama starring Garfield as a lawyer for the numbers racket who finds himself in a moral dilemma when his older brother (Gomez) becomes fatally involved. The ending, in which Garfield reclaims his brother's corpse after it has been washed up on the rocks, is memorable. One of the movie people blacklisted in the early fifties, director Polonsky did not make another film until *Tell Them Willie Boy Is Here* in 1969.

FORMULA, THE

★★ MGM/UA, 1980, c, 117 min. Dir: John G. Avildsen. SP: Steve Shagan, b/o his novel. Cast: George C. Scott, Marlon Brando, Marthe Keller, John Gielgud, Beatrice Straight, Richard Lynch, G. D. Spradlin.

An extremely tangled plot is the downfall of this would-be thriller. Scott is a hard-headed L.A. cop whose investigation of a murdered friend leads him to uncover the Formula. This formula, it seems, can turn coal into pollution-free gasoline, and it's the hottest item in the undercover world market. So many involved characters get killed that it's virtually impossible to understand what's happening, and why. Brando actually has only a supporting role (although a key one) as an eccentric oil tycoon.

FORT APACHE, THE BRONX

★★★ Fox, 1981, c, 125 min. Dir: Daniel Petrie. SP: Heywood Gould. Cast: Paul Newman, Edward Asner, Ken Wahl, Rachel Ticotin, Danny Aiello, Kathleen Beller, Pam Grier.

It's merely day-to-day business for veteran cop John Murphy (Newman), but *his* Fort Apache is his precinct in New York's South Bronx, where the neighborhood is overrun with violence and corruption. One of his biggest problems is dealing with a sadistic fellow cop (Aiello) whom he witnessed throwing a boy off a roof. He also has a brief, doomed romance with an addicted nurse (Ticotin). The movie takes a hard, unvarnished look at life in the inner city, and the pace is swift. Newman gives a fine performance as a cop with a conscience.

48 HRS.

★★★ Paramount, 1982, c, 97 min. Dir: Walter Hill. SP: Roger Spottiswoode, Walter Hill, Steven E. de Souza, Larry Gross. Cast: Nick Nolte, Eddie Murphy, Annette O'Toole, James Remar, Frank McRae, David Patrick Kelly, Sonny Landham.

Using the sassy, street-wise persona he perfected (and later overworked), Murphy made his film debut in this fast-moving police story. He plays a crook released from prison for forty-eight hours to help policeman Nolte catch two nasty escaped convicts. You won't be surprised when the mismatched pair's mutual loathing turns to admiration as they pursue the escapees about the city, dodging bullets all the way. Murphy, of course, seems smarter than anyone else in the movie, which, in some sequences, is not very difficult. (He confounds the patrons of a redneck bar by posing as a policeman.) Nolte is top-notch as a cop who is always getting into trouble. A sequel, *Another 48 HRS.*, was released in 1990.

FOUL PLAY

★★★ Paramount, 1978, c, 116 min. Dir and SP: Colin Higgins. Cast: Goldie Hawn, Chevy Chase, Dudley Moore, Rachel Roberts, Burgess Meredith, Eugene Roche, Marilyn Sokol, Billy Barty.

Foul Play is something of a mess, but an entertaining mess. Part comedy, part thriller, and mostly derivative, it stars Hawn as a light-headed San Francisco librarian who becomes entangled in a plot to assassinate visiting Pope Pius XIII. Chase, in his first leading-man role, is the clumsy detective who finally comes to believe her wild stories about the attempts on her life. A number of the sequences, especially a climactic scene in a theater, are Hitchcockian in their intention, if not their execution. As an orchestra conductor and secret swinger who gets caught up in Hawn's escapades, Moore makes a funny debut in a major American film.

FOXY BROWN

★☆ American International, 1974, c, 94 min. Dir and SP: Jack Hill. Cast: Pam Grier, Antonio Fargas, Peter Brown, Terry Carter, Kathryn Loder.

A nurse (Grier) takes revenge against those who killed her lover, an undercover narcotics agent. Before long she has disposed of a loathsome lot of mobsters, pimps, rapists, and a big-time madam, all in the name of personal justice. Very similar but not up to the actress's 1973 movie *Coffy*.

FRAMED

★★☆ Paramount, 1975, c, 106 min. Dir: Phil Karlson. SP: Mort Briskin, b/o novel by Art Powers, Mike Misenheimer. Cast: Joe Don Baker, Conny Van Dyke, Gabriel Dell, John Marley, Brock Peters, Roy Jenson, John Larch.

Standard action fare from the makers and star of the popular *Walking Tall* (1973). Baker is a gambler and nightclub owner who is framed for murder by corrupt cops and sent to prison. When he is finally released he is bent on revenge, and with the help of an admiring gang boss (Marley), he succeeds in routing the framers—of course, not before a few bloody clashes.

FRANTIC

★★★ Warner Bros., 1988, c, 120 min. Dir: Roman Polanski. SP: Roman Polanski, Gerard Brach. Cast: Harrison Ford, Betty Buckley, Emmanuelle Seigner,

John Mahoney, Jimmie Ray Weeks, David Huddleston.

The streets, rooftops, and nightclubs of Paris provide the background for this taut thriller. Attending a convention with his wife (Buckley), a doctor (Ford) suddenly finds himself caught up in a sinister conspiracy when his wife disappears on their first day. He is soon tangling desperately with spies and terrorists and trying to figure out the ambiguous girl (Seigner) who is involved. Shootouts and chases abound, of course, and Ford goes through it all with his usual brooding intensity.

FREEWAY

★ New World, 1988, c, 91 min. Dir: Francis Delia. SP: Darrell Fetty, Francis Delia, b/o novel by Deanne Barkley. Cast: Darlanne Fluegel, James Russo, Michael Callan, Richard Belzer, Billy Drago.

Los Angeles is in a state of panic. A Bible-quoting madman (Drago) has been killing drivers on the freeway at random, and the police are stumped. A determined nurse (Fluegel), whose husband was one of the victims, takes it on herself to ferret out the madman, joined by a mysterious stranger (Russo) and a cop (Callan). Also involved is a radio psychologist (Belzer), the killer's only contact. A wretched thriller, chock full of gaping plot holes, plus a ridiculous climax.

FREEWAY

★★☆ Republic, 1996, c, 102 min. Dir and SP: Matthew Bright. Cast: Kiefer Sutherland, Reese Witherspoon, Brooke Shields, Dan Hedaya, Wolfgang Bodison, Amanda Plummer, Michael T. Weiss, Bokeem Woodbine.

You may or may not be repelled by this twisted, darkly humorous, modern-day version of "Little Red Riding Hood." Fleeing from her prostitute mother (Plummer) and absusive, drug-taking stepfather (Weiss), illiterate fifteen-year-old "Red" (Witherspoon)

takes to the road. She meets the "Wolf": a seemingly kindly school psychologist (Sutherland) who turns out to be a truly nasty serial killer. She shoots him and leaves him for dead, only to have him survive as a grotesque figure, bent on revenge. More grim than Grimm, *Freeway* is a foul-mouthed original for special tastes. And don't even ask about "Grandma."

FRENCH CONNECTION, THE

★★★★ Fox, 1971, c, 104 min. Dir: William Friedkin. SP: Ernest Tidyman, b/o novel by Robin Moore. Cast: Gene Hackman, Roy Scheider, Fernando Rey, Tony LoBianco, Marcel Bozzuffi.

The French Connection may not have warranted an Oscar as the best picture of its year, but it's a crackerjack melodrama nonetheless: tremendously exciting, fast-paced, and expertly staged. The central character is Popeye Doyle (Hackman), a brutish and profane cop, and his adversary is a kingpin drug dealer (Rey) who is determined to bring a big shipment of heroin into New York City. The most famous sequence involves Popeye's

Gene Hackman won an Oscar for his performance as hard-nosed New York City cop Popeye Doyle in The French Connection *(1971).*

Robert Mitchum plays the title role of a tough but hapless Boston Irish hood in The Friends of Eddie Coyle *(1973).*

relentless pursuit of a hijacked elevated train, which becomes a brilliantly edited symphony of screeching brakes, shrieking passengers, and colliding cars. The movie also won four other Oscars, and a much less successful sequel turned up in 1975.

FRENCH CONNECTION II, THE

★★☆ Fox, 1975, c, 119 min. Dir: John Frankenheimer. SP: Robert Dillon, Laurie Dillon, Alexander Jacobs. Cast: Gene Hackman, Fernando Rey, Bernard Fresson, Jean-Pierre Castaldi, Cathleen Nesbitt.

This disappointing sequel to *The French Connection* sends New York's loose-cannon Popeye Doyle (Hackman) to Marseilles to find the elusive drug dealer Charnier (Rey). Some well-staged action sequences are offset by a long midsection in which Doyle is turned into a junkie by Charnier and his hoods and forced to undergo an agonizing detoxification. This harrowing sequence simply stops the movie in its tracks, and it never recovers. Hackman does his best, but Popeye should have stayed on his home turf.

FRENZY

★★★☆ Universal, 1972, c, 116 min. Dir: Alfred Hitchcock. SP: Anthony Shaffer. Cast: Jon Finch, Barry Foster, Alec McCowen, Anna Massey, Barbara Leigh-Hunt, Billie Whitelaw, Jean Marsh, Vivien Merchant.

Hitchcock's next-to-last film is not among his best, but for fans of the master director, it will suffice. In this story of a serial killer (Foster) at large in London, and the innocent man (Finch) who is sought for his crimes, Hitchcock resorts to more graphic violence than usual, but he also trots out his familiar bag of tricks, some of them still effective. There are lapses: one murder scene (with the hero's ex-wife as the prey) is singularly unpleasant, and another crucial sequence, involving the murderer, a corpse, and a truckful of potatoes, goes on for much too long. Hitchcock's macabre sense of humor is very much in evidence, and he also draws some laughs from a Scotland Yard inspector (McCowen) and his wife (Merchant), who fancies herself a gourmet cook.

FRIDAY FOSTER

★★ American International, 1975, c, 89 min. Dir: Arthur Marks. SP: Orville Hampton. Cast: Pam Grier, Yaphet Kotto, Thalmus Rasulala, Eartha Kitt, Geoffrey Cambridge, Jim Backus, Scatman Crothers, Carl Weathers.

A number of well-known black actors turn up in this run-of-the-mill action drama. Grier stars as a magazine photographer with a knack for stumbling into trouble and sniffing out corruption in high places. She finds herself fighting to expose a conspiracy to assassinate black politicians. Kotto is a cop, Kitt a way-out fashion designer, and Cambridge an effeminate crook.

FRIENDS OF EDDIE COYLE, THE

★★★☆ Fox, 1973, c, 102 min. Dir: Peter Yates. SP: Paul Monash, b/o novel by George V. Higgins. Cast:

Robert Mitchum, Peter Boyle, Richard Jordan, Steven Keats, Alex Rocco, Joe Santos, Mitchell Ryan.

A somber, fatalistic tone pervades this exceptionally effective crime drama. Unable to face living the rest of his life behind bars, three-time loser Eddie Foyle (Mitchum) decides to become a police informant and engage in plea bargaining. Yet he continues to work for the mob. The consequences for Eddie are inevitably fatal. Mitchum's world-weary, cynical persona is eminently right for the role, and Boyle is fine as Eddie's friend, a bartender who doubles as a paid assassin.

FUGITIVE, THE

★★★★ Warner Bros., 1993, c, 131 min. Dir: Andrew Davis. SP: Jeb Stuart, David Twohy, b/o story by David Twohy and characters created by Roy Huggins. Cast: Harrison Ford, Tommy Lee Jones, Sela Ward, Julianne Moore, Jeroen Krabbe, Joe Pantoliano, Andreas Katzulas.

Suspend your sense of logic and you'll have a marvelous time at this breathtaking thriller. The movie's premise is derived from the long-running television series in which Dr. Richard Kimble flees after being falsely convicted of murdering his wife and searches for the one-armed man who committed the crime. Here, Dr. Kimble (Ford) is obliged to survive a variety of disasters before he can prove his innocence and uncover the conspiracy that prompted his wife's death. The good doctor seems to have an astonishing capacity to remain in one piece, but one exciting scene follows another so quickly that there is little time for rational thought. Jones brings a measure of irony and sardonic wit to his Oscar-winning role as the deputy marshal who is Kimble's pursuer. The movie itself received an Oscar nomination as Best Picture.

FUNERAL, THE.

★★★☆ October Films, 1996, c, 94 min. Dir: Abel Ferrara. SP: Nicholas St. John. Cast: Christopher Walken, Chris Penn, Annaella Sciorra, Isabella Rossellini, Vincent Gallo, Benicio Del Toro.

Offbeat director Ferrara's strongest film to date, *The Funeral* is characteristically raw and violent, but it's also darkly compelling and exceptionally well acted. Set in the 1930s, the movie traces the criminal careers of three brothers. Ray (Walken) is the most serious-minded, Chez (Penn) is the most dangerously volatile, and Johnny (Gallo), the youngest, is the Communist hoodlum whose funeral at the film's beginning precipitates the action and the flashbacks of the story. Walken manages to repress his usual mannerisms, but the movie belongs to Penn, who gives an astonishing performance.

FURY

★★★☆ MGM, 1936, b/w, 94 min. Dir: Fritz Lang. SP: Bartlett Cormack, Fritz Lang, b/o story by Norman Krasna. Cast: Spencer Tracy, Sylvia Sidney, Walter Abel, Bruce Cabot, Edward Ellis, Walter Brennan, Frank Albertson.

Lang's first American film still packs quite a wallop on a subject that was seldom if ever discussed in movies of the thirties: the wanton lynching of men who were never proven guilty in a court of law. Tracy is the unlucky man who is falsely arrested on a charge of kidnapping and then must face an out-of-control lynch mob. Sidney is his distraught girlfriend. Lang whips up potent scenes of ordinary people goaded into mindless revenge. Tracy's performance reaches its peak in the courtroom, where he vents his bitterness and rage. Krasna's story won an Oscar.

FUZZ

★★☆ Filmways, 1972, c, 92 min. Dir: Richard A. Colla. SP: Evan Hunter, b/o his novel (Ed McBain). Cast: Burt Reynolds, Raquel Welch, Yul Brynner, Jack Weston, Tom Skerritt, James McEachin, Peter Bonerz.

Evidently an attempt to do for the police what *M.A.S.H.* did for the military, *Fuzz* mixes raucous comedy and violent action with only middling results. At a Boston precinct, a quartet of plainclothes detectives headed by Reynolds continue to botch their stakeouts, usually in comic fashion, while searching for criminals. Their main target is a mysterious bomber (Brynner) who keeps killing local officials. Hunter based the screenplay on one of his "87th Precinct" stories written as "Ed McBain."

F/X

★★★ Orion, 1986, c, 106 min. Dir: Robert Mandel. SP: Robert T. Megginson, Gregory Fleeman. Cast: Bryan Brown, Brian Dennehy, Diane Venora, Cliff De Young, Mason Adams, Jerry Orbach.

A clever, twisty, if somewhat far-fetched thriller. Special effects wizard Brown is hired to stage the fake assassination of a big-time mobster (Orbach). Instead he learns that he is the patsy in a deadly conspiracy involving many people. And he himself becomes a target for murder. Now he must use his wizardry to expose the culprits. Dennehy stands out (as usual) as a tough, abrasive cop on the case. A sequel, F/X2, appeared in 1991.

F/X2: THE DEADLY ART OF ILLUSION

★★☆ Orion, 1991, c, 107 min. Dir: Richard Franklin. SP: Bill Condon. Cast: Bryan Brown, Brian Dennehy, Rachel Ticotin, Joanna Gleason, Philip Bosco.

Brown returns as special effects wizard Rollie Tyler, and Dennehy repeats as his gruff cop partner, in this adequate sequel to the 1986 hit FX. Now retired, Rollie is asked to return and apply his skills to a baffling new case. The case involves the theft of some priceless gold coins and other far-flung matters. The movie's real star is a clown robot named Bluey, who can duplicate Rollie's every movement.

GAMES

★★★ Universal, 1967, c, 100 min. Dir: Curtis Harrington. SP: Gene Kearney, b/o story by George Edwards. Cast: Simone Signoret, James Caan, Katharine Ross, Don Stroud, Kent Smith, Estelle Winwood, Marjorie Bennett, Ian Wolfe.

Mysterious, enigmatic Lisa (Signoret) comes to the New York apartment of newlyweds Paul and Jennifer (Caan and Ross). The couple enjoys playing games and staging fantasies, but as Lisa stays on, the "fun" becomes sinister and ultimately deadly. Who is doing what to whom, and why? You may figure it all out well before the end, but the movie makes fascinating viewing, and Signoret is always a compelling actress.

GANGSTER, THE

★★☆ Allied Artists, 1947, b/w, 84 min. Dir: Gordon Wiles. SP: Daniel Fuchs. Cast: Barry Sullivan, Belita, Joan Lorring, Akim Tamiroff, Henry Morgan, John Ireland, Sheldon Leonard, Fifi D'Orsay, Elisha Cook, Jr., Virginia Christine.

A good cast lifts this glum little crime drama a notch above the ordinary. The story traces the rise and fall of an unhappy gangster named Shubunka (Sullivan), who begins by extorting money from gamblers and others and ends up in the gutter, riddled with bullets. Belita is his abused moll who finally turns him in for a rival mob.

GARMENT JUNGLE, THE

★★☆ Columbia, 1957, b/w, 88 min. Dir: Vincent Sherman. SP: Harry Kleiner, b/o articles by Lester Velie. Cast: Lee J. Cobb, Kerwin Mathews, Gia Scala, Richard Boone, Robert Loggia, Valerie French, Joseph Wiseman, Harold J. Stone.

A modestly produced, occasionally effective melodrama concerning a veteran (Mathews) who joins his father's garment business, only to learn that the business is controlled by the mob. Violence dominates the scene until Mathews and his outnumbered forces fight back. Cobb as the hero's weak-willed father and Boone as the mob's ruthless leader give solid performances. Sherman replaced Robert Aldrich as director midway through the filming.

GASLIGHT

★★★ British National (British), 1940, b/w, 84 min. Dir: Thorold Dickinson. SP: A. R. Rawlinson, Bridget Boland, b/o play by Patrick Hamilton. Cast: Anton Walbrook, Diana Wynyard, Frank Pettingell, Cathleen Cordell, Robert Newton, Jimmy Hanley.

It may be difficult to find this film, but it's worth the effort. The first version of Hamilton's play Angel Street, it is much more modest than the better-known MGM 1944 version, also called Gaslight. Yet it compensates with good acting and well-realized atmosphere. Once again the murderous villain (Walbrook) tries to drive his poor wife (Wynyard) insane while feverishly striving to locate some jewels missing in their home. Reportedly MGM tried to destroy the negative when they made their own version, but it surfaced in 1952 under the title Angel Street.

GASLIGHT

★★★☆ MGM, 1944, b/w, 114 min. Dir: George Cukor. SP: John Van Druten, Walter Reisch, John S. Balderston, b/o play by Patrick Hamilton. Cast: Ingrid Bergman, Charles Boyer, Joseph Cotten, Dame May Whitty, Angela Lansbury.

Bergman won her first Academy Award for her intense portrayal of a beleagured wife in this well-wrought Victorian thriller. Boyer is equally fine as her worldly, scheming husband who is desperate to find the jewels hidden in their town house. He has already committed murder for them, and now he is trying to drive his wife insane. Cukor's smooth direction and Joseph Ruttenberg's atmospheric photography help to sustain the movie's menacing tone. Under the title of *Angel Street*, the story had a past history on stage and screen. Look for Lansbury in her movie debut, as a saucy maid.

Sinister Charles Boyer tries to drive wife Ingrid Bergman mad in Gaslight *(1944), the second film adaptation of the play* Angel Street.

GAUNTLET, THE

★ Warner Bros./Malposo, 1977, c, 109 min. Dir: Clint Eastwood. SP: Michael Butler, Dennis Shryack. Cast: Clint Eastwood, Sondra Locke, Pat Hingle, William Prince, Bill McKinney, Mara Corday.

Actor-director Eastwood plays Ben Shockley, a burned-out veteran Phoenix cop, who is given the assignment of guarding a tough-talking prostitute (Locke), the key witness in a big murder trial. As they travel from Las Vegas back to Phoenix, a succession of shootouts, explosions, and chases tells them soon enough that both sides of the law would like to see them very dead. One of Eastwood's worst films, *The Gauntlet* is utterly stupid from beginning to end, and almost totally unbelievable. Dumbest scene: Shockley pretends to place an entire biker gang under arrest, in order to take one of their bikes.

GETAWAY, THE

★★★ First Artists, 1972, c, 122 min. Dir: Sam Peckinpah. SP: Walter Hill, b/o novel by Jim Thompson. Cast: Steve McQueen, Ali MacGraw, Ben Johnson, Al Lettieri, Jack Dodson, Slim Pickens, Dub Taylor, Bo Hopkins, Sally Struthers.

Don't look for any sense of morality in this harsh, fast-moving melodrama from Sam Peckinpah. After a bank robbery that goes badly, parolee "Doc" McCoy (McQueen) and his wife, Carol (MacGraw), find themselves on the lam from the law and from a vengeful confederate (Lettieri). In their flight, they cut a wide swath of mayhem, but do they get their just deserts? Not in a Peckinpah movie. McQueen is an actor who could project attitudes and feelings without saying a word, but MacGraw is amateurish. Fine performance by Struthers as a woman who turns from a bored doctor's wife into a sluttish gun moll. Remade in 1994.

GETAWAY, THE

★★☆ Universal, 1994, c, 115 min. Dir: Roger Donaldson. SP: Walter Hill, Jim Thompson, b/o novel by Jim Thompson. Cast: Alec Baldwin, Kim Basinger, James Woods, Michael Madsen, David Morse, Jennifer Tilly, James Stephens, Richard Farnsworth.

An inferior remake of Sam Peckinpah's 1972 film, *The Getaway* repeats the basic story but adds several large dollops of graphic violence. Once again "Doc" McCoy (Baldwin) and his wife Carol (Basinger) cut a wide swath of lawlessness as they seek their fortune by robbery, treachery, and (if necessary) murder. Soon the police and vengeful confederates are hot on their trail from Texas to New Mexico. Lots of action, little style, and no sympathetic characters.

GET SHORTY

★★★☆ MGM/UA, 1995, c, 105 min. Dir: Barry Sonnenfeld. SP: Scott Frank, b/o novel by Elmore Leonard. Cast: John Travolta, Gene Hackman, Rene Russo, Danny DeVito, Dennis Farina, Delroy Lindo, James Gandolfini, David Paymer, Bette Midler (unbilled), Harvey Keitel (unbilled).

What do movie people and gangsters have in common? More than you would imagine in this wickedly funny, cleverly wrought crime comedy. Travolta is in top form as Chili Palmer, an enterprising and confident loan shark who comes to Los Angeles to collect on a few outstanding debts and becomes intrigued by the film business. He gets involved with "schlock" producer Harry Zimm (Hackman), actress Karen Flores (Russo), and egotistical film star Martin Weir (DeVito). Chili also tangles with a few hard-nosed criminal types, with expectedly violent results. The movie's pace sags at times, but the dialogue is razor-sharp and there are a number of hilarious scenes. Personal favorite: Chili pitches his story to the self-absorbed Weir.

GETTING AWAY WITH MURDER

★ Savoy, 1996, c, 92 min. Dir and SP: Harvey Miller. Cast: Dan Aykroyd, Jack Lemmon, Lily Tomlin, Bonnie Hunt, Brian Kerwin, Jerry Adler, Andy Romano.

Ethics professor Aykroyd comes to believe that his neighbor, Lemmon, is not the benign old German-American he appears to be but a notorious ex-Nazi who is plotting to leave the country. His obsession with "justice" takes the form of murder, and when it seems to be a case of mistaken identity, he does penance for his crime by marrying the old man's rather forbidding daughter (Tomlin). It all unwinds to what was intended as an ironic ending. This ghastly black comedy is a black mark on the careers of all concerned.

GHOST

★★★ Paramount, 1990, c, 122 min. Dir: Jerry Zucker. SP: Bruce Joel Rubin. Cast: Patrick Swayze, Demi Moore, Whoopi Goldberg, Tony Goldwyn, Vincent Schiavelli, Rich Aviles, Gail Boggs, Armelia McQueen, Phil Leeds.

How could this movie miss? It had everything: brash comedy (mostly courtesy of Oscar-winning Goldberg), a tender supernatural romance, and plenty of violent action. If it all seemed calculated, it was fun nevertheless. When Swayze is murdered, his ghost appears to seek out the killer and to protect his grieving wife (Moore). He is aided in his otherworldly tasks by a fake spiritualist (Goldberg), who is astonished to learn that she has real psychic powers. Cluttered and unwieldy, yes, but enjoyable. Rubin's screenplay also won an Academy Award.

GHOSTS OF MISSISSIPPI

★★★ Castle Rock, 1996, c, 120 min. Dir: Rob Reiner. SP: Lewis Colick. Cast: Alec Baldwin, Whoopi Goldberg, James Woods, William H. Macy, Bill Cobbs, Craig T. Nelson, William H. Macy, Virginia Madsen.

In June 1963 Mississippi civil rights leader Medgar Evers was murdered by a rabid racist named Byron De La Beckwith. After two trials with hung juries, De La Beckwith was a free man. Thirty years later, assistant district attorney Bobby DeLaughter (Baldwin) insisted on retrying the case, despite the opposition of virtually everyone, and De La Beckwith was finally found guilty. Well-intentioned but self-congratulatory, *Ghosts of Mississippi* relates this story competently but resorts to every cliché expected in this sort of film. The acting is more earnest than compelling, but Woods gives a juicy performance as the malevolent culprit.

GILDA

★★★ Columbia, 1946, b/w, 110 min. Dir: Charles Vidor. SP: Marion Parsonnet, adapted by Jo Eisington from story by E. A. Ellington. Cast: Rita Hayworth, Glenn Ford, George Macready, Joseph Calleia, Steven Geray, Joe Sawyer, Gerald Mohr, Robert Scott.

Yes, it's all very absurd, but try taking your eyes from the screen when Hayworth, red hair cascading down her back, sings "Put the Blame on Mame." She became a major star and

Steven Geray tends bar for Glenn Ford and Rita Hayworth in Gilda *(1946). Hayworth became a superstar singing "Put the Blame on Mame" in this film.*

one of the icons of the forties with her performance as the new wife of a sinister Argentinean casino owner (Macready). There's trouble and danger afoot when her old flame (Ford) turns up and rekindles their spark of mutual hatred and attraction. When the dialogue starts to get perilously silly, Hayworth punches it all home with her forties glamour.

GIRL HUNTERS, THE

★★☆ Colorama (British), 1963, c, 103 min. Dir: Roy Rowland. SP: Mickey Spillane, Roy Rowland, Robert Fellows, b/o novel by Mickey Spillane. Cast: Mickey Spillane, Shirley Eaton, Lloyd Nolan, Hy Gardner, Scott Peters, Guy Kingsley Poynter, James Dyrenforth.

For the first and last time, author Spillane played his own fictional detective-hero Mike Hammer in this British-made adaptation of his novel. In this version, after seven years of boozing and feeling responsible for the death of his longtime secretary, Velda, Hammer learns that she may be alive. His search for Velda leads him into a case involving an international Communist plot and the murder of a U.S. senator. Nolan is a federal agent, and Eaton is Hammer's new romantic involvement. The usual tough talk and gun play, and Spillane is not bad as Hammer.

GLASS KEY, THE

★★★ Paramount, 1942, b/w, 85 min. Dir: Stuart Heisler. SP: Jonathan Latimer, b/o novel by Dashiell Hammett. Cast: Brian Donlevy, Alan Ladd, Veronica Lake, William Bendix, Joseph Calleia, Bonita Granville, Richard Denning.

Ladd and Lake were not the most expressive actors, but their flat-voiced, understated style seemed to work for them and their on-screen chemistry made them a popular team of the forties. In this remake of the 1935 movie, Ladd plays the chief aide to political boss Donlevy; he becomes enmeshed in a treacherous web when Donlevy is suspected of murder. Lake is the devious sister of the murder victim, who is romantically drawn to Ladd. Bendix veers from his usual amiable persona to play a brutal bodyguard.

GLEAMING THE CUBE

★★☆ Fox/Gladden, 1989, c, 104 min. Dir: Graeme Clifford. SP: Michael Tolkin. Cast: Christian Slater, Steven Bauer, Richard Herd, Le Tuan, Max Perlich, Art Chudabala, Ed Lauter, Peter Kwong, Charles Cyphers, Micole Mercurio.

Some dazzling skateboarding stunts are the best feature of this adequate action film. Brian Kelly (Slater) is a skateboard enthusiast whose adopted Vietnamese brother (Chudabala) is killed when he inadvertently uncovers an international contraband ring. Nobody believes it's murder until Brian investigates with the reluctant help of a cop (Bauer). Standard material, with (you guessed it) a chase climax featuring many cars—and skateboards. Incidentally, "gleaming the cube" means achieving the ultimate ride.

GLIMMER MAN, THE

★★ Warner Bros., 1996, c, 91 min. Dir: John Gray. SP: Kevin Brodbin. Cast: Steven Seagal, Keenan Ivory Wayans, Bob Gunton, John M. Jackson, Michelle Johnson, Stephen Tobolowsky, Peter Jaron.

Good luck if you can figure out what's happening in this muddled, mindless police drama. Seagal, a free-lance New York cop complete with pony tail, colorful shirts, a black belt in martial arts, and a mysterious past, comes to Los Angeles. He's partnered with cop Wayans, and together they try to capture a bizarre serial killer who crucifies his victims. The two men are also the targets of the Russian Mafia in New York's Little Odessa—and somehow both killer and Mafia are connected. Don't even bother to think about it.

GLORIA

★★ Columbia, 1980, c, 121 min. Dir and SP: John Cassavetes. Cast: Gena Rowlands, John Adames, Buck Henry, Julie Carmen, Lupe Guarnica.

There is scarcely a believable moment in this melodrama from Cassavetes—surely one of his poorest. Rowlands is a tough ex-mob mistress moll who suddenly finds herself saddled with a Puerto Rican boy (Adames) when his family is murdered by hit men. This odd couple has several close calls before everything is resolved. Rowlands is game, but the movie is clumsily written and often preposterous. Some sequences are close to parody, which may have been Cassavetes's intention, but none of it works.

G MEN

★★★ Warner Bros., 1935, b/w, 85 min. Dir: William Keighley. SP: Seton I. Miller. Cast: James Cagney, Margaret Lindsay, Robert Armstrong, Ann Dvorak, Barton MacLane, Lloyd Nolan, William Harrigan.

Fast-moving in Warner's typical slambang fashion, G Men puts Cagney on the side of the law for a change. He plays "Brick" Davis, a lawyer who joins the FBI as a G man after his friend is killed by the gang. He succeeds in ousting the crooks, but not before a few noisy gun battles in which an astonishing number of bullets are fired. The movie's best performance comes from Dvorak as the ill-fated wife of nasty thug MacLane.

GODFATHER, THE

★★★★ Paramount, 1972, c, 175 min. Dir: Francis Ford Coppola. SP: Francis Ford Coppola, Mario Puzo, b/o novel by Mario Puzo. Cast: Marlon Brando, Al Pacino, James Caan, Diane Keaton, Richard Castellano, John Cazale, Robert Duvall, Talia Shire, Sterling Hayden, Richard Conte, Abe Vigoda, Morgana King, Alex Rocco, John Marley.

The Godfather (1972): Mafia patriarch Don Corleone (Marlon Brando) and his son Michael (Al Pacino).

One of the great crime films, surpassed only by the first sequel, *The Godfather, Part Two*. Sweeping, magnetic, and beautifully orchestrated by director Coppola, the film takes the viewer deep into the heart of organized crime in America and its roots in the all-important "family." As Vito Corleone, the clan's revered head who draws his sons (Caan, Pacino, and Cazale) into a web of murder and vengeance, Brando is undeniably riveting, yet he seems to be acting in a different film from anyone else. Pacino gives an outstanding performance as the dutiful son who is transformed into the all-powerful don. One bravura scene follows another, and the climactic sequence, in which a baby's baptism is set against a series of blood-soaked vendettas, is unforgettable. Oscars went to the film, to Brando, and to Coppola and Puzo for their screenplay.

GODFATHER, PART II, THE

★★★★ Paramount, 1974, c, 200 min. Dir: Francis Ford Coppola. SP: Francis Ford Coppola, Mario Puzo. Cast: Al Pacino, Robert De Niro, Robert Duvall, Diane Keaton, John Cazale, Talia Shire, Lee Strasberg, Michael V. Gazzo, G. D. Spradlin, Abe Vigoda, Morgana King, Danny Aiello, Troy Donahue, Harry Dean Stanton.

Proof positive that a sequel can surpass the original. A sweeping epic of near-operatic power, this second installment of the Corleone saga moves from the violent Sicilian beginnings in 1901 to 1958, when Michael Corleone (Pacino) assumes his lonely place as the undisputed don. In between, the film shows crime not as a family affair as in *The Godfather* but as a corruption of the American dream. Oscar-winner De Niro excels in the early scenes as young Vito Corleone and Pacino is brilliant as a man who pays a bitter price for placing family ties above personal feelings. The film won six Oscars, including Best Picture.

GODFATHER, PART III, THE

★★★ Paramount, 1990, c, 161 min. Dir: Francis Ford Coppola. SP: Mario Puzo, Francis Ford Coppola. Cast: Al Pacino, Diane Keaton, Talia Shire, Andy Garcia, Eli Wallach, Joe Mantegna, George Hamilton, Bridget Fonda, Sofia Coppola, Raf Vallone, Frank D'Ambrosio, Donal Donnelly, Don Novello.

By far the least effective of the three *Godfather* films, this epic continuation of the Corleone

Michael Corleone (Al Pacino), who will become the undisputed don, meets with the family's consigliore *(Robert Duvall) in* The Godfather, Part II *(1974).*

Ray Liotta, Robert De Niro, Paul Sorvino, and Joe Pesci (left to right) take time for a Mafia family photo opportunity in GoodFellas *(1990).*

saga boasts several bravura sequences. The overall effect, however, is disappointing. The muddled, cluttered story line deals with Michael Corleone's reluctant return to the world of violent crime, and the disastrous consequences to himself and his family. This time he discovers that the links between the Catholic Church and international business can turn treacherous. Some of the scope and grandeur of the first two films is clearly present, but the movie is never fully satisfying. It did receive several Oscar nominations, including one for Best Picture, but it won no awards.

GOODFELLAS

★★★★ Warner Bros., 1990, c, 146 min. Dir: Martin Scorsese. SP: Nicholas Pileggi, Martin Scorsese, b/o book by Nicholas Pileggi. Cast: Robert De Niro, Ray Liotta, Lorraine Bracco, Joe Pesci, Paul Sorvino, Frank Sivero, Tony Darrow, Mike Starr, Chuck Low.

Martin Scorsese's brilliant crime drama takes us deep into the ugly heart of the Mafia and its "wiseguys," or "goodfellas." It relates the true story of half-Irish, half-Italian Henry Hill (Liotta), who goes from trusted mob member to "stoolie" in the witness protection program. We see the machismo, the flamboyant lifestyle, and the mindless violence of these criminals, and the effect is both funny and terrifying. De Niro plays a top "goodfella" with his usual skill, and Oscar-winner Pesci is especially frightening as a short-fused hood. The movie received five other Oscar nominations.

GOOD SON, THE

★★★ Fox, 1993, c, 88 min. Dir: Joseph Ruben. SP: Ian McEwan. Cast: Macauley Culkin, Elijah Wood, Wendy Crewson, David Morse, Jacqueline Brookes, Daniel Hugh Kelly, Quinn Culkin, Ashley Crowe.

If you don't relish the idea of Macauley Culkin, the cute young star of *Home Alone*, as a "bad seed" without a shred of conscience, you should avoid this movie. Otherwise, you may find a rather well-crafted psychological thriller that works up a fair amount of suspense. After his mother dies, young Mark (Wood) comes to spend two weeks with his aunt and uncle (Crewson and Kelly). Nobody believes him when he discovers that his cousin Henry (Culkin) is a remorseless killer, ready to dispatch anyone who threatens him, especially Mark. Culkin's fans were not prepared to accept this idea, but there are some genuinely frightening moments.

GORKY PARK

★★★ Orion, 1983, c, 128 min. Dir: Michael Apted. SP: Dennis Potter, b/o novel by Martin Cruz Smith. Cast: William Hurt, Lee Marvin, Brian Dennehy, Joanna Pacula, Ian Bannen, Alexander Knox.

In Moscow's Gorky Park, the dead bodies of three young people are discovered, their faces horribly mutilated. Chief investigator Renko (Hurt) takes over the case and soon becomes entangled in a web of conspiracy and duplicity that threatens him at every turn. Involved are a powerful American businessman (Marvin) with ties to top Russian officials, an enigmatic girl (Pacula), and a New York detective (Dennehy) whose brother was one of the victims. Based on a best-selling novel, this movie is competently made and absorbing, but its best feature is the unusual locale (Helsinki substituting for Moscow).

GRIFTERS, THE

★★★☆ Cineplex Odeon, 1990, c, 113 min. Dir: Stephen Frears. SP: Donald E. Westlake, b/o novel by Jim Thompson. Cast: Anjelica Huston, John Cusack, Annette Bening, Pat Hingle, Henry Jones, J. T. Walsh.

Three grifters—scam artists—meet on a fatal collison course in this brilliant, and very tough, film noir. One is Huston, in a marvelous, Oscar-nominated performance, as a hardened woman who works her scam at the racetrack. Another is her son (Cusack), to date only a petty swindler. Enter Bening (also nominated) as the perfect noir dame: ambitious, manipulative, and ruthless. As their schemes succeed or backfire, mother and girl become deadly rivals, until the violent climax. Ice-cold and gripping.

GRISSOM GANG, THE

★★ Fox, 1971, c, 127 min. Dir: Robert Aldrich. SP: Leon Griffiths, b/o novel by James Hadley Chase. Cast: Kim Darby, Scott Wilson, Irene Dailey, Tony Musante, Connie Stevens, Ralph Waite, Robert Lansing, Wesley Addy.

An extremely heavy body count marks this overlong, overbaked, and overacted movie, based on the novel that was filmed once before in Great Britain as *No Orchids for Miss Blandish* (1948). In the Depression era, young heiress Barbara Blandish (Darby) is kidnapped by the Grissom family of mental defectives, headed by their vicious mother (Dailey). Slim (Wilson), the dimmest of the bunch, falls for Barbara, and before a blood-splattered shootout ends it all, Barbara has some feelings for Slim. As trigger-happy Mama, Dailey wins the Scenery-Chewing Award. Good period detail is not enough compensation.

GUILTY AS CHARGED

★★ I.R.S., 1992, c, 95 min. Dir: Sam Irvin. SP: Charles Gale. Cast: Rod Steiger, Lauren Hutton, Heather Graham, Lyman Ward, Zelda Rubenstein.

This crackpot thriller tries for a satirical edge but it doesn't come through. Steiger, in full throttle as usual, plays a wealthy meat packer who decides to take it on himself to execute all convicted murderers who escape capital punishment. He even has his very own electric chair, ready for action. Nothing that happens makes much sense, except that the movie seems to want to say somthing about contemporary law.

GUILTY AS SIN

★★☆ Hollywood, 1993, c, 107 min. Dir: Sidney Lumet. SP: Larry Cohen. Cast: Rebecca De Mornay, Don Johnson, Jack Warden, Stephen Lang, Dana Ivey,

Luis Guzman.

The raffish charm that made a television star of Don Johnson on "Miami Vice" is turned in the direction of pure evil in this mediocre thriller. He plays David Greenhill, a smooth, utterly ruthless killer who hires lawyer Jennifer Haines (De Mornay) to defend him against the charge that he murdered his wife. Soon she becomes an unwilling, terrified pawn in his diabolical plan to escape justice. The problem is that Greenhill is a single-note character, so totally reprehensible that he becomes a fantasy villain rather than the chilling threat he should be. As a consequence, the entire movie suffers.

GUN CRAZY

★★★ United Artists, 1949, b/w, 86 min. Dir: Joseph H. Lewis. SP: MacKinlay Kantor, Millard Kaufman (Dalton Trumbo). Cast: John Dall, Peggy Cummins, Berry Kroeger, Anabel Shaw, Morris Carnovsky, Rusty Tamblyn, Nedrick Young.

A relatively early entry in the "doomed criminal lovers" cycle that peaked with *Bonnie and Clyde* in 1967, *Gun Crazy* is a cult film with many admirers. Trimly and economically made, with several well-handled sequences, it revolves about Bart Tare (Dall), a sensitive young man whose obsession with guns fuses fatally with his lust for the truly nasty Annie Laurie Starr (Cummins). Their criminal spree, made even more deadly by Laurie's homicidal impulses, can only end in disaster. Blacklisted author Dalton Trumbo coauthored the script, using Millard Kaufman as his "front."

HAMMETT

★★☆ Orion, 1983, c, 97 min. Dir: Wim Wenders. SP: Ross Thomas, Dennis O'Flaherty, adapted by Thomas Pope from novel by Joe Gores. Cast: Frederic Forrest, Peter Boyle, Marilu Henner, Roy Kinnear, Elisha Cook, Lydia Lei, David Patrick Kelly, R. G. Armstrong, Royal Dano, Sylvia Sidney.

A stylish production that effectively recreates the look of the 1930s is largely wasted on this tangled and not very interesting mystery. Novelist Dashiell ("Sam") Hammett, who wrote *The Maltese Falcon*, becomes the fictional hero of the story, which involves pornography, blackmail, and murder in San Francisco. The movie includes an homage to the *Falcon*, including its very own Fat Man (Kinnear) and gunsel (Kelly). For good measure, the always-reliable Cook, the original gunsel of the 1941 classic, makes an appearance as a cabbie.

HAND THAT ROCKS THE CRADLE, THE

★★★ Hollywood, 1992, c, 110 min. Dir: Curtis Hanson. SP: Amanda Silver. Cast: Annabella Sciorra, Rebecca De Mornay, Matt McCoy, Ernie Hudson, Julianne Moore, Madeline Zima.

Deranged by the death of her doctor-husband (he committed suicide after being accused of molesting patients) and her unborn child, Peyton (De Mornay) decides to exact revenge on Claire (Sciorra), the woman who blew the whistle. She moves into Claire's home as housekeeper-nanny and plots to kill her and take over her family. She wreaks havoc—and commits murder—to get her way until the hair-raising climax. Predictable, but a notch or two better than other "crazy woman" melodramas, with some suspenseful moments.

HAPPY NEW YEAR

★★☆ Columbia, 1987, c, 86 min. Dir: John Avildsen. SP: Warren Lane. Cast: Peter Falk, Charles Durning, Wendy Hughes, Tom Courtenay, Joan Copeland.

A fairly amusing remake of the 1973 French comedy by Claude Lelouche. Relocated from Paris to Palm Beach, Florida, the movie concerns a couple of thieves (Falk and Durning) who decide to rob Harry Winston's jewelry emporium. The caper, of course, turns into a comic shambles. Falk, as the "brains" of the heist, has his best moments when he's casing the store and disguises himself as a Palm Beach socialite and the socialite's sister. The movie was shelved for a year and had limited theatrical release.

HARD-BOILED

★★★ Golden Princess/Milestone (Hong-Kong), 1992, c, 127 min. Dir: John Woo. SP: Barry Wong, b/o story by John Woo. Cast: Chow Yun-Fat, Tony Leung, Teresa Mo, Philip Chan, Anthony Wong, Kwan Hoi-Shan, A-Lung.

Director Woo's second thriller after *The Killer*, this movie is not up to his first, but it boasts several of the most elaborate action sequences you are ever likely to see. (The body count is high enough to populate another film.) The plot is simple: after the murder of his partner, a "hard-boiled" cop (Yun-Fat) is out to destroy the responsible gun-smuggling ring, with the help of an ambiguous hit man (Leung). The story is merely an excuse for the set pieces: massive, bloody shootouts, effectively staged. The long final sequence in a hospital is astonishing. Dubbed in English.

HARD TO KILL

★★ Warner Bros., 1990, c, 95 min. Dir: Bruce Malmuth. SP: Steven McKay. Cast: Steven Seagal, Kelly LeBrock, Bill Sadler, Frederick Coffin, Bonnie Burroughs, Andrew Block.

After detective and martial-arts expert Seagal uncovers a major crime ring, he is shot and left for dead, and his wife is killed. He awakens from a seven-year coma, grimly bent on revenge. Standard of its kind, with the usual chases, stalkings, and bone-crushing fights. And Seagal's acting range is not exactly wide.

HARD WAY, THE

★★☆ Universal, 1991, c, 111 min. Dir: John Badham. SP: Daniel Pyne, Lem Dobbs, b/o story by Lem Dobbs, Michael Kozoll. Cast: Michael J. Fox, James Woods, Anabella Sciorra, Stephen Lang, Delroy Lindo, Luis Guzman, Penny Marshall.

To nab the role of a tough cop, popular action film star Fox decides to do "research" by attaching himself to tough, hot-tempered New York City cop Woods. Predictably, Woods goes from angry resentment to grudging admiration as they pursue a deranged serial killer (Lang). The movie mixes comedy with action and earns a few scattered laughs until the ending, when one climax follows another, each one more ridiculous than the last. Marshall has an amusing cameo as Fox's agent.

HARPER

★★★ Warner Bros., 1966, c, 102 min. Dir: Jack Smight. SP: William Goldman, b/o novel by Ross MacDonald. Cast: Paul Newman, Lauren Bacall, Shelley Winters, Julie Harris, Robert Wagner, Janet Leigh, Arthur Hill, Pamela Tiffin, Robert Webber, Strother Martin.

A detective story in the Dashiell Hammett-Raymond Chandler tradition, *Harper* has a cleverly contrived screenplay and a good cast, but it's not a classic of the genre. Newman is Harper, the cynical detective who is handy with a fist or a wisecrack. When he is asked to find wealthy Bacall's missing husband, he is soon caught up in a plot involving blackmail and murder. Winters plays a has-been movie actress and Harris is something of a surprise as a drug-addicted nightclub pianist.

HEAR NO EVIL

★★ Fox, 1993, c, 98 min. Dir: Robert Greenwald. SP: R. M. Badat, Kathleen Rowell, b/o story by R. M. Badat, Danny Rubin. Cast: Marlee Matlin, D. B. Sweeney, Martin Sheen, John McGinley, Christina Carlisi, Greg Elam, Charley Lang, Marge Redmond.

Another variation on the damsel-in-danger plotline, this one less than convincing, despite the appealing presence of deaf actress Matlin. She plays a personal trainer who unwittingly comes into possession of a rare stolen coin. Sheen (in an uncharacteristic villain's role) is the corrupt cop who wants the coin at any cost, and Sweeney is the resourceful young man who helps her when she is being threatened. The second "surprise" climax doesn't make much sense.

HEAT

★★★☆ Warner Bros., 1995, c, 172 min. Dir and SP: Michael Mann. Cast: Al Pacino, Robert De Niro, Val Kilmer, Jon Voight, Diane Venora, Tom Sizemore, Amy Brenneman, Ashley Judd, Mykelti Williamson.

Place Pacino and De Niro together in the same film and the sparks are sure to fly. In this explosive film, we get an entire conflagration. Pacino is the tough Los Angeles cop out to capture master thief De Niro and his gang. From the start it's clear that both men are alike: totally dedicated to their careers at the expense of any private lives. This idea may not exactly be new, but it adds some weight to the conventional cop-crook confrontations that punctuate the movie. Writer-director Mann brings his characteristically high-tech style to the movie, and it makes many of these confrontations breathlessly exciting. Pacino and De Niro have one face-to-face encounter in a restaurant, and the coiled intensity of these charismatic actors is something to see.

HEAVEN'S PRISONERS

★★☆ New Line, 1996, c, 135 min. Dir: Phil Joanou. SP: Harley Peyton, Scott Frank, b/o novel by James Lee Burke. Cast: Alec Baldwin, Mary Stuart Masterson, Kelly Lynch, Teri Hatcher, Eric Roberts, Vondie Curtis Hall, Badja Djola.

An ex-cop and recovering alcoholic in New Orleans, Dave Robicheaux (Baldwin) plunges into violent and ultimately tragic events after he rescues a young girl from a downed airplane in the Louisiana swamps. His attempt to learn more about one of the plane's shady passengers leads him into an underworld of dangerous drug lords and killer thugs. Baldwin is not ideally cast in this overlong, murky, moderately engrossing attempt at film noir. (Hatcher's role as a duplicitous wife is pure noir.)

HEAVENLY CREATURES

★★★★ Miramax (New Zealand), 1994, c, 98 min. Dir: Peter Jackson. SP: Peter Jackson, Frances Walsh. Cast: Melanie Lynskey, Kate Winslet, Sarah Peirse, Diana Kent, Clive Merrison, Simon O'Connor.

In 1954 two teenage girls living in Christchurch, New Zealand, bludgeoned to death the mother (Peirse) of one of the girls. The brutal true murder shocked the country, especially when the girls showed no remorse and professed to love one another. The story became the basis for this stunning, disturbing film in which the girls (Lynskey and Winslet) are shown living in a world of fantasy that overwhelmed them and led them inexorably to committing the crime. The movie's hallucinatory style meshes perfectly with the subject matter.

HELL ON FRISCO BAY

★★☆ Warner Bros., 1955, c, 98 min. Dir: Frank Tuttle. SP: Martin Rackin, Sydney Boehm, b/o on novel by William P. McGivern. Cast: Alan Ladd, Edward G. Robinson, Joanne Dru, William Demarest, Paul Stewart, Perry Lopez, Fay Wray.

Robinson is up to his old tricks here, bringing some juice and bite to this standard melodrama. He plays the ruthless kingpin of the San Francisco fishing wharves, who tangles with Ladd, a man bent on revenge for being framed by Robinson into San Quentin. The ensuing mayhem is cut from familiar cloth, but with Robinson snarling his way through his role, it all moves at a lively clip. Nobody could gnaw on a cigar like Robinson.

HENRY, PORTRAIT OF A SERIAL KILLER

★★★ Maljack, 1990, c, 90 min. Dir: John McNaughton. SP: Richard Fire, John McNaughton. Cast: Michael Rooker, Tom Towles, Tracy Arnold.

Artfully made and well directed, this cult film is, nevertheless, singularly unpleasant and is not for the squeamish. Loosely based on a true-life Texas mass murderer, the movie centers on Henry (Rooker), a deranged but seemingly normal serial killer who teams up with dull-witted Otis (Towles) in a random orgy of murder. Otis's sister Becky (Arnold) has the bad luck to fall in love with Henry. Henry's motive for killing—his rage at an abusive prostitute mother—is something of a cliché, but the film, if you can stand it, is chilling and riveting. Made in 1986.

HE WALKED BY NIGHT

★★★ Eagle-Lion, 1949, b/w, 79 min. Dir: Alfred Werker (uncredited: Anthony Mann). SP: John C. Higgins and Crane Wilbur, b/o story by Crane Wilbur. Cast: Richard Basehart, Scott Brady, Roy Roberts, Whit Bissell, Jack Webb, Jimmy Cardwell.

A melodrama in the semidocumentary style popular in the late forties, *He Walked by Night* is essentially built around the police's hunt for Ray Morgan (Basehart), a smart, technically skilled thief and murderer who eludes capture by fleeing through the sewers beneath Los Angeles. The movie concentrates on the details of police work, but Basehart still manages to stand out as the lonely, alienated criminal for whom time is running out.

HIDE IN PLAIN SIGHT

★★★ MGM, 1980, c, 98 min. Dir: James Caan. SP: Spencer Eastman, b/o book by Leslie Waller. Cast: James Caan, Jill Eikenberry, Robert Viharo, Joe Grifasi, Barbra Rae, Kenneth McMillan, Danny Aiello, Josef Sommer.

Caan made his director's debut, and also starred in, this straightforward, reasonably absorbing film about the true ordeal of a factory worker named Tom Hacklin. When his ex-wife (Rae) marries a third-rate mobster (Viharo) who is willing to testify against the mob, she and her two children are put into the witness protection program, which obliterates their identities. Most of the movie is devoted to Hacklin's long search for his children. (It actually took him eight years and not eighteen months as in the film.)

HIDER IN THE HOUSE

★ Vestron, 1991, c, 102 min. Dir: Matthew Patrick. SP: Lem Dobbs. Cast: Gary Busey, Mimi Rogers, Michael McKean, Elizabeth Ruscio, Kurt Christopher Kinder, Cindy Hutson, Bruce Glover.

Deeply disturbed by a traumatic past, Tom Sykes (Busey) longs for a "home" of his own. So what does he do? He moves secretly into a hidden part of the new house of a dysfunctional family and schemes to eliminate the father (McKean) and take over the mother (Rogers) and kids. (Don't ask how he manages to live there.) When things go wrong, he turns violent. With a premise this ridiculous, nothing can go right, and it doesn't. The climax is especially silly.

HIGH SIERRA

★★★ Warner Bros., 1941, b/w, 100 min. Dir: Raoul Walsh. SP: John Huston, W. R. Burnett, b/o novel by W. R. Burnett. Cast: Humphrey Bogart, Ida Lupino, Alan Curtis, Joan Leslie, Arthur Kennedy, Henry Hull, Henry Travers, Barton MacLane, Cornel Wilde.

After reprising his stage role as cold-blooded killer Duke Mantee in *The Petrified Forest* in 1936, Bogart largely marked time as an all-purpose secondary lead until he starred in this gangster melodrama. He created a stir playing brooding, doomed Roy ("Mad Dog") Earle, an ex-convict who finds himself out of step with the world around him. He intends to rob again but is sidetracked by his love and concern for a crippled girl (Leslie). His moll (Lupino) remains loyal, and her final, triumphant cry of "He's free! He's free!" is a memorable moment in this competently made film. Remade twice, as a 1949 Western called *Colorado Territory* and as *I Died a Thousand Times* (1955).

HIS KIND OF WOMAN

★★★ RKO, 1951, b/w, 120 min. Dir: John Farrow. SP: Frank Fenton, Jack Leonard. Cast: Robert Mitchum, Jane Russell, Vincent Price, Raymond Burr, Tim Holt, Charles McGraw, Marjorie Reynolds, Jim Backus, Leslye Banning.

This absurd but entertaining tongue-in-cheek melodrama stars Mitchum as a two-bit gambler who is hired by deported gangster Burr to meet him in Mexico. Burr's secret intention is to assume Mitchum's identity and return to the States and regain control of his underworld empire. Along the way Mitchum meets Russell, and the erotic sparks begin to fly. Price plays the ham actor Russell is trying to snare. The movie mixes action with spoofing in-jokes and succeeds in being good fun.

HIT!

★★ Paramount, 1973, c, 134 min. Dir: Sidney J. Furie. SP: Alan R. Trustman, David M. Wolf. Cast: Billy Dee Williams, Richard Pryor, Paul Hampton, Gwen Welles, Warren Kemmerling, Janet Brandt, Sid Melton.

An overlong and hectic caper movie, centering on a federal agent (Williams) who, after his teenaged daughter is killed by drugs, decides to recruit, finance, train, and transport to France a band of private American citizens willing to assassinate the nine leaders of a Marseilles drug syndicate. Are you following this? Much familiar mayhem, and one very curious idea: two members of Williams's band are an old Jewish immigrant couple (Brandt and Melton) who are grateful to America for giving them "a second chance." They show their gratitude by blithely killing three of the band's targets. Now what do they do for an encore?

HITCHER, THE

★ TriStar, 1986, c, 97 min. Dir: Robert Harmon. SP: Eric Red. Cast: Rutger Hauer, C. Thomas Howell, Jennifer Jason Leigh, Jeffrey DeMunn, Billy Greenbush.

A grisly thriller that defies all logic and reason, this utterly depressing movie has C. Thomas Howell as a luckless young man who, on a journey through the desert, picks up the Hitchhiker from Hell (Hauer), a demented serial killer with the almost supernatural

Humphrey Bogart meets with accomplices Arthur Kennedy and Alan Curtis in
High Sierra (1941) as Bogart's moll, Ida Lupino, listens in.

ability to turn up everywhere. The movie grows more preposterous as it goes along, and the climax is beyond belief.

HITCH-HIKER, THE

★★★ RKO, 1953, b/w, 71 min. Dir: Ida Lupino. SP: Collier Young, Ida Lupino, adapted by Robert Joseph from story by Daniel Mainwaring. Cast: Edmond O'Brien, Frank Lovejoy, William Talman, Jose Torvay.

Directed by actress Lupino, *The Hitch-Hiker* is a spare but taut melodrama with the simplest of premises. On a fishing trip in Mexico, two businessmen (O'Brien and Lovejoy) are held hostage by a psychotic serial killer (Talman),

who terrorizes them at gunpoint. Most of the action takes place in the car, which gives the movie a claustrophobic feeling.

HIT LIST

★☆ CineTel Films, 1989, c, 87 min. Dir: William Lustig. SP: John Goff, Peter Brosnan, b/o story by Aubrey K. Rattan. Cast: Jan-Michael Vincent, Lance Henriksen, Rip Torn, Leo Rossi, Jere Burns, Ken Lerner, Harriet Hall.

Though this crime thriller has a passable idea—gangster Rossi is set to be a material witness against crime boss Torn—the movie is sunk by an inept screenplay. Cold-blooded hit

TOUGH GUYS

Every moviegoer (at least of a certain age) knows about the legendary tough guys of the screen: the swaggering, brawling, gun-toting actors such as Humphrey Bogart, Edward G. Robinson, James Cagney, and their later counterparts. But the next time you watch a vintage movie, scan the credits for the following actors; surely you'll remember that you've seen them before, giving sturdy support to the stars on many occasions.

ELISHA COOK, JR. (1902–1995)

Elisha Cook, Jr., will be forever recalled as Wilmer, the scrappy but ineffectual little "gunsel" in John Huston's classic film *The Maltese Falcon* (1941). Through a very long career Cook played an assortment of weak, cowardly, or neurotic lowlifes who often came to a bad end. His drum solo in *Phantom Lady* (1944) was the movie's highlight, and he had a memorable death scene (by poison) in *The Big Sleep* (1946).

BARTON MACLANE (1900–1969)

Barton MacLane was usually (as the song goes) "meaner than a junkyard dog," and even when he was on the side of the law, as in *The Maltese Falcon*, he was not exactly kind of heart. MacLane made scores of movies after his debut in 1924, giving his all to his mostly villainous roles. He was the nasty hood who machine-gunned poor gunmoll Ann Dvorak in a phone booth in *G-Men* (1935), and years later he made the mistake of trying to cheat Humphrey Bogart in *The Treasure of the Sierra Madre* (1947).

MIKE MAZURKI (1909–1990)

Formerly a heavyweight wrestler, giantlike Mike Mazurki will probably best be remembered as Moose Malloy, the dull-witted hulk who sets the ball rolling in *Murder, My Sweet* (1945) by asking Dick Powell's Philip Marlowe to search for "my Velma." Sometimes sympathetic, sometimes not, he loomed large in scores of other movies, including *Nightmare Alley* (1947), *Night and the City* (1950), and *Some Like It Hot* (1959).

MARC LAWRENCE (b. 1910)

If one of the hoods in a gangster movie is swarthy, tight-lipped, and sinister, he may well be Marc Lawrence. He came to Hollywood in 1933 and played nasty types in such noir films as *This Gun for Hire* (1942), *Dillinger* (1945), and *Key Largo* (1948). One of his most memorable roles was as Cobby in *The Asphalt Jungle* (1950). In the fifties he migrated to Europe, where he appeared in many Italian films and also directed some low-budget movies.

GEORGE E. STONE (1903–1967)

George E. Stone was Edward G. Robinson's loyal sidekick, Otero, in *Little Caesar* (1930). And twenty-nine years later he played "Toothpick Charlie," one of the hoods wiped out by George Raft on St. Valentine's Day in *Some Like It Hot* (1959). In between, from as early as 1916, Stone played character roles in nearly two hundred movies, often as a low-level gangster. Among his films were *The Last Mile* (1932), *Bullets or Ballots* (1936), and *Pickup on South Street* (1953). He also played the Runt, dim-witted friend to Chester Morris's gumshoe Boston Blackie, in a dozen "Blackie" movies of the forties.

man Henriksen is hired to kidnap Rossi's young son to keep him from testifying. By mistake Henriksen kidnaps the son of Rossi's neighbor, straight-arrow Vincent. Now Vincent and Rossi join forces to rescue the boy and put Torn away for good. Absurdly, Vincent turns from everyday Joe to sharp-shooting action hero in the flicker of an eye. Silly stuff, with Torn and Henriksen playing roles they could probably do in their sleep.

HITMAN, THE

★★ Cannon, 1991, c, 94 min. Dir: Aaron Norris. SP: Robert Geoffrion, Don Carmody. Cast: Chuck Norris, Al Waxman, Marcel Sabourain, Alberta Watson, Salim Grant.

Formula Chuck Norris action fare, fast-paced and gory. Norris plays a New York cop sent to Seattle after nearly being killed by his corrupt partner. In Seattle he infiltrates a drug-smuggling operation run by the local Mafia. Impressive stunt work, as always, but not much of anything else. The director is Norris's brother.

HIT THE DUTCHMAN

★ 21st Century, 1993, c, 116 min. Dir: Menahem Golan. SP: Joseph Goldman, b/o story by Alex Simon. Cast: Bruce Nozick, Christopher Bradley, Eddie Bowz, Will Kempe, Sally Kirkland, Jennifer Miller, Jeff Griggs, Jack Conley.

A gangster melodrama with one small distinction: it was filmed in Moscow, using Russian sets and costumes. Tracing the rise and fall of vicious gangster Arthur Flegenheimer (Nozick), who called himself Dutch Shultz, the movie is ghastly from start to finish. The familiar underworld figures turn up—"Legs" Diamond (Kempe), "Mad Dog" Coll (Bradley), and others—and even racketbuster Thomas E. Dewey (Conley) makes an appearance. All in vain: the general ineptness is staggering.

HOMICIDE

★★★ Triumph, 1991, c, 102 min. Dir and SP: David Mamet. Cast: Joe Mantegna, William H. Macy, Natalija Nogulich, Ving Rhames, Vincent Gustaferro, Rebecca Pidgeon.

David Mamet tries to graft his style of clipped, cryptic dialogue onto a police drama, with uneven results. Mantegna stars as a tough Jewish cop who undergoes a personal crisis when an old Jewish storekeeper is murdered and he is assigned to the case. Suddenly, his obsessive need to establish his own identity as a Jew leads him to acts of betrayal that have tragic consequences. Mantegna's transforma-tion from self-hating cop to vengeful Jew is never quite believable, but the movie sustains interest, and parts are compelling.

HONEYMOON KILLERS, THE

★★★ Cinerama, 1970, b/w, 108 min. Dir and SP: Leonard Kastle. Cast: Shirley Stoler, Tony LoBianco, Mary Jane Higby, Doris Roberts, Marilyn Chris, Kip McArdle, Barbara Cason.

An overlong but chillingly effective little sleeper based on the Lonely Hearts murder case of the late forties. Sleazy, self-styled "Lothario" LoBianco courts vulnerable women, then steals their money. Along comes Stoler, even sleazier than he is and also insanely jealous, and the couple launch a series of murders, with lonely women as their targets. Despite skimpy production values, this movie is riveting.

HOODLUM PRIEST, THE

★★★ United Artists, 1961, b/w, 101 min. Dir: Irvin Kershner. SP: Don Deer (Don Murray), Joseph Landon, b/o their story. Cast: Don Murray, Keir Dullea, Larry Gates, Cindi Wood, Logan Ramsey, Don Joslyn, Sam Capuano, Vince O'Brien.

An earnest, well-played film, based on the long career of the Reverend Charles Dismas Clark (Murray), a self-effacing Jesuit priest known for his rehabilitation work with former convicts in St. Louis. Dullea, in his film debut, plays Father Clark's doomed charge who ends up in the gas chamber in the movie's most powerful sequence. The anti-capital punishment theme is clear, but the motivations for some of the principal characters are somewhat fuzzy. Murray co-authored the screenplay under the name of Don Deer.

HOT ROCK, THE

★★★ Fox, 1972, c, 105 min. Dir: Peter Yates. SP: William Goldman, b/o novel by Donald E. Westlake. Cast: Robert Redford, George Segal, Ron Leibman, Paul Sand, Zero Mostel, Moses Gunn, William Redford, Topo Swope.

An entertaining comedy-melodrama, quite preposterous but also brightly written and played by a cast expert at this sort of amiable nonsense. Redford heads the cast as a professional thief and newly released convict who sets up a jewel robbery with assorted inept characters, including his brother-in-law (Segal). Of course, everything goes disastrously wrong as events spiral comically out of control. The centerpiece of the movie is the thieves's all-out assault on a police station.

HOT SPOT, THE

★★ Orion, 1990, c, 130 min. Dir: Dennis Hopper. SP: Nona Tyson, Charles Williams, b/o novel by Charles Williams. Cast: Don Johnson, Virginia Madsen, Jennifer Connelly, Charles Martin Smith, William Sadler, Jerry Hardin, Barry Corbin.

Sex and skulduggery in a hot little Texas town, so intense and overwrought that the movie edges into parody. The plot is classic film noir: Not long after Johnson, a handsome drifter with a hidden agenda, arrives in town, he is enjoying steamy sex with Madsen, a bored blonde with a hated husband (Hardin). Murder, blackmail, dark secrets—they're all here and all fairly dull under actor Hopper's indulgent direction. Johnson fails to register as a strong film personality.

HOUND OF THE BASKERVILLES, THE

★★★ Fox, 1939, b/w, 80 min. Dir: Sidney Lanfield. SP: Ernest Pascal, b/o novel by Sir Arthur Conan Doyle. Cast: Richard Greene, Basil Rathbone, Wendy Barrie, Nigel Bruce, Lionel Atwill, John Carradine, Beryl Mercer, Mary Gordon.

This reasonably faithful version of the mystery classic launched the long careers of Basil Rathbone and Nigel Bruce as eccentric sleuth Sherlock Holmes and his befuddled friend, Dr. Watson. Holmes and his colleague find themselves on the fog-shrouded moors, where their mission is to prevent a savage, expertly trained hound from murdering the lord of Baskerville Hall (Greene). Nicely atmospheric in a modest way, the movie was a surprising success, prompting the studio to make *The Adventures of Sherlock Holmes*. There were two other film versions of the story, in 1959 and 1977, and two television movies, in 1972 and 1983.

HOUSE OF GAMES

★★★☆ Orion, 1987, c, 102 min. Dir and SP: David Mamet. Cast: Lindsay Crouse, Joe Mantegna, Mike Nussbaum, Lilia Skala, J. T. Walsh, Steve Goldstein, Willo Hausman.

On the pretext of helping a patient, a highly repressed psychiatrist (Crouse) ventures into the sleazy and dangerous world of conmen and gamblers, with unforseen results. Her guide into this world is a devious conman (Mantegna) whose relationship with Crouse ends in a startling climax at an airport. Author Mamet made his directorial debut with this offbeat melodrama, which fascinates despite a slightly shaky premise.

HOUSE OF STRANGERS

★★★ Fox, 1949, b/w, 101 min. Dir: Joseph L. Mankiewicz. SP: Philip Yordan, b/o novel by Jerome Weidman. Cast: Edward G. Robinson, Susan Hayward, Richard Conte, Luther Adler, Efrem Zimbalist, Jr., Debra Paget, Paul Valentine, Hope Emerson, Esther Minciotti.

Much of the dialogue in this overwrought but absorbing family drama has an amusingly noirish tone, and the acting is good. Embittered Max Minotti (Conte) emerges from prison remembering the events that sent him there: the treachery of his three brothers (Adler, Zimbalist, and Valentine) and especially the despotism of his overbearing father Gino (Robinson). His thirst for revenge is eventually softened by his love for Irene (Hayward). Robinson dominates the movie as the family tyrant. Remade in 1954 as the Western *Broken Lance*.

HOUSE ON 92ND STREET, THE

★★★☆ Fox, 1945, b/w, 88 min. Dir: Henry Hathaway. SP: Charles G. Booth, Barre Lyndon, and John Monks, Jr., b/o story by Charles G. Booth. Cast: Lloyd Nolan, William Eythe, Signe Hasso, Leo G. Carroll, Gene Lockhart, Lydia St. Clair, Paul Ford, Harry Bellaver.

Joining Fox in 1943, producer Louis de Rochemont, creator (with Roy E. Larsen) of the famed "March of Time" series, brought a documentary-like realism to a number of narrative films. *The House on 92nd Street* was one of the first: a smartly executed melodrama, filmed at many actual locations, concerning the efforts of the FBI to uncover and thwart the espionage of Nazi agents bent on stealing part of the atomic bomb formula at the height of

World War II. Nolan brings a crisp authority to his role of Inspector Briggs, and Eythe plays a student of German parentage who risks his life by becoming a counterspy.

HOW TO MURDER YOUR WIFE

★★ Columbia, 1965, c, 118 min. Dir: Richard Quine. SP: George Axelrod. Cast: Jack Lemmon, Virna Lisi, Claire Trevor, Terry-Thomas, Eddie Mayehoff, Mary Wickes, Jack Albertson, Alan Hewitt, Sidney Blackmer, Max Showalter.

A black comedy, hectic and overstated in the style of the sixties, and also vitriolic in its attitude toward women and marriage. Lemmon plays a comic-strip artist and sworn bachelor who marries Italian sexpot Lisi while in a drunken stupor. Aided by his woman-loathing butler (Terry-Thomas), he devises ways (all unsuccessful) of getting rid of her. For reasons too foolish to contemplate, it ends with his trial for murder. A game cast is overpowered by the gamy material.

HUMAN DESIRE

★★ Columbia, 1954, b/w, 90 min. Dir: Fritz Lang. SP: Alfred Hayes, b/o novel by Emile Zola. Cast: Glenn Ford, Gloria Grahame, Broderick Crawford, Edgar Buchanan, Kathleen Case.

Based on Emile Zola's novel *La Bete Humaine* (filmed once before by Jean Renoir, in 1938), this tawdry melodrama has little to recommend it. Ford is the train conductor who is lured by Grahame, the sluttish wife of insanely jealous Crawford. Of course, no good can come of all this, and soon all the heavy breathing is followed by treachery and murder, not to mention some overwrought emoting. Ford and Grahame fared much better the previous year, under the same director, in *The Big Heat*.

HUSH . . . HUSH, SWEET CHARLOTTE

★★★ Fox, 1965, b/w, 133 m. Dir: Robert Aldrich. SP: Henry Farrell, Lukas Heller. Cast: Bette Davis, Olivia de Havilland, Joseph Cotten, Agnes Moorehead, Victor Buono, Mary Astor, Cecil Kellaway, Bruce Dern.

It begins with a grisly prologue: on a Louisiana plantation, Southern belle Charlotte (Davis) is suspected of murdering her lover, John Mayhew (Dern). Many years later, she is a dotty , reclusive old woman given to fearful fantasies. When her cousin Miriam (de Havilland) arrives, ostensibly to help and comfort Charlotte, strange events occur that evoke the terrible past and send her spinning into hysteria. Who is behind it all, and why? Designed to repeat director Aldrich's success with *What Ever Happened to Baby Jane?* (1962), also with Davis, this Grand Guignol thriller is absurd but entertaining. Davis has a field day flamboyantly repeating her madwoman routine from *Baby Jane*, and it's fun to see de Havilland take a brief vacation from her usual sweetness and light.

HUSTLE

★ Paramount, 1975, c, 120 min. Dir: Robert Aldrich. SP: Steve Shagan. Cast: Burt Reynolds, Catherine Deneuve, Ben Johnson, Paul Winfield, Eileen Brennan, Eddie Albert, Ernest Borgnine, Catherine Bach.

A pretentious, terminally bad screenplay sinks this police drama. Once again, as in *Save the Tiger*, writer Shagan has a brooding hero longing for a golden past. This time cop Reynolds dreams of leaving his ugly world for an idyllic life in Rome with his girlfriend, high-priced call-girl Deneuve. Meanwhile he investigates the death of a teenage girl and declares it a suicide. His partner (Winfield) and the girl's unbalanced father (Johnson) think otherwise, leading to trouble. In a word: awful.

I AM A FUGITIVE FROM A CHAIN GANG

★★★☆ Warner Bros., 1932, b/w, 93 min. Dir: Mervyn LeRoy. SP: Sheridan Gibney, Brown Holmes, b/o autobiographical story by Robert E. Burns. Cast: Paul Muni, Glenda Farrell, Helen Vinson, Preston Foster, Edward Ellis, Allen Jenkins.

The title aptly encapsulates the movie: Muni plays a jobless World War I veteran whose bad luck gets worse when he is innocently involved in a robbery and sent to prison.

The prison turns out to be a hellish place that brutalizes its inmates, and when Muni escapes, he becomes a hunted animal. This deep-in-the-Depression drama created quite a stir in its day with its view of a pitiless justice system and even prompted some reform. It may be primitive in the slam-bang Warners style of the early thirties, but the effect is still powerful. You're not likely to forget the movie's last line: now a desperate fugitive, Muni is asked by his fiancée (Vinson) how he manages to live. "I steal!" he hisses, then vanishes into the night.

I AM THE LAW

★★☆ Columbia, 1938, b/w, 83 min. Dir: Alexander Hall. SP: Jo Swerling, b/o stories by Fred Alihoff. Cast: Edward G. Robinson, Barbara O'Neil, John Beal, Wendy Barrie, Otto Kruger, Arthur Loft, Marc Lawrence.

Robinson, one of the screen's most formidable gangsters, turned in his machine gun for a stint as a lawman in this moderate melodrama. He plays a pipe-smoking law professor who is appointed as a special prosecutor against the burgeoning rackets in the city. The problem is that his chief supporter (Kruger) is actually the big-shot behind the rackets, and the man's son (Beal) is Robinson's straight-arrow assistant. Highlight: Robinson takes on three hoodlums with only his fists.

I CONFESS

★★☆ Warner Bros., 1953, b/w, 95 min. Dir: Alfred Hitchcock. SP: George Tabori, William Archibald, b/o play by Paul Anthelme. Cast: Montgomery Clift, Anne Baxter, Karl Malden, Brian Aherne, O. E. Hasse, Dolly Haas, Roger Dann.

Minor Hitchcock, with only a few good points. In Quebec the sexton of a church (Hasse) confesses his crime of murder to Father Michael (Clift). However, Father Michael himself becomes the chief suspect when his involvement with the victim and other circumstantial evidence are exposed. Sworn to silence by his vows, the priest cannot reveal the killer's confession. Some well-handled Hitchcockian moments are offset by the story's heavy-handed treatment and a lack of true suspense. Best feature: the Quebec setting.

I DIED A THOUSAND TIMES

★★☆ Warner Bros., 1955, c, 109 min. Dir: Stuart Heisler. SP: W. R. Burnett, b/o his novel. Cast: Jack Palance, Shelley Winters, Lee Marvin, Lori Nelson, Earl Holliman, Perry Lopez, Lon Chaney, Jr., Howard St. John.

This remake of *High Sierra* (1941) was written by the author of the novel, W. R. Burnett, and though it is more faithful to the book, it is actually inferior to the original verison. This may be due in part to the charisma of the original stars, Humphrey Bogart and Ida Lupino. Once again, Roy ("Mad Dog") Earle (Palance) is a doomed ex-convict, lost in a world he cannot understand. Winters is his loyal moll, Marie.

ILLEGAL

★★☆ Warner Bros., 1955, b/w, 88 min. Dir: Lewis Allen. SP: W. R. Burnett, James R. Webb, b/o story by Frank J. Collins. Cast: Edward G. Robinson, Nina Foch, Hugh Marlowe, Jayne Mansfield, Albert Dekker, Howard St. John, Ellen Corby, Edward Platt.

Robinson gives his usual forceful performance in this middling melodrama. He plays a fast-on-his-feet, double-dealing criminal attorney whose biggest client is ganglord Dekker. When his assistant (Foch) is falsely accused of murder, Robinson must turn on Dekker to defend her, thus risking life and limb. Mansfield appears as Dekker's very blonde and very bosomy moll. A remake of *The Mouthpiece* (1932).

I LOVE YOU TO DEATH

★★☆ Columbia/TriStar, 1990, c, 96 min. Dir: Lawrence Kasdan. SP: John Kostmayer. Cast: Kevin Kline, Tracey Ullman, Joan Plowright, River Phoenix, William Hurt, Keanu Reeves.

A top-notch cast is wasted in this hectic black comedy. Kline (with unconvincing accent) plays Joey Bocca, the Italian owner of a pizza parlor, a compulsively womanizing scoundrel married to Rosalie (Ullman). Rosalie's Yugoslavian mother (Plowright) urges her to kill him, and most of the movie is devoted to their ill-begotten efforts to send him to that great Pizza Parlor in the sky. They even hire two dim-witted hit men (Hurt and Reeves) to dispatch him. It all gets rowdy and out of hand. So much talent, so few laughs.

IMPULSE

★★☆ Warner Bros., 1990, c, 108 min. Dir: Sondra Locke. SP: John De Marco, Leigh Chapman. Cast: Theresa Russell, Jeff Fahey, George Dzunda, Alan Rosenberg, Nicholas Mele, Eli Danker, Lynne Thigpen.

Sexy undercover cop Theresa Russell, badly worn down by her job, makes a dangerous, impulsive error: she goes to the home of a rich, notorious drug dealer. When he is murdered, she evades the killer and desperately covers up her presence. At the same time she begins a torrid affair with a fellow cop (Fahey). Further complications put her romance—and her life—in danger. A good performance by Russell bolsters this not-bad but conventional thriller.

IN A LONELY PLACE

★★★☆ Columbia, 1950, b/w, 91 min. Dir: Nicholas Ray. SP: Andrew Solt, b/o story by Dorothy B. Hughes and adaptation by Edmund H. North. Cast: Humphrey Bogart, Gloria Grahame, Frank Lovejoy, Carl Benton Reid, Art Smith, Jeff Donnell, Martha Stewart, Ruth Gillette.

A dark, brooding melodrama, *In a Lonely Place* offers one of Bogart's more interesting performances. He plays Dixon Steele, an intense screenwriter with a fuse so short he is capable of exploding into a rage at any time. When a hatcheck girl (Stewart) is murdered, he becomes the chief suspect. He also begins an affair with his sultry neighbor (Grahame). Given his volatile nature, their relationship—which is actually more involving than the mystery—takes a possibly dangerous turn. Fans of this movie will recall Bogart's epitaph for the affair: "I was born when she kissed me. I died when she left me. I lived a few weeks while she loved me."

INCIDENT, THE

★★☆ Fox, 1967, b/w, 107 min. Dit: Larry Peerce. SP: Nicholas E. Baehr, b/o his television play. Cast: Tony Musante, Martin Sheen, Beau Bridges, Jack Gilford, Thelma Ritter, Ed McMahon, Jan Sterling, Gary Merrill, Brock Peters, Ruby Dee, Mike Kellin, Donna Mills.

A harrowing tale of urban violence, based on—and clearly showing its origins as—a television play. Two vicious thugs (Musante and Sheen) invade an oddly unattended New York subway car and proceed to terrorize the passengers as they board. One passenger finally opts to be a hero and pays with his life. The beleaguered characters are conveniently chosen to represent different walks of life, but since they are played by an interesting group of actors, the movie is watchable.

IN COLD BLOOD

★★★★ Columbia, 1967, b/w, 134 min. Dir: Richard Brooks. SP: Richard Brooks, b/o book by Truman Capote. Cast: Robert Blake, Scott Wilson, John Forsythe, Paul Stewart, Gerald S. O'Loughlin, Jeff Corey, Will Geer.

A stark, harrowing adaptation of Truman Capote's self-styled "nonfiction novel" concerning the actual murder of a Kansas family by two ex-convicts (Blake and Wilson) and the pursuit, capture and execution of the killers. Superbly photographed by Conrad Hall, the deliberately fragmented screenplay touches on the placid lives of the victimized farm family, the terrible past of the killers, and, in a horrifying flashback, the murders themselves. The film's documentary-like objectivity may be compromised by the grim execution sequence, but all in all this is an outstanding achievement by director-writer Brooks.

INFORMER, THE

★★★★ RKO, 1935, b/w, 91 min. Dir: John Ford. SP: Dudley Nichols, b/o novel by Liam O'Flaherty. Cast: Victor McLaglen, Preston Foster, Heather Angel, Margot Grahame, Wallace Ford, Una O'Connor, Donald Meek, Joseph Sawyer.

The luster of John Ford's classic drama may have dimmed somewhat over the years, but it's still a powerful and deeply moving film. Set during the Irish "troubles" in 1922, it centers on Gypo Nolan (Oscar-winner McLaglen), a brutish and childlike giant who betrays his best friend (Wallace Ford) to the Black and Tan for money to emigrate to America. Gypo's guilty disintegration through one long agonizing night is depicted with much feeling and perhaps too much symbolism. The final scene, in which he begs forgiveness from Ford's grieving mother (O'Connor) is one of the most memorable of the thirties. Ford, Nichols, and Max Steiner's haunting score also won Oscars.

INNOCENT MAN, AN

★★ Touchstone, 1989, c, 113 min. Dir: Peter Yates. SP: Larry Brothers. Cast: Tom Selleck, F. Murray Abraham, Laila Robins, David Rasche, Richard Young, Badja Djola.

Framed by crooked cops for a crime he did not commit, a happily married engineer (Selleck) is sent to prison, where he experiences a three-year nightmare. Helped by a hardened convict (Abraham), he learns the brutal rules of the prison, which help him to exact revenge on his release. This standard prison melodrama has little to recommend and a none-too-credible climax.

INTERNAL AFFAIRS

★★★ Paramount, 1990, c, 115 min. Dir: Mike Figgis. SP: Henry Bean. Cast: Richard Gere, Andy Garcia, Nancy Travis, Laurie Metcalf, Annabella Sciorra, Richard Bradford, William Baldwin, Michael Beach.

A grim, downbeat police drama that falls short on logic but is still quite gripping. Gere stars as Dennis Peck, a corrupt, vicious cop whose nefarious activities become the focal point of an investigation by straight-arrow detective Raymond Avila (Garcia). Eventually Avila uncovers more nastiness than he could ever have imagined, and the atmosphere turns steamy with sex and violence. Like so many similiar movies, *Internal Affairs* hurtles toward an improbably lurid climax, but until then it holds the attention. Best performance: Metcalf as a tough cop.

IN THE HEAT OF PASSION

★★☆ Concorde, 1992, c, 102 min. Dir and SP: Rodman Flender. Cast: Sally Kirkland, Nick Corri, Jack Carter, Michael Greene, Gloria LeRoy, Carl Franklin.

Modestly budgeted film noir with Kirkland as a married, sexually insatiable psychiatrist who picks up a would-be actor (Corri) and begins a torrid affair that inevitably ends in murder. Clearly the gullible Corri has never been to the movies; otherwise he would know that the lady is bad news.

IN THE HEAT OF THE NIGHT

★★★☆ United Artists, 1967, c, 109 min. Dir: Norman Jewison. SP: Stirling Silliphant, b/o novel by

Philadelphia policeman Sidney Poitier investigates a murder in a Southern town with police chief Rod Steiger in the Oscar-winning In the Heat of the Night *(1967).*

Rene Russo and Clint Eastwood are Secret Service agents protecting the presidential motorcade in In the Line of Fire *(1993).*

John Ball. Cast: Sidney Poitier, Rod Steiger, Warren Oates, Lee Grant, James Patterson, Quentin Dean, Larry Gates, William Schallert.

In the Heat of the Night won the Oscar as the Best Picture, but in retrospect this is surprising, since the movie is nothing more—or less—than a well-made melodrama with some social content. The acting, however, is exemplary, particularly by the leading actors: Poitier as a black Philadelphia cop who makes the mistake of visiting his Mississsipi home town when a leading white citizen has been murdered, and Steiger as the gum-chewing sheriff on the case. The two men tangle, then come together as uneasy allies while the town explodes with racial tension and violence. Director Jewison keeps the pace swift and the suspense high. Steiger also won an Oscar as Best Actor, as did Silliphant for his screenplay.

IN THE LINE OF FIRE
★★★★ Columbia, 1993, c, 126 min. Dir: Wolfgang Petersen. SP: Jeff Maguire. Cast: Clint Eastwood, John Malkovich, Rene Russo, Dylan McDermott, Gary Cole, Fred Dalton Thompson, John Mahoney.

A crackerjack thriller, exciting from start to finish, *In the Line of Fire* is essentially a cat-and-mouse story, but one with fleshed-out charac-

ters. Eastwood plays a Secret Service agent, a "borderline burnout" who is haunted by past demons, mainly his fatally delayed reaction at the Kennedy assassination. Malkovich is the brilliant psychotic who is planning to kill the current president. The two men enter a nerve-racking collision course that comes to an explosive (and beautifully orchestrated) climax at a posh Los Angeles hotel. Director Petersen keeps the pace swift and relentless, getting full mileage out of the many chase sequences. A top-notch movie of its genre.

INTO THE NIGHT
★★★ Universal, 1985, c, 115 min. Dir: John Landis. SP: Ron Koslow. Cast: Jeff Goldblum, Michelle Pfeiffer, Richard Farnsworth, Irene Papas, Kathryn Harrold, Paul Mazursky, Roger Vadim, Dan Aykroyd, Vera Miles, David Bowie.

Quite a cast was assembled (to play roles or walk-ons) in this entertaining if somewhat ramshackle comedy-melodrama. Goldblum stars as an engineer who becomes perilously involved with some stolen jewels and the assorted thieves and killers who want them. The girl in the case is Michelle Pfeiffer, and many of the offbeat characters are played by Hollywood directors, including Don Siegel,

Lawrence Kasdan, David Cronenberg, and others whom film buffs will enjoy trying to identify. (Even director Landis turns up as an Iranian hood.)

INTRUDER IN THE DUST

★★★ MGM, 1949, b/w, 87 min. Dir: Clarence Brown. SP: Ben Maddow, b/o novel by William Faulkner. Cast: David Brian, Claude Jarman, Jr., Juano Hernandez, Elizabeth Patterson, Charles Kemper, Will Geer, David Clarke.

In a small Southern town, an innocent old black man (Hernandez) is accused of murder and is threatened with lynching at the hands of an angry mob. The only townspeople on his side, who wage a desperate fight to save him, are a young boy (Jarman), a feisty old woman (Patterson), and a lawyer (Brian). Adapted from Faulkner's novel, the movie is an unusual entry from MGM, but it was made with some force and conviction. Highlight: the nighttime search for evidence in a graveyard.

I, THE JURY

★★ Fox, 1982, c, 111 min. Dir: Richard T. Heffron. SP: Larry Cohen, b/o novel by Mickey Spillane. Cast: Armand Assante, Barbara Carrera, Alan King, Laurene Landon, Geoffrey Lewis, Paul Sorvino, Judson Scott, Barry Snider, Julie Barr.

A gory version of the Mickey Spillane novel, previously filmed in 1953. Spillane's hard-boiled detective Mike Hammer (Assante) is out to find the men who murdered his friend, a one-armed policeman. His search puts him in contact with, among others, the beautiful head of a sex clinic (Carrera), a baby-faced psychopath (Scott), and a former-CIA operative (Snider). It ends with Hammer charging a booby-trapped hideaway by himself and without a gun. Violence and nudity prevail throughout.

I WAKE UP SCREAMING

★★★ Fox, 1941, b/w, 82 min. Dir: Bruce Humberstone. SP: Dwight Taylor, b/o novel by Steve Fisher. Cast: Betty Grable, Victor Mature, Laird Cregar, Carole Landis, Allyn Joslyn, Alan Mowbray, Elisha Cook, Jr., William Gargan.

Fox was hardly the studio one would associate with film noir, but this early entry in the genre is passable enough. Landis is a high-living, ambitious young model who is found murdered, and Mature is the sports promoter who is the chief suspect. Grable (in a temporary departure from her musicals) plays Landis's demure sister. There is the usual roster of other suspects, but the only interesting character is Cregar, a strange, obsessive cop who hounds Mature. Curious note: for some reason, the musical score includes frequent reprises of "Over the Rainbow." The movie was remade in 1953 as *Vicki*.

I WALK ALONE

★★☆ Paramount, 1947, b/w, 98 min. Dir: Byron Haskin. SP: Charles Schnee, adapted by Robert Smith, John Bright from play by Theodore Reeves. Cast: Burt Lancaster, Lizabeth Scott, Kirk Douglas, Wendell Corey, Kristine Miller, George Rigaud, Marc Lawrence, Mike Mazurki.

Despite the star power, *I Walk Alone* remains a relentlessly mediocre melodrama. Derived from a flop Broadway play, it stars Lancaster as an ex-convict seeking revenge on his doublecrossing colleague (Douglas), now a nightclub owner. He suffers a brutal beating, sees his best friend (Corey) killed, and shoots it out with Douglas before the cops move in for the kill. Scott is Lancaster's ex-girlfriend, who has taken up with Douglas, but not for long. Routine at best.

I WANT TO LIVE!

★★★ United Artists, 1958, b/w, 120 min. Dir: Robert Wise. SP: Nelson Gidding, Don M. Mankiewicz, b/o articles by Ed Montgomery and the letters of Barbara Graham. Cast: Susan Hayward, Simon Oakland, Theodore Bikel, Virginia Vincent, Philip Coolidge.

Hayward won the Academy Award for her bravura performance as Barbara Graham, a prostitute and crook who went to the gas chamber for a crime she did not commit. It's the sad, sordid story of a hapless woman who drifted into trouble and was sentenced for participating in a murder. The early portions are somewhat overbaked and obvious, making their points with a heavy hand, but then the film moves into a truly harrowing, step-by-step account of the execution in which Hayward pulls out all the stops. Oakland plays the reporter who fought to have Barbara's sentence overturned or commmuted. Remade for television in 1983.

JACK'S BACK

★ Paramount, 1988, c, 97 min. Dir and SP: Rowdy Herrington. Cast: James Spader, Cynthia Gibb, Jim Haymie, Robert Picardo, Rod Loomis, Rex Ryon.

Exactly one hundred years after Jack the Ripper terrorized London, a serial killer is at large in Los Angeles, scrupulously following the *modus operandi* of the Ripper. His target: pregnant prostitutes. This is the jumping-off point for a melodrama so wildly preposterous that it is tempting to give away the surprises of the plot as a cautionary warning. Suffice to say that there are two James Spaders (neither of them convincing) and nothing makes sense. Jack, go away again.

JACKSON COUNTY JAIL

★★☆ New World, 1978, c, 89 min. Dir: Michael Miller. SP: Donald Stewart. Cast: Yvette Mimieux, Tommy Lee Jones, Robert Carradine, Frederic Cook, Severn Darden, Howard Hesseman.

Pity poor Yvette Mimieux. Driving in Arizona on her way to New York, she is robbed of all identification, thrown into prison, and raped by the jailer, whom she kills in self-defense. She escapes, sharing a getaway car with an accused murderer and admitted hijacker (Jones). Mimieux gives an effective performance in this harrowing melodrama, which has developed something of a cult following. The principal flaw is that virtually *everyone* in the town appears to be evil and/or corrupt.

JADE

★★ Paramount, 1995, c, 90 min. Dir: William Friedkin. SP: Joe Eszterhas. Cast: David Caruso, Linda Fiorentino, Chazz Palminteri, Richard Crenna, Michael Biehn, Donna Murphy, Angie Everhart.

Beneath all the kinky sex activity in this movie is a conventional and muddled mystery thriller. David Corelli (Caruso) is an assistant district attorney investigating the brutal murder of a prominent figure. The principal suspect turns out to be Kristina Gavin (Fiorentino), a psychologist married to lawyer Matt Gavin (Palminteri), and a former lover of David's. The case involves blackmail, pornography, adultery, and other topics dear to the hearts of writers like Eszterhas. The movie's denouement is exceptionally murky, and please, no more chase scenes through San Francisco's Chinatown. (At least this one triggers casualties and rage from the area's citizens.)

JAGGED EDGE

★★☆ Columbia, 1985, c, 108 min. Dir: Richard Marquand. SP: Joe Eszterhas. Cast: Glenn Close, Jeff Bridges, Peter Coyote, Robert Loggia, John Dehner, Leigh Taylor-Young, Karen Austin, Lance Henriksen.

Did wealthy publisher Jack Forrester (Bridges) brutally murder his wife and maid? Lawyer Teddy Barnes (Close) takes his case, believing he is innocent, then swiftly (and improbably) falls in love with him. Now evidence mounts that he may indeed be guilty. Close and Bridges are superb actors, but they cannot surmount the glaring lapses of logic in the screenplay. Loggia won an Oscar nomination for his performance as a street-smart investigator for Barnes.

JANUARY MAN, THE

★★ MGM, 1989, c, 97 min. Dir: Pat O'Connor. SP: John Patrick Shanley. Cast: Kevin Kline, Susan Sarandon, Mary Elizabeth Mastrantonio, Harvey Keitel, Rod Steiger, Danny Aiello, Alan Rickman.

Kline is an eccentric fireman who was once a police detective. When a serial killer is loose, Kline's police commissioner brother (Keitel) is forced to rehire him to track down the killer. Sarandon is Keitel's wife and Kline's former girlfriend. Steiger plays the mayor. Don't worry if you're not following all this. This mixture of comedy and melodrama is a mess, inexplicably from the writer of that wonderful 1988 comedy *Moonstruck*.

JENNIFER EIGHT

★★☆ Paramount, 1992, c, 127 min. Dir and SP: Bruce Robinson. Cast: Andy Garcia, Uma Thurman, Lance Henriksen, Graham Beckel, Kathy Baker, Kevin Conway, Bob Gunton, John Malkovich.

A displaced Los Angeles cop (Garcia), tense and brooding after a nervous breakdown, comes to a small town and becomes convinced that a serial killer is on the loose, murdering blind women. The latest potential victim is a sightless girl (Thurman), with whom he falls in love. Of course nobody believes him until it is almost too late. This thriller begins sluggishly but picks up momentum in the second half. Malkovich, who can make even the most pleasant character seem malevolent, has a small role as a relentless police investigator.

J.F.K.

★★★☆ Warner Bros., 1991, c, 188 min. Dir: Oliver Stone. SP: Oliver Stone, Zachary Sklar, b/o book by Jim Garrison, other sources. Cast: Kevin Costner, Sissy Spacek, Joe Pesci, Tommy Lee Jones, Jay O. Sanders, Michael Rooker, Jack Lemmon, Walter Matthau, Donald Sutherland, Kevin Bacon, John Candy, Edward Asner.

Writer-director Stone's take on the Kennedy assassination, based on unsubstantiated evidence, would have us believe that it was a massive conspiracy involving the CIA, the military, the FBI, the mob, and even the White House. The chief proponent of this theory, a New Orleans district attorney named Jim Garrison (Costner) is portrayed as a courageous truth-seeker. You will probably regard this film as either a splendidly orchestrated exercise in special pleading, or an irresponsible effort that offers only speculative material. Either way, it's a vivid, absorbing movie with a large, impressive cast.

JIGSAW

★★ United Artists, 1949, b/w, 70 min. Dir: Fletcher Markle. SP: Fletcher Markle, Vincent McConnor, b/o story by John Roeburt. Cast: Franchot Tone, Jean Wallace, Myron McCormick, Marc Lawrence, Winifred Lenihan, Betty Harper, Hedley Rainnie, Walter Vaughn, George Breen.

Some atmospheric location photography in New York City is the sole virtue of this routine melodrama. Investigating two murders, assistant D.A. Tone uncovers a vicious hate group and places his life in jeopardy. Star gazers may enjoy spotting celebrities such as Henry Fonda, John Garfield, and Marlene Dietrich in tiny roles.

JOHNNY APOLLO

★★★ Fox, 1940, b/w, 93 min. Dir: Henry Hathaway.

SP: Philip Dunne, Rowland Brown, b/o story by Samuel G. Engel, Hal Long. Cast: Tyrone Power, Dorothy Lamour, Edward Arnold, Lloyd Nolan, Charley Grapewin, Lionel Atwill, Marc Lawrence.

A competent gangster yarn from a studio not exactly noted for that genre. Power is the devil-may-care college youth who becomes embittered and turns to crime when his father (Arnold) is sent to prison for embezzlement. Many complications later, father and son are involved in a prison break. Lamour plays a nightclub thrush with a yen for Power, and Grapewin does a nice turn in the cliché role of the erudite but alcoholic mouthpiece for the mob.

JOHNNY DANGEROUSLY

★★☆ Fox, 1984, c, 89 min. Dir: Amy Heckerling. SP: Norman Steinberg, Bernie Kukoff, Harry Colomby, Jeff Harris. Cast: Michael Keaton, Joe Piscopo, Marilu Henner, Maureen Stapleton, Peter Boyle, Griffin Dunne, Glynnis O'Connor, Danny DeVito, Dom DeLuise, Ray Walston.

A send-up of the old gangster movies that, like most movie spoofs, is a hit-and-miss affair. As a cautionary tale to a young boy, pet shop owner Johnny Dangerously (Keaton) tells the story of his rise and fall as a kingpin gangster of the thirties. All the clichéd characters are trotted out: the snarling mobster named Vermin (Piscopo); Johnny's resilient mother (Stapleton), racked by every ailment known to man, or woman; Johnny's straight-arrow brother (Dunne), and so on. Some of the gags are funny, but more often they fall flat.

JOHNNY EAGER

★★★ MGM, 1942, b/w, 107 min. Dir: Mervyn LeRoy. SP: John Lee Mahin, James Edward Grant. Cast: Robert Taylor, Lana Turner, Van Heflin, Edward Arnold, Robert Sterling, Patricia Dane, Glenda Farrell, Henry O'Neill.

The ads proclaimed, "Taylor 'n' Turner, Terrific Together!" Well, not exactly, but this typically glossy MGM melodrama can be fun to watch. Taylor is a big-time gangster who falls for a sociology student (Turner) who just happens to be the daughter of a prosecuting attorney (Arnold). What good can come of all this? No good at all. Taylor 'n' Turner are glamorous and lifeless, and acting honors go to Van Heflin as Taylor's alcoholic sidekick.

He won a Supporting Oscar for his performance.

JOHNNY HANDSOME

★★ TriStar, 1989, c, 94 min. Dir: Walter Hill. SP: Ken Friedman, b/o novel by John Godey. Cast: Mickey Rourke, Ellen Barkin, Elizabeth McGovern, Morgan Freeman, Forest Whitaker, Lance Henriksen, Scott Wilson, Yvonne Bryceland.

A gangster movie with a single gimmick but scant originality. Rourke is a grotesquely ugly man who is betrayed by his fellow thieves. In prison he undergoes surgery that transforms him into . . . well, Mickey Rourke. He gets his revenge, but it costs him his life. Barkin startles as the most vicious, unredeemable female ever to wander into this sort of film, but other characters are banal: Freeman as Johnny's Javert-like nemesis; Whitaker as a sympathetic doctor. And why does Rourke remain unkempt after surgery?

JUDGMENT NIGHT

★★★ Universal, 1990, c, 110 min. Dir: Stephen Hopkins. SP: Lewis Colick, b/o story by Lewis Colick, Jere Cunningham. Cast: Emilio Estevez, Cuba Gooding, Jr., Denis Leary, Stephen Dorff, Jeremy Piven, Erik Schrody, Peter Greene.

The premise is simple: during a night on the town, four suburban friends wander into Chicago's worst neighborhood and witness a gangland murder. Now they are pursued relentlessly by the gang members, until they must finally take a stand. As the violence increases, the situation becomes more improbable (where *is* a single soul who is willing to help them?), but there is an undeniable visceral excitement about a basic movie such as this, and it's quite well done. Leary makes a genuinely frightening gang leader.

JUICE

★★☆ Paramount, 1992, c, 94 min. Dir: Ernest R. Dickerson. SP: Gerard Brown, Ernest R. Dickerson, b/o story by Dickerson. Cast: Omar Epps, Tupac Shakur, Jermaine Hopkins, Khalil Kain, Cindy Herron, Samuel L. Jackson.

In Harlem vernacular, "juice" means power, nerve, bravado, and the four friends who seek it in abundance find that the price is terribly high. Q (for Quincy), played by Epps, is the most responsible—he dreams of becoming a disc jockey—while Bishop (Shakur) is the dangerous loose cannon, who triggers the tragic events. Directing for the first time, Spike Lee's cinematographer Dickerson gives the movie a visual flair but the material is basically trite, and the implied anticrime message is too submerged to be effective amid all the violent action.

JULIE

★★ MGM, 1956, b/w, 99 min. Dir and SP: Andrew L. Stone. Cast: Doris Day, Louis Jourdan, Barry Sullivan, Frank Lovejoy, Jack Kelly, Ann Robinson, Jack Kruschen.

An absurd lady-in-distress thriller, with Day as the wife of jealous, psychopathic Jourdan. She marries him unwittingly after he's strangled her first husband, then spends most of the movie being chased by him from Carmel to San Francisco. The climax, in which she must land a plane by herself after a deadly shootout in the cockpit, is unintentionally hilarious. The California scenery, however, is striking.

JUMPIN' JACK FLASH

★ Fox, 1986, c, 100 min. Dir: Penny Marshall. SP: David H. Franzoni, J. W. Melville, Patricia Irving, Christopher Thompson. Cast: Whoopi Goldberg, Jonathan Pryce, Jim Belushi, Carol Kane, Annie Potts, Michael Goetz, Jon Lovitz, Phil Hartman, Tracy Reiner.

Just another in the string of bad movies made by Whoopi Goldberg after her triumph in *The Color Purple* (1985). She plays a computer programmer who becomes involved in international intrigue when a British spy (Pryce) who is trapped behind the Iron Curtain locks into her terminal. Various odd characters emerge from the woodwork, none of them interesting or funny. Marshall made her directing debut with this movie and went on to better things.

JUROR, THE

★★★ Columbia, 1996, c, 118 min. Dir: Brian Gibson. SP: Ted Tally, b/o novel by George Dawes Green. Cast: Demi Moore, Alec Baldwin, Joseph Gordon-Levitt, Anne Heche, James Galdofini, Lindsay Crouse, Tony LoBianco, Michael Constantine.

Baldwin gives a convincing portrayal of

consummate evil in this not very plausible but frequently scary melodrama. Often speaking in a malevolent whisper, he plays the Teacher, a professional killer hired to intimidate a jury member in the murder trial of a major Mafioso (LoBianco). The jury member is a feisty single mother and aspiring sculptor (Moore) who undergoes her own trial by terror. Until midpoint the situation is tense and harrowing, but then the movie goes haywire, with one climax following another, culminating in a rather silly showdown in, of all places, Guatemala. Okay of this kind, but don't expect common sense.

JUST CAUSE

★★ Warner Bros., 1995, c, 102 min. Dir: Arne Glimcher. SP: Jeb Stuart, Peter Stone, b/o novel by John Katzenbach. Cast: Sean Connery, Laurence Fishburne, Kate Capshaw, Blair Underwood, Ed Harris, Ruby Dee, Ned Beatty, Lynn Thigpen, Hope Lange, Kevin McCarthy.

Fine actor Connery seems miscast in this contrived and rather preposterous melodrama. He plays a Harvard law professor, once a prominent lawyer, who is asked to represent a young black man (Underwood), on Death Row for eight years, convicted of the rape and murder of a young girl in a small Florida town. The man professes his innocence, and what Connery finds during his investigation is hostility from everyone and a maze of danger and deception. There's a surprise toward the end, but none of the film is believable, and the climax in a Florida swamp is ludicrous. A worthy cast deserves much better material.

KALIFORNIA

★★ Gramercy, 1993, c, 117 min. Dir: Dominic Sena. SP: Tim Metcalfe, b/o story by Stephen Levy, Tim Metcalfe. Cast: Brad Pitt, Juliette Lewis, David Duchovny, Michelle Forbes.

Pitt's consummate portrait of pure evil and Bojan Bazelli's fine camerawork are the only virtues of this oppressive movie. It has an original but none too credible premise: writing a book on serial killers, Brian (Duchovny) sets out with girlfriend Carrie (Forbes) on a cross-country tour of sites where the murders occurred. Stupidly, they pick up psychopath Early (Pitt) and Adele (Lewis), his brainless girl-of-the-moment, and soon liberal, intelligent Brian is overwhelmed by Early's brutality and wanton killings. (The irony is as heavy-handed as it sounds.) One revolting scene follows another, ending with yet another climactic shootout in that favorite movie site: a house filled with mannequins. (This time it's a nuclear test site—get the symbolism?)

KANSAS

★★ Cannon/Trans World, 1988, c, 108 min. Dir: David Stevens. SP: Spencer Eastman. Cast: Matt Dillon, Andrew McCarthy, Leslie Hope, Brent Jennings, Arden Dean Snyder, Kyra Sedgwick, Andy Romano.

Some pleasing Kansas scenery is the sole virtue of this too-familiar drama. Stranded in Kansas, McCarthy takes up with dangerous drifter Dillon and becomes the unwilling accomplice in a bank robbery. Fleeing with the money, he takes refuge on a farm, where he falls for the farmer's daughter (Hope). Then Dillon shows up, with fatal consequences. Tired, predictable, and not very interesting.

KANSAS CITY

★★★ Fine Line, 1996, c, 110 min. Dir: Robert Altman. SP: Robert Altman, Frank Barhydt. Cast: Jennifer Jason Leigh, Miranda Richardson, Harry Belafonte, Michael Murphy, Dermot Mulroney.

A marvelous jazz score is the best feature of this flavorsome if minor Altman film. In 1934 Kansas City, a girl named Blondie O'Hara (Leigh) kidnaps the wife (Richardson) of a bigwig politician (Murphy), hoping to exchange her for her errant husband (Mulroney). He is being held prisoner by a vicious underworld kingpin called Seldom Seen (Belafonte) for betraying a local black mob boss. Blondie's kidnapping caper leads to events both comic and violent. The movie has color and vigor, but Leigh grates with her usual mannered performance. (She always seems to be in private communion with herself.) Good work by Richardson and Belafonte, who surprises with a full-bodied performance.

KANSAS CITY CONFIDENTIAL

★★☆ United Artists, 1952, b/w, 98 min. Dir: Phil Karlson. SP: George Bruce, Harry Essex, b/o story by Harold Greene, Rowland Brown. Cast: John Payne, Coleen Gray, Preston Foster, Lee Van Cleef, Neville Brand, Jack Elam.

Actor Payne was deep in his tough-guy phase, after years of playing leads in Fox musicals, when he starred in this routine, competently made crime drama. He plays a bitter ex-con who must clear himself of participating in a bank robbery, executed by a quartet of masked hoodlums. Foster is the true criminal mastermind, and Gray is Foster's daughter. As is often the case in movies until the sixties, the police are even nastier than the criminals.

KEY LARGO

★★★☆ Warner Bros., 1948, b/w, 101 min. Dir: John Huston. SP: John Huston, Richard Brooks, b/o play by Maxwell Anderson. Cast: Humphrey Bogart, Edward G. Robinson, Lauren Bacall, Claire Trevor, Lionel Barrymore, Thomas Gomez, Jay Silverheels.

Anderson's Broadway play became a typically hard-driving Warners melodrama, with some of the play's high-flying sentiments diluted but not removed. Bogart is a cynical World War II hero who comes to a decrepit Florida hotel, where he clashes with a vicious gangster (Robinson) and finds love with the owner's widowed daughter (Bacall). Oscar-winner Trevor excels as Robinson's alcoholic mistress. Despite the symbolic underpinnings (democracy vs. Fascism), there is plenty of action to keep viewers awake.

KIDNAPPING OF THE PRESIDENT, THE

★★ Setel (U.S.-Canadian), 1980, c, 113 min. Dir: George Mendeluk. SP: Richard Murphy, b/o novel by Charles Templeton. Cast: Hal Holbrook, William Shatner, Ava Gardner, Van Johnson, Miguel Fernandes, Cindy Girling.

Nonsensical thriller in which U.S. President Holbrook is abducted by two terrorists, a Mexican (Fernandes) and a Radcliffe girl (Girling). Their goal: to teach America humility. ("Our leaders are all so arrogant.")

The cool-headed Secret Service chief (Shatner) springs into action. It is rather depressing to see two famous MGM alumni—Johnson and Gardner—in minor roles as the anxious vice president and his ambitious wife.

KILLER, THE

★★★☆ Circle Films (Hong Kong), 1989, c, 110 min. Dir and SP: John Woo. Cast: Chow Yun-Fat, Danny Lee, Sally Yeh, Chu Kong, Kenneth Tsang.

A veteran hit man (Yun-Fat) wants to end his killing career after one last job, and a relentless cop (Lee) is determined to capture him at any cost. When the mob double-crosses the hit man, he vows revenge. Soon bullets are flying as the bodies mount up. Sound familiar? Maybe, but the differences from other gangland melodramas are significant. This movie, filmed in Hong Kong, features a series of brilliantly staged, if improbable, shootouts and chases, plus some surprising depth in the main characters. Exhausting, but also undeniably exciting. Available with subtitles or dubbed in English.

KILLER INSIDE ME, THE

★★☆ Warner Bros. 1976, c, 99 min. Dir: Burt Kennedy. SP: Edward Mann, Robert Chamblee, b/o novel by Jim Thompson. Cast: Stacy Keach, Susan Tyrrell, Tisha Sterling, Keenan Wynn, Charles McGraw, John Dehner, Julie Adams, Royal Dano, John Carradine, Don Stroud.

Keach stars in this oddball film about a Montana lawman teetering at the edge of psychosis. Flashbacks reveal the traumatic childhood that brought him to this sorry state, which culminates in his killing several people. Keach gives a strong performance, but he is unable to surmount some of the shaky plot elements. Good support from some veteran actors, and Tyrrell stands out as a hooker who is one of Keach's victims.

KILLERS, THE

★★★☆ Universal, 1946, b/w, 105 min. Dir: Robert Siodmak. SP: Anthony Veiller, John Huston (uncredited), b/o story by Ernest Hemingway. Cast: Burt Lancaster, Ava Gardner, Edmond O'Brien, Albert Dekker, Sam Levene, Virginia Christine, William Conrad, Charles McGraw.

The movie begins with an artful replica of the original Hemingway story: two menacing

In a tense moment from The Killers *(1946), Burt Lancaster (with gun) confronts Albert Dekker (arms raised) and his thugs.*

gunmen come to a small-town diner, ready to seek out and kill the unresisting boxer called Swede (Lancaster). The rest is a darkly brooding, well-constructed extension of the story, flashing back to Swede's ill-starred criminal activities, especially his involvement with the seductive, treacherous Kitty Collins (Gardner) and kingpin crook Big Jim Colfax (Dekker). The 1964 remake starred Lee Marvin and featured Ronald Reagan's last movie appearance.

KILLERS, THE

★★☆ Universal, 1964, c, 95 min. Dir: Don (Donald) Siegel. SP: Gene L. Coon, b/o story by Ernest Hemingway. Cast: Lee Marvin, Angie Dickinson, John Cassavetes, Ronald Reagan, Clu Gulager, Claude Akins, Norman Fell.

Ronald Reagan as a ruthless crime lord? That's exactly what he plays in his last movie role, in this very free adaptation of Hemingway's story. This version has the two hit men (Marvin and Gulager) piecing together the story of the man (Cassavetes) they have just killed. Naturally a femme fatale (Dickinson) is involved, but otherwise the script bears little resemblance to the Hemingway story. Color and graphic violence add little to the mix. Stay with the very good 1946 version.

KILLER'S KISS

★ United Artists, 1955, b/w, 64 min. Dir and SP: Stanley Kubrick. Cast: Frank Silvera, Irene Kane, Jamie Smith, Jerry Jarret.

Admirers of director Kubrick will not find much evidence of his talent in his second feature film, a cheaply made film noir. A boxer (Smith) gets into deep trouble when he falls for a dance hall hostess (Kane) and arouses the murderous wrath of her jealous boss (Silvera). Perfectly awful dialogue and acting, plus a wild climax in a warehouse filled with mannequins.

KILLING, THE

★★★☆ United Artists, 1956, b/w, 83 min. Dir: Stanley Kubrick. SP: Stanley Kubrick, Jim Thompson, b/o novel by Lionel White. Cast: Sterling Hayden, Coleen Gray, Vince Edwards, J. C. Flippen, Marie Windsor, Ted de Corsia, Elisha Cook, Joe Sawyer, Tim Carey.

Director Kubrick finally attracted the critics's attention with this, his third film. A modest but suspenseful, well-crafted crime melodrama, it concerns the robbery of a racetrack by a group of sleazy men led by ex-con Hayden. Their plans go awry due to bad timing, bad luck, and a bit of treachery. All hands contribute to the movie's documentary-like feeling, but special kudos go to Cook and Windsor as a couple whose marriage is obviously doomed. The narration is intrusive, but *The Killing* moves relentlessly to a taut climax.

KILLING OF A CHINESE BOOKIE, THE

★★ Faces, 1976, c, 109 min. Dir and SP: John Cassavetes. Cast: Ben Gazzara, Seymour Cassel, Timothy Carey, Robert Phillips, Morgan Woodward, John Red Kullers, Meade Roberts.

Another self-indulgent exercise from director Cassavetes, who also wrote the screenplay. Gazzara, the owner of a shabby Hollywood nightclub, is forced to commit a contract murder as payment for a long-standing gambling debt. The movie is less concerned with the plot than with the characters who flock around Gazzara: the people who work at his club, the mobsters, and so on. A few gleams of insight emerge from the general incoherence, but that's about all.

KILLING ZOE

★ Davis Films, 1994, c, 98 min. Dir and SP: Roger Avary. Cast: Eric Stoltz, Jean-Hugues Anglade, Julie Delpy, Tai-Thai, Bruce Ramsey, Kario Salem, Salvator Xurev, Gary Kemp.

Avary, who co-authored *Pulp Fiction* with Quentin Tarantino, wrote and directed this utterly repellent and worthless movie, which may remind you of Tarantino's *Reservoir Dogs*. Safecracker Stoltz arrives in Paris to join his deranged friend (Anglade) and other low-life men in a bank robbery. The robbery turns into a horrifying bloodbath. The violence quotient is way over the top, and the movie's sole redeeming feature is Anglade's scary performance. Considering the film's events, even the title makes no sense at all. Quentin Tarantino coproduced.

KILL ME AGAIN

★★☆ MGM/UA, 1989, c, 95 min. Dir: John Dahl. SP: John Dahl, David W. Warfield. Cast: Val Kilmer, Joanne Whalley-Kilmer, Michael Madsen, Jonathan Gries, Michael Greene, Bibi Besch, Joseph Carberry.

Virtually every film noir cliché is trotted out for this rather laughable thriller, but in this case the laughs may have been intended. Kilmer is the dumb detective who is entrapped by wicked femme fatale Whalley-Kilmer. Soon they are fleeing from the police, the mob, and the lady's vicious boyfriend (Madsen), with double crosses waiting at every turn. Director Dahl fared much better a few years later with the excellent *Red Rock West* (1993).

KINDERGARTEN COP

★★★ Universal, 1990, c, 111 min. Dir: Ivan Reitman. SP: Murray Salem, Herschel Weingrod, Timothy Harris, b/o story by Murray Salem. Cast: Arnold Schwarzenegger, Penelope Ann Miller, Pamela Reed, Linda Hunt, Richard Tyson, Carroll Baker, Cathy Moriarty, Park Overall.

If you think this movie will be warm and fuzzy, judging by its title, think again. Schwarzenegger plays a tough undercover cop who is forced to impersonate a kindergarten teacher in Oregon in order to find and protect the ex-wife and small son of a killer on the loose (Tyson). The first part of the movie is amusing if predictable, with Arnold rising above kindergarten chaos to become a good teacher. Sentiment is thick, until the killer turns up, bent on kidnapping his son.

The resulting violence will frighten young children, so beware.

KING OF NEW YORK

★★ New Line, 1990, c, 103 min. Dir: Abel Ferrara. SP: Nicholas St. John. Cast: Christopher Walken, David Caruso, Larry Fishburne, Wesley Snipes, Victor Argo, Janet Julian, Giancarlo Esposito, Steve Buscemi, Theresa Randle.

As with *Bad Lieutenant* (1992), director Ferrara's flashy style is used to cover up the essential banality of his extremely violent tale of the rise and fall of a kingpin drug dealer. But here he has no central bravura performance —as he did with Harvey Keitel's *Lieutenant*— to keep us interested. Walken is lifeless as an ex-convict who destroys his rivals in a blood-splattered bid to become the criminal "King of New York." Warners' primitive gangster movies of the thirties did it all better, faster, and more economically.

KING OF THE ROARING TWENTIES

★★☆ Allied Artists, 1961, b/w, 106 min. Dir: Joseph M. Newman. SP: Jo Swerling, b/o book by Leo Katcher. Cast: David Janssen, Diane Foster, Mickey Rooney, Jack Carson, Diana Dors, Dan O'Herlihy, Mickey Shaughnessy, Keenan Wynn, Joseph Schildkraut, William Demarest, Regis Toomey.

An exceptional number of noted actors are caught up in this standard, fictionalized version of the rise and fall of notorious gambler Arnold Rothstein. Janssen in no way resembles the real-life Rothstein, and his laconic personality is ill suited to the role. Rooney has some good moments as Rothstein's ill-fated friend.

KISS BEFORE DYING, A

★★ Fox, 1991, c, 93 min. Dir and SP: James Dearden, b/o novel by Ira Levin. Cast: Matt Dillon, Sean Young, Max Von Sydow, Diane Ladd, James Russo, Martha Gehman, Joy Lee.

A tepid remake of the 1956 thriller, *A Kiss Before Dying* has Dillon in the Robert Wagner role of Jonathan Corliss, the charming psychopath who murders his rich, pregnant girlfriend (Young) and then sets his sights on her twin sister. He also kills everyone who can identify him as Young's secret boyfriend. The movie suffers from too many improbable, shaky plot points, and also from a poor performance by Young in a double role.

KISS ME DEADLY

★ United Artists, 1955, b/w, 105 min. Dir: Robert Aldrich. SP: A. I. Bezzerides, b/o novel by Mickey Spillane. Cast: Ralph Meeker, Albert Dekker, Paul Stewart, Maxine Cooper, Gaby Rodgers, Wesley Addy, Cloris Leachman, Percy Helton, Fortunio Bonanova.

Yes, *Kiss Me Deadly* is regarded as one of the seminal noir films of the fifties, hailed as "years ahead of its time" and "one of the genre's classics." Look again, and you'll find a dull, pretentious, and badly acted melodrama. Driving to Los Angeles, detective Mike Hammer (Meeker) is flagged down by a distraught woman (Leachman) who is apparently nude under her raincoat. From then on, he is plunged into an underworld of dangerous mobsters, wicked women, and sinister doctors. You may admire the busy camerawork, or it may give you a splitting headache. The ending is ridiculous, and so is this cult movie.

KISS OF DEATH

★★★ Fox, 1947, b/w, 98 min. Dir: Henry Hathaway. SP: Ben Hecht, Charles Lederer, b/o story by Eleazar Lipsky. Cast: Victor Mature, Brian Donlevy, Richard Widmark, Coleen Gray, Taylor Holmes, Robert Keith, Karl Malden, Anthony Ross, Mildred Dunnock, Millard Mitchell.

This crime melodrama may have lost some of its punch over the years, but the memory of Oscar-nominated Widmark in his first movie role as giggling psychotic killer Tommy Udo lingers on. The central figure is not Tommy but Nick Bianco (Mature), a hoodlum who keeps himself out of prison and near his daughters by spilling the goods on Udo and the gang. He becomes a target for revenge, leading to an explosive climax. Everyone recalls the shocking scene in which Udo pushes an old wheelchair-bound woman (Dunnock) down a flight of stairs. Filmed in actual New York City locations and remade in 1995.

In Kiss of Death *(1947), Richard Widmark (right) made a sensational film debut as crazed killer Tommy Udo, here on his way to prison with Victor Mature.*

KISS OF DEATH

★★★ Fox, 1995, c, 98 min. Dir: Barbet Schroeder. SP: Richard Price. Cast: David Caruso, Nicolas Cage, Samuel L. Jackson, Kathryn Erbe, Philip Baker Hall, Stanley Tucci, Michael Rapaport.

A remake of the 1947 melodrama, this movie uses only the broadest outline of the original story: thief Jimmy Gilmartin (Caruso) is caught in an attempted robbery and is sent to prison. When his wife is killed fleeing from an attemped rape, he instigates the mob's murder of the culprit by giving up names to the police and then hinting that the culprit was the "squealer." Three years later, he is promised his freedom if he will help to convict the kingpin gangster "Little Junior" Brown (Cage). His betrayal by the authorities leads to further mayhem. Caruso, making his debut as a leading man in films, displays the combination of toughness and angst he had as a cop on television's *NYPD Blue,* but he lacks big-screen charisma. Cage plays "Junior," the rough equivalent of the role that made Richard Widmark a star in his debut in 1947.

KISS TOMORROW GOODBYE

★★ Warner Bros., 1950, b/w, 102 min. Dir: Gordon Douglas. SP: Harry Brown, b/o novel by Horace McCoy. Cast: James Cagney, Barbara Payton, Helena Carter, Ward Bond, Luther Adler, Barton MacLane.

James Cagney followed his triumphant performance in *White Heat* by playing yet another vicious gangster in this poorly done melodrama. He plays a prison escapee who hides out in a small town where he plots robbery and murder with corrupt policemen and other unsavory types. He also has a jealous moll (Payton), who is ultimately responsible for his demise. As usual, Cagney dominates the movie with his galvanic performance, but the dull material defeats him. His brother William, who produced the movie, also has a small role.

KLUTE

★★★☆ Warner Bros., 1971, c, 114 min. Dir: Alan J. Pakula. SP: Andy K. Lewis, Dave Lewis. Cast: Jane Fonda, Donald Sutherland, Charles Cioffi, Roy Scheider, Dorothy Tristan, Rita Gam, Jean Stapleton.

Fonda won the Best Actress Oscar for her remarkable performance as Bree Daniel, a tough, cynical call girl who becomes the target of a serial killer. The movie is essentially a murder mystery, but the screenplay also dwells on Bree's relationship with an enigmatic detective named Klute (Sutherland), whose investigation of a missing friend leads him to Bree. The characterization of this odd couple gives added weight to the movie's thriller aspects, which end with a prolonged climax in a deserted garment factory.

K-9

★☆ Universal, 1989, c, 102 min. Dir: Rod Daniel. SP: Steven Siegel, Scott Meyers. Cast: James Belushi, Mel Harris, Kevin Tighe, James Handy, Ed O'Neill, Jerry Lee.

A misguided comedy-action movie in which loose-cannon cop Belushi teams with a German shepherd named Jerry Lee to bring down a vicious drug lord (Tighe). The joke is that Belushi treats the dog as if he were human, and the dog is made to react as if he really *were* human. A bad joke that went out with Dagwood's Daisy a half century ago. (Older movie buffs will explain.)

KNOCK ON ANY DOOR

★ Columbia, 1949, b/w, 100 min. Dir: Nicholas Ray. SP: Daniel Taradash, John Monks, Jr., b/o novel by Willard Motley. Cast: Humphrey Bogart, John Derek, George Macready, Allen Roberts, Susan Perry, Mickey Knox, Cara Williams.

"Live fast. Die young. And make a good-looking corpse." That's the motto of young Nick Romano (Derek), and sadly, he fulfills his aspirations. Bogart is the lawyer trying to keep him out of the electric chair by evoking the "society-is-to-blame" gambit. Based on a best-selling novel, the movie is poorly written, crudely staged, and noisily scored. Bogart tries hard, to no avail. Sequel: *Let No Man Write My Epitaph* (1960).

KRAYS, THE

★★★☆ Rank/Parkfield (British), 1990, c, 119 min. Dir: Peter Medak. SP: Philip Ridley. Cast: Billie Whitelaw, Gary Kemp, Martin Kemp, Tom Bell, Susan Fleetwood, Charlotte Cornwell, Steven Berkoff, Jimmy Jewel.

If you think that British movies are all gentility, tea, and crumpets, think again. This grim gangster film is based on the true-life careers of the Krays (Gary and Martin Kemp), twin brothers who were England's most notorious, most vicious gangster kingpins in the fifties and sixties. The violence quotient is exceptionally high as the pair scheme and murder their way to the top, then fall ignominiously in the time-honored fashion of these films. The movie spends considerable (perhaps too much) time on the psychological underpinnings of their criminal behavior but it's gripping nonetheless. Whitelaw is superb as the Krays's tough-minded mother.

LADY BEWARE

★★ Scotti Brothers, 1987, c, 108 min. Dir: Karen Arthur. SP: Susan Miller, Charles Zev Cohen. Cast: Diane Lane, Michael Woods, Cotter Smith, Viveca Lindfors, Peter Nevargic, Edward Penn, Tyra Ferrell.

Turned on by window dresser Lane's slightly kinky displays, married creep Woods begins by making obscene telephone calls and moves to breaking into her loft apartment. As the danger increases, so does her anger, and she eventually takes matters into her own hands. Just another of your basic man-stalks-woman movies.

LADY FROM SHANGHAI, THE

★★★ Columbia, 1948, b/w, 89 min. Dir: Orson Welles. SP: Orson Welles, b/o novel by Sherwood King. Cast: Rita Hayworth, Orson Welles, Everett Sloane, Glenn Anders, Ted de Corsia, Erskine Sanford, Gus Schilling.

Welles performed triple duty in this film noir, and the result is intriguing but also puzzling. Actor Welles sports an Irish brogue nearly as thick as Barry Fitzgerald's, and director Welles uses an assortment of stylistic flourishes to tell writer Welles's tale of an easily duped sailor who becomes murderously involved with a seductive woman (Hayworth) and her crippled husband (Sloane). The stunning, justly famous climax involves a shootout in an amusement park's hall of mirrors.

The Lady from Shanghai *(1948) features Orson Welles and Rita Hayworth in a famous "hall of mirrors" sequence.*

In Lady in a Cage *(1964), Olivia de Havilland finds herself trapped in her home elevator, a victim of vicious thugs. Veteran actress Ann Sothern (right) plays a blowsy accomplice.*

LADY IN A CAGE

★☆ Paramount, 1964, c, 94 min. Dir: Walter Grauman. SP: Luther Davis. Cast: Olivia de Havilland, James Caan, Ann Sothern, Jeff Corey, Jennifer Billingsley, Rafael Campos.

In the early sixties, a few of the movie queens of earlier decades, including Bette Davis and Joan Crawford, opted to appear in Grand Guignol melodramas, either as monsters or their hapless victims. In some cases this turned out to be a bad career move. Witness de Havilland in *Lady in a Cage*, in which she plays a wealthy, imperious widow who finds herself trapped in an elevator in her own home, the victim of a vicious trio of thugs who invade the premises. The actress is professional as always, but the movie is singularly repellent, wallowing in its ugly details. Caan makes his film debut, as the gang's nasty leader.

LADY IN CEMENT

★ Fox, 1968, c, 93 min. Dir: Gordon Douglas. SP: Marvin H. Albert, Jack Guss, b/o novel by Marvin H. Albert. Cast: Frank Sinatra, Raquel Welch, Richard Conte, Martin Gabel, Lainie Kazan, Dan Blocker, Pat Henry.

This inept sequel to *Tony Rome* (1967) has private eye Rome (Sinatra) entangled with another assortment of shady characters and buxom women in Miami Beach. Naturally there are several murder victims, including the blonde of the title whose nude body is discovered underwater by Tony at the movie's start. Much flippant dialogue for Sinatra, but very dull stuff indeed.

LADY IN RED, THE

★★★ New World, 1979, c, 93 min. Dir: Lewis Teague. SP: John Sayles. Cast: Pamela Sue Martin, Robert Conrad, Louise Fletcher, Robert Hogan, Laurie Heineman, Glenn Withrow, Rod Gist, Christopher Lloyd.

A fanciful but surprisingly brisk variation on the gangster genre, *The Lady in Red* centers on the woman, here called Polly Franklin (Martin), who was supposed to have fingered Public Enemy John Dillinger in 1934. Polly goes from small-town girl to prostitute, to Dillinger mistress, and then to her very own life of crime, finally ending up in Hollywood. The director keeps the pace lively and the atmosphere colorful, despite a limited budget. A.k.a. *Guns, Sin, and Bathtub Gin*.

LADY IN THE LAKE

★★☆ MGM, 1947, b/w, 105 min. Dir: Robert Montgomery. SP: Steve Fisher, b/o novel by Raymond Chandler. Cast: Robert Montgomery, Audrey Totter, Lloyd Nolan, Tom Tully, Leon Ames, Jayne Meadows, Morris Ankrum.

For this one film only, Montgomery took on the role of detective Philip Marlowe that Humphrey Bogart, Dick Powell, and others had assumed in other years. (He also directed.) The movie's single distinction is that it uses a subjective camera to tell its story—we follow the events as if we were Marlowe. This time the cynical private eye gets involved in murder and other skulduggery when he is called on to investigate the whereabouts of a missing woman. Some good film noir touches but the novelty soon wears thin.

LADY KILLER

★★★ Warner Bros., 1933, b/w, 74 min. Dir: Roy Del Ruth. SP: Ben Markson, Lillie Hayward, b/o story by Rosalind Keating Shaffer. Cast: James Cagney, Mae Clarke, Leslie Fenton, Margaret Lindsay, Henry O'Neill, Raymond Hatton, George Chandler.

A lively Warners programmer, with Jimmy Cagney as a New York mobster turned Hollywood movie star. He flees from the law to the West Coast, where he takes bit roles to stay in the background (Cagney as an Indian!), then makes it to the top by writing his own fan mail. When his old cronies arrive to rob Hollywood houses, he has to decide: gangster or movie star? Cagney punches it all home in his familiar cocky style.

LADY OF BURLESQUE

★★☆ United Artists, 1943, b/w, 91 min. Dir: William A. Wellman. SP: James Gunn, b/o novel by Gypsy Rose Lee. Cast: Barbara Stanwyck, Michael O'Shea, J. Edward Bromberg, Iris Adrian, Gloria Dickson, Victoria Faust, Marion Martin, Stephanie Bachelor, Charles Dingle, Pinky Lee, Janis Carter.

Stanwyck plays a star stripper determined to uncover the madman who is killing the other strippers in her company, in this fairly entertaining adaptation of a novel by famed ecdysiast Gypsy Rose Lee. She places herself in jeopardy but also finds time for a spot of romance with the company's chief comic, Michael O'Shea. Moviegoers of a certain vintage will enjoy seeing "tough" girls Adrian and Martin in supporting roles.

LADY ON A TRAIN

★★☆ Universal, 1945, b/w, 93 min. Dir: Charles David. SP: Edmund Beloin, Robert O'Brien, b/o story by Leslie Charteris. Cast: Deanna Durbin, Ralph Bellamy, Edward Everett Horton, George Coulouris, Allen Jenkins, David Bruce, Patricia Morison, Dan Duryea, Elizabeth Patterson.

Having shed her girlish ways, singing star Durbin was now free to play more conventional women's roles. Here she's a skittish young woman who is convinced that she has witnessed a murder from the window of a train. In the hoary tradition of "damsel-in-distress" movies, nobody believes her, and she sets out to solve the crime herself. Durbin gets to sing, of course, but she shows little aptitude for farce, which this sort of comedy mystery requires.

LAST BOY SCOUT, THE

★★☆ Warner Bros., 1991, c, 105 min. Dir: Tony Scott. SP: Shane Black, b/o story by Shane Black, Greg Hicks. Cast: Bruce Willis, Damon Wayans, Chelsea Field, Noble Willingham, Taylor Negron, Danielle Harris, Halle Berry.

Two men (one black, one white) bicker noisily and profanely as they barrel their way through explosions, chases, and shootouts—until the villains are defeated. No, this isn't *Lethal Weapon*, but not too surprisingly the author is the same, Shane Black. Featuring excessive carnage even by today's standards, *The Last Boy Scout* has ex-Secret Service agent-turned-detective Willis and ex-football-star-turned-druggie Wayans join together reluctantly to fight corruption in high places. The wildly incredible climax takes place at a football game.

LAST DANCE

★★☆ Touchstone, 1996, c, 103 min. Dir: Bruce Beresford. SP: Ron Koslow, b/o story by Steven Haft, Ron Koslow. Cast: Sharon Stone, Rob Morrow, Randy Quaid, Peter Gallagher, Jack Thompson, Don Harvey, Jayne Brook, Pamela Tyson.

As Robert De Niro's self-destructive wife in *Casino*(1995), Stone proved that she could act. Here she goes even further, eschewing all glamor to play death-row inmate Cindy Liggett in this extremely grim and unsparing but ultimately unsatisfying drama. Scheduled to be executed for a double murder, Cindy finds a last-ditch friend in lawyer Rick Hayes (a rather bland Morrow), who does not dispute her guilt but who does come to believe that she should not be executed. For all the emotional upheaval, the characters lack a fully rounded dimension, and the screenplay comes across as curiously underdeveloped and hollow. Stone, however, is just fine.

LAST EMBRACE

★★ United Artists, 1979, c, 102 min. Dir: Jonathan Demme. SP: David Shaber, b/o novel by Murray Teigh Bloom. Cast: Roy Scheider, Janet Margolin, John Glover, Sam Levene, Charles Napier, Christopher Walken.

Can a movie try to out-Hitchcock Alfred Hitchcock and come close to parody instead? Yes, and a case in point is *Last Embrace*. A series of ominous events tells government agent Harry Hannan (Scheider) that somebody is out to kill him. But who and why? Then he receives a note in ancient Hebrew that translates to "Avenger of Blood." Everyone is a suspect, including a graduate student (Margolin) who becomes his lover. Hitchcock could cover gaping plot holes with dazzling style, and he could make the preposterous seem credible. No such luck here. The climax at Niagara Falls is almost a shameless rip-off.

LAST MAN STANDING

★★ New Line, 1996, c, 100 min. Dir and SP: Walter Hill, b/o story by Akira Kurosawa, Ryuzo Kikushima. Cast: Bruce Willis, Christopher Walken, Bruce Dern, Alexandra Powers, David Patrick Kelly, William Sanderson, Karina Lombard, Ned Eisenberg.

Some day *Last Man Standing* may become a cult film, but for now it seems to be a serious mistake. So stylized that it comes close to parody, the movie stars Willis as a loner who comes to a ghost town in Depression Texas and finds two rival gangs—Irish and Italian—vying for control. He pits one side against the other until (you guessed it) he's the "last man standing." The movie is so relentlessly glum that the entertainment quotient is virtually nil. Based on Akira Kurosawa's classic *Yojimbo*, which itself inspired Sergio Leone's "spaghetti Western" *A Fistful of Dollars*. Indeed, *Last Man Standing* plays very much like a Western.

LAST MILE, THE

★★★ World Wide, 1932, b/w, 70 min. Dir: Sam Bischoff. SP: Seton I. Miller, b/o play by John Wexley. Cast: Preston Foster, Howard Phillips, George E. Stone, Noel Madison, Alan Roscoe, Paul Fix.

From the early sound years, a primitive but still fairly pungent prison drama, based on a 1930 play. The setting is a prison's Death Row, and Foster (billed as Preston S. Foster) plays the aptly named convict Killer Mears, who heads a murderous breakout of his cellblock. Phillips is the wrongly charged convict who witnesses the Death Row horrors. Remade in 1959 with (of all people) Mickey Rooney as Killer Mears.

LAST OF SHEILA, THE

★★★ Warner Bros., 1973, c, 119 min. Dir: Herbert Ross. SP: Stephen Sondheim, Anthony Perkins. Cast: James Coburn, Joan Hackett, James Mason, Richard Benjamin, Dyan Cannon, Ian McShane, Raquel Welch.

A wickedly clever mystery (perhaps a bit too clever for its own good), written by puzzle aficionadoes Sondheim and Perkins. Nasty jet-setter Coburn, whose wife Sheila was killed in a hit-and-run accident some time earlier, invites his friends to spend a week on his yacht. They will play an intricate game that will expose their dark, long-buried secrets, one by one. But then murder interferes to provide a new kind of diabolical fun for these self-absorbed people. The movie resembles those all-star Agatha Christie mysteries, this time lacquered over with a veneer of sardonic wit.

LAST OF THE FINEST, THE

★★☆ Orion, 1990, c, 106 min. Dir: John Mackenzie. SP: Jere Cunningham, Thomas Lee Wright, George Armitage, b/o story by Jere Cunningham. Cast: Brian Dennehy, Joe Pantoliano, Jeff Fahey, Bill Paxton, Guy Boyd, Lisa Jane Persky.

Able actor Dennehy can't do much with this passable police melodrama. He plays a dedicated cop who is suspended, along with three young protégés, after a drug investigation turns deadly. Nevertheless they stay with the case, until they have uncovered a major drug and gun-running operation devised to pay for contralike forces in Central America. (The parallels to the Iran-Contra affair are obvious.) Director John Mackenzie had a much better film in *The Long Good Friday*.

LAST SEDUCTION, THE

★★★ Oakwood Films, 1994, c, 110 min. Dir: John Dahl. SP: Steve Barancik. Cast: Linda Fiorentino, Peter Berg, Bill Pullman, J. T. Walsh, Bill Nunn.

In the great tradition of Barbara Stanwyck and Jane Greer, Fiorentino plays a classic film noir woman—seductive, amoral, and extremely dangerous—in this twisty thriller from the director of the clever *Red Rock West*. Adept at "bending the rules" and "playing with people's brains" (as someone says), she double-crosses her husband (Pullman) in a drug deal, seduces a restless small-town nerd (Berg), and causes a few deaths, all with cold-blooded aplomb. The movie is not as good as *Red Rock West*, but it's wicked fun.

LATE SHOW, THE

★★★ Warner Bros., 1977, c, 94 min. Dir and SP: Robert Benton. Cast: Art Carney, Lily Tomlin, Bill Macy, Eugene Roche, Joanna Cassidy, John Considine, Howard Duff, Ruth Nelson.

It may surprise you to find two first-rate comic actors like Carney and Tomlin in a violent crime thriller. But they acquit themselves very well as an aging detective and his very peculiar client. They join together to solve a series of murders, and as the plot twists and turns, a number of familiar noir types emerge to give them trouble or grief. The bodies pile up, but in the end the unlikely duo manages to survive the mayhem.

LAUGHING POLICEMAN, THE

★★☆ Fox, 1974, c, 111 min. Dir: Stuart Rosenberg. SP: Thomas Rickman, b/o novel by Per Wahloo, Maj Sjowall. Cast: Walter Matthau, Bruce Dern, Lou Gossett, Albert Paulsen, Anthony Zerbe, Val Avery, Joanna Cassidy, Cathy Lee Crosby.

It begins with the horrifying massacre of all passengers aboard a bus. When policeman Matthau arrives on the scene, he discovers that one of the victims is his fellow cop and partner. What was he doing on the bus? Matthau's investigation takes him into the city's grimmest neighborhoods, where he meets an assortment of unsavory citizens. A decent premise, but the movie tends to sputter in the unfocused, hectic style of the seventies.

LAURA

★★★★ Fox, 1944, b/w, 85 min. Dir: Otto Preminger. SP: Jay Dratler, Samuel Hoffenstein, Betty Reinhardt, b/o novel by Vera Caspary. Cast: Gene Tierney, Dana Andrews, Clifton Webb, Vincent Price, Judith Anderson.

"I shall never forget the weekend Laura died." With these words, spoken by acerbic, snobbish newspaper columnist and radio commentator Waldo Lydecker (Webb), this tantalizing film gets under way. One of the most stylish mysteries to come out of Hollywood, *Laura* involves a group of morally dubious New York society types in the apparent murder of a beautiful career woman (Tierney). A definite whiff of decadence hovers over such characters as Lydecker, a weak-natured gigolo (Price), and the victim's aunt (Anderson) who, by her own admission, is "not very nice." Strangest of all is the detective on the case (Andrews), who harbors romantic feelings for the victim, a girl he's never met. Preminger's direction is firm and smooth, and David Raksin's haunting theme permeates the movie. But it's Webb, making his sound-film debut, who steals it all with his caustic or egotistical quips. ("In my case, self-absorption is completely justified.") He was nominated for a Supporting Oscar. Joseph LaShelle won the statuette for his shimmering black-and-white cinematography.

Detective Dana Andrews (right) is about to accuse Gene Tierney of murder in the silken mystery Laura *(1944). Looking on are Clifton Webb and maid Dorothy Adams.*

LAWS OF GRAVITY

★★★ Island, 1991, c, 100 min. Dir and SP: Nick Gomez. Cast: Peter Greene, Adam Trese, Edie Falco, Arabella Field, Paul Schulzie.

A low-budget but gritty, absorbing Scorsese wannabe, this movie tracks a group of friends as they swagger, fight, and steal their way through the mean streets of Brooklyn. Under the surface is a tension that threatens to explode into violence at any moment. Jimmy (Greene) is the most responsible, and Johnny (Trese) the most volatile, and the three days in which we follow them and their friends end tragically, if predictably.

LEAVE HER TO HEAVEN

★★☆ Fox, 1945, c, 110 min. Dir: John M. Stahl. SP: Jo Swerling, b/o novel by Ben Ames Williams. Cast: Gene Tierney, Cornel Wilde, Jeanne Crain, Vincent Price, Ray Collins, Mary Philips, Gene Lockhart, Darryl Hickman, Chill Wills.

Pure pulp, gorgeously photographed by Oscar winner Leon Shamroy. In this adaptation of a best-selling novel, Tierney plays a woman so pathologically possessive and jealous of her adored husband (Wilde) that she attempts to destroy everyone around her. Crain is her vacuous sister and the target of her jealousy. Since these actors are barely adequate, the unfolding drama has little impact. The climactic trial sequence is a total absurdity.

LEGAL EAGLES

★★★ Universal/Northern Lights, 1986, c, 114 min. Dir: Ivan Reitman. SP: Jim Cash, Jack Epps, Jr. Cast: Robert Redford, Debra Winger, Darryl Hannah, Brian Dennehy, Terence Stamp, Steven Hill.

Mystery, comedy, and romance are stirred together in moderately entertaining fashion in this film. Redford is a lawyer assigned to prosecute the daughter (Hannah) of a famous artist for trying to steal one of her dead father's paintings. Winger is the court-appointed defense attorney. When some devious skulduggery seems to be behind it all, the two join forces to expose the truth. Lightweight but airily amusing.

LEPKE

★★☆ Warner Bros., 1975, c, 98 min. Dir: Menahem Golan. SP: Wesley Lau, Tamar Hoffs, b/o story by Wesley Lau. Cast: Tony Curtis, Anjanette Comer, Michael Callan, Warren Berlinger, Vic Tayback, Milton Berle, Barry Miller.

Curtis seems an odd choice for Louis ("Lepke") Buchalter, the notorious true-life mobster, but he gains in force and conviction as the movie progresses. Unfortunately too many sequences in the movie play like parodies of the gangster genre, weakening the overall impact. Comer plays Lepke's wife, who stays with him through thick and thin (more thick than thin), and Berle takes on a surprising straight role as her father.

LETHAL WEAPON

★★★ Warner Bros., 1987, c, 110 min. Dir: Richard Donner. SP: Shane Black. Cast: Mel Gibson, Danny Glover, Gary Busey, Mitchell Ryan, Tom Atkins, Darlene Love, Traci Wolfe.

Don't look for much sense and you might enjoy this noisy, ultra-violent police story. It's all slambang action as cops Gibson and Glover investigate a murder that leads to a powerful drug ring. Gibson is a loose cannon, teetering at the edge of a breakdown and suicidal with grief over his wife's death; by way of contrast, Glover is a happily married family man. Naturally their hostility turns to friendship and mutual support as they carry out their good cop-bad cop routine. Fast-paced, brutal, and extremely popular. Two sequels followed.

LETHAL WEAPON 2

★★★ Warner Bros., 1989, c, 113 min. Dir: Richard Donner. SP: Jeffrey Boam, b/o story by Shane Black, Warren Murphy. Cast: Mel Gibson, Danny Glover, Joe Pesci, Joss Ackland, Patsy Kensit, Derek O'Connor.

More of the same in this sequel to the hugely popular *Lethal Weapon*. Two policemen—loose cannon Martin Riggs (Gibson) and dependable family man Roger Murtagh (Glover)—battle a vicious smuggling ring headed by a suave but nasty South African diplomat (Ackland). Pesci is amusing as a motor-mouthed material witness placed in their protective custody. Nonstop mindless action and fun if you don't take it seriously.

LETHAL WEAPON 3

★★ Warner Bros., 1992, c, 117 min. Dir: Richard Donner. SP: Jeffrey Boam, Robert Mark Kamen, b/o story by Jeffrey Boam. Cast: Mel Gibson, Danny Glover, Rene Russo, Joe Pesci, Stuart Wilson, Steve Kahan, Darlene Love.

Less a movie than a series of action sequences sometimes laced with comedy, this third entry in the *Lethal Weapon* series has little to recommend it. Murtagh (Glover) is about to retire, but of course manic Riggs (Gibson) gets him involved in a case concerning the hijacking of a large cache of police guns. Pesci is on board again for comic relief. Russo is the tough cop with whom Riggs has an inevitable love-hate relationship. Their one erotic scene has a new wrinkle: they compare wounds received in the line of duty.

LET HIM HAVE IT

★★★☆ New Line (British), 1991, c, 115 min. Dir: Peter Medak. SP: Neal Purvis, Robert Wade. Cast: Chris Eccleston, Paul Reynolds, Tom Bell, Eileen Atkins, Clare Holman, Michael Gough, Murray Melvin.

A true story, and an exceedingly grim one. In England, in the early fifties, a young man

Bette Davis, in one of her best roles, is lying murderer Leslie Crosbie in The Letter *(1940).*

named Derek Bentley (Eccleston) was hanged for a crime he did not commit. Basically decent but mildly retarded and epileptic, he had been present when a volatile young friend (Reynolds) murdered a policeman during the course of an attempted robbery. Despite public outcry and desperate measures by his family, young Bentley was convicted and sentenced to death. Well made and engrossing, with especially fine performances by Bell and Atkins as Bentley's parents.

LETTER, THE

★★★★ Warner Bros., 1940, b/w, 95 min. Dir: William Wyler. SP: Howard Koch, b/o play by W. Somerset Maugham. Cast: Bette Davis, Herbert Marshall, James Stephenson, Frieda Inescort, Gale Sondergaard, Willie Fung, Bruce Lester, Cecil Kellaway.

From its famous moonstruck beginning, in which Davis shoots her lover, to the final moment in which she meets her fate, Wyler's peerless melodrama will rivet your attention. Davis gives one of her best performance as the wife of Malayan plantation owner Marshall, who claims self-defense in the murder until circumstances reveal her true, sexually thwarted nature. Stephenson is especially good as her lawyer, whose loyalty is mingled with contempt for his client and self-loathing. But Davis dominates the movie in her best flamboyant style. Originally filmed in 1929, remade in 1947 as *The Unfaithful* and again for television in 1982.

LIGHT SLEEPER

★★★ New Line, 1992, c, 103 min. Dir and SP: Paul Schrader. Cast: Willem Dafoe, Susan Sarandon, Dana Delany, David Clennon, Victor Garber.

Like other protagonists in Schrader's films, John LeTour (Dafoe) is an isolated figure in a nightmare world. He's an oddity—an ex-junkie with a conscience, who now works as a courier for a lusty, big-hearted drug dealer (Sarandon). LeTour is unhappy with his lot, and when the girl he loved most (Delany) comes back into his life, it may be time for change. Ultimately, however, he can find redemption only in violence. An odd, pretentious, but curiously absorbing movie, with some good and some murky moments.

Down on his luck, gangster Caesar Enrico Bandello (Edward G. Robinson) regales the flophouse crowd with tales of his prowess in Little Caesar *(1930).*

LIST OF ADRIAN MESSENGER, THE

★★☆ Universal, 1963, c, 98 min. Dir: John Huston. SP: Anthony Veiller, b/o novel by Philip MacDonald. Cast: George C. Scott, Dana Wynter, Clive Brook, Herbert Marshall, Gladys Cooper, Marcel Dalio, Tony Curtis, Kirk Douglas, Burt Lancaster, Robert Mitchum, Frank Sinatra.

A gimmick involving a number of major stars playing minor roles in heavy makeup is the main, or perhaps the only reason to watch this middling mystery film. Sleuth Scott investigates the "accidental" deaths of several people hovering in and around an estate in Ireland. Of course murder is afoot, and the culprit is finally revealed. The principal occupation in the area appears to be fox hunting, which takes up much of the movie's footage. Not one of director Huston's triumphs.

LITTLE CAESAR

★★★☆ Warner Bros., 1930, b/w, 80 min. Dir: Mervyn LeRoy. SP: Francis Edwards Faragoh, others, b/o novel by W. R. Burnett. Cast: Edward G. Robinson, Douglas Fairbanks, Jr., Glenda Farrell, Stanley Fields, Sidney Blackmer, George E. Stone, Ralph Ince, William Collier, Jr.

"Mother of Mercy, is this the end of Rico?" The last words of kingpin mobster Caesar Enrico Bandello (Robinson) have become part of movie lore, and rightly so. They mark the epitaph for a brutal killer whose infamous story still packs a wallop after nearly seven decades. *Little Caesar* traces Rico's life from his rise to the top of the Chicago underworld to his wretched defeat and death. Much of the action is undeniably crude in the style of many early sound movies, but Robinson's galvanic performance holds it all together.

LITTLE GIANT, THE

★★★ Warner Bros., 1933, b/w, 74 min. Dir: Roy Del Ruth. SP: Robert Lord, Wilson Mizner, b/o story by Robert Lord. Cast: Edward G. Robinson, Mary Astor, Helen Vinson, Kenneth Thomson, Russell Hopton.

In 1930 Edward G. Robinson achieved stardom with his blistering portrayal of *Little Caesar*. Only a few years later, he was spoofing that image in this lively comedy. He plays bootleg kingpin James Francis ("Bugs") Ahearn who decides to retire when Prohibition is repealed. He moves into high society to learn how the polo set behaves, but becomes the victim of a stock swindle. Naturally "Bugs" settles the score. Old-fashioned fun, with Robinson in fine fettle.

LITTLE MURDERS

★★★ Fox, 1971, c, 110 min. Dir: Alan Arkin. SP: Jules Feiffer, b/o his play. Cast: Elliott Gould, Marcia Rodd, Elizabeth Wilson, Vincent Gardenia, Alan Arkin, Jon Korkes, Donald Sutherland, Lou Jacobi.

Adapted by Feiffer from his own play, *Little Murders* is a jet-black satirical comedy that depicts an embattled, nightmarish New York City in which chaos rules and people are more than a little demented. Photographer Gould takes up with Rodd and her wildly dysfunctional family and his life becomes a living hell in which random murders are an everyday occurrence. Eventually he himself becomes a cheerful assassin. The events depicted are too ugly to be really funny, but some of the crackpot characters draw laughs. Funniest: Jacobi as a judge.

LITTLE ODESSA

★★★☆ Live, 1994, c, 98 min. Dir and SP: James Gray. Cast: Tim Roth, Edward Furlong, Moira Kelly, Vanessa Redgrave, Maximilian Schell, Paul Guilfoyle.

An extremely bleak, somber, but well-made drama, *Little Odessa* focuses on Joshua Schapira (Roth), a cold-blooded hit man for the Russian Mafia, who has roots in the Russian-Jewish community in Brooklyn's Brighton Beach. When he returns for a "hit" to his old neighborhood, his encounters with his bitter, weary father (Schell), his dying mother (Redgrave), and a younger, worshipping brother (Furlong) are ultimately tragic. Roth gives an exemplary performance, and the last view of his stricken face will probably haunt you for a long time. The other cast members are equally good. Writer-director Gray was only twenty-six when this was made.

LOAN SHARK

★★ Lippert, 1952, b/w, 74 min. Dir: Seymour Friedman. SP: Eugene Ling, Martin Rackin, b/o story by Martin Rackin. Cast: George Raft, Dorothy Hart, Paul Stewart, Helen Westcott, John Hoyt, Henry Slate.

As an actor, Raft had all the animation of a block of granite. Here he plays an ex-convict bent on wreaking revenge at a crime syndicate that murdered a relative. The climax has Raft and the leading hood shooting it out in an empty theater, a favorite site for movies of this kind.

LOCK UP

★★ White Eagle/Carolco, 1989, c, 105 min. Dir: John Flynn. SP: Richard Smith, Jeb Stuart, Henry Rosenbaum. Cast: Sylvester Stallone, Donald Sutherland, John Amos, Sonny Landham, Tom Sizemore, Frank McRae.

Stallone meets the Warden from Hell in this brutal, preposterous prison melodrama. With only six months to go on his prison sentence, convict Sly gets transported to a nightmarish prison where sadistic Sutherland is the man in charge. To bring Sly to heel, Sutherland draws on his Nazi-like henchmen and a really nasty lifer (Landham) for some horrific punishment. Will our hero succumb? No way. With one violent sequence after another, the movie makes not a whit of sense.

LONE STAR

★★★☆ Castle Rock, 1996, c, 138 min. Dir and SP: John Sayles. Cast: Chris Cooper, Elizabeth Peña, Miriam Colon, Kris Kristofferson, Matthew McConaughey, Clifton James, Frances McDormand, Joe Morton, Ron Canada.

In a small Texas border town, the remains of a body have been unearthed. Most likely the body is that of Charley Wade (Kristofferson), the much-hated, bullying sheriff who disappeared and was probably murdered twenty-five years earlier. The discovery sets in motion a chain of events that links the past with the present and involves racial, cultural, and familial tensions. Sayles's intricately plotted, utterly fascinating drama keeps a variety of characters, even minor ones, in perfect balance. One or two of the plot elements seem a bit worn, but on the whole the movie offers a pungent new point of view. Good acting by all.

LONGEST YARD, THE

★★★ Paramount, 1974, c, 121 min. Dir: Robert Aldrich. SP: Tracy Keenan Wynn, b/o story by Albert S. Ruddy. Cast: Burt Reynolds, Eddie Albert, Ed Lauter, Michael Conrad, Jim Hampton, Harry Caesar, John Steadman, Bernadette Peters.

Welcome to yet another movie prison apparently run by disciples of the Marquis de Sade. Brutality and corruption are still rampant, but at least this prison movie has a fresh idea: ex-professional football star Paul Crewe (Reynolds) is sent to a Florida prison, where the nasty warden (Albert) has one obsession: to make national champions out of his football team of mean-spirited guards. He orders Crewe to set up a team of convicts to play against the guards in a single test game, and naturally Crewe's team is expected to lose. But Crewe and his ragtag group of thieves and murderers have different ideas. An enjoyable, offbeat mixture of comedy and drama.

LONG GOODBYE, THE

★★★ United Artists, 1973, c, 113 min. Dir: Robert Altman. SP: Leigh Brackett. Cast: Elliott Gould, Nina Van Pallandt, Sterling Hayden, Mark Rydell, Henry Gibson, Jim Bouton.

Raymond Chandler's hard-boiled, uncorruptible private eye Philip Marlowe had been portrayed by Humphrey Bogart, James Garner, and others. In *The Long Goodbye*, Gould's Marlowe is a different sort: a grungy, shambling loner who seems to be a patsy to the world. He is accused of being an accessory to murder, gets beaten up by the hoods of a vicious gangster (Rydell), and is invited to find the alcoholic husband (Hayden) of a beautiful socialite (Van Pallandt). Marlowe is roused to action only by a friend's betrayal. Some critics championed this movie; other viewers found it disappointing.

LONG GOOD FRIDAY, THE

★★★☆ Calendar/Black Lion (British), 1982, c, 114 min. Dir: John Mackenzie. SP: Barrie Keefe. Cast: Bob Hoskins, Helen Mirren, Eddie Constantine, Dave King, Brian Hall.

Harold Shand (Hoskins) has it all. A top figure in the London waterfront underworld, he lives in a penthouse, has a devoted mistress (Mirren), and is setting up a really big real estate deal. Then, on Easter weekend, his life starts coming apart as a series of bombs kill his chauffeur and demolish his pub. Who is out to get him—and why? Shand learns the truth and exacts his revenge, but it may be too late. Hoskins achieved worldwide stardom in this gritty, brutal British gangster movie that is far removed from the country's tradition of gentility.

LONG KISS GOODNIGHT, THE

★★★ New Line, 1996, c, 120 min. Dir: Renny Harlin. SP: Shane Black. Cast: Geena Davis, Samuel L. Jackson, Patrick Malahide, Craig Bierko, Brian Cox, David Morse, G. D. Spradlin.

Samantha Caine (Davis) appears to be a cheerful, cookie-baking, small-town schoolteacher with a young daughter. But no: she's suffered from amnesia for eight years, and her true identity is as Charly Baltimore, a trained government assassin. And when this identity resurfaces after a car accident, everyone wants to see her dead. Soon, with low-life detective Mitch Hennessy (Jackson) as her reluctant, then willing, ally, she's dodging bullets, destroying bad guys, and rescuing her kidnapped daughter. A cynical, violent, utterly preposterous action thriller—but at least the makers *know* it's preposterous. Some of the dialogue is funny, and the action sequences (the only reason for movies such as this) are well-handled.

LOOKER

★★ Warner Bros., 1981, c, 94 min. Dir and SP: Michael Crichton. Cast: Albert Finney, James Coburn, Susan Dey, Leigh Taylor-Young, Dorian Harewood, Tim Rossovich, Darryl Hickman, Kathryn Witt.

Novelist turned writer-director Crichton created this silly business for the age of computers. Plastic surgeon Finney begins wondering why the beautiful models on whom he performs surgery are being thrown off tall buildings. It turns out that evil conglomerate head Coburn is responsible—his company produces computerized images of perfect models for television and political campaigns, then disposes of the original subjects. The movie sports some fancy hardware, but it doesn't make much sense.

LOOKING FOR MR. GOODBAR

★★ Paramount, 1977, c, 135 min. Dir: Richard Brooks. SP: Richard Brooks, b/o novel by Judith Rossner. Cast: Diane Keaton, Richard Gere, William Atherton, Tuesday Weld, Richard Kiley, LeVar Burton, Tom Berenger, Brian Dennehy.

Adapted from Rossner's best-selling novel, this film is a grim, sordid, and extraordinarily distasteful excursion into the lowest depths of one woman's life. Keaton plays a teacher of deaf children; her nighttime activities are much less innocent. A repressed Catholic with an abusive father (Kiley) and a wildly unstable sister (Weld), she has given herself over to the bar scene and to many one-night sexual encounters with a variety of men, some of them dangerous. One last encounter proves to be fatal. Without a single palatable character, *Looking for Mr. Goodbar* is a depressing viewing experience.

LOOSE CANNONS

★ TriStar, 1990, c, 94 min. Dir: Bob Clark. SP: Richard Christian Matheson, Richard Matheson, Bob Clark. Cast: Gene Hackman, Dan Aykroyd, Dom DeLuise, Ronny Cox, Nancy Travis, Robert Prosky, Paul Koslo, Dick O'Neill.

Another cop-buddy movie, and a pretty awful one. Hackman is a veteran of the vice squad; Aykroyd is a forensic expert who happens to be emotionally unstable. When he can't cope, Aykroyd assmes other identities, from Goofy to the Lone Ranger. Together the mismatched cops go after the villains in a hopelessly confusing case. A few car chases, no laughs.

LOVE AND BULLETS

★★ ITC/Grade (British), 1979, c, 103 min. Dir: Stuart Rosenberg. SP: Wendell Mayes, John Melson. Cast: Charles Bronson, Jill Ireland, Rod Steiger, Strother Martin, Bradford Dillman, Henry Silva, Michael V. Gazzo.

Sent to Switzerland by the FBI to bring back a gangster's moll (Ireland), police detective Bronson spends most of the movie evading or battling the hit men out to kill them both. Along the way he also falls in love with her. Ordinary fare for Bronson diehards.

LOVE CRIMES

★ Miramax, 1992, c, 92 min. Dir: Lizzie Borden. SP: Allan Moyle, Laurie Frank, b/o story by Allan Moyle. Cast: Sean Young, Patrick Bergin, Arnetia Walker, James Read, Ron Orbach, Wayne Shorter.

Young gives a flat performance in this ghastly film. She plays an assistant district attorney on the trail of Bergin, a photographer who seduces, abuses, and humiliates his women subjects. Young has her own sexual fantasies and problems, which emerge when Bergin takes her prisoner. The screenplay makes no sense whatever, and Young's climactic speech, in which she spews out her sexual hangups, is embarrassing.

LOVELY WAY TO DIE, A

★★☆ Universal, 1968, c, 103 min. Dir: David Lowell Rich. SP: A. J. Russell. Cast: Kirk Douglas, Sylva Koscina, Eli Wallach, Kenneth Haigh, Gordon Peters, Martyn Green.

Convinced that crooks are being coddled, tough detective Douglas resigns from the force. Attorney Wallach hires him to guard Koscina, whom he is defending on a charge of murdering her husband. Surprise!: Douglas falls for Koscina, and there's plenty of trouble ahead. Routine mystery tale of no particular interest.

MACHINE-GUN KELLY

★★☆ American-International, 1958, c, 80 min. Dir: Roger Corman. SP: R. Wright Campbell. Cast: Charles Bronson, Susan Cabot, Morey Amsterdam, Jack Lambert, Connie Gilchrist.

Add Machine-Gun Kelly to the roster of true-life gangsters (including Baby Face Nelson, Legs Diamond, Dutch Schultz, and others) who took their place in the movie sun during the fifties. One of the most notorious hoods of the thirties, Kelly is played here by Bronson, who moves from small-time robbery to big-time kidnapping without ever changing his expression. Following the usual pattern, he becomes crazier and more ruthless until he is finally captured.

MACK, THE

★★ Cinerama, 1973, c, 110 min. Dir: Michael Campus. SP: Robert J. Poole. Cast: Max Julien, Richard Pryor, Don Gordon, Carol Speed, Roger E. Mosely.

A highly popular black action movie (possibly because it was one of the first), *The Mack* centers on Max Julien, a street hustler and ex-convict who sets himself the task of cleaning up a corrupt California city. He is helped by Pryor, in one of his first films.

MACON COUNTY LINE

★★☆ American International, 1974, c, 89 min. Dir: Richard Compton. SP: Max Baer, Richard Compton, b/o story by Max Baer. Cast: Alan Vint, Cheryl Waters, Geoffrey Lewis, Joan Blackman, Jesse Vint, Max Baer.

Not exactly a travelogue for the South, *Macon County Line* relates a true story of two luckless brothers (Alan and Jesse Vint) who, along with their traveling companion (Waters), find themselves suspected of the brutal murder of a sheriff's wife in the rural Georgia of 1954. The movie is crudely made for the most part, and it takes too long to work up some genuine suspense. The outcome is decidedly grim, but apparently these are the facts.

MAD DOG AND GLORY

★★★ Universal, 1993, c, 96 min. Dir: John McNaughton. SP: Richard Price. Cast: Robert De Niro, Bill Murray, Uma Thurman, David Caruso, Mike Starr, Kathy Baker.

Murray is a dapper modern-day gangster. De Niro is a mild-mannered crime photographer (talk about reverse casting). When De Niro saves Murray's life during a robbery, the gangster rewards him by sending him bartender Thurman as a week-long gift. Inevitably De Niro and Thurman fall in love, and there's big trouble ahead for both of them. A good-natured, offbeat comedy-drama, *Mad Dog and Glory* is no world-beater, but it's entertaining. Caruso appears in one of his bigger pre-*NYPD* roles.

MADIGAN

★★★☆ Universal, 1968, c, 101 min. Dir: Don Siegel. SP: Henri Simoun, Abraham Polonsky, b/o novel by Richard Dougherty. Cast: Richard Widmark, Henry Fonda, Inger Stevens, Harry Guardino, James Whitmore, Susan Clark, Don Stroud, Michael Dunn, Steve Ihnat.

A solid police drama, made with crisp authority and close attention to detail, *Madigan* stars Widmark as a conscientious Manhattan detective on the trail of a serial killer. The movie seems to be as concerned with the day-to-day operations of the police department as it is with the manhunt, and this makes for some fascinating insights. Fonda is highly effective as the dogged police commissioner, and there is able support from Guardino as Widmark's partner and from Whitmore as a compromised chief inspector who is also Fonda's best friend.

MAGIC

★★ Joseph E. Levine, 1978, c, 107 min. Dir: Richard Attenborough. SP: William Goldman, b/o his novel. Cast: Anthony Hopkins, Ann-Margret, Burgess Meredith, Ed Lauter, David Ogden Stiers.

Viewers who remember one segment of the classic British film *Dead of Night* will recognize the plot of this rather dull and preposterous thriller. Hopkins is Corky Withers, a deranged magician-ventriloquist whose abusive, malevolent dummy takes on a life of its own, which Corky cannot control. The consequences include a double murder. Ann-Margret plays the woman—a long-ago high school friend—who becomes dangerously involved with Corky. Rent *Dead of Night* instead.

MAGNUM FORCE

★★☆ Warner Bros., 1973, c, 124 min. Dir: Ted Post. SP: John Milius, Michael Cimino, b/o story by John Milius. Cast: Clint Eastwood, Hal Holbrook, Mitchell Ryan, David Soul, Felton Perry, Robert Urich, Kip Niven.

A follow-up to the hugely successful *Dirty Harry* (1971), this second installment has Detective Harry Callahan (Eastwood) fighting to expose a secret band of vigilantes in San Francisco's police department. Since Harry himself was a sort of vigilante in his first movie, his stance as defender of the system is rather curious. The movie has the usual assortment of violent encounters, and Eastwood is his usual clenched-teeth enforcer of the law.

MAKE HASTE TO LIVE

★★☆ Republic, 1954, b/w, 90 min. Dir: William Seiter. SP: Warren Duff, b/o novel by the Gordons. Cast: Dorothy McGuire, Stephen McNally, Mary Murphy, Edgar Buchanan, John Howard, Carolyn Jones.

Eight years after being menaced by a maniac in *The Spiral Staircase*, poor Dorothy McGuire is having similar trouble in this oddly titled melodrama. Here's she's the editor of a newspaper in a small New Mexico town whose criminal husband (McNally) returns after eighteen years in prison, seeking vengeance. Now she must keep his identity a secret from her daughter (Murphy), while managing to stay alive. McGuire is, as always, appealing, but the material defeats her.

MALICE

★★☆ Columbia, 1993, c, 107 min. Dir: Harold Becker. SP: Aaron Sorkin, Scott Frank. Cast: Alec Baldwin, Nicole Kidman, Bill Pullman, Peter Gallagher, Bebe Neuwirth, George C. Scott, Anne Bancroft.

This tricky, would-be film noir thriller has a few surprises up its sleeve, but you will believe them only if you accept the surgical act that triggers the plot. Pullman and Kidman are a happily married couple who take in a boarder: a wildly egocentric surgeon (Baldwin). When Baldwin performs an emergency operation on Kidman that leaves her sterile, the lady seems bent on revenge. But of course much more is involved, including treachery and, ultimately, murder. The plot has a few twists that are baffling or make little sense. At least Baldwin seems to be enjoying himself.

MALONE

★★ Orion, 1987, c, 92 min. Dir: Harley Cokliss. SP: Christopher Frank, b/o novel by William Wingate. Cast: Burt Reynolds, Cliff Robertson, Cynthia Gibb, Kenneth McMillan, Scott Wilson, Lauren Hutton, Philip Anglim, Tracey Walter.

A subtitle might be: Burt Reynolds Saves America. He plays an ex-CIA agent who comes upon a high-level conspiracy to take over the country, led by an egomaniacal, power-mad right-winger named Delaney (Robertson). The taciturn Malone kills off Delaney's thugs one by one and also helps a nice young couple being strong-armed by the powerful Delaney. Anyway, *Malone* moves quickly, even if its hero doesn't.

MALTESE FALCON, THE

★★★ Warner Bros., 1931, b/w, 80 min. Dir: Roy Del Ruth. SP: Maude Fulton, Lucien Hubbard, Brown Holmes, b/o novel by Dashiell Hammett. Cast: Ricardo Cortez, Bebe Daniels, Dudley Digges, Una Merkel, Robert Elliot, Thelma Todd.

A decent and in some ways interesting first version of the Hammett novel. Inferior in most ways to the 1941 classic, it still has its moments. The plot is the same: detective Sam Spade and some unsavory characters grapple over the legendary black bird, but here Spade (Cortez) is much more of a womanizer, and the treacherous Brigid (Daniels), here called Ruth Wonderly, is much coarser than Mary Astor's sleek lady. Other differences point up the superiority of John Huston's version. Also remade in 1936 as *Satan Met a Lady*.

MALTESE FALCON, THE

★★★★ Warner Bros, 1941, b/w, 100 min. Dir: John Huston. SP: John Huston, b/o novel by Dashiell Hammett. Cast: Humphrey Bogart, Mary Astor, Sydney

Greenstreet, Peter Lorre, Elisha Cook, Jr., Lee Patrick, Gladys George, Jerome Cowan, Barton MacLane.

By now this third film version of Hammett's novel has earned well-deserved classic status. Huston's screenplay and direction are trim and taut, and the legendary performances bring Hammett's characters to vivid life. A tough, cynical private eye with his own code of behavior in an unsavory world, Bogart's Sam Spade tangles with a nest of vipers bent on murder and treachery in their pursuit of the priceless statue of a black bird. They include devious Brigid O'Shaughnessy (Astor), falsely hearty Kasper Gutman (Greenstreet), and effete Joel Cairo (Lorre). The movie was nominated for an Oscar as Best Picture.

Mary Astor is duplicitous Brigid O'Shaughnessy and Humphrey Bogart is detective Sam Spade in John Huston's classic mystery The Maltese Falcon *(1941).*

MANHATTAN MURDER MYSTERY

★★★ TriStar, 1994, c, 108 min. Dir and SP: Woody Allen. Cast: Woody Allen, Diane Keaton, Alan Alda, Anjelica Huston, Jerry Adler, Joy Behar, Ron Rifkin.

A minor but moderately amusing Woody Allen exercise, *Manhattan Murder Mystery* fits comfortably in the *Thin Man* mode of urban-couple-solves-mystery. Allen and Keaton play a Manhattan duo whose relationship is starting to fray. Then a woman neighbor dies suddenly, and Keaton begins to suspect that she was murdered by her husband. Trailed by a dithering Allen ("I'm not a night person!"), she follows all clues, until they are both in mortal danger. Inevitably the adventure revitalizes their relationship. Allen gets off some good quips, but it's all airily inconsequential. The climax in a movie theater draws on the famous "hall of mirrors" scene from Orson Welles's *The Lady from Shanghai*.

MANHUNTER

★★★ De Laurentiis/Roth, 1986, c, 119 min. Dir: Michael Mann. SP: Michael Mann, b/o novel by Thomas Harris. Cast: William L. Petersen, Kim Greist, Joan Allen, Brian Cox, Dennis Farina, Stephen Lang, Tom Noonan.

Writer-director Michael Mann, who launched the *Miami Vice* television series in 1984, applied the same flashy style to this odd and sometimes effective thriller. Petersen is a former FBI agent who has the weird ability to project himself into the mind of a killer. He becomes obsessed with destroying a particularly noxious serial killer (Noonan), with the aid of the last killer he captured, the deranged Dr. Hannibal Lecktor (Cox). (Yes, that's the same madman—here spelled differently—of *Silence of the Lambs*.) Things turn sinister, of course, and there are some macabre moments along the way.

MAN ON THE EIFFEL TOWER, THE

★★★ RKO, 1949, c, 97 min. Dir: Burgess Meredith. SP: Harry Brown, b/o novel by George Simenon. Cast: Charles Laughton, Franchot Tone, Burgess Meredith, Robert Hutton, Jean Wallace, Patricia Roc, Belita, William Phipps.

Actor Burgess Meredith tried his hand at directing with this atmospheric cat-and-mouse thriller. Laughton plays novelist Simenon's famous Inspector Maigret, who is tracking suspected killer Radek (Tone) all over Paris. There are a few suspenseful twists and turns in the story, but the real star of the movie is the City of Lights, where it was filmed. The famous landmarks shine much brighter than the plot. The director himself has a role as a near-blind knife-grinder.

MAN WHO KNEW TOO MUCH, THE

★★★ Paramount, 1956, c, 120 min. Dir: Alfred Hitchcock. SP: John Michael Hayes, b/o story by Charles Bennett, D. B. Wyndham-Lewis. Cast: James Stewart, Doris Day, Brenda De Banzie, Bernard Miles, Christopher Olsen, Ralph Truman, Daniel Gelin, Alan Mowbray, Hillary Brooke.

Hitchcock's remake of his own 1934 British film, this thriller may be less than vintage work from the director, but it sets a lively pace and boasts a few exciting sequences. As a doctor traveling in French Morocco with his wife (Day) and son (Olsen), Stewart has the misfortune of learning about the planned assassination of a leading political figure in London. To ensure his silence, the culprits kidnap his son, and now he must not only rescue his son but also prevent the assassination. In the Hitchcock way of suspense, the tension mounts as he sprints from one locale to another. On temporary leave from her frothy Technicolor musicals, Day gives a fine performance as the distraught mother. Oscar song: "Que Sera, Sera."

MAN WITH BOGART'S FACE, THE

★★★ Fox, 1980, c, 106 min. Dir: Robert Day. SP: Andrew J. Fenady, b/o his novel. Cast: Robert Sacchi, Franco Nero, Michelle Phillips, Olivia Hussey, Misty Rowe, Victor Buono, Herbert Lom, Sybil Danning, Jay Robinson.

A sometimes amusing, sometimes silly send-up of movie detective thrillers, this movie is explained by its title. Sacchi plays a man named Sam Marlow (a composite of "Sam Spade" and "Philip Marlowe"), who has plastic surgery to resemble his idol, Humphrey Bogart. After he opens a detective agency, Sam is called upon to find missing jewels called the Eyes of Alexander. Not surprisingly, a group of sinister or mysterious people are also after the jewels. Movie buffs will have fun spotting some old-time actors, including Yvonne De Carlo, Martin Kosleck (every other movie Nazi), and George Raft, in his last film.

MARATHON MAN

★★★ Paramount, 1976, c, 125 min. Dir: John Schlesinger. SP: William Goldman, b/o his novel. Cast: Dustin Hoffman, Laurence Olivier, Marthe Keller, Roy Scheider, William Devane, Fritz Weaver.

Most viewers will remember this movie for its almost unwatchable scene in which evil ex-Nazi—and dentist—Christian Szell (Olivier) tortures graduate student Babe Levy (Hoffman) with dental instruments. The plot: After Babe's brother (Scheider) is murdered, Babe is plunged into a nightmare world of international skulduggery, with Szell at the center. Szell has come to New York to retrieve a hidden cache of diamonds, and he and his cohorts would like to learn what Babe knows, or better yet, see him as dead as his brother. Some gaping plot holes—and a few excessively violent scenes—outweigh the genuine moments of suspense.

MARKED FOR DEATH

★★ Fox, 1990, c, 96 min. Dir: Dwight H. Little. SP: Michael Grais, Mark Victor. Cast: Steven Seagal, Basil Wallace, Keith David, Tom Wright, Joanna Pacula, Bette Ford.

After federal drug agent (and martial arts expert) Seagal retires from the Drug Enforcement Administration to a sleepy small town, the town is invaded by Jamaican drug dealers. It's not long before Seagal and his family are marked for extinction. Not to worry—Seagal is on the case, crunching bones, gouging eyes, and shattering glass. Only good feature: music from reggae star Jimmy Cliff.

MARKED WOMAN

★★★ Warner Bros., 1937, b/w, 99 min. Dir: Lloyd Bacon. SP: Robert Rossen, Abem Finkel. Cast: Bette Davis, Humphrey Bogart, Eduardo Ciannelli, Jane Bryan, Lola Lane, Isabel Jewell, Henry O'Neill, Mayo Methot, Rosalind Marquis, Allen Jenkins.

Tough and gritty in the pounding Warners

In Marked Woman (1937), "hostess" Bette Davis is grilled on the witness stand by district attorney Humphrey Bogart.

style, this movie stars Bette Davis as a dance hall "hostess" (read prostitute) in thrall, along with other girls, to a big-time gangster (Ciannelli). When she threatens to squeal to the police, her sweet kid sister (Bryan) is murdered. Davis exacts her revenge, but with terrible consequences. The actress pulls out all the stops in her bravura, sometimes over-the-top style, and Ciannelli, one of the best movie villains, is chilling as the Lucky Luciano-like hood. But Bogart is merely adequate as a crusading district attorney.

MARLOWE

★★ MGM, 1969, c, 100 m. Dir: Paul Bogart. SP: Stirling Silliphant, b/o novel by Raymond Chandler. Cast: James Garner, Gayle Hunnicut, Carroll O'Connor, Rita Moreno, Sharon Farrell, William Daniels, Jackie Coogan.

Humphrey Bogart, Elliott Gould, and George Montgomery, among others, have tried their hand at playing Chandler's hard-boiled detective, Philip Marlowe. This time it's Garner's turn, and despite the actor's genial, laid-back personality, the result is negligible. It begins with Marlowe being asked by a girl named Orfamae (Farrell) to locate her missing brother, and before it ends, Marlowe confronts an assortment of odd characters and several dead bodies. The movie tries to evoke a sense of the high-voltage detective thrillers of the forties, but it's an incoherent mess. Moreno fares best, as a strip dancer.

MARNIE

★★ Universal, 1964, c, 129 min. Dir: Alfred Hitchcock. SP: Jay Presson Allen, b/o novel by Winston Graham. Cast: Tippi Hedren, Sean Connery, Diane Baker, Martin Gabel, Louise Latham, Bob Sweeney, Alan Napier, Mariette Hartley, Bruce Dern.

Hitchcock buffs may be intrigued by *Marnie*, but the movie is proof that the director could come a cropper. A heavy-handed melodrama, it stars a wooden Tippi Hedren as a young woman whose psychological hangups could fill a new chapter of Krafft-Ebing. A compulsive thief who changes identities as often as her wardrobe, she has strong aversions, with men heading the list. Along comes Connery, who loves her and is determined to uncover the source of her illness. Hitchcockian themes may be present,

but the Master's skill is hardly in evidence. Look for Bruce Dern in a climactic scene.

MARRIED TO THE MOB

★★★ Orion, 1988, c, 103 min. Dir: Jonathan Demme. SP: Barry Strugatz, Mark Burns. Cast: Michelle Pfeiffer, Matthew Modine, Dean Stockwell, Mercedes Ruehl, Alec Baldwin, Joan Cusack, Trey Wilson.

Poor Michelle Pfeiffer cannot get away from her mob connections. A gangster's widow, she is being lusted after by the mob boss (Stockwell) who killed her husband and trailed by a likable but clumsy FBI agent (Modine) who would like to nail the boss. Many misunderstandings ensue, leading to comic chaos. The movie is likable and frequently funny, but the biggest laughs may come from the sets, especially the hideously overdecorated Mafia houses. Pfeiffer is delightful, but acting honors go to Ruehl as the mob boss's wildly jealous, vindictive wife.

MARY REILLY

★★ TriStar, 1996, c, 108 min. Dir: Stephen Frears. SP: Christopher Hampton, b/o novel by Valerie Martin. Cast: Julia Roberts, John Malkovich, George Cole, Michael Gambon, Kathy Staff, Glenn Close.

An atmospheric but also rather dreary and repellent thriller that tries a new spin on the Dr. Jekyll and Mr. Hyde story. The horrific tale is now related through the eyes of Mary Reilly (Roberts), an Irish maid in the Jekyll household. Curiously drawn to the brooding doctor, she follows him about until she surmises the terrible secret of his relation to his murderous "assistant," Mr. Hyde. Malkovich plays both Jekyll and Hyde with virtually no change in makeup or voice, so that Mary's inability to realize the truth any sooner makes her seem dull-witted. Close gives a peculiar performance in a small role as a madam.

MASQUERADE

★★★ MGM/UA, 1988, c, 91 min. Dir: Bob Swaim. SP: Dick Wolf. Cast: Rob Lowe, Meg Tilly, Kim Cattrall, Doug Savant, John Glover, Dana Delany.

Olivia (Tilly), a wealthy Long Island heiress, has a new suitor: a handsome boat captain named Tim (Lowe). Does he truly love her, or is he seeking to marry her and then murder her for the inheritance? And what roles are being played by her odious stepfather (Glover), the local cop (Savant) who has always loved her, and others? You may not be totally convinced by the answers, but a few of the plot twists are surprising, and the posh Hamptons setting is attractive.

MAXIMUM RISK

★★ Columbia, 1996, c, 101 min. Dir: Ringo Lam. SP: Larry Ferguson. Cast: Jean-Claude Van Damme, Natasha Henstridge, Jean-Hugues Anglade, Zach Grenier, Stephane Audrane.

The only surprising thing about this action melodrama is how so many extras could have escaped injury during the many car chases and shootouts that punctuate the movie. (They scramble for safety with the greatest dexterity.) Van Damme is a French cop who comes to New York to learn more about his murdered twin brother and walks into a hornet's nest involving the Russian Mafia in Brooklyn's Little Odessa, along with corrupt FBI agents. Bullets fly, cars careen and crash, and Van Damme remains stoic through it all. Ho hum.

MCQ

★★☆ Warner Bros., 1974, c, 116 min. Dir: John Sturges. SP: Lawrence Roman. Cast: John Wayne, Eddie Albert, Diana Muldaur, Colleen Dewhurst, Clu Gulager, David Huddleston, Al Lettieri, Julie Adams.

Late in his career, Wayne went the cops-and-robbers route for this standard action film. He plays a tough cop who is out for revenge when some of his fellow officers are killed. On his own after leaving the force, he seeks out the corrupt cops who are responsible. Wayne goes through the requisite chase sequences with dispatch but seems ill at ease in some of the quieter moments. He would make three more movies before his death in 1979.

MEAN SEASON, THE

★★★ Orion, 1985, c, 103 min. Dir: Philip Borsos. SP: Leon Piedmont, b/o novel by John Katzenbach. Cast: Kurt Russell, Mariel Hemingway, Richard Jordan, Richard Masur, Andy Garcia, Joe Pantoliano.

A serial killer is on the loose in Florida, and in his craving for publicity, he telephones *Miami Journal* reporter Malcolm Anderson

(Russell) to say that Mal will be his "conduit to the public." As the murders occur, Mal becomes a celebrity, the one person to whom the killer will talk. Soon even Mal's girlfriend (Hemingway) becomes dangerously involved, leading to a frightening climax. *The Mean Season* touches lightly on the topic of journalistic ethics—is Mal reporting the news or participating in it?—but the movie is really more concerned with churning up a number of teasing fright sequences, perhaps one too many. As such, it's an enjoyable if unremarkable thriller.

MEAN STREETS

★★★☆ Warner Bros., 1973, c, 110 min. Dir: Martin Scorsese. SP: Martin Scorsese, Mardik Martin. Cast: Robert De Niro, Harvey Keitel, David Proval, Amy Robinson, Richard Romanus, Cesare Danova, George Memmoli, Robert Carradine, David Carradine.

Early Scorsese, and the first of the director's many collaborations with De Niro, *Mean Streets* offers a searing portrait of life in New York's Little Italy. Keitel plays a small-time Mafia hood who spends much of his time looking after his dangerously out-of-control cousin, De Niro. At other times he romances De Niro's epileptic cousin (Robinson) or broods about his wavering Catholicism. With De Niro's debts mounting, violence is not far away. Scorsese carries off some electrifying scenes, and the entire movie pulsates with his nervous energy.

MECHANIC, THE

★ United Artists, 1972, c, 100 min. Dir: Michael Winner. SP: Lewis John Carlino. Cast: Charles Bronson, Jan-Michael Vincent, Keenan Wynn, Jill Ireland, Linda Ridgeway, Frank de Kova.

"Murder is killing without a license. And everyone kills." This is the philosophy of hit man—or "mechanic"—Arthur Bishop (Bronson). Wealthy and thoroughly professional at his job, Bishop is also extremely angst-ridden. When he takes on an apprentice (Vincent), a clash between them is inevitable, and it finally comes in a surprising double-twist ending. The first Hollywood-based movie by British director Winner, *The Mechanic* is appallingly bad. Determined to be trendy in the style of early seventies films, it ends up being ludicrous.

MENACE II SOCIETY

★★★☆ New Line, 1993, c, 97 min. Dir: Allen Hughes, Albert Hughes. SP: Allen Hughes, Albert Hughes, Tyger Williams. Cast: Tyrin Turner, Larenz Tate, Samuel L. Jackson, Glenn Plummer, Julian Roy Doster, Jada Pinkett, Marilyn Coleman, Arnold Johnson.

Allen and Albert Hughes, twenty-one-year-old twins from Detroit, made an impressive feature-film debut with this riveting social drama set in Los Angeles's mean streets. Tyrin Turner stars as eighteen-year-old Caine Lawson, a street-smart hustler in the explosive Watts district, who cannot escape the cycle of crime and misery he and his friends have inherited from other generations. An opening violent incident in a Korean grocery store triggers the grim events that follow, leaving little in the way of hope for young black men. Vivid performances by all, especially Larenz Tate as Caine's trigger-happy friend O-Dog.

MEN OF RESPECT

★★ Columbia, 1991, c, 113 min. Dir and SP: William Reilly, b/o play by William Shakespeare. Cast: John Turturro, Katherine Borowitz, Peter Boyle, Dennis Farina, Rod Steiger, Lilia Skala, Steven Wright, Stanley Tucci.

Back in 1955 Ken Hughes directed *Joe Macbeth*, a British film that attempted to turn Shakespeare's play *Macbeth* into a modern-day gangland melodrama. It didn't work then, and it didn't work again with this overcooked and often unintentionally funny movie. Normally a fine actor, Turturro gives an eye-bulging, over-the-top performance as an ambitious hood who is goaded by his wife (Borowitz) into murdering the head of the crime family (Steiger). You know the rest, but the attempts to combine Shakespeare and the Mafia are foolish and heavy-handed. Trying to match the riddle of "no man of woman born" from *Macbeth* is the final straw that causes the whole enterprise to collapse in unintended laughter.

MESSENGER OF DEATH

★★☆ Cannon, 1988, c, 93 min. Dir: J. Lee Thompson. SP: Paul Jarrico, b/o novel by Rex Burns. Cast: Charles Bronson, Trish van Devere, Laurence Luckinbill, John Ireland, Jeff Corey, Marilyn Hassett, Daniel Benzali.

A rather offbeat entry in the Bronson cycle, but with enough violent action to please his fans. He plays a Denver reporter who is covering the murder of the entire family (three wives, six children) of a Mormon farmer. The farmer is a member of an expelled Mormon sect involved in a bitter feud with another sect. Bronson never even carries a gun, but he nabs the perpetrators.

METRO

★★☆ Touchstone, 1997, c, 117 min. Dir: Thomas Carter. SP: Randy Feldman. Cast: Eddie Murphy, Michael Rapaport, Michael Wincott, Carmen Ejogo, Denis Arndt, Art Evans.

After scoring a success with *The Nutty Professor*, Murphy returned to the shoot-and-chase crime world of his *Beverly Hills Cop* movies with this cliché-ridden action film. This time he's a top cop negotiator whose nemesis is a vicious jewel thief (Wincott). Murphy plays his role without the grinning impudence of Axel Foley, and he's an acceptable action hero. The movie, however, has too many climaxes and the requisite chase scene (once again over the hills of San Francisco) is one of the most destructive and improbable in recent memory. The final sequence is ridiculous.

MIAMI BLUES

★★☆ Orion, 1990, c, 99 min. Dir and SP: George Armitage, b/o novel by Charles Willeford. Cast: Alec Baldwin, Fred Ward, Jennifer Jason Leigh, Nora Dunn, Charles Napier, Shirley Stoler, Jose Perez, Paul Gleason.

In some of his roles, Baldwin has proven adept at combining charm with a certain amount of sleaze. Here he draws on both to play an ex-convict who reverts to his old ways as thief, conman, and murderer. In Miami he steals the identity of a grubby, none-too-bright detective (Ward) and uses it for his own nefarious ends. He also hooks up with a trusting girl (Leigh) for a half-hearted attempt at domesticity. Baldwin is good at playing this nasty and vicious character, and the movie has some darkly comic undertones, but at best it's merely mediocre.

MIDNIGHT EXPRESS

★★★ Columbia, 1978, c, 121 min. Dir Alan Parker. SP: Oliver Stone, b/o book by Billy Hayes, William Hoffer. Cast: Brad Davis, Irene Miracle, Bo Hopkins,

Randy Quaid is brutalized by Turkish prison guards in Alan Parker's harsh drama
Midnight Express *(1978).*

Randy Quaid, John Hurt, Mike Kellin, Paul Smith.

A harrowing story, and ostensibly true, but what is the truth? At a time when Turkey was exceptionally harsh on Americans caught smuggling drugs, young Billy Hayes (Davis) was apprehended with drugs strapped to his body and sentenced to prison. The movie deals with his nightmarish experiences in prison and his daring escape. The prison guards are portrayed as sadists, and Turkey is seen as an evil society. Exceptionally violent but undeniably well made, the film still raises doubts about its veracity, especially when one compares Hayes's own published account of his ordeal with the movie version. Stone's screenplay and Giorgio Moroder's score won Oscars.

MIDNIGHT LACE

★★☆ Universal, 1960, c, 108 min. Dir: David Miller. SP: Ivan Goff, Ben Roberts, b/o play by Janet Green. Cast: Doris Day, Rex Harrison, Myrna Loy, Roddy McDowall, John Gavin, Herbert Marshall, John Williams, Natasha Parry, Hermione Baddeley.

Posh London decor and a strong cast compensate in part for this rather obvious thriller. Day is happily married to suave Harrison until she is suddenly threatened with death by a strange disembodied voice in a neighborhood park. Attempts on her life accelerate and suspects are everywhere until an improbable climax that has her climbing across the girders of a construction site. You should be able to guess the culprit early in the proceedings. An always welcome Myrna Loy is on hand as Day's solicitous aunt.

MIDNIGHT MAN, THE

★★☆ Universal, 1974, c, 117 min. Dir and SP: Roland Kibbee, Burt Lancaster, b/o novel by David Anthony. Cast: Burt Lancaster, Susan Clark, Cameron Mitchell, Morgan Woodward, Harris Yulin, Catherine Bach, Joan Lorring, Linda Kelsey.

Out on parole after serving a sentence for killing his wife's lover, ex-cop Lancaster is reduced to becoming a security guard on a campus. The murder of a coed (Bach) compels him to investigate, leading to trouble and danger. Susan Clark plays the parole officer with whom he becomes involved. Overlong but serviceable mystery.

MIDNIGHT RUN

★★★ City Lights, 1988, c, 122 min. Dir: Martin Brest. SP: George Gallo. Cast: Robert De Niro, Charles Grodin, Yaphet Kotto, John Ashton, Dennis Farina, Joe Pantoliano, Wendy Phillips, Richard Foronjy.

Bounty hunter De Niro has a big problem. After capturing an embezzling accountant (Grodin), he has to contend not only with the FBI but also with the mob from which Grodin embezzled the money. To add to his troubles, Grodin turns out to be a neurotic, preachy nuisance. As the two scramble by train, car, and foot from New York to Los Angeles, their fortunes—and their attitude toward each other—are constantly changing, until, predictably, they end up as buddies. This action-comedy runs too long, but it's never dull, and the obligatory chase scenes are well staged. De Niro curbs his usual intensity to give a relaxed, funny performance as the ex-cop turned bounty hunter, and Grodin confirms his skill at playing holier-than-thou types.

MIGHTY QUINN, THE

★★★ MGM, 1989, c, 98 min. Dir: Carl Schenkel. SP: Hampton Fancer, b/o novel by A.H.Z. Carr. Cast: Denzel Washington, Robert Townsend, James Fox, Mimi Rogers, M. Emmet Walsh, Sheryl Lee Ralph, Art Evans, Esther Rolle.

On a Caribbean island, a prominent citizen is found brutally murdered, and the chief suspect is Maubee (Townsend), the island's well-loved thief and hustler. Police chief Xavier Quinn (Washington), Maubee's boyhood friend, believes that he's innocent, and sets about proving it, though the investigation may cost him his job and his life. A colorful background and lively Caribbean music keep the ordinary plot spinning, and Washington's assured presence also helps. As the villain, Walsh is his usual scruffy and sinister self.

MIKE'S MURDER

★★ Ladd Company, 1984, c, 97 min. Dir and SP: James Bridges. Cast: Debra Winger, Mark Keyloun, Darrell Larson, Brooke Alderson, Paul Winfield.

Perhaps not quite as awful as its reputation, *Mike's Murder* is still pretty bad, all the more surprising since it was directed by Bridges (*The China Syndrome*, among others). A thriller without thrills, the movie deals with Betty (Winger), a bank teller whose lover Mike (Keyloun) is brutally murdered by the mob. Her decision to investigate on her own brings her to danger, although not as much as dealing with Mike's off-the-wall friend (Larson), who practically devours the entire set in a crackpot climax.

MIKEY AND NICKY

★★☆ Castle Hill, 1976, c, 116 min. Dir and SP: Elaine May. Cast: Peter Falk, John Cassavetes, Ned Beatty, Rose Arrick, Carol Grace, Joyce Van Patten.

At first glance this very odd movie seems to be another self-indulgent exercise by director Cassavetes (*Faces*, *Husbands*, and others), but no, it was written and directed by Elaine May, who uses Cassavetes as her costar. During one long night, terrified, unstable Nicky (Cassavetes) expects to be rubbed out by mobsters whose money he has stolen. He turns for help to Mikey (Falk), his best friend, but Mikey may, in fact, be setting him up for the hit man (Beatty). Through the night, Mikey and Nicky exchange revelations and recriminations as they flee from place to place. The ending is truly harrowing, but by that time both men have worn out their welcome and we long for the film to end.

MILDRED PIERCE

★★★ Warner Bros., 1945, b/w, 109 min. Dir: Michael Curtiz. SP: Ranald MacDougall, b/o novel by James M. Cain. Cast: Joan Crawford, Ann Blyth, Zachary Scott, Jack Carson, Eve Arden, Butterfly McQueen.

Until the midforties, Crawford was MGM's Queen of Glamour, playing many tough-as-nails shopgirls who slept or battled their way to riches. Then she moved to Warners, played a noble waitress/restauranteur/mother named Mildred, and won an Oscar. She is not really *that* good, but she manages to be reasonably convincing in this glossy melodrama. Her Mildred Pierce will do anything to pamper or protect her vicious, unloving daughter Veda (Blyth), and this comes to include covering up a murder. The noir aspects of the film are all present—gunshots in the night, desperate women, caddish men—but the story is also awash in self-sacrificial soap suds. As Mildred's friend, Arden provides some welcome humor with her caustic remarks.

MILLER'S CROSSING

★★★ Fox, 1991, c, 114 min. Dir: Joel Coen. SP: Joel Coen, Ethan Coen. Cast: Gabriel Byrne, Marcia Gay Harden, Albert Finney, John Turturro, Jon Polito, J. E. Freeman.

Count on the Coen brothers always to come up with something different. After *Blood Simple* and *Raising Arizona*, they devised this intriguing variation on the gangster melodrama. The familiar characters (mob boss, moll, henchmen, and the like) are all there but they are given odd twists and turns in a convoluted plot that is sometimes hard to follow. Byrne plays the main figure: a hired gun for top hood Finney, who survives the mayhem of a gang war. Best feature: Barry Sonnenfeld's cinematography.

MIRAGE

★★★ Universal, 1965, c, 109 min. Dir: Edward Dmytryk. SP: Peter Stone, b/o story by Walter Ericson. Cast: Gregory Peck, Diane Baker, Walter Matthau, Kevin McCarthy, Leif Ericson, Walter Abel, Jack Weston, Anne Seymour, George Kennedy.

Who is David, and why are assassins trying to kill him? David himself (Peck) would like to know, since he's suffering from amnesia. And is he implicated in the death of the head (Abel) of a peace organization? Before all questions are answered, there are suspenseful sequences, some set against actual New York City locations. Baker is the mysterious woman who is somehow involved. A painless Hitchcock imitation, nicely handled all around.

MIRROR CRACK'D, THE

★★☆ EMI (British), 1981, c, 105 min. Dir: Guy Hamilton. SP: Jonathan Hales, Barry Sandler, b/o novel by Agatha Christie. Cast: Angela Lansbury, Elizabeth Taylor, Rock Hudson, Kim Novak, Tony Curtis, Geraldine Chaplin, Maureen Bennett.

Another entry in the series of Agatha Christie adaptations, this one rather resembling the sort of old-fashioned genteel British mystery parodied in the opening sequence. A group of Hollywood people gather at an English village to make a movie, and a young local woman is murdered. On the scene is canny Miss Jane Marple (Lansbury), who exposes the culprit. The movie's best feature is the verbal war between two aging rival actresses (Taylor and Novak) who detest each other.

MISERY

★★★ Castle Rock, 1990, c, 107 min. Dir: Rob Reiner. SP: William Goldman, b/o novel by Stephen King. Cast: James Caan, Kathy Bates, Frances Sternhagen, Richard Farnsworth, Lauren Bacall.

Not much more than a two-character cat-and-mouse game, *Misery* transforms Stephen King's best-selling novel into a reasonably exciting thriller. Caan is the author of a series of popular novels about a character named Misery Chastaine. When he's stranded in Colorado's snowbound wilderness, he's rescued by a woman (Bates) who is a devoted fan of his books. She also turns out be a dangerous psychotic, determined to keep him a prisoner at all costs. Can he escape from her clutches? The situation is terrifying, but not totally believable. High praise goes to Bates's Oscar-winning performance.

MOBSTERS

★★☆ Universal, 1991, c, 104 min. Dir: Michael Karbelnikoff. SP: Michael Mahern and Nicholas Kazan. Cast: Christian Slater, Anthony Quinn, Patrick Dempsey, Richard Grieco, Costas Mandylor, Lara Flynn Boyle, F. Murray Abraham.

A highly attractive production design (by Richard Sylbert) of New York in the twenties turns out to be the sole virtue of this mediocre crime drama. The fanciful idea: in that blood-soaked era, four young hoodlums named Charlie ("Lucky") Luciano (Slater), Meyer Lansky (Dempsey), Benjamin ("Bugsy") Siegel (Grieco), and Frank Costello (Mandylor) use double crosses, executions, and treacherous scheming to reach the top of the crime world. Everyone tries, including Quinn as a mob godfather, but the screenplay lets them down.

MONA LISA

★★★ HandMade Films (British), 1986, c, 106 min. Dir: Neil Jordan. SP: Neil Jordan, David Leland. Cast: Bob Hoskins, Cathy Tyson, Michael Caine, Robbie Coltrane, Clarke Peters, Kate Hardie, Sammi Davis.

Bob Hoskins won an Oscar nomination for his performance as George, an ex-convict who is assigned by mob boss Mortwell (Caine) to chauffeur high-priced call girl Simone (Tyson). At first hostile to the girl, George finds himself falling for her and being drawn ever deeper into the ugly and dangerous night world of criminal London. Inevitably the climax is violent. Hoskins is the main reason to watch this film; he is riveting as a man who retains a degree of decency and romantic feeling even in the most sordid surroundings. Caine makes a good reptilian villain.

MONEY FOR NOTHING

★★ Set For Life/Buena Vista, 1993, c, 100 min. Dir: Ramon Menendez. SP: Ramon Menendez, Tom Musca, Carol Sobieski. Cast: John Cusack, Debi Mazar, Michael Madsen, Benicio Del Toro, Michael Rapaport, Maury Chaykin, Fionnula Flanagan.

Based on a true story but not very interesting, *Money for Nothing* is a standard-cut comedy melodrama. Unemployed longshoreman Cusack finds a bag containing one million dollars, which has fallen off an armored vehicle driven by two careless couriers. He tries to hold onto the money, which gets him into big trouble with everyone on both sides of the law. Eventually he is apprehended. The real character died not long after the movie's release.

MONEY TRAIN

★★☆ Columbia, 1996, c, 103 min. Dir: Joseph Ruben. SP: Doug Richardson, David Loughery, b/o story by Doug Richardson. Cast: Wesley Snipes, Woody Harrelson, Jennifer Lopez, Robert Blake, Chris Cooper, Joe Grifasi, Vincent Pastore, Scott Sowers.

Noisy, virtually nonstop action in a movie that reunites Snipes and Harrelson. This time, however, they fail to duplicate the success of *White Man Can't Jump*. They play transit cops who are also foster brothers. The two bicker continually and fall for the same woman (Lopez), but things get out of hand when debt-ridden Harrelson decides to rob the "money train," the train that holds all subway revenue. A few well-staged action sequences (including a protracted subway climax), but not much else.

MONSIEUR VERDOUX

★★★☆ United Artists, 1947, b/w, 123 min. Dir and SP: Charles Chaplin. Cast: Charlie Chaplin, Martha Raye, Isobel Elsom, Marilyn Nash, Mady Correll, Fritz Leiber.

The virtues of Charlie Chaplin's macabre comedy-drama surpass its shortcomings. Chaplin's Verdoux is a debonair gentleman and loving family man with a secret life's mission: he woos, weds, and then kills rich and foolish women for their money. If mass killings can be tolerated in wartime, Chaplin insists, why should we execute a man for simply supporting his family? This black comedy suffers from cheap sets, some mediocre performances, and a few talky passages, but it also has hilarious moments, most often when Raye, a gifted comic actress, is on the scene as one of Verdoux's victims. Verdoux's efforts to dispatch the lady are uproariously funny.

MORNING AFTER, THE

★★☆ Fox/Lorimar, 1986, c, 103 min. Dir: Sidney Lumet. SP: James Hicks. Cast: Jane Fonda, Jeff Bridges, Raul Julia, Diane Salinger, Richard Foronjy, Geoffrey Scott, Kathleen Wilhoite, Rick Rossovich.

Fonda's intense performance cannot save this mystery thriller from basic mediocrity. She's an alcoholic actress who wakes up one morning with a murdered man next to her in bed. In a panic she removes all traces of his presence, never calls the cops, and heads for the airport. But her trouble's just beginning. Bridges is the friendly redneck who helps her, and Julia is her estranged husband, who wants to divorce her and marry an heiress. Not awful, but it should have been better.

MORTAL THOUGHTS

★★☆ Columbia, 1991, c, 104 min. Dir: Alan Rudolph. SP: William Reilly and Claude Kerven. Cast: Demi Moore, Glenne Headly, Bruce Willis, John Pankow, Harvey Keitel, Billie Neal.

Was this movie intended as thriller or black comedy? At times it's hard to know. In a flashback format, housewife Moore tells the police her tale of helping best friend Headly murder and dispose of her abusive husband (Willis). But what is the real truth about what happened? The film tries to keep up the suspense, but by the time the switch ending comes around, you may not particularly care, since none of the characters is especially interesting.

MOTHER'S BOYS

★☆ Dimension, 1994, c, 95 min. Dir: Yves Simoneau. SP: Barry Schneider, Richard Hawley, b/o novel by Bernard Taylor. Cast: Jamie Lee Curtis, Peter Gallagher, Joanne Whalley-Kilmer, Vanessa Redgrave, Luke Edwards.

Curtis is badly miscast in this singularly unbelievable thriller. She plays Jude, a deeply disturbed woman who abandoned her husband and children three years earlier and has now returned to reclaim them. ("I want my family back. All of it.") Trouble is that her husband (Gallagher) has a new love interest (Whalley-Kilmer) and wants no part of Jude. The demented lady goes from playing mind games with the eldest son (Edwards) to precipitating violence. It all ends with a wildly preposterous climax. And what on earth is the gifted Redgrave doing in this movie?

MR. ARKADIN

★★☆ Filmorsa (Spanish, French), 1955, b/w, 99 min. Dir and SP: Orson Welles. Cast: Orson Welles, Robert Arden, Paola Mori, Patricia Medina, Akim Tamiroff, Michael Redgrave, Katina Paxinou, Mischa Auer, Suzanne Flon.

There are flashes of brilliance (but only a few) in this bizarre melodrama from Orson Welles. A mysterious billionaire (Welles) hires an adventurer (Arden) to find out about the past he claims to have forgotten. His real goal: to kill all those who know the ugly truth about the man he used to be. Soon Arden realizes that his own life is in danger. A number of veteran actors (including Redgrave and Tamiroff) appear in weird roles. Some *Citizen Kane*-like flourishes, but the movie is mostly odd, murky, and finally baffling. Also known as *Confidential Report*.

MR. MAJESTYK

★★☆ Mirisch, 1974, c, 103 min. Dir: Richard Fleischer. SP: Elmore Leonard. Cast: Charles Bronson, Al Lettieri, Linda Cristal, Lee Purcell, Alejandro Rey, Richard Erdman.

A notch or two above the usual Bronson gorefest, this movie begins as a social drama, with Bronson in the title role of a watermelon farmer determined to fight the crooks who would like to take over his business. But then it switches gears when he runs afoul of the vicious mob leader (Lettieri) who wants to kill him for harboring damaging evidence. Standard chases and shootouts follow until the final showdown.

MRS. SOFFEL

★★☆ MGM/UA, 1984, c, 110 min. Dir: Gillian Armstrong. SP: Ron Nyswaner. Cast: Diane Keaton, Mel Gibson, Matthew Modine, Edward Herrmann, Trini Alvarado, Jennie Dundas, Terry O'Quinn.

Pittsburgh, 1901. In prison with his brother (Modine) on Death Row, Ed Riddle (Gibson) has become a rallying point for doting young women who believe he should not be executed. Along comes Kate Soffel (Keaton), the warden's neurasthenic wife, who falls in love with Ed and helps him escape. They become fugitives from the law, with ultimately devastating consequences. Based on a true story, *Mrs. Soffel* is too gloomy to qualify as entertainment, and not interesting or provocative enough to qualify as anything else. The acting, however, is first-rate.

MS. 45

★★☆ Navaron, 1981, c, 90 min. Dir: Abel Ferrara. SP: Nicholas St. John. Cast: Zoe Tamerlis, Steve Singer, Jack Thibeau, Peter Yellen, Editta Sherman.

This early film from director Abel Ferrara (*Bad Lieutenant*) shows that he always had a capacity for excess and shock. In this lurid thriller, mute New Yorker Tamerlis is raped twice in one evening, and, in retaliation, she murders and dismembers the second rapist, a thief. In no time at all she becomes a cold-blooded assassin, killing men at random, even if they are merely flirtatious. Ferrara displays signs of talent, but the material is off-putting.

MULHOLLAND FALLS

★★☆ MGM/UA, 1996, c, 107 min. Dir: Lee

Tamahori. SP: Pete Dexter, b/o story by Pete Dexter, Floyd Mutrux. Cast: Nick Nolte, Melanie Griffith, Chazz Palminteri, Michael Madsen, Chris Penn, John Malkovich, Treat Williams, Andrew McCarthy, Jennifer Connelly.

If production values were all, *Mulholland Falls* would be a clear winner. The settings, the costumes, and the cinematography are all stunning. But then there's the plot, and this moody crime drama fails to score on this point. In 1950s Los Angeles, four cops known as the "Hat Squad," headed by Max Hooper (Nolte), consider themselves above the law, brutalizing people at will. (There actually was such a squad.) The murder of a call girl (Connelly) sets in motion a shocking case that the squad pursues to the highest level of the military establishment. It also has a personal impact on Max and his wife (Griffith). There are effective moments, but the movie never makes it clear how we should respond to these strong-arm cops. Although it obviously aspires to be another *Chinatown*, *Mulholland Falls* never comes close.

MURDER AT 1600

★★★ Warner Bros., 1997, c, 110 min. Dir: Dwight Little. SP: Wayne Beach, David Hodgin. Cast: Wesley Snipes, Diane Lane, Alan Alda, Ronny Cox, Dennis Miller, Daniel Benzali.

Was this the beginning of a small trend? Once again, as in *Absolute Power*, a beautiful woman is found murdered in the White House. This time the suspects include the president's dissolute son, and even the president (Cox) himself. Hard-headed Washington cop Snipes sniffs out a sinister cover-up, and joined by Secret Service agent Lane, he works to ferret out the culprits. Naturally both their lives are soon in jeopardy. The far-fetched climax takes place in the secret tunnels underneath the White House. The movie doesn't make much sense, but it's handled competently, and the suspense heats up at appropriate points. Alda,

Christopher Penn, Nick Nolte, Michael Madsen, and Chazz Palminteri (left to right), the detectives nicknamed the "Hat Squad," pose for a photograph in 1950s Los Angeles in Mulholland Falls *(1996).*

as the president's national security adviser, has the strangest role of his career to date.

MURDER IN THE FIRST

★★☆ Warner Bros., 1995, c, 122 min. Dir: Marc Rocco. SP: Dan Gordon. SP: Christian Slater, Kevin Bacon, Gary Oldman, Embeth Davidtz, Brad Dourif, Kyra Sedgwick, William H. Macy, R. Lee Ermey.

Suggested by a true incident in 1938 that helped to bring down the old Alcatraz prison, this grim prison drama tells an undoubtedly harrowing story. A prisoner named Henri Young (Bacon, in a fine performance), brutally treated for years, is accused of killing a fellow inmate. Brought to trial, he is defended by lawyer Slater, who accuses the prison and its vicious assistant warden (Oldman) of destroying Henri's humanity. Henri's fate is affecting, but the movie is defeated by its overwrought musical score and its show-off camerawork.

MURDER, MY SWEET

★★★☆ RKO, 1944, b/w, 95 min. Dir: Edward Dmytryk. SP: John Paxton, b/o novel by Raymond Chandler. Cast: Dick Powell, Claire Trevor, Anne Shirley, Otto Kruger, Mike Mazurki, Esther Howard, Miles Mander.

After many years of playing the dimpled juvenile tenor in Warners musicals, Powell decided to change his image completely. Launching his new career, he starred as hard-boiled detective Philip Marlowe in this tangled but fascinating adaptation of Chandler's novel *Farewell, My Lovely*. Grizzled and sardonic, Marlowe makes his way through a dangerous nest of vipers, most notably the rich, deadly Mrs. Grayle (Trevor). The movie is first-rate noir, smartly written and directed. Chandler's story was previously filmed in 1942 as *The Falcon Takes Over* and remade in 1975 under the novel's title, with Robert Mitchum as Marlowe. This 1944 version remains the winner.

MURDER ONE

★★★ Miramax, 1988, c, 83 min. Dir: Graeme Campbell. SP: Fleming B. Fuller. Cast: Henry Thomas, James Wilder, Stephen Shellen, Errol Shue.

Based on a true story, *Murder One* takes the viewer into the cold heart of the murderous mind, and does it with a surprising amount of style. Half-brothers Wilder and Shellen escape from prison, and joined by another escapee (Shue) and their fifteen-year-old brother (Thomas), begin an interstate murder spree. Young Thomas (a long way from the innocent boy of *E.T.*), watches with mounting horror as the killings occur. Good performances and artful photography raise this grim tale a notch or two above others of its kind.

MURDER ON THE ORIENT EXPRESS

★★★ Paramount, 1974, c, 127 min. Dir: Sidney Lumet. SP: Paul Dehn, b/o novel by Agatha Christie. Cast: Albert Finney, Lauren Bacall, Martin Balsam, Ingrid Bergman, Jacqueline Bisset, Jean-Pierre Cassel, Sean Connery, John Gielgud, Wendy Hiller, Anthony Perkins, Vanessa Redgrave, Rachel Roberts, Richard Widmark, Martin York, Colin Blakely, George Coulouris.

A truly stellar cast and a flavorsome thirties atmosphere are the principal virtues of this entertaining Agatha Christie mystery, the first of several Christie adaptations. A group of disparate people are aboard the Orient Express when rich, nasty American Widmark is murdered. Also aboard is Belgian detective Hercule Poirot (Finney, heavily disguised and nearly unintelligible), who proceeds to solve the case. The denouement is tricky but not a total surprise, and the cast performs expertly. Bergman won a Supporting Oscar as a timid missionary.

MURPHY'S LAW

★ Cannon, 1986, c, 100 min. Dir: J. Lee Thompson. SP: Gail Morgan Hickman. Cast: Charles Bronson, Kathleen Wilhoite, Carrie Snodgress, Robert F. Lyons, Angel Tompkins, Richard Romanos.

Par for the Bronson course. This time Bronson is a cop framed for murders by a psychopathic ex-convict (Snodgress) he sent to prison ten years earlier. As usual there is much blood-letting before it's all resolved, with one encounter more violent than the next. It's rather sad to see Snodgress, once so marvelous in *Diary of a Mad Housewife* (1970), playing a mad murderer in this depressing movie.

MUTE WITNESS

★★★ Comet/Avrora, 1995, c, 98 min. Dir and SP: Anthony Waller. Cast: Marina Sudina, Fay Ripley, Evan Richards, Oleg Jankowskij, Alec Guinness (unbilled).

A thriller with a familiar premise but some genuinely terrifying scenes. In Moscow, a mute American prop girl (Sudina) at a film studio witnesses a brutal "snuff" murder during the making of a pornographic movie. Of course the police don't believe her, and soon she is the frightened victim of a number of attempts on her life. The sections involving the girl's sister (Ripley) and her gauche director-boyfriend (Richards) are less successful—the couple resembles Woody Allen and Diane Keaton on a bad day. A British-German-Russian coproduction, filmed in Moscow.

NADINE

★★★ TriStar, 1987, c, 82 min. Dir and SP: Robert Benton. Cast: Jeff Bridges, Kim Basinger, Rip Torn, Gwen Verdon, Glenne Headly, Jay Patterson, Jerry Stiller.

In Austin, Texas, in 1954, manicurist Nadine Hightower (Basinger) is trying to retrieve some nude photographs she posed for in a rash moment. Instead she witnesses a murder and is soon on the run from the culprits, joined by her estranged husband Vernon (Bridges). The pursuit ends in a salvage yard, where Buford Pope (Torn) and his hoods are trying to kill them both. An amusing comedy-thriller with a Texas twang, *Nadine* benefits from Bridges's usual solid performance as the unreliable but resourceful hero.

NAKED CITY, THE

★★★☆ Universal-International, 1948, b/w, 96 min. Dir: Jules Dassin. SP: Albert Maltz, Malvin Wald, b/o story by Malvin Wald. Cast: Barry Fitzgerald, Don Taylor, Dorothy Hart, Howard Duff, Ted de Corsia, House Jameson, Adelaide Klein.

The plot is routine: a shady blonde is found

murdered, and the New York police, led by Lieutenant Dan Muldoon (Fitzgerald) begins a large-scale manhunt to find the killer. Still, *The Naked City* earns the distinction of being the first movie to be filmed largely on location in New York City. The use of actual streets and neighborhoods gives the story added excitement, especially in a climax at the Williamsburg Bridge, where the killer has been trapped. Director Dassin was reputedly not happy with the result—he felt that the realism was undercut by too-heavy editing—but ironically the editor, Paul Weatherwax, won an Oscar. This film influenced many others, including many made for television.

NAKED EDGE, THE

★★☆ United Artists, 1961, c, 99 min. Dir: Michael Anderson. SP: Joseph Stefano, b/o novel by Max Ehrlich. Cast: Gary Cooper, Deborah Kerr, Eric Portman, Diane Cilento, Hermione Gingold, Peter Cushing, Michael Wilding, Wilfrid Lawson, Ronald Howard.

Cooper's final film, *The Naked Edge* is a competent but none too credible melodrama, set in England, concerning a wife (Kerr) who suspects her husband (Cooper) may be a thief and murderer. When a blackmail note seems to confirm her suspicions, she lives in terror that she may be his next victim. After a long career of playing taciturn men of integrity, it was difficult to accept Cooper as a potentially nasty killer, and the premise failed to convince audiences.

NAKED FACE, THE

★ Cannon, 1985, c, 106 min. Dir and SP: Bryan Forbes, b/o novel by Sidney Sheldon. Cast: Roger Moore, Rod Steiger, Elliott Gould, Anne Archer, David Hedison, Art Carney.

Psychiatrist Judd Stevens (Moore) is living in a nightmare: shadowy figures are attempting to kill him, and he doesn't know why. The mystery deepens as other people (a patient, his receptionist) are murdered around him. And he is getting no help whatever from an explosively vindictive cop (Steiger, in another hammy performance). This utterly preposterous mystery thriller wastes a good cast. The climax, appropriately, takes place in a garbage disposal plant.

NAKED GUN, THE: FROM THE FILES OF POLICE SQUAD!

★★☆ Paramount, 1988, c, 85 min. Dir: David Zucker. SP: Jerry Zucker, Jim Abrahams, David Zucker, Pat Proft. Cast: Leslie Nielsen, Priscilla Presley, Ricardo Montalban, George Kennedy, Nancy Marchand, O. J. Simpson.

Derived from *Police Squad,* a failed but hugely supported 1982 TV program, this scattershot parody of police shows finds no gag too old, too lame, or too outrageous for its screenplay. The surprise is that some of the jokes provoke reluctant laughter. Nielsen repeats his TV role as dull-witted Lt. Frank Dreben, causing havoc wherever he goes and inadvertently uncovering a plot to assassinate the visiting queen of England. Most of the material is merely silly but everyone plays in the proper deadpan spirit. The movie was successful and prompted two sequels.

NAKED GUN 2 1/2: THE SMELL OF FEAR

★★☆ Paramount, 1991, c, 85 min. Dir: David Zucker. SP: David Zucker, Pat Proft. Cast: Leslie Nielsen, Priscilla Presley, George Kennedy, O. J. Simpson, Robert Goulet, Richard Griffiths, Anthony James, Jacqueline Brookes.

This second entry in the "Police Squad" series is more of the same: a compilation of gags, some funny, most crude, revolving around the spectacular clumsiness of Lt. Frank Dreben (Nielsen). This time a group of nefarious energy leaders headed by Goulet are out to keep a new government policy from being adopted, and Lt. Dreben stops them in his own disastrous fashion. Funniest gag: a sentimental assassin who cannot resist singing "The Way We Were" along with his showering victim.

NAKED GUN 33 1/3: THE FINAL INSULT

★★☆ Paramount, 1994, c, 83 min. Dir: Peter Segal. SP: Pat Proft, David Zucker, Robert LoCash. Cast: Leslie Nielsen, Priscilla Presley, Fred Ward, Anna Nicole Smith, O. J. Simpson.

Third entry in the raucous, gag-laden series of spoofs of cop and crime films. Relentlessly stupid and inept Lt. Frank Dreben (Nielsen) is back, causing havoc in his wake. Now he's out to prevent a disaster at the Oscar ceremonies and ends up creating his own. Many obvious jokes aimed at *The Untouchables, Thelma and Louise,* and other movies. Funniest bit: "Geriatric Park."

NAKED KISS, THE

★★★ Allied Artists, 1954, b/w, 93 min. Dir and SP: Samuel Fuller. Cast: Constance Towers, Anthony Eisley, Michael Dante, Virginia Grey, Patsy Kelly, Betty Bronson.

A lurid melodrama, guided by a director who has become a cult figure in recent years. Towers plays a tough, angry prostitute who tries to reform by building a new small-town life as a nurse to handicapped children. When the well-regarded man (Eisley) she intends to marry turns out to be a child molester, she kills him and earns the town's wrath. Boldly, Fuller touches on topics usually avoided in films of the fifties, and if his style is crude and sometimes excessive, it also has undeniable vitality.

NAME OF THE ROSE, THE

★★☆ Fox, 1986, c, 128 min. Dir: Jean-Jacques Annaud. SP: Andrew Birkin, Gerard Brach, Howard Franklin, Alain Godard, b/o novel by Umberto Eco. Cast: Sean Connery, F. Murray Abraham, Christian Slater, Elya Baskin, William Hickey, Feodor Chaliapin, Jr.

Stripped of its dense scholastic material, Umberto Eco's best-selling novel becomes an ordinary mystery with an extraordinary setting. Set in a remote abbey in northern Italy in 1327, the movie centers on the investigation into a murder at the abbey by an English monk named Brother William (Connery). All the familiar trappings of the mystery are here—hidden doors, secret staircases, and the like—but the movie never springs to life. The cast and setting, however, are noteworthy.

NANNY, THE

★★☆ Hammer Films (British), 1965, b/w, 93 min. Dir: Seth Holt. SP: Jimmy Sangster, b/o novel by Evelyn Piper. Cast: Bette Davis, William Dix, Wendy Craig, Jill Bennett, James Villiers, Pamela Franklin, Maurice Denham.

Did the nanny (Davis) poison the infant sister of her young charge (Dix)? Or is this merely a dark imagining of the ten-year-old boy's disturbed mind? A cat-and-mouse game ensues as the story unfolds. You may have figured out the solution before the ending, but there are a few chilling moments along the way in this British-made thriller. Best scene: a coolly oblivious Davis refuses to help Craig, who is dying of a heart attack.

NARROW MARGIN, THE

★★★☆ RKO, 1952, b/w, 70 min. Dir: Richard Fleischer. SP: Earl Felton. Cast: Charles McGraw, Marie Windsor, Jacqueline White, Queenie Leonard, Don Beddoe.

One of the true "sleepers" of the fifties, this modest little melodrama manages to squeeze a considerable amount of suspense out of a single situation. A sharp-eyed policeman (McGraw) and his partner (Beddoe) are assigned to protect a key witness (Windsor), the widow of a kingpin gangster, on the train ride from Chicago to Los Angeles. When Beddoe is murdered by the mob, McGraw alone must risk his life to protect the woman from the hoods swarming all over the train. The brisk action is confined to the train as the plot takes a few surprising twists and turns. In light of the obviously low budget, the movie's direction, photography, screenplay, and performances are all exemplary. A remake was released in 1990.

NARROW MARGIN

★★★ Carolco, 1990, c, 97 min. Dir and SP: Peter Hyams. Cast: Gene Hackman, Anne Archer, James B. Sikking, J. T. Walsh, M. Emmet Walsh, Susan Hogan.

A remake of the modest but exemplary thriller of the fifties, Narrow Margin has ingredients that the original could not claim: color, scope, and a sturdy male star. Yet it's not as good. The story is essentially the same: assistant D.A. Hackman is assigned to protect a gangster's widow (Archer), who will testify against the mob. Their lives are in danger on a wild train ride through the Canadian Rockies. The climactic battle on top of the train is exciting.

NATIONAL LAMPOON'S LOADED WEAPON I

★★ New Line, 1993, c, 83 min. Dir: Gene Quintano. SP: Gene Quintano, Don Holley, b/o story by Don Holley, Tori Tellem. Cast: Emilio Estevez, Samuel L. Jackson, Jon Lovitz, Tim Curry, Kathy Ireland, William Shatner, Dr. Joyce Brothers, F. Murray Abraham.

The title says it all: a send-up of the Lethal Weapon movies, this knockabout farce throws together every gag it can muster, whether it's mildly funny or simply awful. Inevitably it manages to wring out a few laughs, but they are few and far between. Estevez and Jackson play the Mel Gibson and Danny Glover roles as cops out to recover a microfilm containing the formula for turning cocaine into cookies. Steady moviegoers will recognize the takeoffs of scenes from Basic Instinct, 48 HRS., and other popular movies.

NATIVE SON

★★ American Playhouse/Cinecom/Cinetudes, 1986, c, 112 min. Dir: Jerrold Freedman. SP: Richard Wesley, b/o novel by Richard Wright. Cast: Matt Dillon, Elizabeth McGovern, Oprah Winfrey, Carroll Baker, Geraldine Page, John McMartin, John Karlen, Victor Love.

A second film version of Wright's novel (the first was in 1950, with the author himself in the lead; there was also a successful stage play in 1941), Native Son comes off as well intentioned but also bombastic and heavy-handed. In late forties Chicago, a black teenager (Love) accidentally kills the wild daughter (McGovern) of the rich family he works for. With the cards stacked against him, he is convicted and sentenced to death. Much of the movie seems hollow and forced, and the acting is overemphatic.

NATURAL BORN KILLERS

★ Warner Bros., 1994, c & b/w, 119 min. Dir: Oliver Stone. SP: David Veloz, Richard Rutowski, Oliver Stone. Cast: Woody Harrelson, Juliette Lewis, Tommy Lee Jones, Robert Downey, Jr., Rodney Dangerfield, Tom Sizemore, Pruitt Taylor Vance, Joe Grifasi.

The operative word for this movie is repellent. Ostensibly a savage attack on America's tolerance and even reverence for violence, as well as its mindless worship of instant "celebrities," Natural Born Killers wallows brazenly in the gore that it claims to abhor. Harrelson and Lewis play Mickey and Mallory, two vicious, moronic youngsters who commit multiple murders as they roam the country. They become nationwide media heroes, but end up in prison, where Mickey precipitates a blood-soaked riot. By this time, the film has gone so far out of control that it seems like a nasty hallucination. Using a variety of styles, from animation to cinema verité, Stone attempts to create a satiric, apocalyptic vision of a nation reveling in the violent behavior of its more unruly citizens. The satire, however, is heavy-handed and old-hat, and the virtually nonstop brutality will turn off most viewers. The film may be intended as a chilling modern-day parable but it's more of a Stone-cold disaster.

NATURAL ENEMIES

★★ Cinema 5, 1979, c, 100 min. Dir and SP: Jeff Kanew, b/o novel by Julius Horwitz. Cast: Hal Holbrook, Louise Fletcher, Jose Ferrer, Viveca Lindfors, Peter Armstrong, Beth Berridge, Steve Austin.

Paul Steward (Holbrook) is in a deep, deep depression. He is tired of his wife and sick of his children. On one crucial day, he considers killing them all, after dinner. Will he or won't he? By the time this rather dreary psychological drama concludes, you may not even care. At one point Paul visits a brothel, where he insists that some prostitutes listen to his tale of woe. Some very able actors are on hand, but the film sinks quickly under its weight.

NET, THE

★★★ Columbia, 1995, c, 118 min. Dir: Irwin Winkler. SP: John Brancato, Michael Ferris. Cast: Sandra Bullock, Jeremy Northam, Dennis Miller, Diane Baker, Wendy Gazelle, Ken Howard, Ray McKinnon.

Pity Angela Bennett (Bullock). A lonely computer wizard, she discovers that she has accidentally locked into a secret computer program that involves top-level skulduggery. Soon her entire identity has been obliterated, and she is being pursued by both a suave assassin (Northam) and the police. A fanciful thriller for the computer age, *The Net* defies belief, especially when Angela is the beleaguered heroine of a new *Perils of Pauline*. Still, the movie is fun on a basic level, and the actress is appealing.

NEVER TALK TO STRANGERS

★★☆ TriStar, 1996, c, 96 min. Dir: Peter Hall. SP: Lewis Green, Jordan Rush. Cast: Rebecca De Mornay, Antonio Banderas, Dennis Miller, Len Cariou, Harry Dean Stanton, Beau Starr, Tim Kelleher.

Sarah Taylor (De Mornay) is a psychologist with several serious hangups of her very own. Then she meets Tony Ramirez (Banderas) and enters into a passionate affair. Suddenly sinister things begin to happen to her, including threats to her life. Who is stalking her, and why? The movie appears to be a conventional damsel-in-distress melodrama with some explicit sex scenes, until a startling—and preposterous—resolution and climax that will certainly leave most viewers depressed and/or angry.

NEW JACK CITY

★★☆ Warner Bros., 1991, c, 97 min. Dir: Mario Van Peebles. SP: Thomas Lee Wright, Barry Michael Cooper, b/o story by Thomas Lee Wright. Cast: Wesley Snipes, Ice-T, Chris Rock, Judd Nelson, Mario Van Peebles, Allen Payne, Russell Wong, Bill Nunn.

There's an antidrug message to be found in this churning movie, but it's mostly buried under tons of melodramatic action, including the requisite shootouts. Snipes gives a strong performance as a powerful drug lord named Nino Brown, who is brought down by police operatives but nearly escapes justice. Rapper Ice-T plays an undercover cop on Nino's trail, and Rock is a loose-cannon drug addict. Virtually nonstop rap music and good photography by Francis Kenny of New York City's badly deteriorating neighborhoods.

NEXT OF KIN

★★☆ Warner/Lorimar, 1989, c, 108 min. Dir: John Irvin. SP: Michael Jenning, Jeb Stuart. Cast: Patrick Swayze, Liam Neeson, Adam Baldwin, Helen Hunt, Andreas Katsulas, Bill Paxton, Ben Stiller, Michael J. Pollard, Ted Levine.

A tough Chicago cop (Swayze) with roots back in Appalachia is out for revenge when his younger brother, also a cop, is murdered by gangsters. Joined by his taciturn hillbilly brother (Neeson), he goes on a mission to destroy the top hood responsible for the killing. Along the way there is much bloodletting and violent behavior, but only one surprise. In the bizarre climax in a cemetery, Swayze resorts to using a bow and arrow to nab his prey!

NIAGARA

★★☆ Fox, 1953, c, 89 min. Dir: Henry Hathaway. SP: Charles Brackett, Walter Reisch, and Richard Breen. Cast: Marilyn Monroe, Joseph Cotten, Jean Peters, Casey Adams, Don Wilson, Lurene Tuttle, Richard Allen.

As breathy and voluputous as ever, Marilyn Monroe is one of the two scenic attractions in this fairly taut but essentially mediocre melodrama. She's the bored, sluttish wife of an unstable war veteran (Cotten), who conspires with her current lover (Allen) in a plot to kill him. The setting is Niagara Falls, and Jean Peters is a wife on her belated honeymoon, who becomes dangerously involved in Monroe's scheme. There's not much suspense, except in the sequence in which Cotten stalks the terrified Monroe, at the site of the Falls. The lady herself, poured into the tightest dresses possible, does her usual minimal acting (mostly pouts and wiggles), which is all the role required. Niagara Falls, however, never looked more stunning.

NICK OF TIME

★★☆ Paramount, 1995, c, 89 min. Dir: John Badham. SP: Patrick Sheane Duncan. Cast: Johnny Depp, Christopher Walken, Charles S. Dutton, Marsha Mason, Peter Strauss, Roma Maffia, Gloria Reuben, G. D. Spradlin.

Filmed in real time, *Nick of Time* is a thriller with a simple premise: straight-arrow accountant Depp (forgoing his usual eccentric roles) is arbitrarily chosen by Walken (malevolent, as usual) for an onerous job: he must assassinate the governor (Mason) of the state within ninety minutes, or his little daughter will be killed. Frantically, Depp tries to avoid committing the deed while alerting the authorities and saving his daughter. The movie is gripping for a while, then loses its grip entirely with some unbelievable heroics on Depp's part.

NIGHT AND THE CITY

★★★ Fox, 1950, b/w, 101 min. Dir: Jules Dassin. SP: Jo Eisinger, b/o novel by Gerald Kersh. Cast: Richard Widmark, Gene Tierney, Googie Withers, Hugh Marlowe, Francis L. Sullivan, Herbert Lom, Stanslaus Zbyszko, Mike Mazurki.

A brooding film noir set in an unsavory section of London. Widmark stars as Harry Fabian, an American hustler bent on cornering the wrestling racket. To this end he uses—and abuses—an old Greek wrestler (Zbyszko), with dire consequences. Ultimately Fabian is a lost and hunted man in London's underworld. Tierney has little to do as Fabian's girlfriend and British actor Sullivan stands out as a slimy nightclub owner. The movie was remade in 1992, with the setting changed to New York and Robert De Niro starring as Fabian.

NIGHT AND THE CITY

★★★ Fox, 1992, c, 104 min. Dir: Irwin Winkler. SP: Richard Price. Cast: Robert De Niro, Jessica Lange, Alan King, Cliff Gorman, Jack Warden, Eli Wallach.

A remake of Jules Dassin's 1950 film noir, which starred Richard Widmark, *Night and the City* moves the setting from London to New York, but retains the basic story of Harry Fabian (De Niro), the fast-talking, sleazy lawyer and would-be boxing promoter who finds himself in deep trouble. Harry uses everyone, but when he goes against coldly vicious big-time promoter "Boom-Boom" Grossman (King), his goose is cooked. Lange, in a thankless role, plays the woman who loves Harry despite his corrupt ways. The movie captures the tawdry atmosphere of lower-depths New York, but its main interest lies in De Niro's galvanic performance. Babbling incessantly (sometimes to save his neck or his life), he is an unleashed force that keeps the movie from sagging.

NIGHT FALLS ON MANHATTAN

★★★☆ Paramount, 1987, c, 115 min. Dir: Sidney Lumet. SP: Sidney Lumet, b/o novel by Robert Daley. Cast: Andy Garcia, Richard Dreyfuss, Lena Olin, Ian Holm, Ron Leibman, James Gandolfini, Colm Fore, Sheik Mahmud-Bey.

Director Lumet's penchant for films about inner-city police corruption (*Serpico, Prince of the City, Q & A*) gets a fresh workout in this compelling if slightly uneven drama. Garcia stars as a newly appointed assistant distict attorney who is assigned to prosecute a murderous, big-time drug dealer (Mahmud-Bey). The dealer's trial and conviction opens up a Pandora's Box of police corruption that threatens to engulf Garcia and his veteran-cop father (Holm). Dreyfuss plays the dealer's William Kunstler-like lawyer, and Olin is his lawyer-colleague who involves Garcia in a perfunctory romance. Lumet directs ably and his screenplay raises moral and legal issues in interesting fashion. Best performance: Leibman as a politically ambitious district attorney.

NIGHTHAWKS

★★☆ Universal, 1981, c, 99 min. Dir: Bruce Malmuth. SP: David Shaber, b/o story by David Shaber, Paul Sylbert. Cast: Sylvester Stallone, Billy Dee Williams, Lindsay Wagner, Persis Khambatta,

Nigel Davenport, Rutger Hauer, Joe Spinell.

Stallone and Williams are two decoy cops on the trail of sadistic international terrorist Hauer in this fast-paced, mindless thriller. Stallone (known as "The Gung Ho Lone Ranger of the Street Crime Unit") is supposed to be reluctant to use violence, yet we are told that he killed no less than fifty-two men in Vietnam. Still, character is not the issue when you have such flashy set-pieces as a subway chase and a frightening hostage sequence on the Roosevelt Island tram.

NIGHT MOVES

★★★ Warner Bros., 1975, c, 95 min. Dir: Arthur Penn. SP: Alan Sharp. Cast: Gene Hackman, Susan Clark, Jennifer Warren, Edward Binns, Harris Yulin, Kenneth Mars, Janet Ward, James Woods, Melanie Griffith.

Penn's interesting but muddled thriller is two films not meshed successfully: a familiar study of a detective confronting his failed life, and a murder melodrama which is tricky and grimly fascinating. Hackman plays a small-time detective who is hired by actress Ward to find her missing daughter (Griffith). Heading to the Florida Keys, he finds much more than he bargained for, including smuggling, murder, and even a tentative romance with the duplicitous Warren. By the end his life doesn't look much better. Some riveting moments, but not one of Penn's best films.

NIGHT OF THE FOLLOWING DAY, THE

★★ Universal, 1969, c, 93 min. Dir and SP: Hubert Cornfield, b/o novel by Lionel White. Cast: Marlon Brando, Richard Boone, Rita Moreno, Pamela Franklin, Jess Hahn, Gerard Buhr.

It's hard to say what might have attracted Brando to this surprisingly boring melodrama. He plays a chauffeur who, along with two other men and a woman (Moreno), kidnaps his rich young charge (Franklin) and holds her for ransom. Inevitably the unsavory group has a falling out that leaves Brando as the sole survivor. Boone is the most sadistic of the kidnappers. The movie has an enigmatic trick ending that leaves the viewer baffled.

NIGHT OF THE GENERALS, THE

★★★ Columbia, 1967, c, 148 min. Dir: Anatole Litvak. SP: Joseph Kessel, Paul Dehn, b/o novel by

Hans Helmut Kirst. Cast: Peter O'Toole, Omar Sharif, Tom Courtenay, Donald Pleasance, Joanna Pettet, Philippe Noiret, Christopher Plummer, Charles Gray.

An unusual—and somewhat underrated—wartime mystery melodrama. In Nazi-occupied Warsaw during 1942, a prositute has been murdered, and her killer has been seen wearing the uniform of a German general. A major from Military Intelligence (Sharif) is assigned to investigate the three leading suspects, most especially a ruthless general (O'Toole) who destroys part of Warsaw as a lesson in discipline. The material is admittedly uneven but fascinating, and O'Toole etches a convincing portrait of consummate evil.

NIGHT OF THE HUNTER, THE

★★★☆ United Artists, 1955, b/w, 93 min. Dir: Charles Laughton. SP: James Agee, b/o novel by Davis Grubb. Cast: Robert Mitchum, Shelley Winters, Lillian Gish, Evelyn Varden, Peter Graves, James Gleason, Billy Chapin, Sally Jane Bruce.

Some arty barnacles do cover this intriguing drama but it still has an unmistakable power. In the rural South a smooth-talking, psychotic preacher named Powell (Mitchum) weds and murders a gullible widow (Winters) and then terrorizes her two children (Chapin and Bruce) in order to locate a hidden cache of money. Enter a gentle spinster (Gish) who protects them from Powell. Actor Laughton directed the film as a tribute to pioneer D. W. Griffith, and it's a one-of-a-kind effort.

NIGHT OF THE JUGGLER

★☆ Columbia, 1980, c, 101 min. Dir: Robert Butler. SP: Bill Norton, Sr., Rick Natkin, b/o novel by William P. McGivern. Cast: James Brolin, Cliff Gorman, Richard Castellano, Abby Bluestone, Dan Hedaya, Linda G. Miller, Julie Carmen, Barton Heyman, Sully Boyar.

There's not a believable moment in this inept thriller. Harboring a grievance against New York City, a deranged man (Gorman) plots to kidnap the daughter of a real estate developer. But he kidnaps the wrong girl, the daughter (Bluestone) of an ex-cop (Brolin). The movie becomes one long chase as Brolin tries desperately to rescue his daughter. He's hampered mainly by a vengeful cop (Hedaya) who would like to blow Brolin's head off because of his own past grievance. Don't bother to figure it out.

NIGHT OF THE RUNNING MAN, THE

★ Trimark, 1995, c, 95 min. Dir: Mark L. Lester. SP: Lee Wells, b/o his novel. Cast: Scott Glenn, Andrew McCarthy, Janet Gunn, John Glover, Wayne Newton.

McCarthy, a Las Vegas cab driver, suddenly finds himself with a million dollars in stolen mob money, and top-ranking hit man Glenn is assigned to find him and retrieve the money. Soon McCarthy is in full flight, threatened with death at every turn. A dreadful movie in which able actor Glenn is called on to play a killer of exceptional viciousness, as well as someone with an uncanny ability to ferret out McCarthy's whereabouts.

NIGHT WATCH

★★☆ Avco-Embassy (British), 1973, c, 105 min. Dir: Brian G. Hutton. SP: Tony Williamson, b/o play by Lucille Fletcher. Cast: Elizabeth Taylor, Laurence Harvey, Billie Whitelaw, Bill Dean, Robert Lang, Tony Britton, Rosario Serrano.

Wealthy, beautiful Ellen Wheeler (Taylor) claims that she has seen two murdered corpses, at intervals, through the window of her plush London house. Did she, or is she going mad? Or is something else going on? Also involved are her husband (Harvey), her best friend (Whitelaw), and a caustic police inspector (Dean). The familiar story shows its stage origins, but there's a surprise twist at the end.

99 AND 44/100% DEAD

★★ Fox, 1974, c, 98 min. Dir: John Frankenheimer. SP: Robert Dillon. Cast: Richard Harris, Edmond O'Brien, Bradford Dillman, Ann Turkel, Constance Ford, David Hall, Katherine Baumann, Chuck Connors, Janice Heiden.

A very bizarre gangster melodrama that mixes dollops of graphic violence with crackpot satire and soon becomes indigestible. Hit man Harris is hired by aging gang boss O'Brien to kill rival gangster Dillman. The movie soon goes seriously haywire, and you have a sewer full of albino alligators, a river cluttered with cement-shoed corpses, and, best of all, a character named Claw (Connors). Claw, it seems, has a metal stump for a hand that can be fitted with dozens of detachable appliances, some of which are deadly. Maybe you can figure it out.

NOBODY LIVES FOREVER

★★☆ Warner Bros., 1946, b/w, 100 min. Dir: Jean Negulesco. SP: W. R. Burnett. Cast: John Garfield, Geraldine Fitzgerald, Walter Brennan, Faye Emerson, George Coulouris, George Tobias.

Garfield plays an ex-con artist who returns to his old ways after leaving the army. Spurred on by top con-man Coulouris, he attempts to swindle a wealthy widow (Fitzgerald) but ends up falling in love with her instead. In retaliation, Coulouris kidnaps the lady, and Garfield must rescue her in a climactic shootout. A standard Warners entry, sparked by Garfield's intensity.

NOCTURNE

★★☆ RKO, 1946, b/w, 88 min. Dir: Edwin L. Marin. SP: Jonathan Latimer, b/o story by Frank Fenton, Rowland Brown. Cast: George Raft, Lynn Bari, Virginia Huston, Joseph Pevney, Myrna Dell, Edward Ashley.

When a composer is found dead, the official ruling is suicide, but detective Joe Warne (Raft) is convinced it's murder. His dogged investigation gets him suspended, but he continues on his own and finally gets to the truth. Bari and Huston are sisters under suspicion. Raft is his usual laconic self in this routine mystery.

NO MAN'S LAND

★★ Orion, 1987, c, 106 min. Dir: Peter Werner. SP: Dick Wolf. Cast: D. B. Sweeney, Charlie Sheen, Lara Harris, Randy Quaid, Bill Duke, M. Emmet Walsh, Arlen Dean Snyder.

Cop Sweeney goes undercover to expose a stolen-car ring headed by wealthy young Sheen. He finds that he likes Charlie, has a yen for Charlie's sister (Harris), and even likes stealing Porsches. Together D. B. and Charlie go after the members of a rival gang, who are mean and murderous. Routine stuff, but okay if you go for car chases.

NO MERCY

★★☆ TriStar, 1986, c, 105 min. Dir: Richard Pearce. SP: Jim Carabatsos. Cast: Richard Gere, Kim Basinger, Jeroen Krabbe, George Dzunda, Gary Basaraba, William Atherton.

Routine for all its flashy production, *No Mercy* stars Gere as a cop who travels to Louisiana to track down and capture the big-shot mobster (Krabbe) who murdered his partner. He ties in with the mobster's girlfriend (Basinger), and soon they are not only in love but in desperate flight from the mobster. Lively enough but not very credible, and the fiery climax in a decrepit hotel is rather preposterous.

NO PLACE TO HIDE
★ Cannon, 1993, c, 95 min. Dir and SP: Richard Danus. Cast: Kris Kristofferson, Drew Barrymore, Martin Landau, O. J. Simpson, Dey Young, Bruce Weitz.

Emotionally dead since his family was killed by a drunk driver, tough cop Joe Garvey (Kristofferson) investigates the bizarre murder of a young ballerina. He becomes attached to the victim's fourteen-year-old daughter (Barrymore), who also appears to be the target of assassins. Landau is a police captain with a secret agenda. An inane thriller that stirs together elements of other, better movies into an unpalatable brew.

NORMAL LIFE
★★★ New Line, 1996, c, 106 min. Dir: John McNaughton. SP: Peg Haller, Bob Schneider. Cast: Ashley Judd, Luke Perry, Bruce Young, Jim True, Dawn Maxey, Scott Cummins, Kate Walsh.

Another doom-laden variation on the Bonnie and Clyde theme, this one stars Perry as Chris, a straight-arrow cop who has the misfortune to meet and fall madly in love with seriously disturbed Pam (Judd), who craves a life of excitement. They marry, and before long he's a debt-ridden ex-cop who must rob banks to keep his addled wife happy. When she joins him in his life of crime, the results are deadly. The movie is not as good as some critics would have you believe, but Judd plays hedonistic Pam with utter conviction, and Perry's flat, uninflected acting style seems just right for his unheeding character. Director McNaughton's earlier film *Henry: Portrait of a Serial Killer* is worth a look.

NORTH BY NORTHWEST
★★★★ MGM, 1959, c, 136 min. Dir: Alfred Hitchcock. SP: Ernest Lehman. Cast: Cary Grant, Eva Marie Saint, James Mason, Jessie Royce Landis, Leo G. Carroll, Martin Landau, Adam Williams, Philip Ober.

One of Hitchcock's most entertaining movies, *North by Northwest* has thrills, romance, comedy, and at least two of the great director's amazing set-pieces. Grant is in top form as Roger Thornhill, a suave New Yorker who is mistaken for one George Kaplan and pursued across the country by enemy agents and the FBI. His roller coaster ride finally takes him for a hair-raising climb across the faces on Mount Rushmore. Saint is the mysterious woman who may be friend or foe, and Mason makes a silkenly persuasive villain. The famous crop-dusting sequence (no crops but a deadly plane) is a real nail-biter.

NOTORIOUS
★★★★ RKO, 1946, b/w, 101 min. Dir: Alfred Hitchcock. SP: Ben Hecht. Cast: Ingrid Bergman, Cary Grant, Claude Rains, Louis Calhern, Madame

Claude Rains, Cary Grant, and Ingrid Bergman are the three principal players in Alfred Hitchcock's dazzling melodrama Notorious *(1946).*

Konstantin, Reinhold Schunzel, Moroni Olsen.

Sleek, suspenseful, and eminently satisfying, *Notorious* is one of Hitchcock's very best films, a romantic melodrama that never wears out its welcome. Ravishingly beautiful Bergman plays the daughter of a convicted Nazi spy, who is recruited to infiltrate a band of Nazi refugees in Rio de Janeiro. She must marry the band's leader (Rains) in order to expose their scheme for another world war. Grant is the American agent who falls in love with her during the dangerous mission. Many of the film's moments are legendary: the marathon kiss between Bergman and Grant; the scene between Oscar-nominated Rains and his ice-cold mother (Konstantin), and others. Watch for the party sequence, and the camera's descent to a crucial key.

NO WAY OUT

★★★ Fox, 1987, c, 116 min. Dir: Roger Donaldson. SP: Robert Garland, b/o novel by Kenneth Fearing. Cast: Kevin Costner, Gene Hackman, Sean Young, Will Patton, George Dzunda, Jason Bernard, Iman, Fred Dalton Thompson.

In the Washington hotbed of politics and intrigue, Navy Commander Tom Farrell (Costner) is in big trouble: it seems that the sexy woman (Young) he is dating is also the secret mistress of David Brice (Hackman), the new Secretary of Defense. When Brice murders the woman in a jealous rage, Farrell is set up as the fall guy for the crime. Soon his life and the lives of others are in jeopardy as he sprints about the nation's capital. A loose remake of *The Big Clock* (1948), the movie generates enough tension to keep you guessing. Best performance: Patton as Brice's malevolent, overly dedicated aide. Unfortunately, the surprise ending is a cheat that left at least one viewer deflated and angry.

NO WAY TO TREAT A LADY

★★★ Paramount, 1968, c, 108 min. Dir: Jack Smight. SP: John Gay, b/o novel by William Goldman. Cast: Rod Steiger, George Segal, Lee Remick, Eileen Heckart, Murray Hamilton, Michael Dunn, Barbara Baxley, Ruth White, Doris Roberts, David Doyle.

Never noted for his acting restraint, Steiger gets the chance to pull out all stops in this enjoyable, black-humored melodrama. He's a theatrical producer who murders gullible middle-aged women as an expression of his hang-up over his late actress-mother. For each murder, he impersonates another character. Segal is the Jewish cop on the case. Part of the movie concerns Segal's romance with Remick, and his relationship with his badgering mother (Heckart). This material is amusing enough, but Steiger steals the show with a flamboyant performance.

NOWHERE TO RUN

★★ Columbia, 1993, c, 95 min. Dir: Robert Harmon. SP: Joe Eszterhas, Leslie Bohem, Randy Feldman, b/o story by Joe Eszterhas, Richard Marquand. Cast: Jean-Claude Van Damme, Rosanna Arquette, Kieran Culkin, Ted Levine, Joss Ackland, Edward Blatchford, Tiffany Taubman.

Martial-arts whiz Van Damme added some "heart" to his usual action mix but the material is much too stale to really work. He's an escaped convict who miraculously finds his way to the home of widow Arquette and her two small children. Her land is being sought by a ruthless developer (Ackland) whose hired thugs are getting nasty. Guess who defends her, falls for her, and returns to prison. Right. This plot would have been rejected by *The Fugitive* television series of three decades ago.

NUTS

★★★ Columbia, 1988, c, 116 min. Dir: Martin Ritt. SP: Tom Topor, Darryl Ponicsan, Alvin Sargent, b/o play by Tom Topor. Cast: Barbra Streisand, Richard Dreyfuss, Maureen Stapleton, Karl Malden, Eli Wallach, James Whitmore, Robert Webber, Leslie Nielsen, William Prince.

Streisand at full throttle—that's how one might describe this film. She plays an aggressive, high-priced hooker who demands the right to stand trial on a charge of manslaughter. Everyone (including parents Stapleton and Malden) believes that she is not in her right mind and needs medical treatment instead of jail. A Legal Aid lawyer (Dreyfuss) who agrees to defend her uncovers a dark and long-buried family secret. Streisand's performance will provoke either applause or alarm, but it's the heart of the movie. She gets good support from a superior cast.

OBSESSION

★★☆ Columbia, 1976, c, 98 min. Dir: Brian De Palma. SP: Paul Schrader. Cast: Cliff Robertson, Genevieve Bujold, John Lithgow, Sylvia Kuumba Williams, Wanda Blackman.

Deep in his Hitchcock phase, director De Palma uses many of the master's stylistic devices to tell a *Vertigo*-like story, but despite some effective moments, the movie doesn't jell. Robertson is a New Orleans real estate tycoon whose wife and daughter are kidnapped and apparently killed. Years later in Florence, he meets a young woman (Bujold) who is a dead ringer for his late wife. What is the nefarious plot behind it all? Robertson seems exceptionally slow to realize what is happening to him, and the plot holes are so large that the movie's entire structure eventually collapses.

OCEAN'S ELEVEN

★★☆ Warner Bros., 1960, c, 127 min. Dir: Lewis Milestone. SP: Harry Brown and Charles Lederer, b/o story by George Clayton Johnson and Jack Golden Russell. Cast: Frank Sinatra, Dean Martin, Peter Lawford, Sammy Davis, Jr., Joey Bishop, Angie Dickinson, Richard Conte, Cesar Romero, Patrice Wymore.

A flippant caper comedy, with the well-known "Rat Pack" of the period playing wartime buddies who join together to rob five major Las Vegas casinos on New Year's Eve. It all goes easily (too easily to be believable) until a wily hijacker (Romero) takes over. Sinatra is Danny Ocean, the breeziest and most visible of the bunch, and the other cast members perform with nonchalant aplomb. Eventually, however, they all wear out their welcome.

ODDS AGAINST TOMORROW

★★★☆ United Artists, 1959, b/w, 95 min. Dir: Robert Wise. SP: John O. Killens, b/o story by William P. McGivern. Cast: Harry Belafonte, Robert Ryan, Shelley Winters, Ed Begley, Gloria Grahame, Will Kulava, Richard Bright.

An expert cast, well directed by Wise, brings some surprising punch and vitality to this crime drama. During the course of a bank robbery in a Hudson Valley town, two of the robbers find themselves at odds with each other when one (Ryan) proves to be a raging bigot with contempt for his black confederate (Belafonte). Their ultimate fate is clearly intended as irony. Fine actor Ryan is especially good as the vicious Southern drifter, recalling the unsavory anti-Semitic villain he portrayed a dozen years earlier in *Crossfire*.

OFF LIMITS

★☆ Fox, 1988, c, 102 min. Dir: Christopher Crowe. SP: Christopher Crowe, Jack Thibeau. Cast: Willem Dafoe, Gregory Hines, Fred Ward, Amanda Pays, Scott Glenn, Keith David, Kay Tong Lim, David Alan Grier.

In the strife torn city of Saigon in 1968, a sadomasochist has been murdering prostitutes, all of whom had babies by American servicemen. Two tough-talking plainclothes cops (Dafoe and Hines) are assigned to the army's Criminal Investigation Detachment to investigate the murders. Soon the men find themselves knee-deep in danger in a sleazy, sinister world. The identity of the culprit—who appears to be high up in the military—is not much of a surprise. An exceptionally ugly and unsavory thriller, steeped in the apparently mutual loathing of American and Vietnamese forces.

ONCE UPON A TIME IN AMERICA

★★★ Ladd Company, 1984, c, 139 min. (also available in full version of 227 min.). Dir: Sergio Leone. SP: Leonardo Benvenuti, Piero de Bernardi, Enrico Medioli, Franco Arcalli, Franco Ferrini, Sergio Leone, b/o novel by David Aaronson (Harry Grey). Cast: Robert De Niro, James Woods, Elizabeth McGovern, Tuesday Weld, Joe Pesci, Danny Aiello, William Forsythe, Burt Young.

Italian director Leone's sweeping vision of the American gangster film has two main virtues: a stunning physical production and a finely shaded performance by De Niro. Moving back and forth in time, from 1921 to 1968, the film relates the story of four Jewish friends (De Niro is "Noodles") who move from reckless young punks on the take to big-shot gangsters during Prohibition. Major faults include too many tediously protracted scenes (especially in the long version) and some ludicrously miscalculated sequences. Warning: the long version contains several graphic rape sequences.

ON DANGEROUS GROUND

★★★ RKO, 1952, b/w, 82 min. Dir: Nicholas Ray. SP: A. I. Bezzerides, adapted by A. I. Bezzerides, Nicholas Ray from novel by Gerald Butler. Cast: Ida Lupino, Robert Ryan, Ward Bond, Charles Kemper, Anthony Ross, Ed Begley, Sumner Williams.

A moody melodrama, expertly directed by Ray, *On Dangerous Ground* stars Robert Ryan as a burned-out, dangerously brutal cop who is called on to investigate a girl's molestation and murder by a disturbed teenager (Williams). He forms an emotional attachment with the teenager's blind sister (Lupino), which promises to break the shell of isolation and alienation he has built around him. Filmed in 1950.

ONE FALSE MOVE

★★★☆ I.R.S. Media, 1992, c, 105 min. Dir: Carl Franklin. SP: Billy Bob Thornton, Tom Epperson. Cast: Bill Paxton, Cynda Williams, Billy Bob Thornton, Michael Beach, Jim Meltzer, Earl Billings.

Former actor Franklin won critical praise for this first feature, a small but taut, clever crime thriller with a twisty plot. After murdering some partygoers, two drug dealers (Thornton and Beach), accompanied by Thornton's girlfriend (Williams), travel to a small Arkansas town to hide out. Waiting for them are the town's sheriff (Paxton) and two cops from Los Angeles. Viewers are on their own from this point, as the story takes unexpected turns, and one surprise follows another. Not every scene works, but this movie will keep you on your toes.

ONE GOOD COP

★★ Hollywood, 1991, c, 114 min. Dir and SP: Heywood Gould. Cast: Michael Keaton, Rene Russo, Anthony LaPaglia, Kevin Conway, Rachel Ticotin, Tony Plana, Charlaine Woodard.

Artie Lewis (Keaton) is a dedicated, happily married cop. When his partner is killed, he takes over the care of his three orphaned little girls. Then mounting pressures cause him to commit a criminal act. An uneasy mix of fami-ly sentiment and police action, the movie takes a disastrous turn when Artie goes improbably bad, and it never recovers. Keaton, however, is a genial actor who deserves better material.

ONION FIELD, THE

★★★ Avco Embassy, 1979, c, 122 min. Dir: Harold Becker. SP: Joseph Wambaugh, b/o his novel. Cast: John Savage, James Woods, Franklyn Seales, Ted Danson, Ronny Cox, Dianne Hull, Priscilla Pointer, Christopher Lloyd.

A bleak true story concerning Carl (Savage), a decent young cop whose life comes apart after a shattering incident in which his partner is killed before his eyes by a psychotic gunman (Woods). Racked by guilt that he was negligent in preventing the murder, he watches with mounting despair as Woods's trial drags on for many years due to Woods's machinations. Ultimately, there is a closure for Carl. The movie is certainly well intentioned but it is also meandering and unfocused, and the irony between the status of the cop and the killer is heavy-handed.

ON THE WATERFRONT

★★★★ Columbia, 1954, b/w, 108 min. Dir: Elia Kazan. SP: Budd Schulberg, b/o articles by Malcolm Johnson. Cast: Marlon Brando, Eva Marie Saint, Karl Malden, Lee J. Cobb, Rod Steiger, Martin Balsam, Pat Henning.

After more than four decades, *On the Waterfront* remains one of the screen's most memorable urban dramas, brilliantly directed by Kazan and played with passion and urgency by an exemplary cast. On the wharves of New York City, Terry Malloy (Brando) is lackey to ruthless dock boss Johnny Friendly (Cobb). He turns stoolie when he learns of Friendly's murderous power, and also falls in love with the sister (Saint) of the man killed by the mob. His defiance costs him dearly, but he survives. Many legendary scenes in Schulberg's screenplay are abetted by Boris Kaufman's photography and Leonard Bernstein's score. The film won eight Oscars, including one for Best Picture.

ON THE YARD

★★★ Midwest, 1979, c, 102 min. Dir: Raphael D. Silver. SP: Malcolm Braly, b/o his novel. Cast: John Heard, Thomas Waites, Mike Kellin, Joe Grifasi,

Marlon Brando and Eva Marie Saint both won Oscars for their performances as a conflicted dock worker and his girl in Elia Kazan's powerful drama On the Waterfront *(1954).*

Richard Bright, Lane Smith, Richard Hayes.

Interesting prison drama has many characters familiar from others in the genre, but it's worth watching. The story centers mainly on four prisoners: Chilly (Waites), the acknowledged king of the yard; Juleson (Heard), a wife-killer who makes the mistake of tangling with Chilly; Morris (Grifasi), a prison jack-of-all-trades; and Red (Kellin), an aging convict fearful of the world outside the walls. Kellin takes the acting honors, especially in the scene in which he appears before the parole board.

ORDEAL BY INNOCENCE

★ Golan-Globus, 1984, c, 91 min. Dir: Desmond Davis. SP: Alexander Stuart, b/o novel by Agatha Christie. Cast: Donald Sutherland, Christopher Plummer, Faye Dunaway, Ian McShane, Diana Quick, Annette Crosbie, Michael Elphick.

By far the weakest of the Agatha Christie adaptations to date; extremely dull and less diverting than the average weekly television mystery. Sutherland arrives at a coastal British village to learn that *he* is the true alibi for a young man who has already been hung for murdering his mother. Sutherland takes it on himself to ferret out the actual killer among the many suspects. Before he can expose the culprit, two more murders are committed. Nobody wins here.

ORIGINAL GANGSTAS

★★ Orion, 1996, c, 96 min. Dir: Larry Cohen. SP: Aubrey Rattan. Cast: Fred Williamson, Jim Brown, Pam Grier, Paul Winfield, Richard Roundtree, Isabel Sanford, Ron O'Neal, Robert Forster, Charles Napier, Wings Hauser.

As this movie would have it, Gary, Indiana is a depressed, dangerous city where black gangs rule by terror and homicide. Back into the neighborhood comes Johnny (Williamson), no longer young but still tough, who organizes his old friends (Brown, Grier, and Roundtree) into a fighting unit bent on wresting control from the gangs. The film seems like little more than an attempt to round up the black action stars of the seventies for one last righteous fling. Yet their righteousness is highly compromised: they respond to violence with their own violence. It doesn't work in the nineties.

OUT COLD

★★★ Hemdale, 1988, c, 92 min. Dir: Malcolm Mowbray. SP: Leonard Glasser, George Malko, b/o story by Leonard Glasser. Cast: John Lithgow, Teri Garr, Randy Quaid, Bruce McGill, Lisa Blount, Alan Blumenfeld.

There are some droll, unexpected twists in this black comedy (from the same director as *A Private Function*). Fed up with her nasty, womanizing butcher-husband Ernie (McGill), Sunny (Garr) locks him in his freezer, where his dead body is discovered by his timid partner Dave (Lithgow). Dave has always loved Sunny, and together they try to dispose of Ernie's body. A dimwitted detective (Quaid) stirs up some comic misunderstandings. Garr sends up the usual wicked film noir woman with an expert performance.

OUTFIT, THE

★★☆ MGM, 1974, c, 103 min. Dir and SP: John Flynn, b/o novel by Richard Stark (Donald E. Westlake). Cast: Robert Duvall, Robert Ryan, Karen Black, Joe Don Baker, Timothy Carey, Richard Jaeckel, Sheree North, Marie Windsor, Jane Greer, Henry Jones, Joanna Cassidy, Elisha Cook, Jr.

The cast for this violent crime movie is highly impressive, but the movie is strictly routine. Able actor Duvall plays a just-released ex-con who learns that his brother has been murdered by the syndicate as reprisal for their ripping off a bank controlled by the syndicate. He and longtime friend Baker join forces to destroy the syndicate headed by Ryan. The pace is fast as the bodies pile up, but the material is shopworn.

OUT FOR JUSTICE

★★ Warner Bros., 1991, c, 90 min. Dir: John Flynn. SP: David Lee Henry. Cast: Steven Seagal, William Forsythe, Jerry Orbach, Jo Champa, Shareen Mitchell, Sal Richards, Gina Gershon.

Another Seagal bone-crusher, with the star as the toughest, meanest cop in Brooklyn, out to avenge the brutal murder of his best friend by the neighborhood psycho (Forsythe). The story is merely a framework for Seagal to demolish scores of hoods with punches, kicks, and any handy weapon. Actually he seems to be almost as deadly and out-of-control as the mobsters he massacres. His fans will not care.

OUT OF BOUNDS

★ Columbia, 1986, c, 93 min. Dir: Richard Tuggle. SP: Tony Kayden. Cast: Anthony Michael Hall, Jenny Wright, Jeff Kober, Glynn Turman, Raymond J. Barry, Pepe Sarna, Meat Loaf.

Iowa farm boy Hall comes to Los Angeles, and at the airport he mistakenly picks up a bag containing heroin. In a flash he is caught in the line of fire between the police and a sadistic drug dealer. A waitress (Wright), appropriately named Dizz, offers to help him. The climax takes place atop an old Art Deco highrise on the Sunset Strip. A brain-dead action movie that makes less than no sense.

OUT OF THE PAST

★★★☆ RKO, 1947, b/w, 97 min. Dir: Jacques Tourneur. SP: Geoffrey Homes (Daniel Mainwaring), b/o his novel. Cast: Robert Mitchum, Jane Greer, Kirk Douglas, Rhonda Fleming, Steve Brodie, Dickie Moore.

A classic example of film noir, complete with a detective (Mitchum) with wavering morals, a nasty gangster (Douglas), and above all, a memorable example of the femme fatale (Greer), a treacherous lady indeed. Mitchum is sent by Douglas to Mexico to find girlfriend Greer, and the consequences are deadly when Mitchum and Greer fall hard for each other. The plot is very convoluted, but the dialogue is sharp. Remade in 1984 as *Against All Odds*.

OUTSIDE MAN, THE

★★★ United Artists, 1973, c, 104 min. Dir: Jacques Deray. SP: Jacques Deray, Jean-Claude Carriere. Cast: Jean-Louis Trintignant, Ann-Margret, Roy Scheider, Angie Dickinson, Georgia Engel, Michel Constantin, Ted de Corsia, Talia Shire, John Hillerman.

This offbeat French-U.S. action movie stars Trintignant as a French hit man who comes to

The defining moment in The Ox-Bow Incident *(1943): three innocent men (Anthony Quinn, Dana Andrews, and Francis Ford) are about to be hung by a lynch mob. At far right is cowpoke Henry Fonda.*

America to kill mob boss de Corsia and finds himself being hunted by hit man Scheider. This "outside man" is in deep trouble since he doesn't understand the language or the customs. Most bizarre sequence: at de Corsia's wake, he is embalmed in a sitting position on a funeral parlor throne, and a shootout breaks out around him. The dialogue is in English, with occasional subtitled French.

OUTSIDERS, THE

★★☆ Warner Bros., 1983, c, 91 min. Dir: Francis Coppola. SP: Kathleen Knutsen Rowell, b/o novel by S. E. Hinton. Cast: Matt Dillon, Ralph Macchio, C. Thomas Howell, Patrick Swayze, Rob Lowe, Emilio Estevez, Tom Cruise, Diane Lane, Leif Garrett.

An impressive number of young actors who would later become famous appears in Coppola's rather pretentious, self-conscious adaptation of Hinton's popular novel. Set in Tulsa, Oklahoma, in the sixties, the movie concerns a group of lower-class youngsters ("greasers") who seem to engage in constant "rumbles" with rich society kids. The clichés are all in place: one greaser (Howell) is sensitive; another (Dillon) is a walking timebomb; still another (Macchio) is needy. For some it ends tragically. Coppola smothers

the slight story in arty photography (countless closeups, silhouettes, and the like).

OVER THE EDGE

★★★ Orion, 1979, b/w, 95 min. Dir: Jonathan Kaplan. SP: Charlie Haas, Tim Hunter. Cast: Michael Kramer, Pamela Ludwig, Matt Dillon, Vincent Spano, Tom Fergus, Andy Romano, Ellen Geer, Lane Smith, Harry Northrup.

A nightmarish view of alienated youth, *Over the Edge* deserved wider attention than it received at its release. In a planned suburban community, the young people, seething with anger and resentment, are knee-deep in vandalism, drugs, and alcohol. Violence finally occurs, and the tense situation explodes into an apocalyptic orgy of destruction. As in most movies of this sort, parents, teachers, and police are depicted as heedless or witless, and the fiery climax, while unsettling, also seems contrived for the sake of shock. But *Over the Edge* is still a fairly honest and worthy effort.

OX-BOW INCIDENT, THE

★★★☆ Fox, 1943, b/w, 75 min. Dir: William A. Wellman. SP: Lamar Trotti, b/o novel by Walter Van Tilburg Clark. Cast: Henry Fonda, Dana Andrews, Mary Beth Hughes, Anthony Quinn, William Eythe,

Henry (Harry) Morgan, Jane Darwell, Frank Conroy, Harry Davenport.

A most unusual film to have come from Fox, this spare, grim Western drama is actually a blunt attack on mob rule and violence. Set in a bleak frontier town, it centers on the lynching of three hapless men by an angry mob that wrongly believes them to be guilty of rustling and murdering a rancher. The main voice of reason is a roving cowpoke (Fonda) who watches the event with mounting aversion. The movie has little subtlety, and the closing, in which Fonda reads a parting letter from one of the victims to his wife, is patently phoney. As a whole, however, the film has a chilling power that makes it difficult to forget.

PACIFIC HEIGHTS
★★★ Morgan Creek, 1990, c, 102 min. Dir: John Schlesinger. SP: Daniel Pyne. Cast: Melanie Griffith, Matthew Modine, Michael Keaton, Laurie Metcalf, Carl Lumbly, Mako, Dorian Harewood, Nobu McCarthy, Beverly D'Angelo (unbilled).

Meet the Tenant from Hell, as played by Keaton in a surprising change from his usual affable persona. Deadly and deranged, he rents a studio apartment in a Victorian house in San Francisco, only recently bought by unmarried couple Griffith and Modine. Soon this psychotic gent has them fighting for their home and eventually for their lives. (A switch: Griffith is the more resourceful of the two.) The movie builds up some suspense but loses its footing toward the end. The violent climax is a nail-biter.

PANIC IN THE STREETS
★★★ Fox, 1950, b/w, 93 min. Dir: Elia Kazan. SP: Richard Murphy, adapted by Daniel Fuchs from story by Edward and Edna Anhalt. Cast: Richard Widmark, Paul Douglas, Barbara Bel Geddes, Walter Jack

Palance, Zero Mostel, Guy Thomajan.

When the victim of a homicide in New Orleans turns out to be infected with pneumonic plague, the search is on for his killer, who can spread the virulent disease on a frightening scale. The search is led by a Navy doctor (Widmark) with the U.S. Public Health Service and a seasoned police captain (Douglas). This intriguing premise for a manhunt thriller is carried out with dispatch under Kazan's direction. In one of his early sympathetic roles, Richard Widmark is adequate as the frantic doctor, but acting honors go to Palance (billed here as Walter Jack Palance, in his first movie role), who is properly scary as the trigger-happy killer.

PAPILLON
★★☆ Allied Artists, 1973, c, 150 min. Dir: Franklin J. Schaffner. SP: Dalton Trumbo, Lorenzo Semple, Jr., b/o book by Henri Charriere. Cast: Steve McQueen, Dustin Hoffman, Don Gordon, Anthony Zerbe, Victor Jory, George Coulouris, Robert Deman, Gregory Sierra.

A grim account—overlong and utterly depressing—concerning the true ordeal of one Henri Charriere, known as the "Butterfly" (Papillon), in a monstrous penal colony on Devil's Island. McQueen is Charriere, who made more than one desperate effort to escape this waking nightmare, and finally succeeded. Hoffman plays France's "best counterfeiter," who becomes Papillon's friend. Most of the movie is difficult to watch, and curiously the last part—dealing with the final escape—turns silly and implausible, despite the "true" basis.

PARADINE CASE, THE
★★☆ Selznick, 1948, b/w, 116 min. Dir: Alfred Hitchcock. SP: David O. Selznick, adapted by Alma Reville, James Bridie from novel by Robert Hichens. Cast: Gregory Peck, Charles Laughton, Alida Valli, Ann Todd, Ethel Barrymore, Charles Coburn, Louis Jourdan, Leo G. Carroll, Joan Tetzel, Isobel Elsom.

A fine cast cannot bring this courtroom drama up to Hitchcock's usual level. There are some striking, artfully photographed sequences, but the screenplay is verbose and largely devoid of subtlety. Peck plays a British lawyer who defends the mysterious Mrs. Paradine (Valli) against the charge of murdering her blind husband. He falls in love with his client, but subsequent events leave his career in ruins. He is left with only the unwavering loyalty of his wife (Todd). Best performance: Barrymore as the cowed, tippling wife of lecherous judge Laughton.

PARTNERS

★ Paramount, 1982, c, 98 min. Dir: James Burrows. SP: Francis Veber. Cast: Ryan O'Neal, John Hurt, Kenneth McMillan, Robyn Douglass, Jay Robinson, Denise Galik, Rick Jason.

The first feature film for television director Burrows, and a bad mistake. Two Los Angeles cops (O'Neal and Hurt) are assigned to investigate a series of homosexual-related murders. Hurt is proudly gay, and O'Neal is aggressively straight but must now assume a gay disguise. Can you figure out the rest? A silly and offensive movie, written by the author of *La Cage Aux Folles*.

PARTY GIRL

★★★ MGM, 1958, c, 99 min. Dir: Nicholas Ray. SP: George Wells, b/o story by Leo Katcher. Cast: Robert Taylor, Cyd Charisse, Lee J. Cobb, John Ireland, Kent Smith, Claire Kelly, Corey Allen, David Opatashu.

Standard gangster material, all dressed up in CinemaScope and Technicolor, and given a stylish spin by director Ray. Taylor is the crippled, cynical "mouthpiece" for racketeer big-shot Cobb. When he falls for dancer Charisse and her life is threatened, he decides to tell all to the crusading prosecutor. The result, inevitably, is a barrage of gunplay. You've seen it all before, but Ray makes it work reasonably well again.

PASSENGER 57

★★☆ Warner Bros., 1995, c, 84 min. Dir: Kevin Hooks. SP: David Loughery, Dan Gordon, b/o story by Dan Gordon, Stewart Raffill. Cast: Wesley Snipes, Bruce Payne, Tom Sizemore, Alex Datcher, Bruce Greenwood, Elizabeth Hurley, Robert Hooks, Ernie Lively.

Long on fast-moving action and short on plausibility, this melodrama stars Snipes as a superconfident security agent ("I'm the best!"), who just happens to be on the same plane as one of the world's leading terrorists (Payne). A clash of wits and wills ensues as Snipes tries to figure out how to deal with the nasty, dangerous Payne and his cohorts. Characters

are cliché (the helpful stewardess, the kibitzing colleague of Snipes) but the movie seldom pauses to catch its breath.

PAST MIDNIGHT

★★☆ CineTel, 1990, c, 100 min. Dir: Jan Eliasberg. SP: Frank Norwood. Cast: Rutger Hauer, Natasha Richardson, Clancy Brown, Guy Boyd, Ernie Lively, Tom Wright.

A lurid thriller with an overly familiar plot line but a few jolting sequences. Released from prison after serving fifteen years for murdering his pregnant wife, Ben Jordan (Hauer) meets his assigned social worker, Laura Mathews (Richardson). Intrigued and attracted, Laura is finally convinced that Ben is innocent of the crime. But is he, or is he a deranged killer? She finds out in a violent and scary climax.

PAST TENSE

★★ Republic, 1994, c, 91 min. Dir: Graeme Clifford. SP: Scott Frost and Miguel Tejada-Flores. Cast: Scott Glenn, Anthony LaPaglia, Lara Flynn Boyle, David Ogden Stiers, Sheree Wilson.

A veteran detective and aspiring mystery writer, Gene Ralston (Glenn) finds himself in a waking nightmare when his beautiful new neighbor (Boyle) is murdered. Or was she? Is he going mad, or is he trapped in some sort of monstrous conspiracy? The puzzle is intriguing, until the movie becomes so hopelessly incoherent you may not care to wait for the solution.

PATTY HEARST

★★☆ Atlantic/Zenith, 1988, c, 110 min. Dir: Paul Schrader. SP: Nicholas Kazan, b/o book by Patricia Campbell Hearst. Cast: Natasha Richardson, William Forsythe, Ving Rhames, Francis Fisher, Jodi Long, Olivia Barash, Dana Delany, Marek Johnson.

In February 1974 Patty Hearst, daughter of a wealthy California family and granddaughter of newspaper tycoon William Randolph Hearst, was kidnapped by self-styled "urban guerrillas" who called themselves the Symbionese Liberation Army. Depending on your point of view, she became either a pathetic brainwashed victim or a willing accomplice who joined the SLA ranks and took part in a bank robbery. She was arrested and served time in prison until receiving a presidential pardon. Written by director Elia Kazan's son Nicholas, the movie tries to be objective about Hearst, blending both the tragic and comic aspects of her story, but it comes across as cold, detached, and oddly uninvolving. Richardson is fine, however, as Patty.

PAY OR DIE

★ Allied Artists, 1960, b/w, 109 min. Dir: Richard Wilson. SP: Richard Collins, Bertram Millhauser. Cast: Ernest Borgnine, Zohra Lampert, Alan Austin, Robert F. Simon, Renata Vanni, Bruno Della Santina, Robert Ellenstein.

A crime drama, based on fact, concerning Joe Petrosino (Borgnine), a New York Italian police detective, who formed a special squad to battle the infamous Black Hand in the early years of the century. There are some colorful details of New York Italian life during this period, but the movie, unfortunately, is ineptly written, clumsily staged, and (except for Borgnine) weakly acted.

PELICAN BRIEF, THE

★★★ Warner Bros, 1993, c, 125 min. Dir: Alan J. Pakula. SP: Alan J. Pakula, b/o novel by John Grisham. Cast: Julia Roberts, Denzel Washington, Sam Shepard, John Heard, William Atherton, Robert Culp, John Lithgow, Tony Goldwyn, Hume Cronyn.

Another adaptation of a Grisham novel, far-fetched but watchable. The premise: two Supreme Court Justices have been murdered and law student Darby Shaw (Roberts) would like to know why. She uncovers some pertinent evidence which she puts into a report she calls the Pelican Brief. Soon her life is in terrible danger and she turns to savvy journalist Gray Grantham (Washington) for help. Now they both become targets of mysterious forces. Nonsensical stuff, but Roberts glows, and the chases and narrow escapes should keep you awake. Good supporting cast.

PENITENTIARY

★★☆ Gross, 1979, c, 99 min. Dir and SP: Jamaa Fanaka. Cast: Leon Isaac Kennedy, Thommy Pollard, Floyd Chatman, Gloria Delaney, Donovan Womack, Hazel Spears, Alicia J. Dhanifu, Albert Shepard.

A crudely made prison drama that manages to generate moments of power by sheer persistence. Unjustly convicted of murder, streetwise "Too Sweet" Johnson (Kennedy) is sent to a hellish prison inhabited largely by blacks, where a violent power struggle never ends. "Too Sweet" manages to save himself by his prowess in the boxing ring. This very peculiar prison has a warden who offers a "conjugal" visit from a woman as the boxing prize! Sequels turned up in 1982 and 1987.

PERFECT WORLD, A

★★★☆ Warner Bros., 1993, c, 130 min. Dir: Clint Eastwood. SP: John Lee Hancock. Cast: Kevin Costner, Clint Eastwood, T. J. Lowther, Laura Dern, Keith Szarabajka, Wayne Dehart.

A film that deserved much more attention than it received, A Perfect World is the surprisingly touching and perceptive tale of the relationship between an escaped killer (Costner) and a small boy (Lowther). In one of his best performances, Costner plays a convicted killer with a damaged past who takes young Lowther as his hostage and, through events that come to a devastating conclusion, teaches him about right and wrong. Eastwood takes the much smaller role of the Texas Ranger assigned to track down Costner and the boy. The familiar story is given superior treatment by director Eastwood.

PETRIFIED FOREST, THE

★★★ Warner Bros., 1936, b/w, 83 min. Dir: Archie Mayo. SP: Charles Kenyon and Delmer Daves, b/o play by Robert E. Sherwood. Cast: Leslie Howard, Bette Davis, Humphrey Bogart, Genevieve Tobin, Dick Foran, Charley Grapewin, Porter Hall.

In this, his eleventh film, Bogart repeated his stage role of gangster "Duke" Mantee and walked off with the movie. Ice-cold, tough, and vicious, he holds a group of people hostage at a desert restaurant. Davis is the yearning waitress and Howard the sensitive poet who find a human connection despite their predicament. The movie is clearly stagebound, and also dilutes some of the symbolism of Sherwood's play in favor of melodrama. But Bogart is riveting. Remade as Escape in the Desert (1945).

PHANTOM LADY

★★☆ Universal, 1944, b/w, 87 min. Dir: Robert

Siodmak. SP: Bernard C. Schoenfeld, b/o novel by
William Irish. Cast: Franchot Tone, Ella Raines, Alan
Curtis, Thomas Gomez, Elisha Cook, Jr., Fay Helm,
Andrew Tombes, Regis Toomey.

Over the years this movie has acquired an
unwarranted reputation as a sleeper. There are
a few flashes of style in the artful camerawork,
but on the whole it is not very impressive.
Curtis is an engineer convicted of murdering
his wife, and Raines is the girl determined to
prove his innocence. But who, and where, is
the "phantom lady" with the peculiar hat—
and the alibi? Wait for Cook's orgasmic drum
solo. The rest is surprisingly humdrum.

PHYSICAL EVIDENCE
★★ Columbia, 1989, c, 99 min. Dir: Michael
Crichton. SP: Bill Phillips, b/o story by Steve
Ransohoff, Bill Phillips. Cast: Burt Reynolds, Theresa
Russell, Ned Beatty, Kay Lenz, Ted McGinley, Tom
O'Brien, Kenneth Welch.

Joe Paris (Reynolds) is in deep trouble. A
suspended cop with a history of violent
behavior, he is now the prime suspect in a
murder. His court-appointed lawyer, Jenny
Hudson (Russell), is blocked at every turn
when potential witnesses either change their
story or are killed. It takes over ninety rather
dull minutes for Jenny to prove Joe's
innocence and to reveal the culprit. A
thoroughly routine and rather clumsily
executed melodrama.

PICKUP ON SOUTH STREET
★★★ Fox, 1953, b/w, 80 min. Dir: Samuel Fuller. SP:
Samuel Fuller, b/o story by Dwight Taylor. Cast:
Richard Widmark, Jean Peters, Thelma Ritter, Murvyn
Vye, Richard Kiley, Willis B. Bouchey, Milburn Stone.

A tense if not entirely credible Cold War
melodrama, Pickup on South Street stars
Widmark as a tough New York pickpocket
who inadvertently gains possession of some
top-secret microfilm wanted by Communist
spies. Before long, spies, detectives, and
various lowlife characters are swirling around
him in violent contention. Rather improbably,
he turns patriotic at the end, helping the police
to catch the Communist villains. Jean Peters
plays the girl whose handbag carrried the
microfilm, and who gets slapped around by all
sides at one time or another. As a streetwise
stool-pigeon, Ritter gives the movie's best

performance.

PITFALL
★★★ United Artists, 1948, b/w, 84 min. Dir: Andre
de Toth. SP: Karl Kamb, b/o novel by Jay Dratler.
Cast: Dick Powell, Lizabeth Scott, Raymond Burr, Jane
Wyatt, John Litel, Byron Barr, Jimmy Hunt, Ann
Doran.

Insurance agent John Forbes (Powell) seems to
be leading the good suburban life with his
wife and son, but he's bored and restless.
Enter seductive Mona Stevens (Scott), with
whom he begins an affair. Everything begins
to unravel when a private eye (Burr), who also
covets Mona, sets in motion a plan to entrap
Forbes that ends in a fatal shooting. A shamed
Forbes tries to restore his marriage. Later
movies would pick up the theme of the
ominous shadows in sunny suburbia.

PLACE IN THE SUN, A
★★★☆ Paramount, 1951, b/w, 122 min. Dir: George
Stevens. SP: Michael Wilson, Harry Brown, b/o novel
by Theodore Dreiser and play by Patrick Kearney.
Cast: Montgomery Clift, Elizabeth Taylor, Shelley
Winters, Anne Revere, Raymond Burr, Keith Brasselle.

Time has slightly tarnished this second
adaptation of Theodore Dreiser's novel, but it
remains a gripping, disturbing drama. Clift is
the ambitious young man who is saddled with
a drab—and pregnant—working-class
girlfriend (Winters). When he meets and falls
in love with a rich girl (Taylor at her most
exquisitely beautiful), his fate is sealed. Some
of the film is plodding, and the conclusion is
dubious (should a man be executed if he only
thought of murder?), but the power is
cumulative, and the acting is exemplary. The
movie won six Oscars, including one for
director Stevens.

PLAIN CLOTHES
★★ Paramount, 1988, c, 98 min. Dir: Martha
Coolidge. SP: A. Scott Frank. Cast: Arliss Howard,
Suzy Amis, George Wendt, Diane Ladd, Seymour
Cassell, Larry Pine, Jackie Gayle, Abe Vigoda, Robert
Stack, Alexandra Powers.

This run-of-the-mill action comedy has
Howard as an undercover cop who pretends
to be an overage high school student in order
to find the killer of a teacher. He gives himself
the name of Nick Springsteen and claims to be

distantly related to rock star Bruce. The movie tries to combine high school frivolity with serious police business but it doesn't work. Good supporting cast, however.

PLAY MISTY FOR ME

★★★ Universal/Malposo, 1972, c, 103 min. Dir: Clint Eastwood. SP: Jo Helms and Dean Riesner, b/o story by Jo Helms. Cast: Clint Eastwood, Jessica Walter, Donna Mills, John Larch, Jack Ging, Irene Hervey, Clarice Taylor, Donald Siegel.

Eastwood's first feature as a director-star shows that he still had a long way to go but it's still a riveting movie with some scary moments. Eastwood plays a radio disc jockey whose life is disrupted when an infatuated but deranged listener (Walter) refuses to disappear. She goes from distraught to dangerously violent, putting his life and those of his friends in jeopardy. Walter is frightening as the obsessed fan, her smiles turning to snarls in an instant, and the Monterey-Carmel setting is beautiful.

POINT BLANK

★★★☆ MGM, 1967, c, 92 min. Dir: John Boorman. SP: Alexander Jacobs, David Newhouse, Rafe Newhouse, b/o novel by Richard Stark (Donald E. Westlake). Cast: Lee Marvin, Angie Dickinson, Carroll O'Connor, Keenan Wynn, Lloyd Bochner, John Vernon, Michael Strong, Sharon Acker.

Some critics regard this film as one of the best melodramas of the sixties, and it's not hard to see why. Tough-minded and stylish, it stars Marvin as Walker, an ex-convict bent on revenge for being betrayed and left for dead by his wife (Acker) and her lover (Vernon). He also wants the $93,000 he is owed. Of course a bloodbath ensues, with Walker at the center and his seductive sister-in-law (Dickinson) standing by ambiguously. The movie does get a bit overfancy, but there's an exciting climax at the deserted Alcatraz prison.

POISON IVY

★★ New Line, 1992, c, 94 min. Dir: Katt Shea Ruben. SP: Andy Ruben, Katt Shea Ruben. Cast: Tom Skerritt, Sara Gilbert, Cheryl Ladd, Drew Barrymore.

A sordid, unconvincing little melodrama of the teenager-from-hell school. Rich, lonely Gilbert becomes friends with sexy Barrymore, who proceeds to seduce daddy Skerritt. She also has worse things on her nasty mind. Ladd is Gilbert's manic-depressive mother. Barrymore will be remembered as the enchanting little girl in the classic E.T.. My, how the girl has grown!

POPE OF GREENWICH VILLAGE, THE

★★★ MGM/UA, 1984, c, 120 min. Dir: Stuart Rosenberg. SP: Vincent Patrick, b/o his novel. Cast: Mickey Rourke, Eric Roberts, Darryl Hannah, Geraldine Page, Kenneth McMillan, Tony Musante, M. Emmet Walsh, Burt Young.

A long, rambling comedy-drama with some pungent flavor and some good performances. In New York's Little Italy, down-on-his-luck Charlie (Rourke) is conned into committing a robbery by his loose-cannon cousin Paulie (Roberts). The problem is that the money belongs to the Mafia, and soon the two are in big trouble. Roberts has the showiest role as the crazy Paulie, but there are juicy character turns, especially by Oscar-nominated Page as the blowsy mother of a crooked cop.

PORTRAIT IN BLACK

★★ Universal, 1960, c, 112 min. Dir: Michael Gordon. SP: Ivan Goff, Ben Roberts, b/o their play. Cast: Lana Turner, Anthony Quinn, Sandra Dee, John Saxon, Richard Basehart, Lloyd Nolan, Ray Walston, Anna May Wong.

Dark deeds in glitzy surroundings—that's what this hard-breathing melodrama is all about. It seems that the glamorous Turner, sheathed in her Jean-Louis gowns, not only has contempt for her nasty husband (Nolan) but is also carrying on a torrid affair with the family doctor (Quinn). Together, wife and doctor murder the husband, but someone has their number. Who is it, and who could possibly care? The dialogue is ludicrous, the performances leaden, and the plot riddled with holes.

POSSESSED

★★★ Warner Bros., 1947, b/w, 108 min. Dir: Curtis Bernhardt. SP: Silvia Richards, Ranald MacDougall, b/o story by Rita Weiman. Cast: Joan Crawford, Van Heflin, Raymond Massey, Geraldine Brooks, Stanley Ridges.

Overwrought but fascinating, Possessed begins with a dazed woman (Crawford) wandering through the city streets at night. Admitted to a psychiatric ward, she turns out to be a schizophenic former nurse with a troubled past. A lengthy flashback reveals a wealthy husband (Massey) she doesn't love, a heel (Heflin) who spurns her amorous advances, and a stepdaughter (Brooks) who is her rival for Heflin. It doesn't help that her husband's first wife committed suicide while under her nursing care. Small wonder that the lady is driven to murder. The movie is a decent example of Hollywood's infatuation with psychiatry in the late forties, and Crawford gives it her all in her usual intense style.

POSTMAN ALWAYS RINGS TWICE, THE

★★★☆ MGM, 1946, b/w, 112 min. Dir: Tay Garnett. SP: Harry Ruskin, Niven Busch, b/o novel by James M. Cain. Cast: Lana Turner, John Garfield, Cecil Kellaway, Hume Cronyn, Leon Ames, Audrey Totter.

The minute drifter Frank (Garfield) spots Cora (Turner), you know there's going to be trouble. Seductive in white shorts, halter, and turban, she's the restless wife of elderly Nick (Kellaway), who owns a California diner. Trouble comes fast in this steamy, provocative version of Cain's novel. The two plot Nick's murder, and that's only the beginning of their tangled relationship. The two leads are

Joan Crawford's obsession with Van Heflin eventually leads to murder in the melodrama Possessed *(1947).*

perfectly cast as the star-crossed lovers, and they get expert support, especially from Cronyn as a crafty lawyer. The 1981 remake was twice as explicit and not even half as good.

POSTMAN ALWAYS RINGS TWICE, THE
★★☆ Paramount, 1981, c, 123 min. Dir: Bob Rafelson. SP: David Mamet, b/o novel by James M. Cain. Cast: Jack Nicholson, Jessica Lange, John

Lana Turner and John Garfield exude sexuality in The Postman Always Rings Twice *(1946), a supercharged version of the James Cain novel.*

Colicos, Michael Lerner, Anjelica Huston, John P. Ryan, William Traylor, Tom Hill.

Despite its greater faithfulness to Cain's novel, this adaptation is not nearly as good as the 1946 version with John Garfield and Lana Turner. The movie is photographed handsomely (by Sven Nykvist), and the acting is expert, but the tale of lust, murder, and ironic retribution seems rather dreary in this incarnation. Nicholson is the drifter and Lange the bored, sluttish wife who share some highly explicit sex scenes as they plot to kill her husband (Colicos). The ending has been changed from the novel and the 1946 film.

PRESIDIO, THE

★★★ Paramount, 1988, c, 97 min. Dir: Peter Hyams. SP: Larry Ferguson. Cast: Sean Connery, Mark Harmon, Meg Ryan, Jack Warden, Mark Blum, Dana Gladstone, Jenette Goldstein.

A murder has been committed on the Presidio, a military base near San Francisco. Investigating the crime are a policeman (Harmon) and an officer (Connery) who was once Harmon's nemesis when he was with the military police. The men despise each other, and compounding the problem is Harmon's attraction to Connery's daughter (Ryan). The movie pays much more attention to these tangled relationships than to solving the murder, but there's a burst of action toward the end. Standard material, but Connery, as always, pitches it with professional aplomb.

PRESUMED INNOCENT

★★★ Warner Bros., 1990, c, 127 min. Dir: Alan J. Pakula. SP: Frank J. Pierson, Alan J. Pakula, b/o novel by Scott Turow. Cast: Harrison Ford, Brian Dennehy, Raul Julia, Bonnie Bedelia, Greta Scacchi, John Spencer, Joe Grifasi.

Shock waves occur when a beautiful young lawyer (Scacchi) is found murdered, and the principal suspect is Ford, a prosecuting attorney and colleague with whom she was having a clandestine affair. As the incriminating evidence mounts, Ford becomes the center of a firestorm involving his politically ambitious boss and others with their own agenda. With Ford's loyal wife (Bedelia) waiting in the wings, the trial gets under way. Based on Turow's best-selling novel, *Presumed Innocent* is an overlong but reasonably gripping melodrama that gains momentum after a sluggish opening. The denouement is surprising but not at all believable. As the beleaguered attorney, Ford is understandably dour and intense, but then he is almost *always* dour and intense.

PRETTY POISON

★★★ Fox, 1968, c, 89 min. Dir: Noel Black. SP: Lorenzo Semple, Jr., b/o novel by Stephen Geller. Cast: Anthony Perkins, Tuesday Weld, Beverly Garland, John Randolph, Dick O'Neill.

Released with little fanfare in 1968, this chilling film has now acquired a durable reputation as an offbeat melodrama. Perkins stars as a disturbed young man who leaves prison after serving a stretch as an arsonist. He encounters Weld, whose air of sunny small-town innocence conceals a murderous nature. She lures him into a tangled web that ends with double murder. Drawing on a mostly effective screenplay, first-time director Black offers a riveting portrait of an amoral monster, and Weld plays her expertly.

PRIMAL FEAR

★★★☆ Paramount, 1996, c, 130 min. Dir: Gregory Hoblit. SP: Steve Shagan, Ann Biderman, b/o novel by William Diehl. Cast: Richard Gere, Laura Linney, John Mahoney, Edward Norton, Alfre Woodard, Frances McDormand.

A gripping, smoothly turned out courtroom drama, *Primal Fear* will keep viewers on their toes. In one of his best roles, Gere plays an arrogant, grandstanding Chicago lawyer defending a young choir boy (Norton) against the charge of brutally murdering a beloved archbishop. The case moves in many directions, some shocking and sinister, until the startling denouement. Some plot devices smack of contrivance, but a good cast performs expertly, especially Norton, who is chillingly believable as the defendant.

PRIME CUT

★★ Cinema Center, 1972, c, 86 min. Dir: Michael Ritchie. SP:Robert Dillon. Cast: Lee Marvin, Gene Hackman, Angel Tomkins, Gregory Walcott, Sissy Spacek, Janet Baldwin.

Over the titles, *Prime Cut* begins with a scene in which a gangster is reduced to a package of sausages in a meat-processing plant. The movie proceeds downhill from there. Marvin is a Chicago enforcer who comes to Kansas City to collect a large debt from nasty Hackman, who runs a drug-and-prostitution empire from his plant. After many blood-splattered encounters, guess who winds up dead. Flashy camerawork and elaborately staged scenes of destruction do not help. Film debut of Spacek.

PRINCE OF THE CITY

★★★ Warner Bros., 1981, c, 167 min. Dir: Sidney Lumet. SP: Jay Presson Allen, Sidney Lumet. Cast: Treat Williams, Jerry Orbach, Richard Foronjy, Don Billett, Kenny Marino, Carmine Caridi, Bob Balaban, Lindsay Crouse.

Much too long but still compelling, *Prince of the City* is based on the true story of a cop, here named Danny Ciello (Williams), who agreed to cooperate with a committee investigating police corruption. Despite assurances that he need not involve fellow policemen, his testimony tightened the net around friends and colleagues, with devastating consequences for himself and others. The movie raises interesting moral questions, and Williams gives an intense performance, but the movie's extreme length weakens its forcefulness.

PRINCIPAL, THE

★★ TriStar, 1987, c, 110 min. Dir: Christopher Cain. SP: Frank Deese. Cast: James Belushi, Lou Gossett, Jr., Rae Dawn Chong, Michael Wright, J. J. Cohen, Esai Morales, Troy Winbush.

As punishment for vandalism on the car of his estranged wife's boyfriend, hot-headed teacher Belushi is given a new assignment as principal of the district's worst school. Here he must not only confront the dregs of inner-city youth but a gang leader (Wright) who is vicious and dangerous. After much violence, he prevails with the help of his security head (Gossett). A shrill, heavy-handed melodrama, not believable for a minute.

PRIVATE HELL 36

★★☆ Filmmakers, 1954, b/w, 81 min. Dir: Don Siegel. SP: Collier Young, Ida Lupino. Cast: Ida Lupino, Steve Cochran, Howard Duff, Dean Jagger, Dorothy Malone.

An adequate but also rather drab and sluggish police drama. Duff and Cochran are two cops who come upon a large cache of mob money in pursuit of a suspect. They pocket some of the money, but Duff is a basically honest sort soon racked with guilt, while Cochran is essentially crooked, wanting the money to impress nightclub singer Lupino. The climax is predictable.

PRIZZI'S HONOR

★★★☆ ABC Pictures, 1985, c, 129 min. Dir: John Huston. SP: Richard Condon and Janet Roach, b/o novel by Richard Condon. Cast: Jack Nicholson, Kathleen Turner, Anjelica Huston, Robert Loggia, William Hickey, John Randolph, Lee Richardson.

Prizzi's Honor, Huston's extremely black—and very funny—comedy-melodrama, brought the director new acclaim at the end of his long career. In this wicked satire of the gangster subgenre, Jack Nicholson plays Charlie Partanna, a none-too-bright hit man for a powerful Mafia family, who falls for Irene Walker (Turner), only to discover she is a hit woman with her own agenda. Anjelica Huston, in an Oscar-winning performance, steals the movie as Maerose Prizzi, a scorned Mafia daughter who sets in motion her own elaborate plan of revenge, with startling results. The tongue-in-cheek dialogue and comically convoluted situations keep the laughs coming despite the ample violence. The movie's Oscar nominations included one for Best Picture.

PROFESSIONAL, THE

★★ Columbia, 1994, c, 119 min. Dir and SP: Luc Besson. Cast: Jean Reno, Natalie Portman, Gary Oldman, Danny Aiello, Peter Appel, Ellen Greene.

French-born Leon (Reno) is a different kind of hit man: he likes milk, plants, and Gene Kelly movies. And when the family next door is slaughtered by renegade cops in a drug deal gone sour, he befriends the only survivor, a sullen, street-smart preteenager named Matilda (Portman). The movie is an odd and far-fetched mixture of graphic violence and sentimentality, and despite a few stylish flourishes, it doesn't work. Oldman chews the scenery to bits as a vicious, pill-popping villain.

Hit persons Kathleen Turner and Jack Nicholson dispose of a victim in John Huston's jet-black crime comedy Prizzi's Honor *(1985).*

PSYCHO

★★★☆ Paramount, 1960, b/w, 109 min. Dir: Alfred Hitchcock. SP: Joseph Stefano, b/o novel by Robert Bloch. Cast: Anthony Perkins, Janet Leigh, Vera Miles, John Gavin, Martin Balsam, John McIntire, Frank Albertson.

Is *Psycho* an horrific shocker spawned by Hitchcock's wicked mind? Or is it, as the director himself has called it, "a serious comedy told with tongue in cheek?" However you view it, you are not likely to forget Norman Bates (Perkins), his "mother," or his motel. Early on, the director plays with the audience's expectations—the ostensible heroine (Leigh) steals her company's payroll and flees, only to make the fatal mistake of stopping at the Bates Hotel. From then on, all bets are off as Hitchcock offers one jolt after another. The famous set-pieces—the shower scene, the attack on the stairs—will haunt your dreams, but the ending is simplistic. There have been two sequels and a television movie, all revolving around Norman and his hang-ups.

PUBLIC ENEMY, THE

★★★☆ Warner Bros., 1931, b/w, 84 min. (originally 96 min.) Dir: William Wellman. SP: Kubec Glasmon, John Bright, b/o story by John Bright. Cast: James Cagney, Jean Harlow, Edward Woods, Joan Blondell, Mae Clarke, Donald Cook, Beryl Mercer.

A crude but still powerful gangster melodrama, *The Public Enemy* startled audiences in its day, and also propelled Cagney to stardom, with its no-holds-barred view of a murderous thug's rise and fall. Cagney may be homicidal as Tom Powers, but he also has a sort of

James Cagney's explosive performance in The Public Enemy *(1931) established him as a major star.*

cocky-bantam charm. Of course this is the movie in which, annoyed at breakfast, he pushes a grapefruit into the face of girlfriend Clarke. You are sure to remember the uncompromising ending in which his mummified corpse, bound in rope, topples onto the floor before the eyes of his horrified brother (Cook). Harlow is briefly on hand, giving a hilariously inept performance as Powers's society moll.

PUBLIC EYE, THE

★★☆ Universal, 1992, c, 99 min. Dir and SP: Howard Franklin. Cast: Joe Pesci, Barbara Hershey, Stanley Tucci, Jerry Adler, Jared Harris, Dominic Chianese, Richard Foronjy, Bob Gunton.

Pesci plays Leon ("Berzini") Bernstein, a freelance tabloid photographer modeled on the famed "Weegee," the photographer who recorded life in the raw in New York of the forties. Asked to do a favor by an alluring nightclub owner (Hershey), Berzini suddenly finds himself in the middle of a mob war in which his own life in danger. Pesci's Berzini is completely amoral, and Hershey's slinky femme fatale is pure film noir. Atmospheric but oddly lethargic, the movie is watchable without being especially good.

PULP FICTION

★★★☆ Miramax, 1994, c, 149 min. Dir and SP: Quentin Tarantino, b/o stories by Quentin Tarantino, Roger Avary. Cast: John Travolta, Samuel L. Jackson, Bruce Willis, Uma Thurman, Harvey Keitel, Tim Roth, Amanda Plummer, Eric Stoltz, Rosanna Arquette, Ving Rhames, Christopher Walken, Maria de Medeiros.

A startlingly original piece of work, *Pulp Fiction* combines the blackest of comedy with the most graphic of violence. The movie brings together an odd group of lowlifes in a series of interlocking stories in which time is deliberately splintered. (Some events occur out of sequence.) Characters include two eccentric hit men (Travolta and Jackson, both excellent), a boxer (Willis) on the run from a ruthless gangster (Rhames), and the gangster's drugged-out wife (Thurman). Writer-director Tarantino's technique is to throw the audience off guard by punctuating discussions of mundane matters—a good cup of coffee, pigs as food—with sudden bursts of ultra-violent activity. Most of the time it works. Oscar winner for Best Original Screenplay.

PUSHOVER

★★☆ Columbia, 1954, b/w, 88 min. Dir: Richard Quine. SP: Roy Huggins, b/o stories by Thomas Walsh, William S. Ballinger. Cast: Fred MacMurray, Kim Novak, Phil Carey, Dorothy Malone, E. G. Marshall, Allen Nourse.

Kim Novak made her film debut in this standard-cut melodrama about a cop (MacMurray) who murders for money and a blonde. MacMurray went the same route a decade earlier in Billy Wilder's *Double Indemnity*, but now he seems more tired at the game. Here he is seduced by a wily gangster's moll (Novak) into a conspiracy that results in two murders. Inevitably the plan comes unraveled and MacMurray meets his doom. In no way can Novak match the chilling amorality of Barbara Stanwyck in the earlier Wilder classic.

Q & A

★★★ TriStar, 1990, c, 132 min. Dir: Sidney Lumet. SP: Alan Smithee (Sidney Lumet), b/o novel by Edwin Torres. Cast: Nick Nolte, Timothy Hutton, Armand Assante, Patrick O'Neal, Jenny Lumet, Lee Richardson.

Tough, gritty, but also meandering and sometimes difficult to follow, *Q & A* stars Nolte as Mike Brennan, a man certain to win the Nastiest Cop of the Year Award. A vicious racist and killer, Brennan becomes the target of a police investigation after he shoots a drug suspect in cold blood. Leading the investigation is a naive assistant district attorney (Hutton) who uncovers buried layers of corruption in the department. His knowledge places him in danger and leads to an inevitably violent climax. Nolte gives a fine performance as the loathsome cop, and other cast members are good as well. But the movie is unfocused and too long. Director Lumet also wrote the screenplay under the familiar pseudonym of Alan Smithee.

QUICK CHANGE

★★★ Warner Bros., 1990, c, 89 min. Dir: Howard Franklin, Bill Murray. SP: Howard Franklin, b/o novel by Jay Cronley. Cast: Bill Murray, Geena Davis, Randy Quaid, Jason Robards, Philip Bosco, Bob Elliott, Phil Hartman, Tony Shalhoub, Stanley Tucci.

A far-fetched but sometimes amusing crime comedy starring Murray as a stressed-out New Yorker who robs a bank disguised as a clown. He and his cohorts, girlfriend Davis and infantile friend Quaid, try to leave the city with the loot, but they are thwarted at every turn. By turns they use a car, a cab, a bus, and finally a plane, finding unexpected trouble all along the way. Murray is in his usual put-on mode, and there are some clever swipes at the perils of urban life. The novel was previously filmed in 1985 as *Hold-Up*, with Jean-Paul Belmondo.

QUICKSAND

★★☆ United Artists, 1950, b/w, 79 min. Dir: Irving Pichel. SP: Robert Smith. Cast: Mickey Rooney, Jeanne Cagney, Peter Lorre, Barbara Bates, Taylor Holmes, Art Smith, Wally Cassel.

In the late forties and early fifties, after playing bumptious young men (mainly Andy Hardy) in scores of MGM movies, Rooney took on some serious dramatic roles. Here he plays a luckless fellow who, in trying to impress a girl (Cagney), gets ever deeper into criminal activity. It's strictly routine material; only Lorre (as a penny arcade operator) contributes some color.

RACKET, THE

★★☆ RKO, 1951, b/w, 88 min. Dir: John Cromwell. SP: William Wister Haines, W. R. Burnett, b/o play by Bartlett Cormack. Cast: Robert Mitchum, Lizabeth Scott, Robert Ryan, William Talman, Ray Collins, Robert Hutton, Joyce MacKenzie, William Conrad.

The cobwebs really show in this film version of a 1927 play that was filmed before, in 1928. By this time the story of a fearless, honest police captain (Mitchum) and his clash with a politically ambitious gangster (Ryan) had shown up in many variations, and this version was not exactly fresh. Mitchum brings a good hard edge to his stalwart policeman, but Ryan is best as the Al Capone-like mobster.

RADIOLAND MURDERS

★ Universal, 1994, c, 108 min. Dir: Mel Smith. SP: Willard Huyck, Gloria Katz, Jeff Reno, Ron Osborn. Cast: Brian Benben, Mary Stuart Masterson, Ned Beatty, Brion James, Michael Lerner, Jeffrey Tambor, Larry Miller, Corbin Bersen, Stephen Tobolowsky, Christopher Lloyd, Harvey Korman, Robert Klein, Anita Morris, Michael McKean.

A misbegotten attempt to resuscitate vintage farce, which was probably not all that hilarious when it was vintage. On an evening in 1939, at a Chicago radio station making its network debut, a number of people are murdered, and the station's head writer (Benben) is the chief suspect. Frantic and painfully unfunny, the movie has an impressive cast of players, all trapped in the dreadful material. Lloyd provides the only laughs, as a hard-working sound effects man.

RAGE IN HARLEM, A

★★☆ Miramax, 1991, c, 108 min. Dir: Bill Duke. SP: John Toles-Bey and Bobby Crawford, b/o novel by Chester Himes. Cast: Forest Whitaker, Gregory Hines, Robin Givens, Danny Glover, Zakes Mokae, Badja Djola.

When smooth operator Givens brings a stolen cache of gold from Mississippi to Harlem in 1956, various low-life characters scramble to latch onto it, including hustler Hines and big-shot gangster Glover. Whitaker is Hines's stepbrother, a pious, nerdy undertaker's assistant who fancies himself in love with Givens. Another filming of a Chester Himes novel (*Cotton Comes to Harlem* and others); atmospheric, violent, and ultimately tiresome.

RAISING ARIZONA

★★★☆ Fox, 1987, c, 92 min. Dir: Joel Coen. SP: Ethan Coen, Joel Coen. Cast: Nicolas Cage, Holly Hunter, John Goodman, Trey Wilson, William Forsythe, Sam McMurray, Frances McDormand, Randall "Tex" Cobb.

The Coen brothers followed their clever film noir *Blood Simple* with this off-the-wall crime comedy. When thief Cage and ex-policewoman Hunter learn that they cannot have children, Cage pleases his distraught wife by kidnapping one of the new quintuplets of a furniture mogul. Chaos results when other bizarre characters enter the picture. Cage and Hunter are funny as the misguided couple, and one sequence involving a foiled robbery is inspired slapstick.

RAISING CAIN

★ Universal, 1992, c, 91 min. Dir and SP: Brian De Palma. Cast: John Lithgow, Lolita Davidovich, Steven Bauer, Frances Sternhagen, Gregg Henry, Mel Harris, Tom Bower.

Director-writer De Palma makes an unwise return to his Hitchcock mode for this lurid and utterly preposterous thriller. Lithgow has an actor's field day playing a world-class lunatic who will do anything to find children for his father's scientific experiments. How much is "anything" is for viewers to discover, should they choose to see this awful movie. It is so far over the top that De Palma may have intended it as satire, but don't bother to find out. And how many times did the director see *Psycho*?

RAMPAGE

★★ Miramax, 1992, c, 97 min. Dir and SP: William Friedkin, b/o novel by William P. Wood. Cast: Michael Biehn, Alex McArthur, Nicholas Campbell, Deborah Van Valkenburgh, John Harkins, Art Le Fleur, Grace Zabriskie, Royce D. Applegate.

More of a polemic than a thriller, *Rampage* argues against the use of an insanity plea in murder cases. McArthur gives a chilling performance as a deranged young killer who faces the gas chamber for grisly mass murder, unless his defense can have him confined for life in an asylum. Biehn plays the prosecuting attorney determined to secure the maximum sentence. Early portions of the movie are almost unwatchable in their horror, and the movie has little merit aside from its message. Based on a true story. Made in 1987.

RANSOM

★★★ Touchstone, 1996, c, 119 min. Dir: Ron Howard. SP: Richard Price, Alexander Ignon, b/o story by Cyril Hume, Richard Maibaum. Cast: Mel Gibson, Rene Russo, Gary Sinise, Delroy Lindo, Lili Taylor, Brawley Nolte, Liev Schreiber, Donnie Walhberg, Evan Handler.

A slickly made, undeniably riveting nail-biter that somehow fails to convince as drama. Gibson stars as a wealthy airline executive whose young son (Nolte) is kidnapped by renegade cop Sinise and his scruffy cohorts. When he is unable to recover his son, Gibson startles everyone by offering the ransom money as a reward to anyone who can help him apprehend the kidnappers. One high-voltage sequence follows another, but credibility keeps seeping away as gaping holes appear in the narrative. The all-stops-out climax simply defies belief, but you won't be bored. Loosely based on a 1956 movie and television play of the same name.

RAW DEAL

★★☆ Eagle-Lion, 1948, b/w, 79 min. Dir: Anthony Mann. SP: Leopold Atlas, John C. Higgins, b/o story by Arnold B. Armstrong, Audrey Ashley. Cast: Dennis O'Keefe, Claire Trevor, Raymond Burr, John Ireland, Marsha Hunt, Curt Conway.

The "raw deal" in this competent melodrama goes to Trevor, who loyally aids boyfriend O'Keefe in his desperate prison break, then gets shunted aside when he meets another girl (Hunt) while on the lam. O'Keefe breaks out to exact revenge on the sadistic man (Burr) who double-crossed him. Matters do not turn out well for our hero. Tough stuff in the hard-bitten late-forties style of director Mann.

RAW DEAL

★★ De Laurentlis, 1986, c, 97 min. Dir: John Irvin. SP: Gary M. DeVore, Norman Wexler, b/o story by Luciano Vincenzoni, Sergio Donati. Cast: Arnold Schwarzenegger, Kathryn Harrold, Darren McGavin, Sam Wanamaker, Paul Shenar, Steven Hill, Joe Regalbuto, Robert Davi, Ed Lauter.

Additional proof, as if more were needed, that Schwarzenegger is a maximum action hero with minimum acting ability. In this rather dumb entry, he plays a dismissed FBI agent who has a chance at getting his old job back if he will single-handedly destroy an infamous crime czar (Wanamaker) and his gang. The catch: he will get no help or protection from any law enforcement agency. In one unintentionally hilarious climax after another, he shoots or disables every bad guy without getting a scratch. Way to go, Arnold.

REAR WINDOW
★★★★ Paramount, 1954, c, 112 min. Dir: Alfred Hitchcock. SP: John Michael Hayes, b/o story by Cornell Woolrich. Cast: James Stewart, Grace Kelly, Wendell Corey, Thelma Ritter, Raymond Burr, Judith Evelyn.

One of the Hitchcock's best films, *Rear Window* is a stylishly handled thriller, a bold cinematic experiment, and a cautionary tale on the dangers of prying too deeply into the private lives of people. Stewart is a photographer confined to a wheelchair with a broken leg. Gazing out his window (we see everything from his point of view), he comes to believe that his neighbor (Burr) has strangled his wife. He insists on investigating, with the help of his ravishing fiancée (Kelly) and his sharp-tongued nurse (Ritter). It all becomes very dangerous, and very suspenseful. "We've all become Peeping Toms," the nurse remarks. Today's tabloid journalists, take note.

REBECCA
★★★★ Selznick International, 1940, b/w, 130 min. Dir: Alfred Hitchcock. SP: Robert E. Sherwood, Joan Harrison, b/o novel by Daphne du Maurier. Cast: Laurence Olivier, Joan Fontaine, Judith Anderson, George Sanders, Nigel Bruce, Florence Bates, Gladys Cooper, Reginald Denny.

Hitchcock made his auspicious American film debut with this first-rate, tantalizing drama. What is the mystery behind the death of the beautiful Rebecca? Our heroine (Fontaine) would like to know, since she has married the late Rebecca's brooding husband (Olivier) and inherited the ancestral manor of Manderley. And why is Manderley's housekeeper (Anderson) so hostile to her? All questions are answered in a swirl of melodrama and romance. Fontaine won stardom in her first major role but her Oscar came a year later for Hitchcock's *Suspicion*. *Rebecca* won Oscars for Best Picture and Best Cinematography.

RECKLESS MOMENT, THE
★★★ Columbia, 1949, b/w, 82 min. Dir: Max Opuls (Ophuls). SP: Henry Garson, Robert Soderberg, adapted by Mel Dinelli, Robert E. Kent from story by Elisabeth Sanxay Holding. Cast: Joan Bennett, James Mason, Geraldine Brooks, Henry O'Neill, Shepperd Strudwick, David Bair, Roy Roberts.

Although born in Germany, noted director Ophuls (Opuls in America) brings a special feeling for the California locale to this suspense tale of a beleaguered mother (Bennett). When she believes (erroneously) that her daughter (Brooks) has killed a man, she hides the body, only to confront a smooth Irish blackmailer (Mason). Complications ensue when he falls for Bennett. The story is well handled, but the lady's morally dubious behavior does not make for a sympathetic heroine.

RED HEAT
★★ Columbia/TriStar, 1988, c, 106 min. Dir: Walter Hill. SP: Harry Kleiner, Walter Hill, Troy Kennedy Martin, b/o story by Walter Hill. Cast: Arnold Schwarzenegger, James Belushi, Peter Boyle, Ed O'Ross, Larry Fishburne, Gina Gershon, Richard Bright.

Loud, fast-moving, and entirely predictable, *Red Heat* has the distinction of being the first American production to receive permission to film in Moscow's Red Square, even if only for establishing shots. Stone-faced Schwarzenegger is a top Russian detective who is sent to Chicago to bring back a vicious drug dealer (O'Ross) who has fled to America. When the dealer escapes, Schwarzengger teams with foul-mouthed cop Belushi to capture him. Inevitably their mutual hostility turns to friendship as they barrel through the usual chases and shootouts.

RED HOUSE, THE
★★ United Artists, 1947, b/w, 100 min. Dir and SP: Delmer Daves, b/o novel by George Agnew Chamberlain. Cast: Edward G. Robinson, Lon McAllister, Allene Roberts, Judith Anderson, Julie London, Rory Calhoun, Ona Munson.

Even Robinson's reliable professionalism cannot do much for this awkward, overwrought melodrama. He plays a farmer tormented by a deadly secret involving his misdeed in the past. His curious young ward (Roberts) and a local farmhand (McAllister) investigate the mystery buried deep in the adjoining woods, sending the farmer over the edge. Apart from Robinson the cast is barely adequate, and Anderson, as Robinson's sister, is nobody's idea of a plain-speaking farm drudge.

RED ROCK WEST

★★★☆ Propaganda Films, 1993, c, 97 min. Dir: John Dahl. SP: John Dahl, Rick Dahl. Cast: Nicolas Cage, Dennis Hopper, Lara Flynn Boyle, J. T. Walsh, Timothy Carhart, Dan Shor.

This modestly scaled but superb film noir for the nineties makes all the right moves. Twisty and intriguing, it centers on Mike (Cage), a decent but not overly bright Texas drifter who comes to dusty Red Rock, Wyoming, where he is mistaken for a hit man. The prospective victim is the devious wife (Boyle) of the town's nasty sheriff (Walsh), who has ordered the hit. By the time the real hit man (Hopper) turns up with murder on his mind, Mike is in great danger, and so is virtually everyone else. There are some surprises along the way, plus many neatly rendered noir touches. Hopper gives his by-now standard performance as a hair-trigger nutcase, and Boyle is effectively slinky as an Ava Gardner-like seductress.

RELENTLESS

★ New Line, 1989, c, 93 min. Dir: William Lustig. SP: Jack T. D. Robinson. Cast: Judd Nelson, Leo Rossi, Robert Loggia, Meg Foster, Patrick O'Bryan, Ken Lerner, Angel Tompkins.

Driven over the edge by an abusive father, deranged serial killer Nelson selects his victims from the telephone pages, while L.A. cops Rossi and Loggia work to catch him. A good part of this odious film is taken up with graphic depictions of Nelson's murders; much of the rest consists of dull banter between the cops. An ugly and reprehensible thriller, yet somehow it inspired three sequels.

RENT-A-COP

★★ Kings Road, 1988, c, 96 min. Dir: Jerry London. SP: Dennis Shryack, Michael Blodgett. Cast: Burt Reynolds, Liza Minnelli, James Remar, Richard Masur, Dionne Warwick, Bernie Casey, Robby Benson.

The body count is high and the believability low in this tired melodrama. Minnelli (in an unnerving performance) plays a hooker who inadvertently becomes a material witness when a drug bust turns sour and a number of people, including cops, are killed. Now the killer (a sleazy Remar) is stalking her, and she turns to ex-cop Reynolds for help. Together, after some unlikely turns of the plot, they manage to set things right. Nothing much works here.

REPORT TO THE COMMISSIONER

★★☆ United Artists, 1975, c, 112 min. Dir: Milton Katselas. SP: Abby Mann, Ernest Tidyman, b/o novel by James Mills. Cast: Michael Moriarty, Yaphet Kotto, Susan Blakely, Hector Elizondo, Tony King, Dana Elcar, William Devane, Vic Tayback, Stephen Elliott, Richard Gere.

"What am I doing here anyway—on this planet?" A good question from rookie cop Bo Lockley (Moriarty), but the answer is tragic. He is naive and idealistic, and also a sitting duck for a department cover-up. When Bo accidentally kills an undercover cop (Blakely), the higher-ups refuse to divulge the circumstances, and the consequences for Bo are devastating. A downbeat, unsettling police drama, marred by a weak screenplay with cloudy or inexplicable motivations. The central sequence—a chase through New York City streets into Saks department store—is flashy but not believable. Gere's film debut.

RESERVOIR DOGS

★★★ Miramax, 1992, c, 100 min. Dir and SP: Quentin Tarantino. Cast: Harvey Keitel, Tim Roth, Chris Penn, Steve Buscemi, Lawrence Tierney, Michael Madsen.

Two years before *Pulp Fiction*, Tarantino attracted critical attention as writer-director of this film. It's a typical Tarantino mixture of ultra-violent action and jet-black comedy, which viewers will find either tasty or unpalatable. After an aborted diamond robbery, a group of thieves gather at their hideout to discuss what went wrong. For one thing, one of the men is a police informer. Occasional flashbacks explain some of the missing pieces. In between conversations on mundane matters, there are a few sudden, unsettling explosions of graphic blood-letting. A striking movie, but proceed at your own risk.

REVENGE

★★ Columbia, 1990, c, 124 min. Dir: Tony Scott. SP: Jim Harrison, Jeffrey Fiskin, b/o novel by Jim Harrison. Cast: Kevin Costner, Anthony Quinn, Madeleine Stowe, Tom Milian, Joaquin Martinez, James Gammon, Miguel Ferrer, Sally Kirkland.

A heavy-handed thriller, starring Costner as a retired Navy pilot who visits Quinn, his rich, tyrannical, and very powerful Mexican friend, and makes the bad mistake of having a steamy affair with his wife (Stowe). Quinn retaliates by beating him senseless and sending his wife into prostitution. Now Costner is out for—you guessed it—revenge. Star power cannot save this dull and unconvincing movie.

REVERSAL OF FORTUNE

★★★☆ Warner Bros., 1990, c, 120 min. Dir: Barbet Schroeder. SP: Nicholas Kazan, b/o book by Alan Dershowitz. Cast: Jeremy Irons, Glenn Close, Ron Silver, Annabella Sciorra, Uta Hagen, Fisher Stevens, Christine Baranski.

Did Claus von Bulow (Irons) attempt to murder his wife Sunny (Close), who now lies in a comatose state? The apparent facts were all in the newspapers, but what is the truth behind the headlines? Headed by von Bulow's lawyer, Alan Dershowitz (Silver), a team of his colleagues and students look into the evidence, the legalities, and the morality of the case. At the same time, a cold, impassive von Bulow (a brilliant performance by Oscar-winner Irons) remains an enigma to everyone, while Sunny is seen in flashback or delivers voice-over narration from her sickbed. A crafty true tale of life and law as practiced among the rich, the movie lacks emotional heat, but it's undeniably fascinating to watch.

RICH MAN'S WIFE, THE

★★ Hollywood, 1996, c, 95 min. Dir and SP: Amy Holden Jones. Cast: Halle Berry, Christopher McDonald, Clive Owen, Peter Green, Clea Lewis, Charles Hallahan, Frankie Faison.

What on earth has happened to poor Josie Potenza (Berry)? Accused of murdering her wealthy husband (McDonald), she has also been involved in (though not necessarily guilty of) the deaths of her duplicitous lover (Owen) and a homicidal fruitcake named Cole (Green). The story leading to Josie's plight is told in flashback, and it makes for a derivative, dreary film noir. Clearly Josie has never seen *Strangers on a Train*—she half-heartedly wishes her husband dead, then meets Cole, the dangerous man most likely to carry out her wish. From that point on she behaves so stupidly that soon she is up to her pretty neck in violence. The surprise ending makes no sense. Lewis stands out as Cole's wily ex-wife.

RICOCHET

★ Warner Bros., 1991, c, 97 min. Dir: Russell Mulcahy. SP: Steven E. de Souza, b/o story by Fred Dekker, Menno Meyjes. Cast: Denzel Washington, John Lithgow, Ice T, Kevin Pollak, Lindsay Wagner, Mary Ellen Trainor.

The body count is exceptionally high in this flashy but lurid and repellent crime drama. Washington is the honorable cop-turned-assistant district attorney who captures psychotic killer Lithgow. Lithgow escapes from prison to exact his revenge on Washington with a diabolical plan of public humiliation, intimidation, and murder. Somehow the movie spins out of control as it progresses, ending in a wildly improbable climax atop a tower. Lithgow has played a few demented killers in his career but none as nasty as this.

RIOT

★★☆ Paramount, 1969, c, 97 min. Dir: Buzz Kulik. SP: James Poe, b/o novel by Frank Elli. Cast: Jim Brown, Gene Hackman, Ben Carruthers, Mike Kellin, Gerald O'Loughlin, Clifford David.

Former football star Jim Brown plays a convict who unwittingly finds himself leading a prison riot in this standard-cut melodrama. The riot starts as a spontaneous demonstration provoked by convict Hackman in the solitary cell block and spreads to the entire prison, where Brown takes over to protect the lives of the guards and to insure the success of a tunneling operation. The movie runs through the familiar gambits of the prison genre and adds a few wrinkles for a later era.

RIOT IN CELL BLOCK II

★★★ Allied Artists, 1954, b/w, 80 min. Dir: Don Siegel. SP: Richard Collins. Cast: Neville Brand, Emile Meyer, Frank Faylen, Leo Gordon, Robert Osterloh, Paul Frees, Whit Bissell, Dan Keefer, Alvy Moore.

Director Siegel brings considerable force and high-powered energy to this prison drama. Filmed at California's Folsom State Prison, the movie used many actual inmates to tell the grim story of prisoners who rebel against intolerable conditions, including crowded quarters, enforced idleness, and the company of deranged men. Brand stands out as the hard-as-nails leader of the riot, and others contribute gritty performances.

RISE AND FALL OF LEGS DIAMOND, THE

★ Warner Bros., 1960, b/w, 101 min. Dir: Budd Boetticher. SP: Joseph Landon. Cast: Ray Danton, Karen Steele, Elaine Stewart, Jesse White, Simon Oakland, Robert Lowery, Warren Oates, Judson Pratt.

The notorious Jack "Legs" Diamond (Danton) cheats, steals, and kills his way to the top of the twenties crime world in this inept and dreary movie. The film obviously hopes to emulate the Warner gangster melodramas of the thirties, but not a single shred of their punch or their drive is evident for a moment, and Danton's overwrought "Legs" is not even on a par with George Raft.

RISING SUN

★★★ Fox, 1993, c, 129 min. Dir: Philip Kaufman. SP: Michael Crichton, Michael Backes, b/o novel by Michael Crichton. Cast: Sean Connery, Wesley Snipes, Harvey Keitel, Tia Carrere, Kevin Anderson, Steve Buscemi, Mako, Cary-Hiroyuki Tagawa, Stan Shaw.

In the offices of a powerful Japanese corporation based in Los Angeles, while a lavish dinner is in progress, a prostitute is found murdered in the board room. Who killed her, and why is her murder being covered up? Detective Webb Smith (Snipes) and seasoned investigator John Connor (Connery) team up to find the answers. Inevitably they uncover skulduggery in high places. The ins and outs of the plot are sometimes difficult to follow, but the intriguing high-tech background helps to sustain interest.

RIVER'S EDGE

★★★ Hemdale, 1987, c, 99 min. Dir: Tim Hunter. SP: Neal Jimenez. Cast: Crispin Glover, Keanu Reeves, Ione Skye Leitch, Daniel Roebuck, Dennis Hopper, Joshua Miller, Roxana Zal.

Based on a true incident that took place in California in 1981, this disturbing but ultimately oppressive film concerns the murder of a teenage girl, and the oddly disengaged, even indifferent way in which her friends respond to the killing. Their leader (Glover, in a bizarre performance) urges them to remain silent and to go about their empty lives. The movie's portrait of amoral young people is somewhat compromised by the apparent absence of *any* happy or productive people in this town, whether child or adult. Hopper appears as a drug-crazed hermit who claims also to have killed a girl twenty years earlier.

RIVER WILD, THE

★★★ Universal, 1994, c, 108 min. Dir: Curtis Hanson. SP: Denis O'Neill. Cast: Meryl Streep, Kevin Bacon, David Strathairn, Joseph Mazzello, John C. Reilly, Benjamin Bratt.

After playing so many neurasthenic women, it must have been something of a relief for Streep to play a strong action heroine in this suspenseful melodrama. She's Gail, unhappily married to Tom (Strathairn), who goes out West with her son (Mazzello) on a rafting trip. The trip becomes a terrifying ordeal when two fleeing killer-thieves (Bacon and O'Reilly) take over and demand that she use her rafting expertise to help them get away. With Tom showing up unexpectedly, the trip becomes not only a test of their relationship but also a harrowing challenge to her family's stamina and resourcefulness. Some character nuances are lost along the way, but the movie holds your attention.

ROARING TWENTIES, THE

★★★ Warner Bros., 1939, b/w, 103 min. Dir: Raoul Walsh. SP: Jerry Wald, Richard Macaulay, Robert Rossen, b/o story by Mark Hellinger. Cast: James Cagney, Priscilla Lane, Humphrey Bogart, Jeffrey Lynn, Gladys George, Frank McHugh, Paul Kelly.

The theme was not exactly new even in 1939. a rejected World War I veteran (Cagney) turns to crime, becomes a kingpin gangster, then meets a violent end. However, Warners slams the story across with its usual vitality, turning Cagney's rise and fall into watchable melodrama. Lane is the demure singer Cagney loves in vain, and Bogart is his nasty nemesis. Blowsy chanteuse George has a classic line after Cagney is gunned down by the police: "He used to be a big shot."

ROBBERY

★★★ Embassy (British), 1967, c, 114 min. Dir: Peter Yates. SP: Edward Boyd, Peter Yates, George Markstein, b/o treatment by Gerald Wilson. Cast: Stanley Baker, Joanna Pettet, James Booth, Frank Finlay, Barry Foster, William Marlowe, Clinton Greyn, George Sewell, Michael McKay.

MOMENTS TO WAIT FOR

From the annals of movie crime come these fifteen startling and memorable images.

- Wrapped in a mummy's shroud, the body of gangster James Cagney topples onto his horrified brother. (*The Public Enemy*, 1931)

- Asked how he lives, desperate escaped convict Paul Muni hisses, "I steal!" then vanishes into the darkness. (*I Am a Fugitive from a Chain Gang*, 1932)

- In the Malayan moonlight, Bette Davis finally comes face to face with the retribution she has so far avoided for killing her lover. (*The Letter*, 1940)

- Racing to the library, Teresa Wright confronts—word by word—a newspaper article that suggests her beloved uncle, Joseph Cotten, is a murderer. (*Shadow of a Doubt*, 1943)

- Having committed cold-blooded murder, lovers Barbara Stanwyck and Fred MacMurray are anxious to flee the scene. Then their car stalls. (*Double Indemnity*, 1944)

- Psychotic hood Richard Widmark, laughing maniacally, pushes wheelchair-bound Mildred Dunnock down a flight of stairs. (*Kiss of Death*, 1947)

- Defying the police, deranged gangster James Cagney straddles a gasoline tank. Shouting, "Made it, Ma! Top of the world!," he fires a bullet into the tank and blows himself up. (*White Heat*, 1949)

- Nasty hood Lee Marvin flings scalding-hot coffee into the face of his moll, Gloria Grahame. (*The Big Heat*, 1953)

- The triple-surprise ending in the courtroom. (*Witness for the Prosecution*, 1957)

- Demented hag Bette Davis serves a repulsive supper to her pitiful crippled sister, Joan Crawford. (*What Ever Happened to Baby Jane?*, 1962)

- A bloodbath concludes the infamous careers of Bonnie Parker and Clyde Barrow. (*Bonnie and Clyde*, 1967)

- In one shocking moment, hit man Jack Nicholson settles the score with his hit woman wife, Kathleen Turner. (*Prizzi's Honor*, 1985)

- During the blistering climactic shootout at Chicago's Union Station, a baby carriage, with baby inside, begins to roll down a long flight of stairs. (*The Untouchables*, 1987)

- In the "social club" of mobsters, volatile, trigger-happy Joe Pesci abruptly shoots and kills a young waiter whom he previously wounded and whom he now feels is mocking him. (*GoodFellas*, 1990)

- In the closing moments, detective Brad Pitt is forced to confront the ultimate horrifying act of the deranged serial killer he has been pursuing throughout the film. (*Seven*, 1995)

An efficiently made, straightforward account of an actual event: the 1963 robbing of over three million pounds from a British night train bound from Glasgow to London. Regarded as the biggest heist in English history, the robbery required a small army of men well trained in their special lines of work. Baker plays the master thief who supervises the operation, Pettet is his troubled wife, and Booth gives a crisp edge to the role of the Scotland Yard detective in pursuit of the thieves. Best scene: the twenty-minute, almost wordless theft and car chase that opens the movie.

ROBOCOP

★★★ Orion, 1987, c, 103 min. Dir: Paul Verhoeven. SP: Edward Neumeier, Michael Miner. Cast: Peter Weller, Nancy Allen, Daniel O'Herlihy, Ronny Cox, Kurtwood Smith, Miguel Ferrer, Robert DoQui, Ray Wise.

An extremely violent futuristic cop movie, with very good special effects and touches of humor. After Detroit cop Murphy (Weller) is killed in the line of duty, a sinister security company reconstructs him into a robot who is programmed to enforce the law. The trouble is that Weller, imbedded in the robot, still seeks revenge on those who murdered him. This hit movie from Dutch director Paul Verhoeven inspired two sequels and both an animated and live-action television series.

ROCK, THE

★☆ Hollywood, 1996, c, 136 min. Dir: Michael Bay. SP: David Weisberg, Douglas S. Cook, b/o story by David Weisberg, Douglas S. Cook, Mark Rosner. Cast: Sean Connery, Nicolas Cage, Ed Harris, Michael Biehn, William Forsythe, David Morse, John Spencer, John C. McGinley, Vanessa Marcil.

A renegade Marine general (Harris), joined by an outlaw brigade, seizes the now-defunct Alcatraz Island, known as the Rock, taking a number of tourists as hostages. Unless reparations are paid to the families of men killed in covert operations, he will fire poison-gas bombs at San Francisco. Two men—an FBI chemical/biological weapons expert (Cage) and a convict (Connery) who is the only man to ever break out of Alcatraz—are sent to defuse the bombs and stop Harris. A long, relentless, terminally stupid action film that defies all logic and reason and wastes its three able leads. High-tech special effects, and nothing more.

ROLLERCOASTER

★★☆ Universal, 1977, c, 119 min. Dir: James Goldstone. SP: Richard Levinson, William Link, b/o story by Sanford Sheldon, Richard Levinson, William Link. Cast: George Segal, Richard Widmark, Timothy Bottoms, Henry Fonda, Harry Guardino, Susan Strasberg, Helen Hunt, Dorothy Tristan.

A good cast gives a bit of a boost to this not-very-good thriller. Bottoms is a cool young extortionist who is sabotaging rollercoasters across the country and causing many deaths.

Segal is the Los Angeles safety inspector who is tracking the killer and is determined to nab him. The suspense drains away by the time of the film's climax, a hair-raising rollercoaster ride.

ROMEO IS BLEEDING

★★★ Gramercy, 1994, c, 108 min. D: Peter Medak. SP: Hilary Henkin. Cast: Gary Oldman, Lena Olin, Annabella Sciorra, Juliette Lewis, Roy Scheider, Will Patton, James Cromwell, Dennis Farina, Julia Migenes.

It's difficult to say how any viewer will react to this lurid, over-the-top film noir, but it's not likely to bore. The characters are as disreputable a lot as one could imagine: a grungy and corrupt cop (Oldman), his dim-bulb mistress (Lewis), a truly vicious hit woman (Olin) with the smile of a shark, and a snakelike kingpin mobster (Scheider). Only Oldman's long-suffering wife (Sciorra) escapes the terminal nastiness. Some of the violent sequences are so excessive that they come close to parody, and the same is true of the hard-breathing film noir dialogue: "Hell is the time you should have walked—but you didn't."

ROOKIE, THE

★☆ Warner Bros., 1990, c, 121 min. Dir: Clint Eastwood. SP: Boaz Yakin and Scott Spiegel. Cast: Clint Eastwood, Charlie Sheen, Raul Julia, Sonia Braga, Lara Flynn Boyle, Tom Skerritt.

They meet, they fight, they bond. Yes, this is yet another buddy-cop movie, and not the Martin and Lewis farce the title seems to suggest. But this entry is more preposterous than usual. Eastwood is the tough veteran cop (we know he's tough because he chomps on cigars), and Sheen is his new partner, a rich kid who has to prove his mettle through a violent rite of passage. Every conceivable cliché of the genre is trotted out, but it's all in vain. Poor Braga plays a German bondage freak who accompanies bad guy Julia on his nasty capers.

ROPE

★★★ Paramount, 1948, c, 80 min. Dir: Alfred Hitchcock. SP: Arthur Laurents; adaptation: Hume Cronyn, b/o play by Patrick Hamilton. Cast: James Stewart, John Dall, Farley Granger, Joan Chandler, Cedric Hardwicke, Constance Collier, Douglas Dick.

Hitchcock's films are almost always interesting, but this peculiar, experimental melodrama—

his first in color— is not among his best. Dall and Granger are two young men who believe themselves to be above the law. Merely for thrills, they murder a friend, then perversely invite their victim's father, aunt, and girlfriend to supper in their apartment, with the body hidden in a chest. Their former headmaster (a miscast Stewart) uncovers the crime. To create eighty seamless minutes of real time, Hitchcock shot the movie in continuous ten-minute takes. Despite his efforts, the movie's stage origin is all too evident.

ROSARY MURDERS, THE

★★ Laurel/First Take, 1987, c, 105 min. Dir: Fred Walton. SP: Elmore Leonard, Fred Walton, b/o novel by William Kienzle. Cast: Donald Sutherland, Charles Durning, Belinda Bauer, Josef Sommer, Kathleen Tolan.

A dreary mystery in which a priest (Sutherland) turns detective after a number of nuns and other priests are brutally murdered. When the killer confesses to the priest, there are suggestions of Alfred Hitchcock's I Confess, but the movie's suspense simply drains away by the fourth or fifth murder. By the time that dark secrets are finally exposed, viewers are not likely to care.

ROXIE HART

★★★ Fox, 1942, b/w, 75 min. Dir: William A. Wellman. SP: Nunnally Johnson, b/o play by Maurice Watkins. Cast: Ginger Rogers, Adolphe Menjou, George Montgomery, Lynne Overman, Nigel Bruce, Spring Byington, William Frawley, Sara Allgood, Iris Adrian.

This raucous satirical comedy gives Rogers a juicy role as a gum-chewing redhead in 1920s Chicago who becomes a media darling after shooting her lover. Menjou is the shyster lawyer ("A simple barefoot mouthpiece") who defends her with a series of hilarious wisecracks. While hardly in a class with Wellman's best work, the movie is sardonic fun. The movie was adapted from Watkins's stage play Chicago, which was first filmed in 1927 and became the basis for the 1975 stage musical and its 1997 revival under that name.

RUBY

★★☆ Polygram, 1992, c, 110 min. Dir: John Mackenzie. SP: Stephen Davis. Cast: Danny Aiello, Sherilyn Fenn, Arliss Howard, Marc Lawrence, Richard Sarafian, Tobin Bell, David Duchovny.

Jack Ruby, the sleazy nightclub owner who killed Lee Harvey Oswald, remains a shadowy figure in the controversy surrounding the assassination of President Kennedy. This elaborate but fairly plodding fictionalization of Ruby's role depicts him as an ambitious lowlife who found himself caught up in a deadly conspiracy shared by the CIA and the Mafia. Aiello gives a fine performance as a small fish in a riverful of sharks, but the movie never catches fire.

RUMBLE IN THE BRONX

★★☆ New Line, 1995, c, 91 min. Dir: Stanley Tong. SP: Edward Tang, Fibe Ma. Cast: Jackie Chan, Anita Mui, Francoise Yip, Marc Akerstream, Garvin Cross, Morgan Lam, Kris Lord.

Chinese film star and martial arts wizard Chan broke into the American market with this crudely made but sometimes amusing action film. He arrives from Hong Kong to attend his uncle's wedding in the Bronx and finds himself the target for a nasty motorcycle gang and then for some equally nasty jewel thieves. The plot is merely an excuse for Chan to demonstrate his amazing Kung Fu prowess, which he does in sequence after sequence. Poorly dubbed in part, but at least it's mostly tongue-in-cheek.

RUN

★★☆ Buena Vista, 1990, c, 91 min. Dir: Geoff Burrowes. SP: Dennis Shryack, Michael Blodgett. Cast: Patrick Dempsey, Kelly Preston, Ken Pogue, James Kidnie, Sean McCann, Michael MacRae.

Nonstop action, lively and wildly improbable, as law student Dempsey runs for his life. Falsely accused of killing the only son of a town's biggest mobster, he must flee not only from the mob but also from corrupt cops. There are at least three separate climaxes as he hurtles from place to place, aided by a pretty casino dealer (Preston). As the bullets fly past his head, he seems to have more lives than a barrelful of cats.

RUNAWAY TRAIN

★★★☆ Cannon, 1985, c, 112 min. Dir: Andrei Konchalovsky. SP: Djordje Milicevic, Paul Zindel, Edward Bunker, b/o screenplay by Akira Kurosawa. Cast: Jon Voight, Eric Roberts, Rebecca De Mornay, Kyle Heffner, John P. Ryan, T. K. Carter, Kenneth McMillan.

A thinking person's action movie, *Runaway Train* can also boast a remarkable performance by Voight and some breathtaking edge-of-the-seat footage. Voight plays Manny, a hardened criminal, choking with rage at society. He escapes from a hellish Alaska prison with his lightheaded fellow convict (Roberts), but makes the mistake of jumping aboard a freight train that has lost its engineer and is out of control. Meanwhile, the sadistic prison warden (Ryan) is determined to recapture the escapees at any cost. The pace is swift and the dialogue is pungent and occasionally even thoughtful. Voight and Roberts both won Oscar nominations.

RUNNING SCARED

★★★ 1986, MGM/UA, c, 106 min. Dir: Peter Hyams. SP: Gary DeVore, Jimmy Huston. Cast: Gregory Hines, Billy Crystal, Steven Bauer, Darlanne Fluegel, Joe Pantoliano, Dan Hedaya, Jimmy Smits.

Hines and Crystal play rowdy Chicago street cops in this unsurprising but fast and entertaining melodrama. The two decide it's time to retire, but not before they nail one more lowlife, would-be Spanish godfather Smits. Naturally that leads to chases, shootouts, and lots of raucous, playful banter between the leads. Hines and Crystal seem to share a genuine rapport, and that adds to the fun. But don't expect anything new.

RUSH

★★ MGM, 1991, c, 120 min. Dir: Lili Fini Zanuck. SP: Pete Dexter. Cast: Jason Patric, Jennifer Jason Leigh, Sam Elliott, Max Perlich, Gregg Allman, Tony Frank, William Sadler.

Talk about giving your all to your job: In mid-seventies Texas, Jim Raynor (Patric) and Kristen Cates (Leigh) are undercover cops who are assigned to bring down a drug lord (Allman). Lovers as well as partners, they must pretend to be junkies and drug dealers, but sadly, caught up in the drug scene, they become desperate junkies for real, with ultimately devastating consequences. Tough, gritty, and grim, *Rush* is also tedious and unconvincing. Patric, however, is good, and Leigh is less mannered than she would become in later roles.

RUTHLESS PEOPLE

★★★ Touchstone, 1986, c, 93 min. Dir: Jim Abrahams, David Zucker, Jerry Zucker. SP: Dale Launer. Cast: Danny DeVito, Bette Midler, Judge Reinhold, Helen Slater, Anita Morris, Bill Pullman, William G. Schilling.

A scatterbrained comedy that earns some laughs, mostly due to Midler, who plays a rich, obnoxious woman who is loathed by her husband (DeVito). He hatches a plan to kill her, but instead she is kidnapped by an inept couple (Reinhold and Slater), who have a business grievance against DeVito. Midler is the Prisoner from Hell for the couple, as others, including DeVito's mistress (Morris) and her idiot boyfriend (Pullman), become involved. Midler is hilarious as the virago who shrieks, "I've been kidnapped by K-Mart!" when the kidnappers keep lowering their ransom price.

SABOTEUR

★★☆ Universal, 1943, b/w, 108 min. Dir: Alfred Hitchcock. SP: Peter Viertel, Joan Harrison, Dorothy Parker. Cast: Robert Cummings, Priscilla Lane, Norman Lloyd, Otto Kruger, Alan Baxter, Alma Kruger, Vaughan Glaser.

Hitchcock's wartime melodrama is not very good, but viewers may enjoy some of the set pieces, especially the famous Statue of Liberty climax. ("The sleeve! The sleeve!") Cummings is miscast as a young factory worker who is falsely accused of espionage. He flees, and with the help of a girl (Lane) whose reluctance turns to love, he finally catches the real saboteur (Lloyd). There are a few nice offbeat touches, but Hitchcock said it best: "The script lacks discipline."

SATAN MET A LADY

★★ Warner Bros., 1936, b/w, 75 min. Dir: William

Dieterle. SP: Brown Holmes, b/o novel by Dashiell Hammett. Cast: Warren William, Bette Davis, Alison Skipworth, Arthur Treacher, Winifred Shaw, Marie Wilson, Porter Hall.

A curiosity, available on video, but don't hurry to find it. In fact, it's a disguised version of Hammett's *The Maltese Falcon*, first filmed in 1931 and then again (classically) in 1941. This time the private eye is Warren William, who tangles with a nest of vipers over, not a gold-encrusted falcon, but a jewel-filled ram's horn. Davis plays the femme fatale, the rough equivalent of Mary Astor's role. Cheaply made and forgettable.

SCARFACE

★★★☆ United Artists, 1932, b/w, 90 min. Dir: Howard Hawks. SP: Seton I. Miller, John Lee Mahin, W. R. Burnett, b/o story by Ben Hecht and novel by Armitage Trail. Cast: Paul Muni, Ann Dvorak, George Raft, Boris Karloff, Karen Morley, Vince Barnett, Osgood Perkins, C. Henry Gordon.

This primitive but still-powerful melodrama remains one of the most influential gangster films of the early thirties. Muni plays Tony Camonte, a cunning and vicious gangster resembling Al Capone, who murders his way to the top and finally gets his just desserts on the gallows. Under Hawks's direction, the movie captures the tawdry, dangerous atmosphere of the underworld and even adds a few surprising twists, such as Tony's disturbingly close attachment to his wild sister (Dvorak). Karloff appears as an unlikely gangster. Censors of the time demanded the addition of a subtitle—*The Shame of the Nation*. The movie was remade in 1983, with Al Pacino.

SCARFACE

★★ Universal, 1983, c, 170 min. Dir: Brian De Palma. SP: Oliver Stone. Cast: Al Pacino, Steven Bauer, Michelle Pfeiffer, Mary Elizabeth Mastrantonio, Robert Loggia, Miriam Colon, Paul Shenar, Harris Yulin.

A long, blood-splattered remake of the famed 1932 gangster film, *Scarface* adheres closely to the plot line of the original. A thug named Tony (Pacino), now a Cuban refugee in 1980, comes to Florida, where he rises to become a powerful, ruthless drug lord. Eventually he is undone by arrogance, greed, and his incestuous love for his sister (Mastrantonio). Drawing on Stone's overinflated, often tedious screen-play, director De Palma tries to give the movie a tragic dimension, but ultimately he adds nothing but a larger body count and a few repellent sequences. Perhaps some political point is being made here (in typical Stone fashion, *everyone* is corrupt), but the movie drowns in its excess, and all of Pacino's emoting cannot save it. De Palma dedicates the movie to Howard Hawks and Ben Hecht, the director and author, respectively, of the original. Talk about chutzpah.

SCARFACE MOB, THE

★★☆ United Artists, 1962, b/w, 102 min. Dir: Phil Karlson. SP: Paul Monash, b/o book by Eliot Ness, Oscar Fraley. Cast: Robert Stack, Keenan Wynn, Barbara Nichols, Pat Crowley, Neville Brand, Bruce Gordon.

In 1959 a two-part program on *Desilu Playhouse* concerning the exploits of thirties crime-buster Eliot Ness and his colleagues led to the popular television series *The Untouchables*. *The Scarface Mob* is the reedited feature-film version of that original program, with intrepid Ness pursuing Al Capone and his gang. As he would in the TV series, columnist Walter Winchell provides the staccato narration. For the best Ness-Capone confrontation, see *The Untouchables* (1987).

SCARLET STREET

★★★ Universal, 1945, b/w, 103 min. Dir: Fritz Lang. SP: Dudley Nichols, b/o play by Georges de la Fourcharliere. Cast: Edward G. Robinson, Joan Bennett, Dan Duryea, Rosalind Ivan, Margaret Lindsay.

To capitalize on the success of *Woman in the Window* in the previous year, the stars and director of that well-turned melodrama were reunited in this lesser but fairly intriguing film. Under Lang's direction, Robinson plays a mousy cashier with a dead-end job and a shrewish wife (Ivan). One fateful night, he meets alluring Bennett, who uses his intense infatuation to extract money for herself and her lowlife boyfriend (Duryea). Her treachery leads inexorably to murder. Robinson plays another of Lang's doomed antiheroes, but this time, in a rare switch, somebody else pays for his crime, and he ends up with only a very guilty conscience. The movie has the dark, sordid atmosphere of midforties film noir, but it's only intermittently interesting.

SCISSORS

★ Paramount, 1991, c, 105 min. Dir: Frank De Felitta. SP: Frank De Felitta, b/o story by Joyce Selznick. Cast: Sharon Stone, Steve Railsback, Ronny Cox, Michelle Phillips, Vicki Frederick.

Living alone in a big city, a deeply repressed woman (Stone) is attacked in an elevator and defends herself with a pair of scissors. Following the attack, a strange series of events, especially a long, terrifying session as a prisoner in a bizarrely rigged apartment, sends her to the brink of madness. Don't ask. An atrocious thriller, lamentable in all departments.

SEA OF LOVE

★★★ Universal, 1989, c, 112 min. Dir: Harold Becker. SP: Richard Price. Cast: Al Pacino, Ellen Barkin, John Goodman, William Hickey, Michael Rooker, Richard Jenkins, Christine Estabrook, Barbara Baxley, Patricia Barry.

A twenty-year veteran of the New York police force, detective Frank Keller (Pacino) is tough, hard-drinking, and wretchedly unhappy (also divorced)—the perfect person to fall dangerously for a sexy murder suspect (Barkin). When several men are slain after answering a "lonely hearts" ad, Frank is forced to wonder: is she the killer? *Sea of Love* is a dark-hued, well-made thriller, but much of the suspense is dissipated by greater concern with the romance than with solving the mystery. Pacino gives a fierce, commanding performance, and Barkin makes a convincing foil.

SECOND WOMAN

★☆ United Artists, 1951, b/w, 91 min. Dir: James V. Kern. SP: Mort Briskin, Robert Smith. Cast: Robert Young, Betsy Drake, John Sutton, Henry O'Neill, Morris Carnovsky, Florence Bates, Steven Geray.

A silly, muddled melodrama, with echoes of *Rebecca*, but not one-tenth of the quality. Young is an architect brooding about the death of his fiancée. Is he paranoid or is his life being systematically destroyed by someone who hates him? Betsy Drake would like to know, since she loves him. Soon both their lives are in danger. Stilted writing and mediocre acting do not help, nor does the Tchaikovsky music, which is merely distracting.

SECRET BEYOND THE DOOR

★★ Universal-International, 1948, b/w, 98 min. Dir: Fritz Lang. SP: Silvia Richards, b/o story by Rufus King. Cast: Joan Bennett, Michael Redgrave, Anne Revere, Barbara O'Neil, Natalie Schafer, Anabel Shaw, Ross Rey.

A shrill melodrama echoing many other wife-in-distress thrillers such as *Rage in Heaven* and *Suspicion*. Bennett is the beleaguered lady who marries the distinctly odd Redgrave and then finds her life in jeopardy in his creepy old mansion. It seems that hubby has a morbid fascination with death, and hers may be the next in line. Or maybe not. Lang directed some classic melodramas, but this is not one of them.

SEDUCTION, THE

★ Avco Embassy, 1982, c, 104 min. Dir and SP: David Schmoeller. Cast: Morgan Fairchild, Michael Sarrazin, Vince Edwards, Andrew Stevens, Colleen Camp, Kevin Brophy, Wendy Smith Howard, Woodrow Parfrey.

Television actress Fairchild made her movie debut in this dreadful thriller. She's a beautiful Los Angeles newswoman with a live-in lover (Sarrazin) and a serious problem. She is being stalked by a psychotic Peeping Tom (Stevens) who turns increasingly dangerous. Not exactly an original idea, and nothing here to spark interest, except views of the leading lady in pool, bath, or steamroom.

SEE NO EVIL, HEAR NO EVIL

★☆ TriStar, 1989, c, 103 min. Dir: Arthur Hiller. SP: Earl Barret, Arne Sultan, Eliot Wald, Andrew Kurtzman, Gene Wilder, b/o story by Earl Barret, Arne Sultan, Marvin Worth. Cast: Richard Pryor, Gene Wilder, Joan Severance, Kevin Spacey, Kirsten Childs, Alan North, Anthony Zerbe.

Amazingly, it took five writers to concoct this frenetic, painfully unfunny farce. The gimmick: Pryor is blind, and Wilder is deaf. Present at the scene of a murder, they become the chief suspects, and soon they are fleeing from both the police and the real killers. Every situation is telegraphed from a mile away, and the jokes revolving around their handicaps become tiresome very quickly. One of the weakest efforts of the Pryor-Wilder team.

SERIAL MOM

★★ Savoy, 1994, c, 93 min. Dir and SP: John Waters. Cast: Kathleen Turner, Sam Waterston, Ricki Lake, Matthew Lillard, Mink Stole, Suzanne Somers.

Beverly Sutphin (Turner) is a sunny Baltimore housewife, with a devoted husband (Waterston) and two great kids (Lake and Lillard). There's one catch: Beverly is a serial killer who murders anyone who displeases her: her son's teacher, her thoughtless neighbor, and so on. When she's caught, she becomes a media celebrity. Notorious filmmaker Waters tried to go mainstream with this black comedy, and some found it hilarious. But the idea becomes wearisome after a while, the satire is applied with a trowel, and much of the humor is a gross-out. Still, Turner seems to be having a good time. If this is your cup of tea, happy sipping.

SERPICO

★★★☆ Paramount, 1973, c, 129 min. Dir: Sidney Lumet. SP: Waldo Salt and Norman Wexler, b/o book by Peter Maas. Cast: Al Pacino, Tony Roberts, John Randolph, Jack Kehoe, Biff McGuire, Barbara Eda-Young, Lewis J. Stadlen, F. Murray Abraham, M. Emmet Walsh.

This grim, depressing, but well-told police drama, based on a true story, takes on added relevance in the light of recent revelations about police corruption. Pacino plays Frank Serpico, an honest, dedicated policeman who finds himself immersed in the corruption of his colleagues, whatever the precinct, and no matter how high the level. His despairing efforts to blow the whistle and reveal the truth meet only with indifference, hostility, and threats on his life. Pacino gives one of his most intense performances—his sorrow and anger are almost palpable—and although the movie has some sluggish stretches, it conveys the plight of a man who was too honest for his own good.

SET IT OFF

★★★☆ New Line, 1996, c, 120 min. Dir: F. Gary Gray. SP: Kate Lanier, Takashi Bufford, b/o story by Takashi Bufford. Cast: Jada Pinkett, Queen Latifah, Vivica A. Fox, Kimberly Elise, John C. McGinley, Blair Underwood.

Vivid performances by four strong black actresses, especially Jada Pinkett and Queen Latifah, spark this grim, often powerful crime drama of bonding and revenge. Each of four Los Angeles women friends has a serious grievance against the establishment, and together they decide to rob a bank. The exhilaration of the robbery provokes them to continue with their crime spree, while the police close in. The final consequences are mostly tragic. There are flaws—the causes for the women's grievances are somewhat arbitrary, and Pinkett's romance with a wealthy young banker (Underwood) seems to come from a different movie—but the movie's sense of doom is palpable, and key action scenes are well staged.

SET-UP, THE

★★★☆ RKO, 1949, b/w, 72 min. Dir: Robert Wise. SP: Art Cohn, b/o poem by Joseph Moncure March. Cast: Robert Ryan, Audrey Totter, George Tobias, Alan Baxter, Wallace Ford, Percy Helton, Darryl Hickman.

Washed-up boxer Stoker Thompson (Ryan) is in deep trouble. Believing that he is "one punch away" from the big time, he has refused to take a fall for the kingpin gangster (Baxter) who owns him. Retaining his pride and dignity, he survives a brutal beating in the ring but must also face the consequences of his action. Obviously made on a shoestring, *The Set-Up* still packs a wallop, with a sterling performance by Ryan and moody photography by Milton Krasner, all under Wise's expert direction. Based on a narrative poem by Joseph Moncure March.

SEVEN

★★★☆ New Line, 1995, c, 125 min. Dir: David Fincher. SP: Andrew Kevin Walker. Cast: Brad Pitt, Morgan Freeman, Gwyneth Paltrow, R. Lee Ermy, John C. McGinley, Richard Roundtree.

A grisly but undeniably well-made thriller, *Seven* revolves around the relentless search for a serial murderer. Detective William Somerset (Freeman), jaded and methodical, joins with detective David Mills (Pitt), young and impetuous, to capture the deranged person whose victims embody (in his sick mind) the Seven Deadly Sins. The doom-laden atmosphere is well realized, with rain constantly falling, and in many scenes, only flashlights pierce the darkness. Freeman, in particular, gives a fine, measured performance. The horrifying climax will leave you shaken. The killer is played by an unbilled actor whom many will recognize.

SEVEN-PER-CENT SOLUTION, THE

★★★☆ Universal, 1976, c, 113 min. Dir: Herbert Ross. SP: Nicholas Meyer, b/o his novel. Cast: Nicol Williamson, Alan Arkin, Robert Duvall, Vanessa Redgrave, Joel Gray, Charles Gray, Georgia Brown, Samantha Eggar, Jeremy Kemp.

Imagine this: celebrated detective Sherlock Holmes (Williamson) has been lured to Vienna so that the eminent Sigmund Freud (Arkin) can cure him of his cocaine addiction. Then imagine the two men joining together to rescue a lady in distress (Redgrave) from a fate worse than death. It's all absurd, of course, but this stylish, fanciful production also makes it highly entertaining. The movie veers distractingly from serious drama to tongue-in-cheek melodrama, but everyone appears to be having a good time. And so will you. Laurence Olivier appears briefly as a prissy old Professor Moriarty.

SEVEN-UPS, THE

★★ Fox, 1973, c, 103 min. Dir: Philip D'Antoni. SP: Albert Rubin, Alexander Jacobs, b/o story by Sonny Grosso. Cast: Roy Scheider, Tony LoBianco, Larry Haines, Richard Lynch.

D'Antoni, the producer of the Oscar-winning, successful *French Connection* (1971), opted not only to produce but also direct this semi-follow-up to that film. Bad idea. *The Seven-Ups* is another fast-moving police drama, replete with car chases, stakeouts, and shoot-outs, but it is merely noisy and relentless, without much style. (One long chase sequence, however, is well-staged.) The title refers to a group of vigilante New York cops, led by Scheider, who make their own rules and are not above using violence to achieve their goals. The movie treats them as heroes, which is interesting in light of the publicity in recent years concerning police behavior.

SHACK OUT ON 101

★☆ Allied Artists, 1955, b/w, 80 min. Dir: Edward Dein. SP: Edward Dein, Mildred Dein. Cast: Terry Moore, Lee Marvin, Frank Lovejoy, Keenan Wynn, Whit Bissell, Jess Barker, Donald Murphy, Frank De Kova.

A tacky, mildly noir-style melodrama that has somehow acquired an undeserved reputation as a cult film. Another product of fifties paranoia about Communism, the movie stars Moore as a waitress in a shabby diner, apparently devoid of customers, where Wynn is the owner and Marvin the cook (called "Slob," no less). To her righteous indignation, Moore learns that Marvin and his nasty cohorts are stealing nuclear secrets for the Communists. Lovejoy is the scientist, amorously involved with Moore, who may or may not be a traitor. Certainly one of a kind, and thank goodness for that.

SHADOW, THE

★★☆ Universal, 1994, c, 108 min. Dir: Russell Mulcahy. SP: David Koepp, b/o Advance Magazine Publishers' character. Cast: Alec Baldwin, John Lone, Penelope Ann Miller, Peter Boyle, Tim Curry, Ian McKellen, Jonathan Winters.

"Who knows what evil lurks in the hearts of men? The Shadow knows!" One of the best-remembered slogans in popular culture, this baleful pronouncement belonged to the Shadow, the mysterious avenger of evil who inhabited America's radio sets for many years. Everyone of a certain age knows, of course, that the Shadow is really New York playboy Lamont Cranston. Brought to the screen in this elaborate production, the Shadow/Cranston (Baldwin) can still "cloud the minds of men" in his fight against crime, but now he's engaged in a monumental war-to-the-death with the evil Shiwan Khan (Lone), who has turned up in New York City in the thirties with one simple objective: to destroy the world. (What else?) The stylized sets and costumes are stunning, but it's hard to say for whom this movie was intended.

SHADOW OF A DOUBT

★★★★ Universal, 1943, b/w, 108 min. Dir: Alfred Hitchcock. SP: Thornton Wilder, Sally Benson, Irma Reville, b/o story by Gordon McDonell. Cast: Teresa Wright, Joseph Cotten, Macdonald Carey, Patricia Collinge, Henry Travers, Hume Cronyn, Wallace Ford, Edna May Wonacott.

Hitchcock regarded this film as his personal favorite, and it's not difficult to see why. A chilling tale of paradise lost and innocence

In Alfred Hitchcock's Shadow of a Doubt *(1943), young Charlie (Teresa Wright) begins to suspect that her beloved Uncle Charlie (Joseph Cotten) is not all he seems to be.*

destroyed, *Shadow of a Doubt* keeps the director's usual stylistic flourishes to a minimum, without sacrificing a moment of suspense. Cotten plays the serial killer who comes to visit his small-town California family, where he is loved and admired by all. When his worshipful niece (Wright) learns the terrible truth, her world is shattered and her life is in jeopardy. The dark side that lurks beneath everyday life has seldom been depicted as skillfully, with ordinary events—a family dinner, a trip to the library, and the like—turning suddenly sinister.

SHADOW OF THE THIN MAN

★★☆ MGM, 1941, b/w, 97 min. Dir: W. S. Van Dyke II. SP: Irving Brecher, Harry Kurnitz, b/o story by Harry Kurnitz. Cast: William Powell, Myrna Loy, Donna Reed, Barry Nelson, Sam Levene, Alan Baxter, Stella Adler.

Nick and Nora Charles are back for their fourth outing in the *Thin Man* series. Here they investigate a murder at a race track, allowing for a tidy batch of colorful characters. By this time the quips are beginning to wear thin, and the mystery itself is none too involving. But the leads are still pretending that it's all a lark, and they are always fun to watch. Note the presence of actress and acting coach Stella Adler in a rare movie role.

SHAFT

★★☆ MGM, 1971, c, 100 min. Dir: Gordon Parks. SP: Ernest Tidyman, John D. F. Black, b/o novel by Ernest Tidyman. Cast: Richard Roundtree, Moses Gunn, Charles Cioffi, Christopher St. John, Drew Bundini Brown, Gwenn Mitchell.

This tough, violent movie spawned many imitations. Roundtree is John Shaft, a sleek, no-nonsense black private eye who is hired to find the kidnapper of a Harlem druglord (Gunn). By the time the movie ends, the landscape is strewn with bodies. Isaac Hayes's theme song won an Oscar. There were two sequels: *Shaft's Big Score!* and *Shaft in Africa*.

SHAFT'S BIG SCORE!

★★☆ MGM, 1972, c, 100 min. Dir: Gordon Parks. SP: Ernest Tidyman, b/o characters created by Ernest Tidyman. Cast: Richard Roundtree, Moses Gunn, Drew Bundini Brown, Joseph Mascolo, Kathy Imrie, Julius W. Harris.

This first sequel to *Shaft* is not up to the original, despite the same director and writer, but Roundtree still demonstrates a good amount of stylish insolence and "smarts" as John Shaft, private detective. This time Shaft tangles with unsavory types, both black and white, who are after a quarter of a million dollars hidden in a coffin in Harlem. The ending involves a long chase from a Long Island graveyard to the Brooklyn waterfront.

SHAFT IN AFRICA

★★☆ MGM, 1973, c, 112 min. Dir: John Guillermin. SP: Stirling Silliphant, b/o characters created by Ernest Tidyman. Cast: Richard Roundtree, Frank Finlay, Vonetta McGee, Neda Arneric.

This second sequel to *Shaft* finds the suave private eye forced to leave his Manhattan luxury apartment to break up a sinister ring smuggling cheap illegal labor out of Africa to the factories of Paris. Posing as a job-seeking tribesman, he tangles with the smugglers and their leader (Finlay). Once again, heavy doses of violent action. Followed by a television series starring Roundtree.

SHAKEDOWN

★★☆ Universal, 1988, c, 90 min. Dir and SP: James Glickenhaus. Cast: Peter Weller, Sam Elliott, Patricia Charbonneau, Antonio Fargas, Blanche Baker, Richard Brooks, David Proval.

Legal aid lawyer Weller takes one last case before joining his future father-in-law's law film: he defends a drug dealer (Brooks) accused of killing a cop. Before long he is joined by a dissipated undercover cop (Elliott) in a much larger undertaking: hunting down a major graft ring run by corrupt policemen. The usual mayhem—gunfights, car chases—but competently done.

SHAMUS

★★☆ Columbia, 1973, c, 106 min. Dir: Buzz Kulik. SP: Barry Beckerman. Cast: Burt Reynolds, Dyan Cannon, John Ryan, Joe Santos, Giorgio Tozzi, Ron Weyand.

A failed attempt at evoking the "private eye" melodramas of the forties, *Shamus* even begins with a sly homage to *The Big Sleep* as Brooklyn detective McCoy (Reynolds) visits a millionaire (Ryan) in his mansion to take on a case. Naturally nothing is as it seems to be, and McCoy is soon being chased, shot at, and beaten up as he encounters various characters. The trouble is that none of these characters holds much interest, and the movie lacks the irony, wit, and excitement of its best predecessors. Another throwback to *The Big Sleep*: McCoy visits a bookstore.

SHARKEY'S MACHINE

★★ Warner Bros., 1981, c, 123 min. Dir: Burt Reynolds. SP: Gerald Di Pego, b/o novel by William Diehl. Cast: Burt Reynolds, Vittorio Gassman, Rachel Ward, Brian Keith, Charles Durning, Earl Holliman, Bernie Casey, Darryl Hickman, Richard Libertini.

The violence virtually never ceases in this basically tiresome, overlong crime drama. Reynolds, who also directed, plays a veteran cop demoted to vice who takes on Mafia bigwig Gassman, especially after he becomes emotionally involved with one of Gassman's

An action moment for cop Burt Reynolds in Sharkey's Machine *(1981).*
Reynolds also directed.

$1,000-a-night hookers (Ward). Gore galore, and movie buffs will recognize the partial rip-off of the classic *Laura*. Durning overplays the clichéd role of the apoplectic police captain.

SHATTERED

★★☆ MGM, 1991, c, 98 min. Dir and SP: Wolfgang Petersen. Cast: Tom Berenger, Greta Scacchi, Bob Hoskins, Joanne Whalley-Kilmer, Corbin Bernsen, Theodore Bikel.

Suffering from amnesia after a devastating auto accident, real estate developer Dan Merrick (Berenger) begins to put together the shattered pieces of his past. Were his seemingly devoted wife (Scacchi) and her mysterious lover trying to kill him, and will they try again? He enlists the help of a private detective (Hoskins) to find the answers. This tricky Hitchcockian thriller stays on course until midpoint, when it crashes on the rocks of implausibility, ending with a surprising but wildly unbelievable denouement.

SHAWSHANK REDEMPTION, THE

★★★ Castle Rock, 1994, c, 142 min. Dir: Frank Darabont. SP: Frank Darabont, b/o novel by Stephen King. Cast: Tim Robbins, Morgan Freeman, Bob Gunton, James Whitmore, William Sadler, Clancy Brown, Gil Bellows, Mark Ralston, David Proval.

Overlong, rambling, but occasionally powerful, this prison drama has both virtues and shortcomings. On the credit side, it relates the intriguing story of Andy Dufresne (Robbins), a banker wrongly sentenced to life imprisonment for murdering his wife and her lover. His nightmarish experiences in Shawshank Prison under a sadistic warden (Gunton) are shown in grim, unsparing detail, and his redemption and revenge after nearly twenty lost years are given equal weight. On the debit side, the film leaves too many basic questions unanswered, and several key scenes ring patently false. Robbins and Freeman are both suitably solemn and repressed in the leading roles.

SHOCK

★★ Fox, 1946, b/w, 70 min. Dir: Alfred Werker. SP: Eugene Ling, b/o story by Albert de Mond. Cast: Vincent Price, Lynn Bari, Frank Latimore, Anabel Shaw, Michael Dunne, Reed Hadley, Charles Trowbridge.

A woman (Shaw) witnesses a murder. In a state of total shock, she is treated by a psychiatrist (Price), but he just happens to be the killer. He attempts to drive her out of her mind and overdose her with insulin. Lynn Bari plays Price's icy partner in crime. A very minor entry in the "psychiatric" cycle of the mid- to late forties.

SHOCK CORRIDOR

★★☆ Allied Artists, 1963, b/w, 101 min. Dir and SP: Samuel Fuller. Cast: Peter Breck, Constance Towers, Gene Evans, James Best, Hari Rhodes, Larry Tucker, Philip Ahn, William Zukert.

Ambitious reporter Breck has an idea: he'll ferret out the murderer at a mental institution by impersonating a patient. Wrong. His confrontation with everything from schizophrenia to nymphomania ends tragically. Despite some gaping holes in logic, there are a few shocking moments along the way. Another entry in the movie industry's fascination with psychiatry, at least as a backdrop for thrillers.

SHOCK TO THE SYSTEM, A

★★☆ Corsair, 1990, c, 88 min. Dir: Jan Egleson. SP: Andrew Klavan, b/o novel by Simon Brett. Cast: Michael Caine, Elizabeth McGovern, Peter Riegert, Will Patton, Swoosie Kurtz, John McMartin, Barbara Baxley, Jenny Wright.

Executive Graham Marshall (Caine) is

saddled with an annoying wife (Kurtz) and a job that's going nowhere. (He loses a top promotion to an obnoxious rival.) Then he discovers, first by accident, then by design, how easy it is to get rid of people who stand in the way of happiness and success. You simply kill them! This black comedy is intended to be wickedly satirical, and it amuses for a while. Then it slides into improbability, and at the end it just leaves behind a sour taste. Caine, however, is always fun to watch.

SHOOT TO KILL

★★☆ Touchstone, 1988, c, 110 min. Dir: Roger Spottiswoode. SP: Harv Zimmel, Michael Burton, Daniel Petrie, Jr., b/o story by Harv Zimmel. Cast: Sidney Poitier, Tom Berenger, Kirstie Alley, Clancy Brown, Richard Masur, Andrew Robinson.

Poitier's first starring role in eight years was hardly a stretch for this fine actor. He plays an FBI special agent who is bent on capturing a serial killer (Brown). When the killer escapes into the rugged Pacific Northwest wilderness, with guide Alley as his hostage, Poitier joins with the girl's boyfriend (Berenger) in pursuit. The scenery is beautiful (actually British Columbia) and the action rugged, but this highly contrived melodrama takes much too long to work up its suspense. Although Poitier gives the role his usual intensity, he might have chosen a sturdier vehicle for his return.

SHORT EYES

★★★☆ The Film League, 1977, c, 104 min. Dir: Robert M. Young. SP: Miguel Pinero, b/o his play. Cast: Bruce Davison, Jose Perez, Nathan George, Don Blakely, Shawn Elliott, Tito Goya, Joseph Carberry, Curtis Mayfield, Freddie Fender, Miguel Pinero.

An exceptionally raw and blistering view of prison life, filmed entirely in New York's former Men's House of Detention, known as the Tombs. In a claustrophic prison where blacks, whites, and Puerto Ricans live in ferocious contention that occasionally explodes into violence, a new prisoner (Davison) arrives—an accused child molester whom the prisoners call Short Eyes. Loathed by all, he becomes the terrible target of their anger and frustration. Obviously a stage play—it was an Off-Broadway hit—the movie is grim and unsettling, not for faint hearts.

SHORT TIME

★★☆ Gladden, 1990, c, 97 min. Dir: Gregg
Champion. SP: John Blumenthal, Michael Berry.
Cast: Dabney Coleman, Matt Frewer, Teri Garr,
Barry Corbin, Joe Pantoliano.

When policeman Burt Simpson (Coleman)
learns that he has only two weeks to live, he
decides to get himself killed in the line of
duty so that his wife (Garr) can get enough
insurance money to sent his ten-year-old son
to Harvard. To nobody's surprise but Burt's,
he finds it hard to carry out his plan. Mixture
of comedy and action (with a dab of
sentiment) doesn't come off, but Coleman is
good.

SHOW THEM NO MERCY!

★★★ Fox, 1935, b/w, 76 min. Dir: George
Marshall. SP: Kubec Glasmon, adapted by Henry
Lehrman from a story by Kubec Glasmon. Cast:
Bruce Cabot, Rochelle Hudson, Cesar Romero,
Edward Norris, Edward Brophy, Warren Hymer.

A fast-paced gangster tale, typical of the era,
Show Them No Mercy! centers on four thugs
who kidnap a young couple (Hudson and
Norris) and their baby. Determined FBI
agents eventually bring the crooks down,
helped by bitter wrangling among the
kidnappers themselves. Cabot stands out as
the vicious and treacherous killer unnerved
by liquor and fear. Based on a true
kidnapping case of the period; later remade
in a Western setting as *Rawhide* (1951).

SILENT FALL

★★ Warner Bros., 1994, c, 104 min. Dir: Bruce
Beresford. SP: Akiva Goldsman. Cast: Richard
Dreyfuss, John Lithgow, Linda Hamilton, Liv Tyler,
Ben Faulkner, J. T. Walsh.

Dreyfuss tries, sometimes a little too hard, to
save this muddled and far from credible
mystery drama. He plays Jake Rainer, a
small-town psychiatrist with a troubled past,
who is asked to deal with an autistic nine-
year-old boy (Faulkner) who has witnessed
the murder of his parents. (The boy's oddest
symptom: he can mimic other voices.) Also
involved is the boy's teenage sister (Tyler).
The story becomes increasingly lurid and
never recovers from several weird and highly
unlikely turns.

SILKWOOD

★★★ Fox, 1983, c, 128 min. Dir: Mike Nichols. SP:
Nora Ephron, Alice Arlen. Cast: Meryl Streep, Kurt
Russell, Cher, Craig T. Nelson, Diana Scarwid, Fred
Ward, Ron Silver, Charles Hallahan, Josef Sommer,
Tess Harper, David Strathairn, Sudie Bond.

The facts are not in dispute: A feisty,
uninhibited woman named Karen Silkwood
(Streep) worked for a plutonium recycling
plant in Oklahoma. When she became troubled
by the dangerously sloppy conditions in the
plant, she threatened to make her concerns
public. She died in a car accident—or was it
murder? The screenplay tries to give some
dramatic shape to Silkwood's life, and
sometimes succeeds. But the lingering
question remains: how much is fact, and how
much fiction? Also, the outcome is never in
doubt, which dissipates any suspense. Streep
gives a fine performance as the imperfect but
tenacious whistle-blower.

SILVER STREAK

★★★ Fox, 1976, c, 113 min. Dir: Arthur Hiller. SP:
Colin Higgins. Cast: Gene Wilder, Jill Clayburgh,
Richard Pryor, Patrick McGoohan, Ned Beatty, Clifton
James, Ray Walston, Richard Kiel.

Hectic, improbable, and sometimes amusing,
this mystery comedy aspires to be in the
tradition of other skulduggery-on-a-train
movies. Wilder is a hapless editor traveling the
Silver Streak who becomes innocently
enmeshed in the nefarious activities of crooked
art dealer McGoohan. Clayburgh is the
obligatory lady-in-distress. The movie receives
a badly needed shot of adrenalin from Pryor
as a resourceful thief who gets involved
reluctantly. The runaway train climax is
spectacular.

SINGLE WHITE FEMALE

★★☆ Columbia, 1992, c, 107 min. Dir: Barbet
Schroeder. SP: Don Roos, b/o novel by John Lutz.
Cast: Bridget Fonda, Jennifer Jason Leigh, Steven
Weber, Peter Friedman, Stephen Tobolowsky, Frances
Bay, Rene Estevez, Ken Tobey.

A not-bad entry in the ever-popular Crazy
Woman division of Urban Thrillers. Career
woman Fonda dumps her erring boyfriend
(Weber) and looks for a new roommate. What
she gets is Leigh, a seriously disturbed woman
with homicidal tendencies. The premise is

psychologically interesting, but somewhere at midpoint the movie turns lurid, violent, and exceedingly improbable. No faulting the lead actresses, and this time Leigh, who is adept at playing loonies (even her "normal" characters are weird), comes across as genuinely chilling.

SISTERS

★☆ American International, 1973, c, 93 min. Dir: Brian De Palma. SP: Brian De Palma, Louisa Rose. Cast: Margot Kidder, Jennifer Salt, Charles Durning, Bill Finley, Lisle Wilson, Barnard Hughes.

Siamese twins who were separated in late adolescence, Danielle and Dominique Breton (Kidder) are in the usual movie-twin quandary: one is good, the other evil. Along comes investigative reporter Grace Collier (Salt), who witnesses a horrifying murder committed by the nasty twin. Of course the police don't believe her. Before all is revealed, Salt experiences her very own nightmare. Director De Palma's first excursion into Hitchcock territory, *Sisters* is gory, crude, and quite preposterous, and the central sequence—Salt imprisoned in an "experimental madhouse"—is silly rather than frightening. Eerie score by frequent Hitchcock composer Bernard Herrmann.

SKYJACKED

★★☆ MGM, 1972, c, 100 min. Dir: John Guillermin. SP: Stanley R. Greenberg, b/o novel by David Harper. Cast: Charlton Heston, Yvette Mimieux, James Brolin, Claude Akins, Jeanne Crain, Susan Dey, Roosevelt Grier, Walter Pidgeon, Mariette Hartley, Leslie Uggams.

Standard melodramatics aloft, as a flight from the West Coast to Minneapolis is hijacked, terrifying the passengers and worrying captain Heston. With the mysterious hijacker threatening to blow up the plane as he diverts it first to Anchorage and then to Russia, there's plenty to worry about. Among the passengers are a U.S. Senator (Pidgeon), a nervous GI (Brolin), a jazz cellist (Grier), and a very pregnant woman (Hartley). Do they survive? What do *you* think?

SLAMDANCE

★ Zenith/Island, 1987, c, 100 min. Dir: Wayne Wang. SP: Don Opper. Cast: Tom Hulce, Mary Elizabeth Mastrantonio, Harry Dean Stanton, Virginia Madsen, Adam Ant, Millie Perkins, Don Opper.

Cartoonist C. C. Drood (Hulce) is in deep trouble. When his ex-girlfriend (Madsen) is found murdered, he is not only a leading suspect but he also becomes the patsy for those in high places who actually killed her. His situation grows steadily worse, until he hangs in the balance. Never mind. This irritating, incoherent, and pretentious movie will not be included on anybody's "must see" list.

SLAUGHTER

★★ American International, 1972, c, 92 min. Dir: Jack Starrett. SP: Mark Hanna, Don Williams. Cast: Jim Brown, Stella Stevens, Rip Torn, Don Gordon, Cameron Mitchell, Marlene Clark, Robert Phillips.

This violent melodrama gets a better supporting cast than it deserves. Brown stars in the title role as an ex-Green Beret soldier who avenges the gangland murder of his father and then continues to demolish scores of bad guys in Central America. Torn is the over-the-top villain, and Stevens is the romantic interest. Followed by *Slaughter's Big Rip-Off* in 1973.

SLAUGHTER'S BIG RIP-OFF

★★ American International, 1973, c, 93 min. Dir: Gordon Douglas. SP: Charles Johnson, b/o character created by Don Williams. Cast: Jim Brown, Ed McMahon, Brock Peters, Don Stroud, Gloria Hendry, Richard Williams, Art Metrano.

The only thing worth noting about this sequel to *Slaughter* is that Ed McMahon, Johnny Carson's sidekick for many years, plays the arch villain. Otherwise, the movie is as dreary as the original, with Brown repeating as the ex-CIA man out to avenge the death of some of his friends at the hands of McMahon.

SLEEPERS

★★☆ Warner Bros., 1996, c, 105 min. Dir and SP: Barry Levinson, b/o book by Lorenzo Carcaterra. Cast: Robert De Niro, Brad Pitt, Dustin Hoffman, Jason Patric, Kevin Bacon, Ron Eldard, Bruno Kirby, Vittorio Gassman, Minnie Driver, Billy Crudup, Brad Renfro.

Slickly produced and well-acted, *Sleepers* still comes up short as drama due to a highly questionable moral stance. Many years after four slum boys have been brutalized by a sadistic reformatory guard (Bacon), two of the boys, now irredeemable hoods, kill the guard. Another of the boys, now a prosecuting attorney (Pitt), concocts an elaborate scheme of revenge that will free the friends on trial and exact retribution from the other culpable reformatory guards. The scheme involves the attorney's subverting the law as well as lying testimony on the witness stand by a supportive priest (De Niro). The story is gripping but it leaves a sour taste. Based on the "controversial" best-seller.

SLEEPING WITH THE ENEMY

★★☆ Fox, 1991, c, 98 min. Dir: Joseph Ruben. SP: Ronald Bass, b/o novel by Nancy Price. Cast: Julia Roberts, Patrick Bergin, Kevin Anderson, Elizabeth Lawrence, Kyle Secor.

This standard-issue "lady-in-peril" thriller is clearly designed as a starring vehicle for Roberts. She plays a young wife who flees from her insanely jealous, abusive husband (Bergin) and settles down in a small Iowa town. Soon enough she meets a nice teacher (Anderson), and all's well until her crackpot husband locates her. At midpoint the movie forgoes all suspense to admire Roberts's undeniable beauty, but it picks up for a nerve-racking climax.

SLEUTH

★★★☆ Fox, 1972, c, 138 min. Dir: Joseph L. Mankiewicz. SP: Anthony Shaffer, b/o his play. Cast: Laurence Olivier, Michael Caine, Alec Cawthorne, Eve Channing, John Matthews, Teddy Martin.

Olivier and Caine give brilliant performances in this smooth and hugely entertaining adaptation of the stage success. Olivier is Andrew Wyke, wealthy author of mystery fiction, and Caine is Milo Tindle, beautician and lover to Wyke's wife. On Wyke's country estate, which he has turned into a fun house, the two act out a diabolically clever, ultimately fatal cat-and-mouse game. The screenplay is little more than a hollow conceit, but watching the two actors sink their teeth into their roles is more than enough compensation.

SLIGHT CASE OF MURDER, A

★★★☆ Warner Bros., 1938, b/w, 85 min. Dir: Lloyd Bacon. SP: Earl Baldwin, Joseph Schrank, b/o play by Damon Runyon, Howard Lindsay. Cast: Edward G. Robinson, Ruth Donnelly, Jane Bryan, Allen Jenkins, Willard Parker, Edward Brophy, John Litel, Harold Huber.

Robinson gives one of his best comedy performances in this tangy, uproarious farce. He's a retired kingpin bootlegger with a problem: his old enemies have been thoughtless enough to leave four dead bodies in a bedroom of his Saratoga home, and his daughter (Bryan) wants to marry a state trooper. The pace is hectic, and the situations funny, with dialogue that captures the flavor of Runyon's agreeably disreputable people.

SLING BLADE

★★★ Miramax, 1996, c, 133 min. Dir and SP: Billy Bob Thornton. Cast: Billy Bob Thornton, Dwight Yoakum, Natalie Canerday, John Ritter, Lucas Black.

Released after twenty-five years in what he calls a "nervous hospital" for killing his mother and her lover, mildly retarded Karl Childers (Thornton) returns to his Arkansas home town. A withdrawn, gentle soul with an ability to fix broken appliances, he befriends a young boy (Black) and his widowed mother (Canerday). Unfortunately, she has a nasty, abusive live-in lover (Yoakum) who delights in mocking Karl. Early on, it becomes obvious that Karl will play avenging angel and revert to his old ways. Many of the small-town characters are clichéd, but one must admire Thornton's skillful, Oscar-nominated performance and his triple role as actor, writer, and director. He won the Oscar for Best Original Screenplay.

SLITHER

★★★ MGM, 1973, c, 97 min. Dir: Howard Zieff. SP: W. D. Richter. Cast: James Caan, Peter Boyle, Sally Kellerman, Louise Lasser, Allen Garfield, Richard B. Shull, Alex Rocco.

A quirkily amusing action comedy, Slither takes a group of eccentric characters on a madcap trailer chase across California. James Caan is an ex-convict who learns about the existence of $300,000 in stolen loot from a dying embezzler (Shull). In his effort to find the money, he is joined by a gun-toting "kook" (Kellerman), a small-time crook (Boyle) with dreams of making it big, and the crook's devoted wife (Lasser). They are all pursued by inept gangsters with their own agenda. For all the spurts of violence, the movie maintains a lighthearted approach to the material that many viewers have found endearing. Funniest scene: a Bingo game.

SLIVER

★☆ Paramount, 1993, c, 106 min. Dir: Phillip Noyce. SP: Joe Eszterhas, b/o novel by Ira Levin. Cast: Sharon Stone, William Baldwin, Tom Berenger, Martin Landau, Polly Walker, Nina Foch, CCH Pounder, Colleen Camp, Keene Curtis.

Book editor Stone moves into a swank New York apartment house where a series of bizarre deaths have occurred. Two men take a shine to her, and one of them may be responsible for the deaths. Is it wealthy Baldwin, whose elaborate hi-tech setup can see into every apartment in the house? Or is it best-selling author Berenger? A handsomely produced but contrived, soporific erotic thriller, not worth your time or attention.

SNEAKERS

★★★ Universal, 1992, c, 125 min. Dir: Phil Alden Robinson. SP: Lawrence Lasker, Walter F. Parkes, Phil Alden Robinson. Cast: Robert Redford, Sidney Poitier, Dan Aykroyd, Ben Kingsley, River Phoenix, Mary McDonnell, David Strathairn, George Hearn, Timothy Busfield.

Basically an old-fashioned caper movie, redesigned for the computer age, *Sneakers* benefits from a high-profile cast and a sense of not taking itself too seriously. Redford plays a once-notorious computer hacker who is now the head of a company that tests security systems. His colleagues all have shady pasts, but they are experts in their fields. Soon Redford and friends are embroiled in a dangerous cat-and-mouse game centering on a black box that can break any existing computer code in the world. The action is fast and lively, and the technology is intriguing, even if it's a bit difficult to follow. *Sneakers* has little substance, but it keeps you watching.

SNIPER, THE

★★★ Columbia, 1952, b/w, 85 min. Dir: Edward Dmytryk. SP: Harry Brown, b/o story by Edna Anhalt, Edward Anhalt. Cast: Adolphe Menjou, Arthur Franz, Gerald Mohr, Marie Windsor, Frank Faylen, Richard Kiley, Mabel Paige.

A small-scale but trimly made, absorbing melodrama centering on a demented killer (Franz) who shoots women at random and the all-out manhunt designed to capture him. The screenplay fails to delve into the motives for his murderous actions but the policework, led by a clean-shaven Menjou, is handled with commendable dispatch. The real San Francisco locales help to give the movie a feeling of authority.

SO I MARRIED AN AXE MURDERER

★★☆ TriStar, 1993, c, 93 min. Dir: Thomas Schlamme. SP: Robbie Fox. Cast: Mike Myers, Nancy Travis, Anthony LaPaglia, Amanda Plummer, Brenda Fricker, Charles Grodin, Phil Hartman, Steven Wright, Alan Arkin (unbilled).

Myers, yet another *Saturday Night Live* alumnus, tried his hand at the big screen with this intermittently amusing comedy. He's a shy young man with a wretched love life, who marries a girl (Travis) whom he begins to suspect might be a notorious axe murderer. Myers has some funny moments playing his own Scottish father, and there are a few clever cameos by Grodin, Hartman, and others.

SOLDIER'S STORY, A

★★★☆ Columbia, 1984, c, 101 min. Dir: Norman Jewison. SP: Charles Fuller, b/o his play. Cast: Howard E. Rollins, Jr., Adolph Caeser, Dennis Lipscomb, Art Evans, Denzel Washington, David Alan Grier, Robert Townsend, Trey Wilson, Patti LaBelle.

Just outside an army base in Louisiana in 1944, a much-hated black sergeant (Caesar) has been found murdered. A black lawyer and captain (Rollins) comes to the base to investigate, and through interrogations and flashbacks he uncovers the guilty party, and also reveals some disturbing facts about racism in the ranks of the blacks themselves. Washington stands out as the most intelligent of the recruits. Fuller adapted his Pulitzer Prize-winning play, and the cast is largely drawn from the original players of the Negro Ensemble Company. Somewhat stage-bound but gripping.

SOMEONE BEHIND THE DOOR

★★ GSF (French), 1971, c, 97 min. Dir: Nicolas Gessner. SP: Jacques Robert, Marc Behm, Lorengo Ventavoli, Nicolas Gessner, b/o novel by Jacques Robert. Cast: Charles Bronson, Anthony Perkins, Jill Ireland, Henri Garcin.

Set in England but filmed in France, this silly little melodrama stars Bronson as an escaped lunatic, suffering from amnesia, who is used by a deranged brain surgeon (Perkins, billed here as "Tony") to kill the lover of the doctor's wife. (Bronson is told he will be getting a personality transplant. Well, it seemed a good idea at the time.)

SOMEONE TO WATCH OVER ME

★★★ Columbia, 1987, c, 106 min. Dir: Ridley Scott. SP: Howard Franklin. Cast: Tom Berenger, Mimi Rogers, Lorraine Bracco, Jerry Orbach, John Rubenstein, Andreas Katsulas.

A beautiful young socialite (Rogers) witnesses a murder, and a detective (Berenger) is assigned to protect her from the killer (Katsulas). He becomes infatuated with her, nearly wrecking his marriage, while trying to keep her alive. Not exactly a new idea, but it is carried out with a degree of style and intelligence. The thriller aspects are not totally convincing, especially toward the end, but the cast acquits itself well.

SOMETHING WILD

★★ Orion, 1986, c, 113 min. Dir: Jonathan Demme. SP: E. Max Frye. Cast: Jeff Daniels, Melanie Griffith, Ray Liotta, Tracey Walter, Dana Preu, Jack Gilpin.

Demme has directed some very good films (*Melvin and Howard, The Silence of the Lambs,* and others), but this combination of dark, eccentric comedy and suspense doesn't come off. Daniels is a straight-arrow Wall Street consultant whose life falls apart when he meets wildly unpredictable Lulu (Griffith), who takes him on a journey of kinky sex, thievery, and a few other surprises. Along comes her dangerously volatile ex-husband (Liotta), who takes the movie into much more sinister territory. Daniels plays such a hopeless fool that it's difficult to sympathize with him, and the movie veers too often from one mood to another.

SONG OF THE THIN MAN

★★☆ MGM, 1947, b/w, 86 min. Dir: Edward Buzzell. SP: Steve Fisher, Nat Perrin, b/o story by Stanley Roberts and characters created by Dashiell Hammett. Cast: William Powell, Myrna Loy, Keenan Wynn, Dean Stockwell, Patricia Morison, Philip Reed, Gloria Grahame, Jayne Meadows, Don Taylor, Leon Ames.

The Charleses, Nick and Nora (Powell and Loy), treading water. This sixth and final entry in the *Thin Man* series has the detective and his wife investigating the murder of a bandleader

aboard a gambling yacht, which leads them to late-night jazz clubs and further shennanigans. Stockwell plays their now eleven-year-old son.

SORRY, WRONG NUMBER

★★★ Paramount, 1948, b/w, 89 min. Dir: Anatole Litvak. SP: Lucille Fletcher, b/o her radio drama. Cast: Barbara Stanwyck, Burt Lancaster, Ann Richards, Wendell Corey, Ed Begley, Leif Erickson, William Conrad.

Essentially a tour de force for Stanwyck, this suspense thriller was adapted from the popular radio play that starred Agnes Moorehead. Stanwyck plays a rich, neurotic woman confined to her bed in her Manhattan apartment. Through crossed wires on her phone, she learns that a murder is being planned, and that she (yes, she!) is the victim. Lancaster is her weak husband, and Richards is the close friend who reveals the truth behind the murder plan. Mostly, the movie consists of Stanwyck's increasingly frantic and terrified calls for help, and the actress rises to the challenge with her usual solid professionalism. She won an Oscar nomination.

SOUTH CENTRAL

★★★ Warner Bros., 1992, c, 99 min. Dir: Steve Anderson. SP: Steve Anderson, b/o book by Donald Bakeer. Cast: Glenn Plummer, Byron Keith Minns, Carl Lumbly, LaRita Shelby, Kevin Best, Christian Coleman.

South Central begins as a conventional gang movie—turf fights, bloodshed, and so on— then veers surprisingly into a Movie with a Message. Bobby Johnson (Plummer) is a black Los Angeles street punk who goes to prison for murder, but emerges a reformed citizen due to the intense teaching of a fellow convict (Lumbly). Learning that "the cycle of hate must be broken," he saves his young son (Coleman) from a life of crime. ("We've got to be there for our children.") Modestly made, but reasonably effective.

SOUTHERN COMFORT

★★☆ Fox, 1981, c, 106 min. Dir: Walter Hill. SP: Michael Kane, Walter Hill, David Giler. Cast: Keith Carradine, Powers Boothe, Fred Ward, Franklyn Seales, T. K. Carter, Lewis Smith, Peter Coyote, Les Lannom.

Director Hill is adept at staging action scenes,

but here he is largely defeated by the material. In 1973 a platoon of National Guardsmen on maneuvers ventures into the Louisiana swampland. Their contemptuous treatment of the local Cajuns has fatal consequences when, one by one, the men are attacked and killed. Forced to survive, the men also confront the implacable force of nature and their own weaknesses. A pale echo of *Deliverance*, the movie also suffers from its highly questionable attitude toward the Louisiana Cajuns.

SPECIALIST, THE

★★ Warner Bros., 1994, c, 108 min. Dir: Luis Llosa. SP: Alexandra Seros. Cast: Sylvester Stallone, Sharon Stone, James Woods, Rod Steiger, Eric Roberts.

Stallone is an ex-mercenary and hired assassin, but we know he's really a nice guy: he has a cat and he beats up men who are harrassing bus passengers. Then he's hired by sultry Stone to kill the men who murdered her parents many years earlier. Ah, but there's more than meets the eye, mostly involving Stallone's bitter enemy (Woods, at his nastiest). Never mind. There are many explosions, yards of improbable dialogue, and one torrid sex scene. Favorite line: as a hotel is being demolished by bombs, and panicked guests are fleeing, a voice announces, "No cause for alarm."

SPEED

★★★☆ Fox, 1994, c, 115 min. Dir: Jon De Bont. SP: Graham Yost. Cast: Keanu Reeves, Dennis Hopper, Sandra Bullock, Joe Morton, Jeff Daniels, Alan Ruck, Glenn Plummer.

Hold on to your seats! If you can toss logic to the winds, this exciting action movie can prove to be quite a ride. The premise: mad but brilliant Howard Payne (Hopper) has rigged a city bus with a bomb that will activate when the bus goes over fifty miles an hour, and then explode if the bus goes under fifty. His price to prevent the mayhem: $37 million. On the scene comes a police SWAT team headed by stalwart Jack Traven (Reeves), who enlists passenger Annie (Bullock) as the driver. The thrills are ample, even when the situation is scarcely believable, and three cheers for the special effects and stunt people. The film took the Oscar for Best Sound and Sound Effects Editing.

SPELLBOUND

★★★ Selznick-United Artists, 1945, b/w, 111 min. Dir: Alfred Hitchcock. SP: Ben Hecht, b/o novel by Francis Beeding. Cast: Ingrid Bergman, Gregory Peck, Leo G. Carroll, Michael Chekhov, Rhonda Fleming, John Emery.

Once widely admired, Hitchcock's melodrama now seems mostly absurd and simplistic in its view of psychiatry. Still, there are enough Hitchcockian moments to warrant a viewing. Bergman is the prim psychiatrist who must delve into Peck's troubled past to convince him that he is not a murderer. Unfortunately, despite her restrained, intelligent performance, she is given too many lines that provoke laughter ("I have done a great deal of research on emotional problems and love difficulties."). And Peck is not much help as her glum costar. The movie's best features are Miklos Rozsa's Oscar-winning score and George Barnes's striking photography.

SPIRAL STAIRCASE, THE

★★★ RKO, 1946, b/w, 83 min. Dir: Robert Siodmak. SP: Mel Dinelli, b/o novel by Ethel Lina White. Cast: Dorothy McGuire, George Brent, Ethel Barrymore, Kent Smith, Rhonda Fleming, Elsa Lanchester, Sara Allgood, Rhys Williams.

On one rainswept evening in 1906 New England, a murderer is on the loose, stalking handicapped young women. In the home of good Dr. Warren (Brent) and his invalid mother (Barrymore), deaf-mute Helen (McGuire) works as a servant and companion. You can guess the rest (and even guess the killer's identity), but it's all handled quite nicely, with some chilling Hitchcockian moments (an eye staring at Helen as she gazes in a mirror, a suddenly extinguished candle in a cellar). Don't look for logic or reason; just savor the suspense. A dreadful remake turned up in 1975.

SPLIT SECOND

★★★ RKO, 1953, b/w, 85 min. Dir: Dick Powell. SP: William Bowers, Irving Wallace, b/o story by Chester Erskine, Irving Wallace. Cast: Stephen McNally, Alexis Smith, Jan Sterling, Keith Andes, Paul Kelly, Arthur Hunnicut, Robert Paige, Richard Egan, Frank de Kova.

Actor Powell made his directorial debut with this contrived but rather taut melodrama with a clever gimmick. A trio of escaped convicts holds a group of people hostage in a Nevada ghost town that just happens to be in a nuclear test area. While the minutes tick by inexorably to a nuclear blast-off, one of the convicts requires an emergency operation. The characters are mostly familiar types, but a good cast gives them some believability.

STAGE FRIGHT

★★★ Warner Bros., 1950, b/w, 110 min. Dir: Alfred Hitchcock. SP: Whitfield Cook, adapted by Alma Reville from novel by Selwyn Jepson. Cast: Jane Wyman, Marlene Dietrich, Alastair Sim, Michael Wilding, Richard Todd, Dame Sybil Thorndike, Kay Walsh.

Suspense laced with comedy is the keynote for this disappointing but moderately entertaining film from Hitchcock, set in London's theater world. Wyman is the drama student who sets about trying to prove her beau (Todd) innocent of murder. But is he? Dietrich is the victim's wife, a glamorous, duplicitous stage star. (Her rendition of "The Laziest Gal in Town" is a highlight.) The movie doesn't hang together, but Sim is delightfully funny as Wyman's father.

STAKEOUT

★★★ Touchstone, 1987, c, 115 min. Dir: John Badham. SP: Jim Kouf. Cast: Richard Dreyfuss, Emilio Estevez, Madeleine Stowe, Aidan Quinn, Dan Lauria, Forest Whitaker, Ian Tracey.

Enjoyable if familiar buddy-cop movie, mixing action and comedy. Dreyfuss and Estevez are Seattle cops and partners: Dreyfuss is a loose cannon; Estevez is a stable family man. Trouble erupts when they are ordered to guard the beautiful ex-girlfriend (Stowe) of an escaped convict (Quinn), especially when Dreyfuss falls for her. Some lively action sequences, and Quinn gives a genuinely chilling supporting performance. Followed by a sequel, *Another Stakeout* (1993).

STAR CHAMBER, THE

★★☆ Fox, 1983, c, 109 min. Dir: Peter Hyams. SP: Roderick Taylor, Peter Hyams. Cast: Michael Douglas, Hal Holbrook, Yaphet Kotto, Sharon Gless, James B. Sikking, Joe Regalbuto.

A variation on the concept of "vigilante justice" that many films seemed to advocate and, in some cases, even admire. In this instance, Judge Steven Hardin (Douglas) uncovers a secret group of judges who, disgusted with the miscarriages of justice they have been forced to endure in their courtrooms, take the law into their own hands by retrying freed criminals and then having them executed. Judge Hardin joins the group, to his lasting regret. Nicely acted, but far-fetched and not helped by an abrupt ending.

STAR 80

★★★ Ladd Company/Warner Bros., 1983, c, 102 min. Dir: Bob Fosse. SP: Bob Fosse, b/o an article by Teresa Carpenter. Cast: Eric Roberts, Mariel Hemingway, Cliff Robertson, Carroll Baker, Roger Rees, David Clennon, Josh Mostel, Sidney Miller, Jordan Christoper, Stuart Damon.

In 1980 *Playboy* model Dorothy Stratten (Hemingway) was brutally murdered by her sleazy mentor and husband, Paul Snider (Roberts), who then committed suicide. Using a deliberately fragmented style, in which friends and acquaintances of the couple recall what they remember, Fosse relates this sordid story with considerable style. Still, the film's message about America's obsession with sex and celebrity is hardly new, and despite some bravura touches we are left with only an unpleasant aftertaste and a feeling of revulsion. As a man fatally obsessed with the "star" he created, Roberts gives a stunning performance.

STAR OF MIDNIGHT

★★☆ RKO, 1935, b/w, 90 min. Dir: Stephen Roberts. SP: Howard J. Green, Anthony Veiller, Edward Kaufman, b/o novel by Arthur Somers Roche. Cast: William Powell, Ginger Rogers, Paul Kelly, Gene Lockhart, Ralph Morgan, Leslie Fenton.

A flippant, mildly amusing mystery-comedy squarely in the *Thin Man* vein. Even the star is the same: Powell as a debonair lawyer who finds himself a murder suspect when a gossip columnist is shot in his apartment. Naturally he must solve the case himself. Rogers plays the giddy heiress determined to lure Powell into marriage.

STATE OF GRACE

★★★ Orion, 1990, c, 134 min. Dir: Phil Joanou. SP: Dennis McIntyre. Cast: Sean Penn, Ed Harris, Gary Oldman, Robin Wright, John Turturro, Burgess

Meredith, R. D. Call, Joe Viterelli.

There are more than a few echoes of Martin Scorsese in this brutal if somewhat rambling gangster movie. Once again, as in Scorsese films, a man knee-deep in inner-city corruption must confront his own inner demons and his divided loyalties. Penn is superb as Terry Noonan, who returns to his old neighborhood in New York's Hell's Kitchen (now known as Clinton) to become part of the Irish Mafia gang headed by Frankie Flannery (Harris). Vicious competition between Irish and Italian gangs sparks much bloodshed, but Terry has to contend with his own dark secret. Fine performances by all, especially Oldman as Frankie's raging, out-of-control brother.

STEPFATHER, THE

★★★ ITC, 1987, c, 98 min. Dir: Joseph Ruben. SP: Donald E. Westlake, b/o story by Carolyn Lefcourt, Brian Garfield, Donald E. Westlake. Cast: Terry O'Quinn, Jill Schoelen, Shelley Hack, Charles Lanyer, Stephen Shellen.

Jerry Blake (O'Quinn) believes in the American dream—and especially the American family. A mild-mannered real estate salesman, he lives comfortably in Washington State with his wife (Hack) and teenage stepdaugher (Schoelen). But there's one small problem: Jerry is also a serial killer who moves in on one fatherless family after another. When his dream of perfection is disturbed, he butchers his family and assumes a new identity. And now his wife and stepdaughter are in terrible jeopardy. *The Stepfather* is a modest, craftily made thriller with a number of bloodcurdling moments and a sense of the banality of evil that suggests the films of Alfred Hitchcock. Two inferior sequels followed, in 1989 and 1992.

STICK

★☆ Universal, 1985, c, 109 min. Dir: Burt Reynolds. SP: Elmore Leonard, Joseph C. Stinson, b/o novel by Elmore Leonard. Cast: Burt Reynolds, Candice Bergen, George Segal, Charles Durning, Jose Perez, Richard Lawson, Alex Rocco, Tricia Leigh Fisher, Dar Robinson.

Reynolds directed himself in this underworld melodrama and came up with a loser. He plays a newly released ex-convict called Stick, who comes to Florida and becomes enmeshed with drug dealers when his friend is murdered by them. The story is handled in clumsy fashion, and while Reynolds fares adequately, Durning and Segal are burdened with embarrassing roles, Durning as a bewigged drug dealer and Segal as an obnoxious Hollywood wheeler-dealer.

STILETTO

★★ Avco Embassy, 1969, c, 98 min. Dir: Bernard Kowalski. SP: A. J. Russell, b/o novel by Harold Robbins. Cast: Alex Cord, Patrick O'Neal, Joseph Wiseman, Britt Ekland, Barbara McNair, John Dehner.

Flat little crime melodrama. Cord is a Mafia assassin, living high on the hog and surrounded by beautiful women. Then he abruptly decides to forsake the mob and go his own way. Should he be surprised when there are repercussions? It all ends with a violent showdown in Puerto Rico.

STILL OF THE NIGHT

★★☆ MGM/UA, 1982, c, 91 min. Dir and SP: Robert Benton, b/o story by David Newman, Robert Benton. Cast: Roy Scheider, Meryl Streep, Jessica Tandy, Joe Grifasi, Sara Botsford, Josef Sommer, Irving Metzman.

Yet another Hitchcock homage, *Still of the Night* goes through the familiar devices—the long tracking shots through dark places, the conventional setting that turns sinister—but it comes up empty, and there's seldom a genuine payoff to the setups. One of the patients of psychiatrist Sam Rice (Scheider) has been murdered. Enter tense, troubled Brooke Reynolds (Streep), who was one of the victim's conquests. Dr. Rice is intrigued and attracted—could she be the killer, or will she be another victim? Loose plotting doesn't help, and you may want to count the number of times Ms. Streep plays with her hair.

STING, THE

★★★☆ Universal, 1973, c, 129 min. Dir: George Roy Hill. SP: David S. Ward. Cast: Paul Newman, Robert Redford, Robert Shaw, Charles Durning, Ray Walston, Harold Gould, Dana Elcar, Eileen Brennan, Robert Earl Jones.

This hugely entertaining caper movie surprised many by winning seven Academy Awards, including Oscars for direction, screenplay, and as the year's best picture. The time: the mid-thirties. The place: Chicago.

Clever conmen Paul Newman and Robert Redford prepare to put a "sting" on their victim in The Sting *(1973).*

Newman and Redford are small-time conmen seeking revenge for the murder of a friend by mob boss Shaw. With the help of friends, they devise an elaborate "sting" that will divest Shaw of a huge sum of money. Contributing greatly to the fun are Marvin Hamlisch's sprightly adaptations of Scott Joplin ragtime tunes. A sequel, *The Sting II* flopped in 1983.

STING II, THE

★★ Universal, 1983, c, 102 min. Dir: Jeremy Paul Kagan. SP: David S. Ward. Cast: Jackie Gleason, Mac Davis, Teri Garr, Karl Malden, Oliver Reed.

A weak sequel to the extremely popular, Oscar-winning film of 1973. This time the roles of Gondorff and Hooker, the two slick con

artists, are played (with different first names) by Gleason and Davis. Already the movie is in trouble. The new sting, or swindle, involves convincing Lonnegan (Reed), the gambler played by Robert Shaw in the earlier film, that Hooker has the potential to be a champion boxer. Only Garr rises above the general mediocrity.

STIR CRAZY

★★★ Columbia, 1980, c, 111 min. Dir: Sidney Poitier. SP: Bruce Jay Friedman. Cast: Gene Wilder, Richard Pryor, Jobeth Williams, George Stanford Brown, Miguelangel Suarez, Craig T. Nelson, Barry Corbin.

Actor Poitier directed this raucously entertaining comedy that brought together

Richard Pryor and Gene Wilder are going Stir Crazy *(1980) as hapless New Yorkers who are thrown into prison.*

hyperactive Wilder and streetwise Pryor in their first teaming since *Silver Streak* (1976). They are two down-on-their luck New Yorkers who, on their drive to California, are mistaken for bank robbers and thrown into prison. Their plight behind bars, where they confront the usual movie assortment of brutes and crackpots, makes up the best part of the movie.

ST. IVES
★ Warner Bros., 1976, c, 93 min. Dir: J. Lee Thompson. SP: Barry Beckerman, b/o novel by Oliver Bleeck. Cast: Charles Bronson, John Houseman, Jacqueline Bissett, Maximilian Schell, Harry Guardino, Dana Elcar, Daniel J. Travanti, Harris Yulin, Dick O'Neill, Elisha Cook, Jr., Jeff Goldblum.

An unusual number of reputable actors are hopelessly trapped in this dreadful movie. Stone-faced Bronson plays an ex-crime reporter turned author who gets caught up in some vaguely defined international skulduggery by way of eccentric millionaire Houseman. Dead bodies keep accumulating around him as he is beaten, chased, or

threatened at every turn. The screenplay is close to parody and the climax is utterly ridiculous. Don't bother.

STONE KILLER, THE
★★☆ Columbia, 1973, c, 98 min. Dir: Michael Winner. SP: Gerald Wilson, b/o novel by John Gardner. Cast: Charles Bronson, Martin Balsam, Norman Fell, Ralph Waite, Stuart Margolin, Jack Colvin, Alfred Ryder, John Ritter.

A routine entry in the "vigilante cop" series of movies in the early seventies, probably triggered by Clint Eastwood's *Dirty Harry* (1971). This time Bronson is a brutal cop who takes on an underworld mob virtually single-handed. As usual he is not above risking everyone else's life and limb in pursuit of a crook. Shootouts, chase scenes, and Martin Balsam as an improbable gangland don.

STOP! OR MY MOM WILL SHOOT
★ Universal, 1992, c, 87 min. Dir: Roger Spottiswoode. SP: Blake Snyder, William Osborne, William Davies. Cast: Sylvester Stallone, Estelle Getty,

JoBeth Williams, Roger Rees, Martin Ferrero, Gailard Sartain, Dennis Buckley.

Here's the joke: Stallone is a California cop who is visited by his mother (Getty) from Newark, a relentlessly pushy, interfering nightmare. Soon she is witness to a murder and meddling dangerously in her son's police activities. Bad joke, bad movie. As the story lurches from one abysmal scene to another, Getty comes across as so obnoxious that the viewer cringes at her every appearance. It is not easy to erase the memory of this ogre singing a nighttime lullaby to her reluctant "boy."

STORMY MONDAY

★★★ Atlantic Entertainment (British), 1988, c, 93 min. Dir and SP: Mike Figgis. Cast: Melanie Griffith, Tommy Lee Jones, Sting, Sean Bean, James Cosmo, Mark Long, Brian Lewis.

A stylish, atmospheric film noir, except that the setting is Newcastle, England, rather than the dark streets of New York or Los Angeles. During a gaudy American festival, a powerful, malevolent American businessman (Jones) comes to Newcastle, bent on carrying out a lucrative real estate plan at any cost. Opposing him is a jazz club owner (Sting), and violence inevitably erupts. Griffith plays a call girl for Jones, who switches sides when she falls for Sting's employee (Bean). Well done.

STORYVILLE

★★☆ Davis Entertainment, 1992, c, 112 min. Dir: Mark Frost. SP: Mark Frost, Lee Reynolds, b/o novel by Frank Galbally, Robert Macklin. Cast: James Spader, Jason Robards, Joanne Whalley-Kilmer, Charlotte Lewis, Michael Warren, Chuck McCann, Woody Strode, Piper Laurie.

Politics, lust, and murder—these are the concerns that tear apart a Louisiana community in this good-looking but essentially mediocre melodrama. Spader is an ambitious young lawyer running for Congress whose one indiscretion with a prostitute (Lewis) triggers a chain of events that endangers his life and career. At the same time, an investigation into his family's past threatens to expose long-buried secrets. The muddled plotline is no help, but the cast works hard at making some sense of it all.

STRAIGHT TIME

★★☆ Warner Bros., 1978, c, 114 min. Dir: Ulu Grosbard. SP: Alvin Sargent, Edward Bunker, Jeffrey Boam, b/o novel by Edward Bunker. Cast: Dustin Hoffman, Theresa Russell, Gary Busey, Harry Dean Stanton, M. Emmet Walsh, Rita Taggart.

In this glum, curiously drab movie, Hoffman plays Max Dembo, a paroled criminal who finds life outside the walls intolerable. Circumstances, especially shabby treatment at the hands of his nasty parole officer (fine character actor Walsh), lead him back into crime. Good performances help, and the action sequences are well staged, but the central character is grossly unappealing. Russell plays his inexplicably sympathetic girl.

STRANGE LOVE OF MARTHA IVERS, THE

★★★ Paramount, 1946, b/w, 117 min. Dir: Lewis Milestone. SP: Robert Rossen, b/o story by Jack Patrick. Cast: Barbara Stanwyck, Van Heflin, Kirk Douglas, Lizabeth Scott, Judith Anderson, Roman Bohnen, Darryl Hickman, Janis Wilson.

"Whisper her name!" the ads proclaimed. And why? Because Martha Ivers (Stanwyck) is a nasty sort, cold, ambitious, and married to a spineless alcoholic (Douglas, in his film debut) who shares a guilty secret with her: years before, as a neurotic teenager, Martha had killed her despised aunt (Anderson). Now, in the present day, along comes Heflin, a figure from their past who may or may not know about the old crime. Soon all three, joined by parolee Scott, are trapped in a maze of blackmail, passion, and inevitable violence. The deafening music, overcooked dialogue, and feverish atmosphere may edge the movie toward parody, but with Stanwyck at her wicked best, it's still fun to watch.

STRANGER, THE

★★★ International-RKO, 1946, b/w, 95 min. Dir: Orson Welles. SP: Anthony Veiller, b/o story by Victor Trivas and Decla Denning. Cast: Edward G. Robinson, Loretta Young, Orson Welles, Philip Merivale, Richard Long, Martha Wentworth, Konstantin Shayne.

There are some bravura flourishes of the master director in this suspense melodrama, but ultimately it is not one of Welles's best films. He also plays a central role as an unregenerate Nazi who disguises himself as a teacher in a quiet Connecticut town. He even

Farley Granger grapples with Robert Walker on a runaway carousel in the breathtaking climax to Alfred Hitchcock's thriller Strangers on a Train *(1951).*

marries the daughter (Young) of a Supreme Court justice (Merivale). Then along comes a federal agent (Robinson) for the Allied War Crimes Commission, who is bent on ferreting out Welles's true identity. Welles manages some good scenes, most notably a murder in the woods, but the story is not very credible, and the climax atop an old clock tower is laughable.

STRANGER AMONG US, A

★★☆ Hollywood, 1992, c, 106 min. Dir: Sidney Lumet. SP: Robert J. Avrech. Cast: Melanie Griffith, Eric Thal, John Pankow, Tracy Pollan, Lee Richardson, Mia Sara, Jamey Sheridan.

When a young Hasidic diamond dealer is found murdered in his close-knit Brooklyn community, detective Emily Eden (Griffith) is sent to invesigate. She decides to go undercover, whereupon she not only learns the customs and laws of the Hasidic community but also falls for the Rebbe's son (Thal), who is destined to take his father's place. Their clearly doomed romance takes much more footage than the undernourished and contrived mystery plot. The scenes of Hasidic activity, especially the Sabbath

observance, are certainly colorful. But usually able director Lumet strikes out here.

STRANGER ON THE THIRD FLOOR

★★★ RKO, 1940, b/w, 64 min. Dir: Boris Ingster. SP: Frank Partos, b/o his story. Cast: Peter Lorre, John McGuire, Margaret Tallichet, Charles Waldron, Elisha Cook, Jr., Charles Halton, Ethel Griffies.

This low-budget thriller actually gives only brief footage to Lorre as the "stranger." McGuire plays the central character, a reporter whose conscience troubles him when he condemns a boy to death for murder with circumstantial evidence. When his neighbor is murdered, McGuire dreams that he is being accused of the crime, and predictably that's what happens. He is saved from execution by his girlfriend (Tallichet), who unmasks the real killer in both crimes (Lorre). Early film noir techniques, combined with expressionistic touches, make for an odd little film.

STRANGERS ON A TRAIN

★★★☆ Warner Bros., 1951, b/w, 101 min. Dir: Alfred Hitchcock. SP: Raymond Chandler, Czenzi Ormonde, adapted by Whitfield Cook from novel by Patricia Highsmith. Cast: Robert Walker, Farley

Granger, Ruth Roman, Leo G. Carroll, Patricia Hitchcock, Marion Lorne.

This taut, suspenseful thriller from Hitchcock may not be numbered among his masterworks, but it should keep viewers enthralled. Tennis star Guy (Granger) meets wealthy psychopath Bruno (Walker), who proposes a pact of mutual killings: Bruno will kill Guy's despised wife and Guy will dispose of Bruno's detested father. Bruno carries out his side of the pact, and suddenly Guy is thrust into Bruno's dark, twisted world, with no way of escape. As usual, Hitchcock carries off some bravura sequences, among them the murder of Guy's wife at an amusement park and the terrifying climax on a runaway carousel.

STRANGLER, THE

★★☆ Allied Artists, 1964, b/w, 89 min. Dir: Burt Topper. SP: Bill S. Ballinger. Cast: Victor Buono, David McLean, Diane Sayer, Davey Davison, Ellen Corby.

Corpulent Victor Buono inherits the mantle of Laird Cregar in this modestly effective thriller. He plays a mother-ridden man who turns to murder, strangling seven women even before the movie begins, then adding four more to his roster of victims. He also has a doll fetish, which eventually does him in.

STRAW DOGS

★★ ABC Pictures, 1971, c, 113 min. Dir: Sam Peckinpah. SP: David Zelag Goodman, Sam Peckinpah. Cast: Dustin Hoffman, Susan George, David Warner, Peter Vaughan, Ken Hutchison, T. P. McKenna, Del Henney, Jim Norton.

Director Peckinpah (*The Wild Bunch* and others) apparently believed that one of the rites of passage for true manhood was accepting, and even committing, acts of violence in defense of home and hearth. This dubious premise received its most overt expression in this British-made film. Hoffman is a mild-mannered American mathematician living in an isolated house in Cornwall, England, with his rather childish but sexy wife (George). Terrible events conspire to turn him into a virtual killing machine, violent and vengeful. Hoffman's conversion from wimp to "macho" man is not convincing, and the whole movie is overbaked, especially in the final, explicitly gory sequence.

STREET WITH NO NAME, THE

★★★ Fox, 1948, b/w, 91 min. Dir: William Keighley. SP: Harry Kleiner. Cast: Mark Stevens, Richard Widmark, Lloyd Nolan, Barbara Lawrence, Ed Begley, Donald Buka, Joseph Pevney, John McIntire, Walter Greaza, Howard Smith.

Widmark followed up his sensational debut performance as Tommy Udo in *Kiss of Death* with a stint as gang leader Alec Stiles in this brisk, competent melodrama. Stevens plays the FBI agent who worms his way into Stiles's gang and is nearly killed for his effort. The movie was made in the semidocumentary style popularized by Fox in the mid- to late forties in such movies as *The House on 92nd Street* (1945) and *Boomerang* (1947).

STRIKING DISTANCE

★★☆ Columbia, 1993, c, 102 min. Dir: Rowdy Herrington. SP: Rowdy Herrington, Martin Kaplan. Cast: Bruce Willis, Sarah Jessica Parker, John Mahoney, Dennis Farina, Robert Pastorelli.

Outspoken fifth-generation Pittsburgh cop Willis has accused his colleagues of corruption and cover-up. He is also convinced that the wrong man was convicted for killing his policeman father (Mahoney) two years earlier. Naturally, he has been demoted to the River Rescue Patrol. Now the real culprit—a serial killer—is menacing him and murdering his old girlfriends, and he must be caught. Parker plays Willis's partner and love interest. The movie is lively but strictly routine. Small bonus: a tour of the Pittsburgh area.

STRIPPED TO KILL

★★☆ Concorde, 1987, c, 88 min. Dir: Katt Shea Ruben. SP: Katt Shea Ruben, Andy Ruben. Cast: Kay Lenz, Greg Evigan, Norman Fell, Pia Kamakahi, Tracey Crowder, Debby Nassar.

Somebody is killing strippers in Los Angeles, and policewoman Lenz would like to nab the culprit. Naturally she goes undercover, so to speak, and poses as a stripper. When she starts to enjoy the job too much, her partner (Evigan) gets concerned. Not to worry—Lenz ferrets out the killer, who turns out to be seriously (and implausibly) weird. Many strip scenes pad out the action, but there are some good touches in this not-bad exploitation movie. A sequel turned up in 1989.

ST. VALENTINE'S DAY MASSACRE, THE

★★ Fox, 1967, c, 100 min. Dir: Roger Corman. SP: Howard Browne. Cast: Jason Robards, George Segal, Ralph Meeker, Jean Hale, Clint Ritchie, Frank Silvera, Bruce Dern.

Fox must have expended its entire supply of bullets to make this elaborate, blood-soaked, but generally inept gangster movie. It purports to relate the events leading up to the notorious 1929 execution of a number of gangsters in a North Side Chicago garage by Al Capone's hoods. Capone is wildly overplayed by a miscast Robards (even his scars look fake), and there are not much better performances by Segal as Peter Gusenberg and Meeker as Bugs Moran.

SUBSTITUTE, THE

★☆ Live, 1996, c, 114 min. Dir: Robert Mandel. SP: Roy Frumkes, Rocco Simonelli, Alan Ormsby. Cast: Tom Berenger, Diane Venora, Ernie Hudson, Glenn Plummer, Mark Anthony, Cliff De Young, Sharron Corley, Richard Brooks, Raymond Cruz.

School was never like this. When mercenary Tom Berenger is temporarily "retired" from covert operations for the CIA, he takes over as substitute teacher for his injured girlfriend (Venora) at an out-of-control Miami high school. He not only tames the kids but (with the help of his fellow mercenaries) also demolishes a drug-smuggling ring operating out of the school. Fast-moving but utterly ridiculous melodrama.

The Moran gang blasts away at Al Capone's hotel in The St. Valentine's Day Massacre *(1967). More than one other movie has depicted the massacre, notably Billy Wilder's* Some Like It Hot *(1959).*

SUDDEN DEATH

★★★ Universal, 1995, c, 111 min. Dir: Peter Hyams. SP: Gene Quintano, b/o story by Karen Baldwin. Cast: Jean-Claude Van Damme, Powers Boothe, Dorian Harewood, Raymond J. Barry, Whittni Wright, Ross Malinger.

Far-fetched it may be, but this apocalyptic thriller is undeniably exciting to watch. At the final game of the Stanley Cup hockey playoffs, a vicious, cold-blooded terrorist (Boothe), with his band of cohorts, holds the vice president hostage and threatens to blow up the arena unless his demands are met. Van Damme, a former fireman with a traumatic experience in his past, turns into a one-man army determined to stop the terrorists, especially when his young daughter (Wright) is taken hostage. The extended climactic sequence is preposterous, but you won't doze.

SUDDEN FEAR

★★★ RKO, 1952, b/w, 110 min. Dir: David Miller. SP: Lenore Coffee, Robert Smith, b/o novel by Edna Sherry. Cast: Joan Crawford, Jack Palance, Gloria Grahame, Bruce Bennett, Virginia Huston, Touch "Mike" Connors.

Crawford emotes all over the place (and won an Oscar nomination) in this suspenseful thriller. She plays a wealthy playwright who marries a struggling actor (Palance), only to learn that he is plotting to kill her with the help of his girlfriend (Grahame). Now she must do everything in her power to avoid being murdered. There are no real surprises, but Crawford is an expert at depicting beleaguered women, and the San Francisco setting makes an effective backdrop. (This was Jack Palance's first movie under that name; previously he had been billed as Walter Jack Palance.)

SUDDEN IMPACT

★★ Warner Bros., 1983, c, 117 min. Dir: Clint Eastwood. SP: Joseph C. Stinson, b/o story by Earl E. Smith, Charles B. Pierce. Cast: Clint Eastwood, Sondra Locke, Pat Hingle, Bradford Dillman, Paul Drake, Audrie J. Neenan, Jack Thibeau.

This fourth entry in Eastwood's *Dirty Harry* series is long, unpleasant, and deplorable in its point of view. This time the cop with his own code of behavior faces a serial killer (Locke) who is seeking out and murdering the men who raped her and her now-catatonic sister

years earlier. When the killer and Harry finally connect late in the film, she is a lady in distress, menaced by nasty hoods, and he is her rescuer! And he allows her to go scot free! Before all this happens, we see Harry in monotonous action, confronting crooks or dodging attempts on his life. Still, Eastwood looks tired and not a little bored with the prospect of directing himself.

SUDDENLY

★★★ United Artists, 1954, b/w, 77 min. Dir: Lewis Allen: SP: Richard Sale. Cast: Frank Sinatra, Sterling Hayden, Nancy Gates, James Gleason, Kim Charney, Christopher Dark, Paul Frees.

Only a year after winning an Oscar for his performance in *From Here to Eternity*, Sinatra confirmed his acting ability by playing an ice-cold, seriously troubled assassin in this compact little thriller. He's the head of a trio of thugs who are plotting to kill the nation's president as he passes through a town called Suddenly. They take an all-American family hostage, and as they wait for the fateful moment, Sinatra reveals the reasons for his bitterness and savage behavior. It's all simplistic but suspenseful, and Sinatra is chillingly effective.

SUGAR HILL

★★★ Fox, 1993, c, 123 min. Dir: Leon Ichaso. SP: Barry Michael Cooper. Cast: Wesley Snipes, Michael Wright, Theresa Randle, Leslie Uggams, Clarence Williams III, Abe Vigoda, Larry Joshua, Sam Bottoms.

Harlem drug lord Roemello Skuggs (Snipes) wants to leave the criminal life behind. As the member of a family destroyed by drugs, he would like to give it all up and settle down with his beautiful girlfriend (Randle). Inevitably, however, violence erupts around him, and he has no choice but to wage a brutal war against his rivals. *Sugar Hill* doesn't use the freshest materials, but it is well made and absorbing. Snipes gives his character some dignity and strength, but also watch for Vigoda, who gives an expert performance as a weary old Italian drug dealer.

SUGARLAND EXPRESS, THE

★★★ Universal, 1974, c, 109 min. Dir: Steven Spielberg. SP: Hal Barwood, Matthew Robbins. Cast: Goldie Hawn, William Atherton, Michael Sacks, Ben Johnson, Gregory Walcott, Louise Latham.

Spielberg's first feature film promises better things to come, but it's enjoyable nonetheless. A free-wheeling comedy-drama, it is based on a true incident that took place in Texas in 1969: a recent female parolee named Lou Jean (Hawn) breaks her husband Clovis (Atherton) out of prison so that they can retrieve their infant son. The couple careens across the state with a highway patrolman (Sacks) as their hostage and many police cars in pursuit. Soon they become a media event. Spielberg has fun with the well-staged chase sequences but the material and some of the characters are a trifle shopworn.

SUNSET

★★ Columbia, 1988, c, 107 min. Dir and SP: Blake Edwards, b/o story by Rod Amateau. Cast: James Garner, Bruce Willis, Mariel Hemingway, Kathleen Quinlan, Jennifer Edwards, Richard Bradford, Patricia Hodge.

In 1929 Hollywood, Western movie star Tom Mix (Willis) joins forces with Western legend Wyatt Earp (Garner), technical adviser on his film, to solve a murder. They encounter various unsavory characters, get into a number of scrapes and jams, and end up in a violent climax at the first Academy Award ceremony. Unfortunately a fanciful idea is aborted by a dull and muddled screenplay that conveys very little of the period's flavor. Even Garner's affable personality can't save the movie.

SUNSET BOULEVARD

★★★★ Paramount, 1950, b/w, 110 min. Dir: Billy Wilder. SP: Charles Brackett, Billy Wilder, D. M. Marshman, Jr., b/o story by Charles Brackett, Billy Wilder. Cast: Gloria Swanson, William Holden, Erich von Stroheim, Nancy Olson, Fred Clark, Jack Webb, Cecil B. DeMille, Hedda Hopper.

Wilder's brilliant film is a mordant study of monstrous self-delusion as well as a bitterly sardonic view of Hollywood as a spinner of elusive dreams. Swanson is Norma Desmond, a silent-screen goddess who has become a deranged recluse in her gloomy mansion. When she takes writer Joe Gillis (Holden) as her lover, she makes an inexorable descent into madness and murder. Famed actor-director von Stroheim plays her doggedly loyal butler and ex-husband. Eyes bulging and teeth flashing, Swanson gives an audacious performance as Norma, and Holden is fine as an ice-cold opportunist who makes the fatal mistake of compassion. The screenplay, art direction, and score for this masterly classic won Oscars.

SUPERFLY

★ Warner Bros., 1972, c, 96 min. Dir: Gordon Parks, Jr. SP: Philip Fenty. Cast: Ron O'Neal, Carl Lee, Sheila Frazier, Julius W. Harris, Charles McGregor.

Highly popular in its time, Superfly is actually a dull and reprehensible movie, unworthy of anyone's attention. O'Neal is the seemingly invulnerable title character, a big-time cocaine dealer with one major problem: he wants to get out of the business. Inevitably he finds himself up against a treacherous partner, corrupt cops, and others who make his goal impossible. Since he is apparently the only character with money, guts, and power, he perseveres: a clear lesson for future drug dealers. There were two sequels: Superfly T.N.T. (1973) and The Return of Superfly (1990).

SUPERFLY T.N.T.

★ Paramount, 1973, c, 87 min. Dir: Ron O'Neal. SP: Alex Haley, b/o story by Sig Shore, Ron O'Neal. Cast: Ron O'Neal, Roscoe Lee Browne, Sheila Frazier, Robert Guillaume, Jacques Sernas.

Even worse than the original Superfly, this tacky little effort finds our cocaine dealer (O'Neal) now reformed and living a dull life in Rome. He accepts an offer to head a gun-running mission for a small, oppressed African country, and the adventure begins. Browne provides the only bright spot, as a fiery African revolutionary. Another sequel, The Return of Superfly, turned up in 1990.

SUSPECT

★★★ TriStar, 1987, c, 121 min. Dir: Peter Yates. SP: Eric Roth. Cast: Cher, Dennis Quaid, Liam Neeson, John Mahoney, Joe Mantegna, Philip Bosco.

A reasonably engrossing thriller with a few too many holes in its plot, Suspect stars Cher as a public defender who is assigned a seemingly hopeless case: Leeson, a deaf mute and a derelict, has been accused of murder. Before long Cher is joined by a scrappy lobbyist (Quaid) in a search for the truth. The search uncovers a top-level conspiracy and places them both in grave danger. Yet for all their sleuthing they find time enough to fall in love. The motives for the characters are not always clear, but the film moves at a fast clip and holds the interest. There's also a surprise ending.

SUSPICION

★★★ RKO, 1941, b/w, 99 min. Dir: Alfred Hitchcock. SP: Samson Raphaelson, Joan Harrison, Alma Reville, b/o novel by Francis Iles. Cast: Cary Grant, Joan Fontaine, Nigel Bruce, Sir Cedric Hardwicke, Dame May Whitty, Leo G. Carroll, Heather Angel.

Fontaine won the Oscar as Best Actress for her performance as a frightened young wife in this medium-range thriller from Hitchcock. A shy heiress-to-be, she has married dashing ne'er-do-well Grant, and her worry about his shady business dealings turns to terror when she starts to believe that he is trying to kill her. The climax, with the two grappling in a speeding auto, is rather absurd. There are a few memorable moments, especially the scene in which Grant brings Fontaine a glass of milk that seems to glow with the poison she suspects he has added. But on the whole, this is not one of the great Hitchcock thrillers. Still, it was nominated for an Academy Award as Best Picture.

TAKE THE MONEY AND RUN

★★★ Cinerama, 1969, c, 85 min. Dir and SP: Woody Allen. Cast: Woody Allen, Janet Margolin, Marcel Hillaire, Lonny Chapman, Jacquelyn Hyde; narrated by Jackson Beck.

Early Allen, and quite funny in a ramshackle way. His first movie as director, *Take the Money and Run* casts Allen as Virgil Starkwell, possibly the world's most inept thief. His efforts at robbery either land him in prison or keep him in flight from the law. Allen takes aim at the clichés of prison and gangster movies: the bank robbery, the prison breakout, and the like, and more often than not, he hits the target. His later films, however, would be more focused and disciplined.

TAKING OF PELHAM ONE-TWO-THREE, THE

★★★ Fox, 1974, c, 104 min. Dir: Joseph Sargent. SP: Peter Stone, b/o novel by John Godey. Cast: Walter Matthau, Robert Shaw, Martin Balsam, Hector Elizondo, Earl Hindman, Dick O'Neill, Jerry Stiller, Tony Roberts, James Broderick.

The premise is simple: three men, led by a coldly fanatical Shaw, hijack a New York City subway train, threatening to kill passengers unless they receive a million dollars in cash—in one hour. Matthau is the detective with the Transit Authority in charge of keeping the passengers alive and foiling the thieves. The screenplay has little time for characterization, but there are plenty of terrifying moments in the race against time, along with some sardonic comedy. (The city's mayor is depicted as a fool.) This sort of movie calls for tight, skillful editing, and it gets just that from Jerry Greenberg.

TANGO & CASH

★★☆ Warner Bros., 1989, c, 98 min. Dir: Andrei Konchalovsky. SP: Randy Feldman. Cast: Sylvester Stallone, Kurt Russell, Jack Palance, Teri Thatcher, Michael J. Pollard, Brion James, James Hong, Michael Jeter.

Two top-ranking Los Angeles cops named Tango (Stallone) and Cash (Russell) are framed by an arch criminal (Palance) and sent to prison. They escape to exact their revenge and win their vindication in this ridiculous but not unentertaining comic-book adventure. The action is virtually nonstop as the two heroes continue to crack jokes even under the direst circumstances. Palance contributes an appropriately hammy performance as the sneering villain.

TARGET

★★ CBS/Zanuck-Brown, 1985, c, 117 min. Dir: Arthur Penn. SP: Howard Berk, Don Petersen, b/o story by Leonard Stern. Cast: Gene Hackman, Matt Dillon, Gayle Hunnicutt, Josef Sommer, Herbert Berghof, Victoria Fyodorova, Ilona Grubel, Guy Boyd.

A fine director and a superb leading man cannot surmount the clumsy, cliché-riddled screenplay of this would-be thriller. Hackman is a prosperous lumber dealer with a resentful son (Dillon). When his wife (Hunnicutt) is kidnapped in Paris, Hackman springs into action. It seems that he was once a top CIA operative, and now someone is seeking revenge for an imagined crime from the past. With his bewildered son in tow, Hackman sprints from one European city to another, renewing old contacts and dodging assassination as he tries to rescue his wife. Only Berghof as a bitter old ex-agent survives the general ineptness.

TARGETS

★★★ Paramount, 1968, b/w, 90 min. Dir: Peter Bogdanovich. SP: Peter Bogdanovich, b/o story by Peter Bogdanovich, Polly Platt. Cast: Boris Karloff, Tim O'Kelly, Peter Bogdanovich, Nancy Kseuh, Sandy Baron.

Bogdanovich's first feature film was obviously made on a shoestring, but within its limitations it proved to be a chilling, often expert effort. O'Kelly stars as an ordinary, sweet-faced, but deranged young man who suddenly launches a killing spree in Los Angeles. A parallel story involves Karloff in his last role, as an aging star of horror films, who has decided to retire. (To him the real world has become more terrifying than any of his films.) Ironically, the serial killer and the star confront each other in the movie's suspenseful climax. The sequences with the stalking O'Kelly dramatize the banality of evil most effectively.

TATTOO

★ Fox, 1981, c, 103 min. Dir: Bob Brooks. SP: Joyce Buñuel, b/o story by Bob Brooks. Cast: Bruce Dern, Maud Adams, Leonard Frey, Rikki Borge, John Getz, Peter Iachangelo.

Shades of William Wyler's *The Collector*. A sleazy erotic thriller, *Tattoo* stars Bruce Dern in one of his patented looney roles. He's a plastic surgeon who is so enraptured by Adams that he kidnaps her and holds her prisoner in an abandoned New Jersey house so that he can tattoo her body at his whim. It turns out that he has a full-body tattoo as well, which seems to turn her on. The ending is violent. The author of the screenplay is Luis Buñuel's daughter-in-law.

TAXI DRIVER

★★★☆ Columbia, 1976, c, 113 min. Dir: Martin Scorsese. SP: Paul Schrader. Cast: Robert De Niro, Cybill Shepherd, Harvey Keitel, Peter Boyle, Jodie Foster, Albert Brooks.

Beware of Travis Bickle (De Niro). A Manhattan cabdriver, he drives the nighttime streets consumed with rage and disgust at the pimps, whores, and criminals he sees everywhere. ("This city is an open sewer!") When an attractive political worker (Shepherd) rejects him, he plots to assassinate her

Robert De Niro is riveting as deranged taxi driver Travis Bickle, dangerously at large in New York City's nighttime jungle in Taxi Driver *(1976). At left is Peter Boyle.*

candidate, but ends up killing the "animals" he loathes in a hideous bloodbath. In light of today's world, the coda that once seemed wildly improbable may have been prophetic after all. Viewers either detest or admire Scorsese's vision of urban hell, but it's a jolting, fascinating film, and De Niro gives a powerhouse performance as a man on the edge. Foster appears as a teenage prostitute, and Keitel plays her pimp. *Taxi Driver* won four Oscar nominations, including one for Best Picture.

TEMP, THE

★★ Paramount, 1993, c, 99 min. Dir: Tom Holland. SP: Kevin Falls, b/o story by Kevin Falls, Tom Engleman. Cast: Timothy Hutton, Lara Flynn Boyle, Faye Dunaway, Dwight Schultz, Oliver Platt, Steven Weber, Colleen Flynn.

She's on the loose again—another Crazy Woman—in this rather obvious and foolish thriller. This time it's Boyle, cool, sexy, and dangerous, who arrives at a cookie company and proceeds to maim or kill her way to the top. Her boss (Hutton) had been prone to paranoid behavior in the past, so naturally nobody believes him when he becomes suspicious. As the plot unravels, all sorts of questions remain unanswered. Dunaway is the steely Boss Lady who gets her comeuppance.

10 RILLINGTON PLACE

★★★ Columbia (British), 1971, c, 111 min. Dir: Richard Fleischer. SP: Clive Exton, b/o book by Ludovic Kennedy. Cast: Richard Attenborough, Judy Geeson, John Hurt, Pat Heywood, Isabel Black.

In 1950 Welshman Timothy Evans was executed for the murder of his infant daughter at 10 Rillington Place, London. Three years later it was revealed that a former policeman named John Reginald Christie had not only committed the murder but had killed many others. Evans was pardoned posthumously, and the death penalty was abolished in England. *10 Rillington Place* is a sensible, straightforward account of the events, often filmed on actual locations.

TEN TO MIDNIGHT

★ Golan-Globus, 1983, c, 100 min. Dir: J. Lee Thompson. SP: William Roberts. Cast: Charles Bronson, Lisa Eilbacher, Gene Davis, Andrew Stevens, Geoffrey Lewis, Wilford Brimley.

Bronson is back on the vigilante trail in this grim, depressingly ugly thriller. When a vicious, deranged serial killer (Davis) seems to be escaping justice through a legal loophole, cop Bronson falsifies evidence against him and is fired from the force. After his daughter (Eilbacher) becomes the killer's next victim, he takes matters into his own hands.

TEQUILA SUNRISE

★★★ Warner Bros., 1988, c, 116 min. Dir and SP: Robert Towne. Cast: Mel Gibson, Michelle Pfeiffer, Kurt Russell, Raul Julia, J. T. Walsh, Gabriel Damon, Arye Gross, Ann Magnuson.

Gibson is a drug dealer who would like to retire but cannot get out of the business. Russell is a cop and Gibson's boyhood friend who is asked to bring him down at any cost. The situation is magnified when both men fall for sexy restaurant owner Pfeiffer. The movie's star chemistry is palpable (Pfeiffer practically defines it), but Julia gives the best performance as a suavely sinister drug lord. The story gets somewhat muddled until the explosive climax.

THELMA & LOUISE

★★★☆ MGM, 1991, c, 128 min. Dir: Ridley Scott. SP: Callie Khouri. Cast: Susan Sarandon, Geena Davis, Harvey Keitel, Michael Madsen, Christopher McDonald, Brad Pitt, Timothy Carhart, Stephen Tobolowsky.

An exhilarating reinvention of the "buddy" movie, given urgency and excitement by an Oscar-winning screenplay, expert direction, and two sterling performances by its stars. Thelma (Davis) is a timid housewife with a boorish husband (McDonald), and Louise (Sarandon) is a smart, hard-headed, but restless waitress. Together they set off on a journey down Western roads that begins as an impulsive lark and ends with them as desperate fugitives from the law. The feminist sensibility is obvious throughout—Keitel, as a detective, plays the only sympathetic male— but the movie is simultaneously gritty, poignant, and funny. Only the ending is questionable.

THEY CALL ME *MISTER* TIBBS!

★☆ United Artists, 1970, c, 107 min. Dir: Gordon Douglas. SP: Alan R. Trustman, James R. Webb, b/o story by Alan R. Trustman and character created by John Ball. Cast: Sidney Poitier, Martin Landau, Barbara McNair, Anthony Zerbe, Edward Asner, Jeff Corey, Norma Crane, Juano Hernandez, David Sheiner, Beverly Todd.

A very poor first sequel to the successful *In the Heat of the Night* (1967). Back on his home turf, detective Virgil Tibbs (Poitier) investigates the murder of a prostitute in which the chief suspect is an activist minister (Landau) who has been Tibbs's good friend for years. The screenplay is surprisingly amateurish, and the domestic interludes with Tibbs and his family are simply excrutiating. Followed by *The Organization* (1971).

THEY LIVE BY NIGHT

★★★☆ RKO, 1949, b/w, 95 min. Dir: Nicholas Ray. SP: Charles Schnee, b/o novel by Edward Anderson. Cast: Farley Granger, Cathy O'Donnell, Howard Da Silva, Helen Craig, J. C. Flippen.

Director Ray made his debut with this modestly scaled but artful and rather touching film in the Bonnie and Clyde tradition. Unable to leave his life of crime, young thief Bowie (Granger) falls in love with and marries farm girl Keechie (O'Donnell). Together they flee from the law, only to meet with betrayal. There are patches of awkward dialogue, but Ray manages to sustain a mood of imminent doom. The movie was made in 1948 and shelved until it scored a success in England and was finally released in the States. Remade by Robert Altman in 1974 under the title of the original novel, *Thieves Like Us*.

THEY MADE ME A CRIMINAL

★★☆ Warner Bros., 1939, b/w, 92 min. Dir: Busby Berkeley. SP: Sig Herzig, b/o story by Bertram Millhauser, Beulah Marie Dix. Cast: John Garfield, Claude Rains, Gloria Dickson, Ann Sheridan, Billy Halop, Bobby Jordan, Leo Gorcey, Huntz Hall, Gabriel Dell.

A routine remake of *The Life of Jimmy Dolan* (1935), this movie gains some added punch through the dynamic presence of Garfield. He plays a tough, cynical boxer framed on a murder charge, who flees to the West, where he takes up residence at May Robson's ranch for delinquent boys. Detective Rains is hot on his trail, but after some dramatic events Garfield finds love and redemption. This was director Berkeley's last movie at Warners before moving to MGM.

THEY ONLY KILL THEIR MASTERS

★★★ MGM, 1972, c, 97 min. Dir: James Goldstone. SP: Lane Slate. Cast: James Garner, Katharine Ross, Hal Holbrook, Peter Lawford, Harry Guardino, Christopher Connelly, June Allyson, Tom Ewell, Ann Rutherford.

A neatly turned out, rather diverting mystery film, with Garner as a policeman investigating the murder of a pregnant woman in a California coastal town. The trail leads to other corpses and to a Doberman pinscher who provides the main clue. Some veteran actors, including Allyson and Lawford (MGM "sweethearts" in the forties), wander in to play small roles.

THEY WON'T BELIEVE ME

★★★ RKO, 1947, b/w, 79 min. Dir: Irving Pichel. SP: Jonathan Latimer, b/o story by Gordon McDonell. Cast: Robert Young, Susan Hayward, Jane Greer, Rita Johnson, Tom Powers, George Tyne, Don Beddoe.

Young discarded his usual affable persona to take the role of a devious scoundrel in this cleverly contrived melodrama. He plays a philandering husband whose lies and machinations get so far out of hand that he becomes an obvious murder suspect. Hayward and Greer are the other women in his life, but Johnson takes the acting honors as his desperate wife. There's an ironic and surprising twist at the movie's end.

THEY WON'T FORGET

★★★☆ Warner Bros., 1937, b/w, 95 min. Dir: Mervyn LeRoy. SP: Robert Rossen, Aben Kandel, b/o book by Ward Greene. Cast: Claude Rains, Gloria Dickson, Otto Kruger, Edward Norris, Allyn Joslyn, Elisha Cook, Jr., Lana Turner, Clinton Rosemond.

Crude as it is in many ways, *They Won't Forget* still retains much of its power as an example of Warner Bros.'s social dramas of the thirties. The movie is based on the true, notorious 1913 case in which Leo Frank, a Jewish factory superintendant from the North, was accused of murdering a young Georgia girl and was summarily lynched by an angry mob. In the movie, the victim is a Northern teacher who is lynched after a prosecuting attorney (Rains) incites a mob to violence. The movie overstates everything, but it pulls no punches in depicting the ugliness of the lynch mob and the corruption of those who exploit the lynchers. Turner, in her first movie role, created quite a stir as the murder victim.

THIEF

★★★ MGM/UA, 1981, c, 123 min. Dir: Michael Mann. SP and story: Michael Mann, b/o novel by Frank Hohimer. Cast: James Caan, Tuesday Weld, Willie Nelson, Robert Prosky, James Belushi, Tom Signorelli.

Television director Mann made his feature film debut with this harsh melodrama, and the flashy style he would later use for his successful TV series *Miami Vice* is very much in evidence. The central figure is Frank (Caan), a highly efficient professional thief who, in order to stay alive, must battle not only a vicious ganglord (Prosky) but corrupt cops as well. Nothing matters to him any more except his wife (Weld) and child. In the end only cataclysmic measures can guarantee his survival. Caan gives one of his best post-*Godfather* performances as Frank.

THIEF WHO CAME TO DINNER, THE

★★☆ Warner Bros, 1973, c, 105 min. Dir: Bud Yorkin. SP: Walter Hill, b/o novel by Terrence L. Smith. Cast: Ryan O'Neal, Jacqueline Bisset, Warren Oates, Jill Clayburgh, Charles Cioffi, Ned Beatty, Austin Pendleton.

Bored computer expert O'Neal decides that being a jewel thief is much more rewarding and he moves into Houston society with that intention. His trademark is leaving a chess piece at the scene of each robbery. Then he falls in love with a society girl (Bisset), and the plot does not exactly thicken—it simmers lightly. This inconsequential caper comedy features Clayburgh in a prestardom role as O'Neal's disgruntled ex-wife.

THIEVES LIKE US

★★★☆ United Artists, 1974, b/w, 123 min. Dir: Robert Altman. SP: Calder Willingham, Joan Tewkesbury, Robert Altman, b/o novel by Edward Anderson. Cast: Keith Carradine, Shelley Duvall, John Schuck, Bert Remsen, Louise Fletcher, Tom Skerritt, Ann Latham.

Altman's take on the Bonnie and Clyde theme is an exceptionally gritty and forceful drama. Based on a novel that was filmed in 1949 as *They Live by Night*, the movie deals with two prison escapees (Carradine and Schuck) and an ex-con (Remsen) in Depression-plagued Mississippi, who hide out with a friend after a string of bank robberies. Bowie (Carradine) falls in love with a plain country girl named Keechie (Duvall), and their doomed affair is the heart of the film. Beautifully photographed and acted with conviction, *Thieves Like Us* is worth your attention.

THIN BLUE LINE, THE

★★★★ (Documentary) American Playhouse, 1988, c, 96 min. Dir and SP: Errol Morris.

Morris's gripping, hypnotic documentary concerns a hideous miscarriage of justice. In Dallas in 1976, a man named Randall Adams was accused and convicted of murdering a policeman, despite substantial evidence that the crime was committed by a teenage punk named David Harris. A combination of outright lies, hypocrisy, self-serving evasiveness, and stupidity resulted in a death sentence for Adams. Using interviews, photo collages, and a recreation of the killing, Morris shows just how rusty the wheels of justice can get. The case was reopened after the film's premiere, and Adams was exonerated. Harris was convicted and sentenced to death for another crime.

THINGS CHANGE

★★★ Columbia, 1988, c, 100 min. Dir: David Mamet. SP: David Mamet, Shel Silverstein. Cast: Don Ameche, Joe Mantegna, Robert Prosky, Mike Nussbaum, J. J. Johnston, Ricky Jay.

In his second effort as a director, playwright Mamet forgoes his usual cryptic, convoluted style to offer a straightforward, amusing comedy. The premise: Gino (Ameche), a simple old Italian-American shoemaker, is hired to "take the fall" for a kingpin mobster he greatly resembles. Jerry (Mantegna), the hood assigned to guard Gino, takes him to Lake Tahoe for a final fling before prison, where the old man is mistaken for a true crime boss. Soon Gino and Jerry are in deep trouble, fleeing the mob. Cleverly wrought if not totally credible, the movie offers a few surprises along the way, and Ameche, deep in his elderly-character phase after years as an insipid leading man, is fully in command of his role as old Gino.

THINGS TO DO IN DENVER WHEN YOU'RE DEAD

★ Miramax, 1995, c, 115 min. Dir: Gary Fleder. SP: Scott Rosenberg. Cast: Andy Garcia, Christopher Walken, Gabrielle Anwar, William Forsythe, Treat Williams, Christopher Lloyd, Jack Warden, Steve Buscemi, Faruka Balk.

A movie with characters named "Jimmy the Saint," "The Man with the Plan," and "Mr. Shush" is bound to be different. But here's proof positive that different is not necessarily good. One of the nastiest, most atrocious crime films in recent memory, *Things to Do* is made worse by a screenplay choked with ludicrously self-conscious dialogue. Garcia plays Jimmy the Saint, a sensitive sort with underworld ties, who is ordered to commit a violent crime by the Man with the Plan (Walken). Jimmy brings along his friends on the job, and when it goes horribly wrong, all the men are doomed. Williams stands out in a showy but not necessarily career-reviving role.

THIN MAN, THE

★★★★ MGM, 1934, b/w, 93 min. Dir: W. S. Van Dyke II. SP: Albert Hackett, Frances Goodrich, b/o novel by Dashiell Hammett. Cast: William Powell, Myrna Loy, Maureen O'Sullivan, Nat Pendleton, Cesar Romero, Minna Gombell, Natalie Moorhead, Edward Ellis, Porter Hall.

The mystery plot was perfunctory and the production modest, but this is the movie that not only launched a popular series but also created a new trend in movie sophistication. Powell is the suave detective Nick Charles, happily married to the charming Nora (Loy). Together they share a fondness for alcohol, wisecracks, and solving murders, and here they get the chance to indulge in all three. The movie was an unexpected hit, as audiences delighted in viewing a marriage that was not only sexy but fun. There were five sequels, none quite up the first but still enjoyable, as well as many imitations. Also: three cheers for the Charleses' dog, Asta.

THIN MAN GOES HOME, THE

★★☆ MGM, 1944, b/w, 100 min. Dir: Richard Thorpe. SP: Robert Riskin, Dwight Taylor, b/o story by Robert Riskin, Harry Kurnitz, and characters created by Dashiell Hammett. Cast: William Powell, Myrna Loy, Lucile Watson, Gloria De Haven, Anne Revere, Harry Davenport, Leon Ames, Helen Vinson, Donald Meek, Edward Brophy.

Fifth film in the *Thin Man* series and another fairly agreeable mix of mayhem and mirth, with emphasis on the latter. Nick (Powell) and Nora (Loy) Charles visit Nick's parents in Sycamore Springs where (surprise!) a local artist is found murdered, followed by the local madwoman (Revere). Nick is soon back playing detective, abetted, of course, by Nora, with their dog, Asta, providing the usual comic relief.

THIS GUN FOR HIRE

★★★ Paramount, 1942, b/w, 80 min. Dir: Frank Tuttle. SP: W. R. Burnett, Albert Maltz, b/o novel by Graham Greene. Cast: Veronica Lake, Robert Preston, Alan Ladd, Laird Cregar, Tully Marshall, Marc Lawrence, Pamela Blake.

After playing minor roles in several films, including *Citizen Kane*, Ladd achieved stardom as the cold-blooded killer Raven in this modestly intriguing melodrama. He's a hired gun who kills without blinking, but his main goal here is to exact revenge on double-crossing Cregar, playing another of his effete and treacherous fat men. Lake is the blonde singer who becomes Ladd's prisoner and his sympathetic sounding board. The two became a popular movie team in the forties, but neither was much of an actor. Remade as *Short Cut to Hell* in 1957, and for cable TV in 1991.

THOMAS CROWN AFFAIR, THE

★★★ United Artists/Mirisch, 1968, c, 102 min. Dir: Norman Jewison. SP: Alan R. Trustman. Cast: Steve McQueen, Faye Dunaway, Paul Burke, Jack Weston, Biff MGuire, Yaphet Kotto.

The use of multiscreen images will be lost on television, but this lightweight romantic caper is still enjoyable. McQueen is a smooth, dapper millionaire who organizes an elaborate—and successful—bank robbery. Enter Dunaway, a glamorous insurance investigator who suspects that McQueen is the prime suspect. They begin a cat-and-mouse game that doesn't end when they become lovers. Best scene: the sexiest chess game in movie annals. The movie's theme song, "The Windmills of Your Mind," won an Oscar.

THREAT, THE

★★☆ RKO, 1949, b/w, 65 min. Dir: Felix Feist. SP: Hugh King, Dick Irving Hyland, b/o story by Hugh King. Cast: Charles McGraw, Michael O'Shea, Virginia Grey, Julie Bishop, Frank Conroy, Robert Shayne, Anthony Caruso.

A tidy little melodrama featuring McGraw, an actor who was skilled at playing hardened criminals. Here he's a prison escapee who kidnaps the policeman (O'Shea) and district attorney (Conroy) who helped to send him to jail, along with the moll (Grey) whom he suspects of betraying him. No surprises, but some brisk action in the sort of movie that used to make double features an occasional pleasure.

THREE DAYS OF THE CONDOR

★★★ Paramount, 1975, c, 118 min. Dir: Sydney Pollack. SP: Lorenzo Semple, Jr., David Rayfiel, b/o novel by James Grady. Cast: Robert Redford, Faye Dunaway, Cliff Robertson, Max Von Sydow, John Houseman, Carlin Glynn.

This suspenseful thriller was another entry in the spate of "government conspiracy" movies that surfaced in the seventies. Redford is a reader for what appears to be a literary society but is actually a front for the CIA. When all his fellow staff members are murdered, he finds that he can trust nobody and that his own life is in danger. He finds refuge, and romance, with a journalist (Dunaway). Robertson plays his duplicitous boss, and Von Sydow is a killer-for-hire.

THROW MOMMA FROM THE TRAIN

★★☆ Orion, 1987, c, 88 min. Dir: Danny DeVito. SP: Stu Silver. Cast: Billy Crystal, Danny DeVito, Anne Ramsey, Kim Greist, Kate Mulgrew, Branford Marsalis, Rob Reiner.

This black comedy must have sounded funny on paper, but it's mostly preposterous as a movie. Crystal is a writer and teacher with a much-hated ex-wife (Mulgrew) who has written a best-selling novel. Into his creative writing class comes dim-witted DeVito, who has a monstrous mother (Ramsey) he would like to see dead. After watching Hitchcock's *Strangers on a Train*, DeVito proposes that he and Crystal "exchange" murders. Every hoary comedy-thriller device is trotted out to keep the movie churning, but to little avail.

THUNDERBOLT AND LIGHTFOOT

★★★ United Artists, 1974, c, 114 min. Dir and SP: Michael Cimino. Cast: Clint Eastwood, Jeff Bridges, George Kennedy, Geoffrey Lewis, Catherine Bach, Gary Busey, Jack Dodson.

Cimino made his directorial debut with this overlong but entertaining crime comedy. Eastwood is the man they call "Thunderbolt," a con-man and thief who is persuaded to restage the robbery of the Montana Armory long after the loot from the original robbery has vanished. He is joined by his former cohorts, nasty Kennedy and nerdy Lewis, and by a new friend, an easy-going young thief named Lightfoot (Bridges). The action is raucous, fast, and often funny, with an unexpectedly poignant ending. Bridges walks away with the movie, hands down.

THUNDERHEART

★★★ TriStar, 1992, c, 119 min. Dir: Michael Apted. SP: John Fusco. Cast: Val Kilmer, Sam Shepard, Graham Greene, Chief Ted Thin Elk, Fred Ward, Sheila Tousey, Fred Dalton Thompson.

When part-Sioux FBI agent Kilmer is assigned to investigate a murder on an Indian reservation in South Dakota, he walks into a violent civil war. Militant radical Indians who want to retain the old ways are battling fiercely with hostile locals. During the course of his investigation, Kilmer not only uncovers the grim truth about the killing but also comes to understand his heritage and his own dark past. An absorbing mystery thriller, with an interesting background. Based on true events.

TIE THAT BINDS, THE

★ Hollywood, 1995, c, 98 min. Dir: Wesley Strick. SP: Michael Auerbach. Cast: Darryl Hannah, Keith Carradine, Moira Kelly, Vincent Spano, Julia Devin, Cynda Williams, Bruce A. Young.

Studio thinking: we had a hit with *The Hand That Rocks the Cradle* and its monster nanny. Let's try Birth Parents from Hell, who terrorize the adoptive parents and their very own troubled daughter. Wrong thinking. This meretricious, reprehensible thriller stars Carradine and Hannah as a psychotic couple who try to wrench their child from her loving adoptive parents (Kelly and Spano), leaving dead bodies in their wake. The movie plays on the very real fears of many adoptive parents and should be shunned at all cost.

TIGHTROPE

★★ Warner Bros., 1984, c, 114 min. Dir and SP: Richard Tuggle. Cast: Clint Eastwood, Genevieve Bujold, Dan Hedaya, Alison Eastwood, Jennifer Beck.

Eastwood has spent much of his acting career being tough, taciturn, and in control. But here he is a New Orleans cop "on the edge," as the ads proclaimed. While tracking down a serial killer, he comes to realize that he shares the same sexual proclivities. And the killer knows it. Soon all the women in Eastwood's life are in dire peril. This darkly photographed movie may be discreet enough not to wallow in the gory details of the murders, but somehow it still comes across as tawdry. And with Eastwood the only character of any dimension, all that film noir atmosphere eventually becomes monotonous and oppressive. Eastwood's true daughter Alison plays his teenage daughter in the movie.

TIGHT SPOT

★★ Columbia, 1955, b/w, 97 min. Dir: Phil Karlson. SP: William Bowers, b/o play by Lenard Kantor. Cast: Ginger Rogers, Edward G. Robinson, Brian Keith, Katherine Anderson, Lorne Greene, Eve McVeagh, Allen Nourse.

Rogers is clearly miscast in this drab, talky little melodrama. She plays a hard-bitten convict who is being asked to risk her life by testifying against a top gangster (Greene). Sequestered in a hotel room, she is guarded by a detective (Keith), a prosecutor (Robinson), and a prison matron (Anderson). There are a few spurts of action, but mostly dull palaver between Rogers and Keith as hostility turns to love. There's also a single surprise, which we will not reveal. Not even Robinson's usual forceful acting can inject life into this movie.

TIME TO KILL, A

★★★ Warner Bros., 1996, c, 145 min. Dir: Joel Schumacher. SP: Akiva Goldsman, b/o novel by John Grisham. Cast: Matthew McConaughey, Sandra Bullock, Samuel T. Jackson, Kevin Spacey, Charles S. Dutton, Brenda Fricker, Patrick McGoohan, Donald Sutherland, Kiefer Sutherland.

In a small Mississippi town, a ten-year-old black girl is brutally raped and tortured by two drunken young rednecks. In a blind rage, her father (Jackson) kills them both, setting off a racial storm that engulfs the community. The movie adapts Grisham's novel into a churning and undeniably absorbing melodrama in which virtually every character is a walking cliché, from the honorable young lawyer (McConaughey in a star-making role) who defends the black man to the remarkably articulate black man himself. Bullock plays a liberal Northern law student in what is essentially a supporting role. A good cast helps.

T-MEN

★★★ Eagle Lion, 1947, b/w, 96 min. Dir: Anthony Mann. SP: John C. Higgins, suggested by story by Virginia Kellogg. Cast: Dennis O'Keefe, June Lockhart, Alfred Ryder, Charles McGraw, Wallace Ford, Mary Meade.

Another feature in the "semidocumentary" style popular at this time, T-Men is a no-nonsense melodrama that revolves around the activities of Treasury Department trouble-shooters. Two T-Men (O'Keefe and Ryder) disguise themselves as hoodlums and worm their way into and expose a big-time counterfeit ring. That's the gist of the story but as crisply directed by Mann, it covers familiar territory with surprising effectiveness. Some footage was shot at actual locations in Detroit and Los Angeles.

TO CATCH A THIEF

★★★ Paramount, 1955, c, 106 min. Dir: Alfred Hitchcock. SP: John Michael Hayes, b/o novel by David Dodge. Cast: Cary Grant, Grace Kelly, Jessie Royce Landis, John Williams, Charles Vanel, Brigitte Auber.

The luscious French Riviera scenery is actually the best feature of this lightweight romantic caper film from Hitchcock. As debonair as ever, Grant plays an ex-burglar who finds that he must return to his old profession when a new thief who imitates his *modus operandi* turns up on the Cote d'Azur. His romantic dalliance with wealthy, beautiful Kelly interferes with his mission, but only for a while. Landis as Kelly's blunt-speaking mother and Williams as an insurance agent lend delightful support to the glamorous leads.

TODD KILLINGS, THE

★★ National General, 1971, c, 95 min. Dir: Barry Shear. SP: Dennis Murphy, Joel Oliansky, b/o story by

Mann Rubin. Cast: Robert F. Lyons, Richard Thomas, Belinda Montgomery, Barbara Bel Geddes, Gloria Grahame, Ed Asner, Meg Foster.

Not for the first time, one is forced to wonder how so many capable actors managed to find their way into a tawdry melodrama. Lyons plays a severely disturbed young man who possesses a strange power over a group of teens in a small California town. He also happens to be a killer, and when he murders one of his dates, two of his awed friends help him hide the body. Weeks later he has chalked up two more victims. Justice finally prevails, but you may not choose to hold out until the end.

TO DIE FOR

★★☆ Columbia, 1995, c, 103 min. Dir: Gus Van Sant. SP: Buck Henry, b/o novel by Joyce Maynard. Cast: Nicole Kidman, Matt Dillon, Joaquin Phoenix, Casey Affleck, Illeana Douglas, Alison Folland, Dan Hedaya, Wayne Knight, George Segal (unbilled).

Perky Barbie doll Suzanne Stone (Kidman) wants to be on television in the worst way—and she finds it: by becoming a calculating, cold-blooded killer. She lures an infatuated teenager (Phoenix) and his dim-witted friend (Affleck) into murdering her nice but in-the-way husband (Dillon). And soon she's a media "celebrity". This caustic satire begins amusingly (although the satire is rather old-hat), then turns sour and unpleasant. Kidman gives her role the proper calculating tone within its one-note limits, but Douglas is best as her skeptical sister-in-law.

TO KILL A MOCKINGBIRD

★★★★ Universal, 1962, b/w, 130 min. Dir: Robert Mulligan. SP: Horton Foote, b/o novel by Harper Lee. Cast: Gregory Peck, Mary Badham, Philip Alford, Robert Duvall, Brock Peters, Rosemary Murphy, John Megna, Collin Wilcox, Frank Overton.

Peck's measured, dignified acting style perfectly matched his role in this film, and he won an Academy Award for his effort. He plays Atticus Finch, a strong but gentle and deeply honorable lawyer in a quiet Southern town of the thirties. A firestorm is created when he is called upon to defend a black man (Peters) accused of raping a white girl (Wilcox). The ugly truth is finally uncovered, but it all ends tragically. The film is flavorsome, touching, and wholly satisfying,

and Badham and Alford are especially fine as Atticus's children. Duvall made his film debut as a mysterious neighbor named Boo Radley. Other Oscars: Best Adapted Screenplay and Best Art Direction/Set Decoration (black-and-white).

TO LIVE AND DIE IN L.A.

★★ MGM/UA, 1985, c, 116 min. Dir: William Friedkin. SP: William Friedkin, Gerald Petievich, b/o novel by Gerald Petievich. Cast: William L. Petersen, Willem Dafoe, John Pankow, Debra Feuer, Dean Stockwell, John Turturro, Darlanne Fluegel.

This downbeat and highly unpleasant crime drama has Petersen as a federal agent whose partner is murdered by evil counterfeiter Dafoe. Petersen vows revenge at all cost, but the movie's central problem is that he turns out to be as bad (or even worse) than Dafoe: a truly nasty, unsympathetic character who is not above breaking the law himself. All the other characters are equally rotten. A few wild chase scenes may keep viewers awake, but the movie's depressingly ugly tone weighs it down.

TONY ROME

★★☆ Fox, 1967, c, 109 min. Dir: Gordon Douglas. SP: Richard Breen, b/o novel by Marvin H. Albert. Cast: Frank Sinatra, Jill St. John, Richard Conte, Gene Rowlands, Simon Oakland, Jeffrey Lynn, Lloyd Bochner, Sue Lyon.

Sinatra went the hard-boiled detective route for this brash, Miami-set mystery. He's Tony Rome, a cryptic private eye who is hired by a wealthy building contractor (Oakland) and soon finds himself knee-deep in criminal activities. During the film's course, he is beaten up, cut up, shot at, and seduced—all in a day's work. The movie is a far cry from *The Maltese Falcon*, and the sequel, *Lady in Cement*, is not much better.

TOO LATE FOR TEARS

★★☆ United Artists, 1949, b/w, 99 min. Dir: Byron Haskin. SP: Roy Huggins, b/o his magazine serial. Cast: Lizabeth Scott, Dan Duryea, Don DeFore, Arthur Kennedy, Kristine Miller, Barry Kelley.

Jane Palmer (Scott) is a bad sort. When $60,000 in cash falls into her lap through a case of mistaken identity, she joins with Danny Fuller (Duryea), the blackmailer for whom it was intended, to get rid of her nice husband

(Kennedy), who wants to turn in the money. Then she double-crosses the blackmailer. Does she get her comeuppance? Was there a movie code? Average, competent melodrama, with husky-voiced Scott at her nasty best.

TOUCH OF EVIL

★★★★ Universal, 1958, b/w, 93 min. Dir: Orson Welles. SP: Orson Welles, b/o novel by Whit Masterson. Cast: Charlton Heston, Janet Leigh, Orson Welles, Marlene Dietrich, Joseph Calleia, Akim Tamiroff, Ray Collins, Dennis Weaver.

One of Welles's most fascinating films, *Touch of Evil* is a quirky, nightmarish melodrama set in a grubby Mexican border town. Heston plays a Mexican narcotics agent who clashes with the town's corrupt, all-powerful chief detective (Welles) in a murder investigation. Heston's new bride (Leigh) becomes the target of Welles's insidious scheme. Deep shadows and odd camera angles, plus baroque decor, attest to the movie's film noir sensibility. Dietrich appears in a small but memorable role as a world-weary madam, and there are unbilled bits by Joseph Cotten, Mercedes McCambridge, and others. Welles's original, 108-minute version is now often shown in theaters.

TOUGH GUYS

★★☆ Touchstone, 1986, c, 104 min. Dir: Jeff Kanew. SP: James Orr, Jim Cruickshank. Cast: Burt Lancaster,

Marlene Dietrich is a fortune-telling madam and Orson Welles is a corrupt sheriff in Welles's brilliant melodrama Touch of Evil *(1958).*

Kirk Douglas, Alexis Smith, Eli Wallach, Dana Carvey, Charles Durning, Billy Barty.

Seasoned professionals who appeared together in six films, Lancaster and Douglas teamed for one last time in this lukewarm caper comedy. They play once-notorious bank robbers who are released from prison after serving thirty years. Treated like retarded children in a bewildering new world, they try returning to a life of crime, with predictably disastrous results. The stars are amiable, and the supporting cast includes some welcome faces, but the screenplay is heavy-handed and contrived.

TOUGH GUYS DON'T DANCE

★ Cannon, 1987, c, 110 min. Dir and SP: Norman Mailer, b/o his novel. Cast: Ryan O'Neal, Isabella Rossellini, Wings Hauser, Debra Sandlund, John Bedford Lloyd, Lawrence Tierney, Frances Fisher, Penn Jillette, Clarence Williams III.

Incomprehensible claptrap from Mailer, based on his novel, that may be intended as a parody of film noir, but who could possibly care? O'Neal is a failed writer and ex-convict who awakens from a long drinking binge unable to remember whether he killed two people. Encounters in flashback and the present involve him with an assortment of bizarre and unsavory people. Mailer has nobody but himself to blame, since he wrote and directed this fiasco.

TRACES OF RED

★★ Goldwyn, 1992, c, 105 min. Dir: Andy Wolk. SP: Jim Piddock. Cast: James Belushi, Lorraine Bracco, Tony Goldwyn, William Russ, Michelle Joyner, Joe Lisi.

A tricky but unsatisfying film noir set in Palm Beach, this film is narrated by detective Belushi, who just happens to be dead. His sordid tale stems from the serial murders of three women, but the plot spins out to encompass many other unsavory characters, including Belushi's politician brother (Russ), his womanizing partner (Goldwyn), and a rich, seductive widow (Bracco). The plot eventually twists itself into a corkscrew, and you may or may not swallow the double-trick ending.

TRAP, THE

★★☆ Paramount, 1959, c, 84 min. Dir: Norman

Panama. SP: Richard Alan Simmons, Norman Panama. Cast: Richard Widmark, Lee J. Cobb, Tina Louise, Earl Holliman, Carl Benton Reid, Lorne Greene.

A fairly taut melodrama, starring Widmark as a conscience-stricken shyster lawyer who decides to turn over his mobster client (Cobb) to the police after his father is killed. His journey through the southern California desert is complicated by the mobster's men, and by his own no-good brother (Holliman). Louise is Holliman's unhappy wife. Nice color scenery but not much else.

TRIAL BY JURY

★★ Warner Bros., 1994, c, 92 min. Dir: Heywood Gould. SP: Jordan Katz, Heywood Gould. Cast: Joanne Whalley-Kilmer, Gabriel Byrne, Armand Assante, William Hurt, Kathleen Quinlan, Margaret Whitton, Ed Lauter.

This unpleasant, unbelievable thriller draws on a premise also used in the later film *The Juror*. Whalley-Kilmer, a divorcée with a young son, is called on for jury duty in the murder trial of mobster Assante. To win his acquittal, Assante's men terrorize her and kidnap her son. A taut situation is wrecked by poorly worked out plot details. For some unaccountable reason, Hurt took the role of an alcoholic ex-cop-turned-hit man.

TROUBLE IN MIND

★★ Alive Films, 1985, c, 111 min. Dir and SP: Alan Rudolph. Cast: Kris Kristofferson, Keith Carradine, Lori Singer, Genevieve Bujold, Joe Morton, George Kirby, Divine.

In a vaguely futuristic, vaguely Fascist place called Rain City, a group of decidedly offbeat people intermingle in bizarre ways. Hawk (Kristofferson) is an ex-cop, just out of prison. Coop (Carradine) is a dull-witted hood, moving ever deeper into crime, and Georgia (Singer) is his tremulous girlfriend who has had his baby. The three form a loose romantic triangle that is never really resolved. Even the crooks are peculiar: Morton as Coop's poetry-spouting crony who comes to a gruesome end, and Divine as a rich, effete crime lord. Another of Rudolph's self-indulgent, pretentious exercises in filmmaking that some viewers seem to enjoy. Good jazz score.

TROUBLE WITH HARRY, THE

★★★ Paramount, 1955, c, 99 min. Dir: Alfred Hitchcock. SP: John Michael Hayes, b/o novel by Jack Trevor Story. Cast: Edmund Gwenn, John Forsythe, Shirley MacLaine, Mildred Natwick, Mildred Dunnock, Jerry Mathers, Royal Dano.

The trouble with Harry is he's dead. His body lies in the New England woods, and several local citizens are claiming responsibility for his demise. A sea captain (Gwenn), a spinster (Natwick), and a pretty young widow (MacLaine, in her movie debut)—each believes that he or she killed Harry for different reasons. With the help of an artist (Forsythe), they alternately bury Harry or dig him up, depending on the circumstances. It's all resolved in the end. A fairly amusing but rather strained piece of whimsy from Hitchcock, the movie boasts some beautiful autumnal photography by Robert Burks, and it's always a pleasure to watch such pros as Gwenn, Natwick, and Dunnock.

TRUCK TURNER

★☆ American International, 1974, c, 91 min. Dir: Jonathan Kaplan. SP: Oscar Williams, Michael Allen, b/o story by Jerry Wilkes. Cast: Isaac Hayes, Yaphet Kotto, Alan Weeks, Annazette Chase, Nichelle Nichols.

A below-par black exploitation movie that stars composer Hayes (he also wrote the score) as Truck Turner, a skip tracer (a detective who tracks down bail jumpers). When they kill his sidekick and maim his bail-bondsman boss, Truck is out for revenge. Chases and shootouts for those who can't get enough.

TRUE BELIEVER

★★★ Columbia, 1989, c, 103 min. Dir: Joseph Ruben. SP: Wesley Strick. Cast: James Woods, Robert Downey, Jr., Margaret Colin, Yuki Okumoto, Kurtwood Smith, Charles Hallahan.

Woods gives an emotionally charged performance in this well-wrought drama. He plays Eddie Dodd, a disillusioned lawyer who was once a radical hero of the sixties but is now mainly defending drug pushers. His worshipful assistant (Downey) goads him into taking on the case of a young Asian American (Okumoto) who has been imprisoned for eight years on a murder charge. The reopened case sets off explosions in high places. The movie was later the basis for a television series called *Eddie Dodd.*

TRUE CONFESSIONS

★★★ United Artists, 1981, c, 108 min. Dir: Ulu Grosbard. SP: Joan Didion, John Gregory Dunne, b/o novel by John Gregory Dunne. Cast: Robert De Niro, Robert Duvall, Charles Durning, Burgess Meredith, Ed Flanders, Rose Gregorio, Cyril Cusack, Kenneth McMillan, Dan Hedaya, Jeanette Nolan.

A dark, gloomy film that raises a number of serious questions, *True Confessions* centers on two brothers: a veteran cop (Duvall) and a Catholic priest (De Niro) who wields considerable power. When a girl is brutally murdered, the two become caught up in the case, which involves questions of church politics and morality. The plot is sometimes difficult to follow, and the entire movie seems to be shrouded in a gray, chilly mist. Some will find it fascinating; others will not.

TRUE ROMANCE

★★★ Warner Bros./Morgan Creek, 1993, c, 121 min. Dir: Tony Scott. SP: Quentin Tarantino. Cast: Christian Slater, Patricia Arquette, Dennis Hopper, Val Kilmer, Gary Oldman, Brad Pitt, Christopher Walken, Bronson Pinchot, Samuel L. Jackson, Michael Rapaport, Saul Rubinek.

The title may suggest a love story, but don't be fooled. It's a twisted love story at best, a typically Tarantino screenplay blending mayhem and laughter. Airhead Alabama (Arquette) meets and falls for Clarence (Slater), and when they come into possession of a rich cache of narcotics, they are soon fleeing from both the mob and the police. Not an original plotline, but Tarantino gives it his own peculiar spin, with offbeat characters behaving in both extremely vicious and comically stupid ways. The direction is by Tony Scott (*Top Gun, Days of Thunder*), but the climax is pure Tarantino, both gory and hilarious.

TRY AND GET ME

★★★ United Artists, 1951, b/w, 90 min. Dir: Cyril Endfield. SP: Jo Pagano, b/o his novel. Cast: Frank Lovejoy, Kathleen Ryan, Richard Carlson, Lloyd Bridges, Katherine Locke, Adele Jergens, Art Smith.

Barely remembered but still worthy, this taut melodrama indicts mob violence and yellow journalism with considerable force. A hapless fellow (Lovejoy), unable to support his family, falls in with a vicious hoodlum (Bridges) up to no good. They kidnap a wealthy young man whom Bridges kills, and when they are caught, a mob, inflamed by the local newspaper, lynches them both. The film is occasionally awkward and preachy, but some scenes convey a genuine jolt.

TURNER & HOOCH

★★ Touchstone, 1989, c, 100 min. Dir: Roger Spottiswoode. SP: Dennis Shryack, Michael Blodgett, Daniel Petrie, Jr., Jim Cash, Jack Epps, Jr. Cast: Tom Hanks, Mare Winningham, Craig T. Nelson. Reginald VelJohnson, Scott Paulin.

It took five credited writers to concoct this routine cop-meets-dog comedy. Don't ask why Hanks is Turner, a fussy cop who finds himself saddled with a supremely ugly dog named Hooch. Hooch witnesses a double murder, and Turner believes that the dog is the only means of identifying and catching the killers. The ending will emphatically not endear the movie to viewers.

12 ANGRY MEN

★★★ United Artists, 1957, b/w, 95 min. Dir: Sidney Lumet. SP: Reginald Rose, b/o his television play. Cast: Henry Fonda, Lee J. Cobb, Ed Begley, Jack Klugman, Martin Balsam, E. G. Marshall, Jack Warden, George Voskovec, Joseph Sweeney, Edward Binns, John Fiedler, Robert Webber.

Well regarded in its day for its single-set compactness and ingenuity, this small drama now seems overly schematic and more than a little obvious. A diverse group of men assemble in a jury room to decide the fate of a boy accused of murdering his father. Soon the men are revealing their attitudes and their prejudices, ranging all the way from Fonda's humane, liberal stance to Begley's nasty bigotry. Fonda is the single holdout against a quick guilty verdict, and not surprisingly he changes everyone's mind. The top-drawer cast is very able, and Lumet directs his first feature film efficiently. But the movie is cut-and-dried.

TWO DAYS IN THE VALLEY

★★☆ Rysher/MGM, 1996, c, 105 min. Dir and SP: John Herzfeld. Cast: Danny Aiello, James Spader, Jeff Daniels, Glenne Headly, Teri Hatcher, Eric

Stoltz, Paul Mazursky, Marsha Mason, Greg Cruttwell, Charlize Theron, Louise Fletcher, Keith Carradine.

Cross Robert Altman with Quentin Tarantino and you might arrive at this extremely odd combination of absurdist comedy and violent melodrama. Your feelings about it may range from loathing to laughter. Intersecting stories bring together a group of wretched (or at least wretchedly unhappy) people in the San Fernando Valley, including a vicious, ice-cold hit man (Spader), an Olympic skiier (Hatcher) with a recently murdered ex-husband, a suicidal has-been writer-director (Mazursky), and many other mixed-up characters. A good cast helps; Aiello is best, as a hit man with a heart.

TWO JAKES, THE

★★ Paramount, 1990, c, 137 min. Dir: Jack Nicholson. SP: Robert Towne. Cast: Jack Nicholson, Harvey Keitel, Meg Tilly, Madeleine Stowe, Eli Wallach, Ruben Blades, Frederic Forrest, David Keith, Richard Farnsworth.

Trying to decipher the convoluted plot of this film is like traveling through an unfamiliar city without a map. A sequel to the seventies classic *Chinatown*, it brings back private eye J. J. Gittes (Nicholson), who once again becomes involved in a tangled web of adultery, corruption, and murder. The year is 1948, and various enigmatic characters swirl about Gittes, none of them very interesting. Nicholson is the director as well as the star, but in no way does this measure up to the original.

TWO MRS. CARROLLS, THE

★★ Warner Bros., 1947, b/w, 95 min. Dir: Peter Godfrey. SP: Thomas Job, b/o play by Martin Vale. Cast: Barbara Stanwyck, Humphrey Bogart, Alexis Smith, Nigel Bruce, Isobel Elsom.

Overwrought nonsense that traps Bogart and Stanwyck in a mystery thriller without thrills. Based on a short-running play that starred Elisabeth Bergner, it has Bogart as a demented artist who paints his first wife as the "Angel of Death" and then murders her when his inspiration runs dry. Stanwyck copes in vain with the role of his second wife and new victim. Filmed in 1945.

UNDERCURRENT

★★ MGM, 1946, b/w, 116 min. Dir: Vincente Minnelli. SP: Edward Chodorov, b/o story by Thelma Stradel. Cast: Katharine Hepburn, Robert Taylor, Robert Mitchum, Edmund Gwenn, Marjorie Main, Jayne Meadows.

One of director Minnelli's mistakes: a well-produced but tired melodrama concerning a small-town girl (Hepburn), the daughter of a noted scientist (Gwenn), who marries a wealthy man (Taylor), only to learn in stages that he is a murderous psychopath. The screenplay works overtime to establish a tense situation that falls apart before long and ends in a foolish climax. Mitchum plays Taylor's sympathetic brother.

UNDERNEATH, THE

★★★☆ Gramercy, 1995, c, 99 min. Dir: Steven Soderbergh. SP: Sam Lowry, Daniel Fuchs, b/o novel by Don Tracy. Cast: Peter Gallagher, Alison Elliott, William Fichtner, Adam Trese, Paul Dooley, Elisabeth Shue, Joe Don Baker, Shelley Duvall.

A remake of Robert Siodmak's 1949 melodrama *Criss Cross*, this oddly titled and unheralded movie is worth your attention. Despite some variations, the plot is virtually the same: Gallagher (in the Burt Lancaster role) makes the mistake of returning to see his ex-wife (Elliott), whom he still loves, and hooking up with her nasty new husband (Fichtner) in the robbery of an armored truck. Director Soderbergh perhaps uses too many stylistic flourishes, but the plot twists will keep you interested, and the hard, cold film noir mood seldom falters. Best scene: the hospital.

UNDER SUSPICION

★★ Columbia, 1992, c, 99 min. Dir and SP: Simon Moore. Cast: Liam Neeson, Laura San Giacomo, Kenneth Granham, Alphonsia Emmanuel, Maggie O'Neill, Martin Grace, Stephen Moore.

A miscast leading lady and a poorly worked out screenplay that only gains momentum near the end combine to sink this tricky melodrama. In Brighton, England, in 1959, Neeson is a seedy private eye who arranges fake adultery cases for his divorce-minded clients. When his wife and a client are murdered together, he becomes a suspect. And so does the victim's seductive mistress (San Giacomo). There are numerous convolutions in the story, many of them unbelievable, before the surprise ending.

UNDERWORLD, U.S.A.

★★☆ Columbia, 1961, b/w, 99 min. Dir and SP: Samuel Fuller. Cast: Cliff Robertson, Dolores Dorn, Beatrice Kay, Robert Emhardt, Larry Gates.

A competently made crime melodrama, with some notable scenes courtesy of producer/director/writer Fuller. Robertson is a small-town crook who has a lifelong obsession with avenging the death of his father at the hands of the crime syndicate. Kay, a popular radio singer of old-time ballads, makes her dramatic debut as a saloon keeper who befriends Robertson.

UNFORGETTABLE

★★☆ MGM/UA, 1996, c, 116 min. Dir: John Dahl. SP: Bill Geddie. Cast: Ray Liotta, Linda Fiorentino, Peter Coyote, Christopher McDonald, David Paymer, Kim Cattrall, Kim Coates, Duncan Fraser.

Director Dahl fared much better with his two previous films, *Red Rock West* (1993) and *The Last Seduction* (1994). A rather delirious thriller, *Unforgettable* stars Liotta as a medical examiner who wants desperately to find his wife's killer. (He has been accused and acquitted.) To this end, he enters into a bizarre medical experiment that allows him to enter the memory of any person, alive or deceased, in the last moments of his or her life and actually become that person. (No explanation here.) The movie has some flashy special effects, but it's too hectic and overwrought to be successful.

UNHOLY WIFE, THE

★ RKO, 1957, c, 94 min. Dir: John Farrow. SP: Jonathan Latimer, b/o story by William Durkee. Cast: Diana Dors, Rod Steiger, Arthur Franz, Beulah Bondi, Tom Tryon, Marie Windsor, Luis Van Rooten, Joe De Santis.

In her American debut, Dors is up to no good,

in a movie that is no good at all. She's the bored wife of wine grower Steiger, who takes up with cowboy Tryon. When she tries to kill her husband and kills a neighbor instead, she schemes to frame her spouse. Ironically she ends up in the gas chamber for a crime that never occurred. Dors sashays seductively, and Steiger chews the scenery—all to no avail.

UNION STATION

★★☆ Paramount, 1950, b/w, 80 min. Dir: Rudolph Mate. SP: Sydney Boehm, b/o story by Thomas Walsh. Cast: William Holden, Barry Fitzgerald, Nancy Olson, Lyle Bettger, Jan Sterling, Allene Roberts, Herbert Heyes.

Coming off the classic *Sunset Boulevard*, actors Holden and Olson might have found a sturdier vehicle than this workmanlike but essentially routine melodrama. When the blind daughter of a local tycoon is kidnapped in a railroad station, transit cop Holden, joined by unlikely police inspector Fitzgerald, goes into action. He finally traps the chief villain (Bettger) in a railroad tunnel. Nothing special.

UNLAWFUL ENTRY

★★★ Fox, 1992, c, 111 min. Dir: Jonathan Kaplan. SP: Lewis Colick, b/o story by George D. Putnam, Jack Katchmer, Lewis Colick. Cast: Kurt Russell, Ray Liotta, Madeleine Stowe, Ken Lerner, Roger E. Mosley, Deborah Offner, Carmen Argenziano.

Suspend your disbelief for nearly two hours, and you may have a good suspenseful time at this urban thriller. Michael (Russell) and Karen (Stowe) are a happy couple until their house is invaded by an intruder. One of the cops summoned is Pete (Liotta), who develops a dangerous fixation on Karen. Pete conspires to wreck

Michael's life, finally resorting to murder. It all hurtles to a terrifying climax. Liotta is genuinely scary as the deranged cop and, despite some plot holes, the movie is a nail-biter.

UNTOUCHABLES, THE

★★★★ Paramount, 1987, c, 120 min. Dir: Brian De Palma. SP: David Mamet. Cast: Kevin Costner, Sean Connery, Robert De Niro, Andy Garcia, Charles Martin Smith, Jack Kehoe, Richard Bradford, Billy Drago, Patricia Clarkson, Brad Sullivan.

Only vaguely derived from the popular television series that ran from 1959 to 1963, *The Untouchables* is a first-

Kevin Costner is federal agent Eliot Ness in Brian De Palma's splendid crime drama The Untouchables *(1987).*

rate example of movie craftsmanship: smartly written, acted, and directed. In the film, the straight-arrow Eliot Ness (Costner) of the television series is thrust into the criminal world of Chicago in 1930, where vicious Al Capone (De Niro) is the undisputed leader. Ness and his Untouchables (Connery, Garcia, Smith) go after Capone and his mob in a number of memorable sequences, the best being a riveting shootout in Chicago's Union Station. Connery won a Supporting Oscar for his assured performance as a seasoned cop.

USUAL SUSPECTS, THE

★★★☆ Gramercy, 1995, c, 106 min. Dir: Bryan Singer. SP: Christopher McQuarrie. Cast: Gabriel Byrne, Chazz Palminteri, Kevin Spacey, Kevin Pollak, Stephen Baldwin, Benicio Del Toro, Pete Postlethwaite, Suzy Amis, Dan Hedaya.

It begins with a massive ship explosion and the discovery of twenty-seven dead bodies. At a police station, a garrulous lowlife appropriately named Verbal Kint (Spacey) explains what led to the disaster. But is he telling the truth? His flashbacks take us into Verbal's peculiar world, where he and his criminal cohorts scheme, rob, and kill, all under the shadow of a mysterious and terrifying figure named Keyser Sose. And just who *is* Sose? The plot twists and turns in this intriguing, clever, and stylishly made thriller. The cast performs expertly, but Oscar-winner Spacey is a standout as the devious Verbal. McQuarrie also won an Oscar for his original screenplay.

VALACHI PAPERS, THE

★★ Columbia (Italian), 1972, c, 125 min. Dir: Terence Young. SP: Stephen Geller, b/o book by Peter Maas. Cast: Charles Bronson, Gerald S. O'Loughlin, Lino Ventura, Joseph Wiseman, Walter Chiari, Jill Ireland.

This Italian-made melodrama has little to recommend and a lot to shun, as Mafia-soldier-turned-informer Joe Valachi (Bronson) exposes the thirty-year activities of the crime "family." In the midst of all the mayhem, Bronson is his usual taciturn self, but Wiseman gives a juicy, over-the-top performance as Cosa Nostra founder Salvatore Maranzano.

VANISHING POINT

★★ Fox, 1971, c, 107 min. Dir: Richard C. Sarafian. SP: Guillermo Cain, b/o story outline by Malcolm Hart. Cast: Barry Newman, Cleavon Little, Dean Jagger, Victoria Medlin, Paul Koslo, Gilda Texter.

A man named Kowalski (Newman) is asked to drive a car from Denver to California, and he decides to make the trip in only fifteen hours. Soon the police are on his trail, and a blind disc jockey named Super Soul (Little) turns him into a national culture hero, "the last American to whom speed means freedom of the soul." Uh-huh. The movie has a cult following, but it's neither interesting nor exciting enough to warrant much attention.

VANISHING, THE

★ Fox, 1993, c, 110 min. Dir: George Sluizer. SP: Todd Graff, b/o novel by Tim Crabbe. Cast: Jeff Bridges, Kiefer Sutherland, Nancy Travis, Sandra Bullock, Park Overall, Maggie Linderman, George Hearn, Lisa Eichhorn.

An odd, singularly ugly, and totally unconvincing remake of the much better 1988 foreign film, helmed, oddly enough, by the same Dutch director. The premise, at least, is frightening: Sutherland's fiancée (Bullock) suddenly vanishes, kidnapped by deranged teacher-scientist Bridges. Several years later Bridges contacts an obsessed Sutherland and the two men are soon locked in a bizarre life-and-death struggle that involves Sutherland's new girlfriend (Travis). Bridges gives one of his few inadequate performances, and the climax is wildly incredible.

VELVET TOUCH, THE

★★☆ RKO, 1948, b/w, 97 min. Dir: John Gage. SP: Leo Rosten, adapted by Walter Reilly from story by William Mercer, Annabel Ross. Cast: Rosalind Russell, Sydney Greenstreet, Leo Genn, Claire Trevor, Leon Ames, Frank McHugh, Walter Kingsford.

A good cast helps this slick but patly contrived

melodrama. Russell stars as a famous stage actress who inadvertently kills her nasty producer (Ames) when he threatens to reveal their past relationship to her newest boyfriend. She spends the rest of the movie with a guilty conscience and the fear of being exposed by a crafty detective (Greenstreet) on the case. Her final appearance onstage in *Hedda Gabler* provides an ironic coda to the story.

VERDICT, THE

★★★☆ Fox, 1982, c, 129 min. Dir: Sidney Lumet. SP: David Mamet, b/o novel by Barry Reed. Cast: Paul Newman, James Mason, Charlotte Rampling, Jack Warden, Milo O'Shea, Edward Binns, Julie Bovasso, Roxanne Hart, Lindsay Crouse.

Newman gives one of his finest performances—assured and well seasoned—in this compelling drama. He plays Frank Galvin, a seedy, disgraced Boston lawyer given one last chance to redeem himself. He takes on the case of a young woman who has fallen into an irreversible coma through hospital negligence. The suit places him in bitter conflict with the church that owns the hospital, the doctors, and a high-powered law firm. The ending may not be legally authentic but it is dramatically satisfying. Good work all around, especially by Mason as a formidable lawyer.

VERTIGO

★★★☆ Paramount, 1958, c, 128 min. Dir: Alfred Hitchcock. SP: Alec Coppel, Samuel Taylor, b/o novel by Pierre Boileau, Thomas Narcejac. Cast: James Stewart, Kim Novak, Barbara Bel Geddes, Tom Helmore, Henry Jones.

Many regard *Vertigo* as Hitchcock's greatest film, but its faults, notably a lack of credibility in some of the plot details, keep it from the very pinnacle of his achievements. Still, it's a fascinating and complex tale involving acrophobia and murder, with Stewart (cast against his usual easy-going type) as a guilt-ridden ex-cop and his dangerous, ultimately fatal obsession with a beautiful, enigmatic woman (Novak). Nothing is exactly what it seems to be, and what it is will not be revealed here. There are surprises along the way, and Stewart gives one of his best, most intense performances. San Francisco never looked more breathtaking. A Hitchcock puzzler worth your close attention.

V.I. WARSHAWSKI

★★ Hollywood, 1991, c, 89 min. Dir: Jeff Kanew. SP: David Aaron Cohen, Nick Thiel, Edward Taylor; story by Edward Taylor, b/o novels by Sara Paretsky. Cast: Kathleen Turner, Jay O. Sanders, Charles Durning, Angela Goethals, Nancy Paul, Frederick Coffin, Stephen Meadows, Wayne Knight.

Novelist Paretsky's tough Chicago private eye V.I. Warshawski is played by Turner in what was probably intended as the first of a series. Too bad. Turner tries, but a mystery plot riddled with clichés sinks the idea for good. Here Warshawski strives to solve the murder of a hockey player, with the help of his young daughter (Goethals) and a reporter boyfriend (Sanders). Another boat chase, another dockside climax. Yawn.

WAIT UNTIL DARK

★★★ Warner Bros., 1967, c, 108 min. Dir: Terence Young. SP: Robert Carrington, Jane-Howard Carrington, b/o play by Frederick Knott. Cast: Audrey Hepburn, Alan Arkin, Richard Crenna, Jack Weston, Julie Herrod, Samantha Jones.

Adapted from a play, *Wait Until Dark* is a fairly adroit thriller with a workable gimmick. A doll stuffed with heroin finds its way into the flight bag of pilot Zimbalist and eventually into the apartment of Crenna's blind young wife (Hepburn). Now a hoodlum (Arkin) and his cohorts (Crenna and Weston) are determined to wrest the doll from Hepburn, who is helpless and alone. They assume a clever series of impersonations and tricks to confuse and frighten her. Ultimately the beleaguered woman must use her resources as a blind person to thwart them, especially the diabolical Arkin. A cat-and-mouse game ensues, culminating in a scary climax in pitch darkness. There are some loopholes in the plot, but also some nail-biting moments as well.

James Stewart and Kim Novak star in Vertigo *(1958), Alfred Hitchcock's multilayered drama of obsessive love and deception.*

Hepburn won an Oscar nomination for her performance.

WALK SOFTLY, STRANGER

★★☆ RKO, 1950, b/w, 81 min. Dir: Robert Stevenson. SP: Frank Fenton, b/o story by Manny Seff, Paul Yawitz. Cast: Joseph Cotten, Alida Valli, Spring Byington, Paul Stewart, Jack Paar, Jeff Donnell, John McIntyre.

Actually made before Carol Reed's *The Third Man* enhanced the star value of its two leading players, *Walk Softly, Stranger* is a modest melodrama with a familiar plot. Small-time crook Cotten holes up in an Ohio town, where he falls for a bitter crippled girl (Valli). Can redemption and a new outlook on life for both parties be far behind? Not before Cotten confronts his enemies.

WALKING TALL

★★☆ Cinerama, 1974, c, 125 min. Dir: Phil Karlson. SP: Mort Briskin. Cast: Joe Don Baker, Elizabeth Hartman, Gene Evans, Noah Beery, Lurene Tuttle, Brenda Benet, John Brascia, Bruce Glover.

A hugely popular, highly ambiguous melodrama, ostensibly based on the true exploits of one Buford Puser, a sheriff who single-handedly fought to bring law and order to a corruption-ridden county in Tennessee. Here Sheriff Puser (Baker) wants peace in his territory, and he will use any means, including virtually nonstop, bone-cracking violence, to achieve it. The movie is crude, but its attitude seemed to appeal to a great many people at the time. Inspired a sequel and a television series.

WANTED DEAD OR ALIVE

★ New World, 1987, c, 104 min. Dir: Gary Sherman. SP: Michael Patrick Goodman, Brian Taggert, Gary Sherman. Cast: Rutger Hauer, Gene Simmons, Robert Guillaume, Mel Harris, William Russ, Susan McDonald.

The only mild note of interest in this cheaply made action thriller is that Dutch actor Rutger Hauer plays Nick Randall, the grandson of Josh Randall, the bounty hunter played by Steve McQueen in the late-fifties television series of the same name. Here bounty hunter Nick pursues an Arab terrorist named Malik (Simmons) Does he get his man? Guess.

WARRIORS, THE

★★★ Paramount, 1979, c, 90 min. Dir: Walter Hill. SP: David Shaber, Walter Hill. Cast: Michael Beck, James Remar, Thomas Waites, Dorsey Wright, Deborah Van Valkenburgh, Mercedes Ruehl.

A striking use of color by cinematographer Andrew Laszlo is a principal virtue of this tough, fast-moving urban melodrama. The plot is simple: a Coney Island gang called the Warriors is blamed for the murder of a hood. Threatened with extinction, they must fight their way out of "enemy" territory and find their way home. The colors of the Warriors's uniforms make a vivid contrast to the bleak, threatening darkness of nighttime New York City. The movie provoked a number of violent incidents in theaters.

WEEDS

★★☆ De Laurentiis, 1987, c, 109 min. Dir: John Hancock. SP: Dorothy Tristan, John Hancock. Cast: Nick Nolte, Rita Taggart, William Forsythe, Ernie Hudson, Joe Mantegna, Lane Smith, Anne Ramsey, Charlie Rich.

Serving a life sentence at San Quentin Prison, convict Lee Umstetter (Nolte) writes a play about the prison world and becomes a national celebrity. Winning his freedom through the efforts of a journalist (Taggart), he forms an acting troupe made up of fellow ex-convicts, and their experiences become the heart of the film. Paradoxically, despite being based on fact, the movie seldom rings true. It's all well intentioned, but until an unexpected prison riot late in the story, there's little to hold an audience. An excellent actor, Nolte brings conviction to his role, but all in vain.

WHAT EVER HAPPENED TO AUNT ALICE?

★★★ Cinerama, 1969, c, 101 min. Dir: Lee H. Katzin. SP: Theodore Apstein, b/o novel by Ursula Curtiss. Cast: Geraldine Page, Ruth Gordon, Mildred Dunnock, Rosemary Forsyth, Robert Fuller.

What's a poor widow to do? Mrs. Marrable (Page) has a solution: to tend her Arizona cottage, she hires a succession of companion-housekeepers with tidy savings accounts and then kills them one by one for their money. This enjoyably nasty melodrama is played to the hilt by eccentric actresses Page and Gordon, with Gordon as Mrs. Marrable's most suspicious victim. Not surprisingly, the movie was produced by Robert Aldrich, who directed *What Ever Happened to Baby Jane?* in 1962.

WHAT EVER HAPPENED TO BABY JANE?

★★★ Warner Bros., 1962, b/w, 132 min. Dir: Robert Aldrich. SP: Lukas Heller, b/o novel by Henry Farrell. Cast: Bette Davis, Joan Crawford, Victor Buono, Marjorie Bennett, Maidie Norman, Anna Lee.

Bitter rivals both on and off the screen, Davis and Crawford, the two reigning queens of old moviedom, compete to take center stage in this outrageous but enjoyable melodrama. They play sisters who were once movie stars, long retired after Blanche (Crawford) was crippled in an auto accident blamed on Jane (Davis). Now they occupy a crumbling old house in which Jane, a grotesque harridan, spends her time tormenting her helpless sister. The plot thickens and curdles as Jane goes further off the deep end, and the movie lumbers from one Grand Guignol situation to another. Still, the ladies are clearly having a high old time, and probably so will you. Davis won an Oscar nomination as Best Actress.

Jane Hudson (Bette Davis) grapples with her dying sister Blanche (Joan Crawford) in What Ever Happened to Baby Jane? *(1962).*

WHAT'S THE MATTER WITH HELEN?

★★☆ United Artists, 1971, c, 101 min. Dir: Curtis Harrington. SP: Henry Farrell. Cast: Debbie Reynolds, Shelley Winters, Dennis Weaver, Agnes Moorehead, Michael MacLiammoir.

Adelle Bruckner (Reynolds) and Helen Hill (Winters) are not-so-young women who run a dance studio in Hollywood during the early thirties. Since their sons committed a hideous murder together years ago, the two are locked

AND I QUOTE . . .

These famous lines are all from movies on crime and punishment. How many of these movies can you identify?

1. "Mother of Mercy, is this the end of Rico?"

2. "I hated her so much I couldn't get her out of my mind for a minute."

3. "Mother, I'm married to an American agent."

4. "You and me, Walter. All the way down the line."

5. "I hope they don't hang you, precious, by that sweet neck."

6. "They call me *Mister* Tibbs!"

7. "I write with a quill pen dipped in venom."

8. "Alligators have the right idea. They eat their young."

9. "This is 'Duke' Mantee, folks. He's a world-famous killer, and he's hungry."

10. "Do I ice her? Do I marry her?"

ANSWERS

1. *Little Caesar* (1930). Mobster Edward G. Robinson's dying words.

2. *Gilda* (1946). Glenn Ford, commenting on his love-hate relationship with Rita Hayworth.

3. *Notorious* (1946). Claude Rains, telling his mother that wife Ingrid Bergman is not what she seems.

4. *Double Indemnity* (1944). Treacherous Barbara Stanwyck, affirming her ties to lover Fred MacMurray.

5. *The Maltese Falcon* (1941). Humphrey Bogart, about to "send up" Mary Astor for murdering his partner.

6. *In the Heat of the Night* (1967). Black detective Sidney Poitier, identifying himself forcefully to the redneck police.

7. *Laura* (1944). Radio commentator Clifton Webb, commenting on his acerbic style.

8. *Mildred Pierce* (1945). Eve Arden's oblique reference to Joan Crawford's grasping, nasty daughter.

9. *The Petrified Forest* (1936). The henchman of vicious gangster "Duke" Mantee introduces his boss to the people who will become his prisoners.

10. *Prizzi's Honor* (1985). Hit man Jack Nicholson wonders what to do about his lover and dangerous rival, Kathleen Turner.

together in an unhealthy dependency. It turns out that Helen is a religious fanatic and quite mad, which leads inevitably to mayhem. Okay entry in the "Crazy Lady" cycle of the period.

WHEN A STRANGER CALLS

★☆ Columbia, 1979, c, 97 min. Dir: Fred Walton. SP: Steve Feke, Fred Walton. Cast: Charles Durning, Carol Kane, Colleen Dewhurst, Tony Beckley, Rachel Roberts, Ron O'Neal.

The opening sequence is frightening: Babysitter Kane is terrorized by a maniac (Beckley) at large in the house, who murders her two little charges. The movie then goes rapidly downhill. After seven years in a sanitarium, the killer escapes and is pursued by detective Durning. Finally he returns to terrorize Kane, who now has two children of her own. Lopsided, unconvincing, and strewn with gaps in logic. A TV sequel, *When a Stranger Calls Back*, was shown in 1993.

WHERE ARE THE CHILDREN?

★★☆ Columbia, 1986, c, 92 min. Dir: Bruce Malmuth. SP: Jack Sholder, b/o novel by Mary Higgins Clark. Cast: Jill Clayburgh, Frederic Forrest, Max Gail, Barnard Hughes, Harley Cross, Elisabeth Harnois, Elizabeth Wilson, Clifton James.

When Clayburgh's two children are kidnapped on Cape Cod, the town starts buzzing. It seems that nine years earlier she was convicted of murdering two other children from her first marriage. Is she guilty again? It takes a while for the characters (but not the audience) to figure out the truth in this contrived but occasionally suspenseful thriller based on a Mary Higgins Clark novel. Forrest plays Clayburgh's very sick former husband. And why is it always raining?

WHERE LOVE HAS GONE

★★☆ Paramount, 1964, c, 114 min. Dir: Edward Dymtryk. SP: John Michael Hayes, b/o novel by Harold Robbins. Cast: Susan Hayward, Bette Davis, Michael Connors, Joey Heatherton, Jane Greer, DeForest Kelley, George Macready, Anne Seymour.

A lushly produced but synthetic and overbaked adaptation of Robbins's best-selling novel, *Where Love Has Gone* stars Hayward as a woman driven to rebellious promiscuity by her cold, overbearing mother (Davis, overacting outrageously). Her life spirals out of control until her teenage daughter (Heatherton) stabs her mother's lover to death with a chisel. The story was clearly derived from a true-life murder case involving a Hollywood star.

WHERE THE SIDEWALK ENDS

★★☆ Fox, 1950, b/w, 95 min. Dir: Otto Preminger. SP: Ben Hecht, adapted by Victor Trivas, Frank P. Rosenberg, Robert E. Kent from novel by William L. Stuart. Cast: Dana Andrews, Gene Tierney, Gary Merrill, Karl Malden, Tom Tully, Ruth Donnelly, Craig Stevens, Bert Freed.

While investigating a murder, tough cop Andrews accidentally kills a suspect and desperately tries to cover his tracks. His agenda changes when he falls for the victim's estranged wife (Tierney) and her father (Tully) is charged with the crime he committed. Considering the talent involved this should have been a better movie, but it's strictly routine. Andrews's motive for his brutal behavior with suspects is Basic Hollywood Psychology (he detested his criminal dad), and the production is drab.

WHILE THE CITY SLEEPS

★★★ RKO, 1956, b/w, 100 min. Dir: Fritz Lang. SP: Casey Robinson, b/o novel by Charles Einstein. Cast: Ida Lupino, Dana Andrews, Vincent Price, Rhonda Fleming, George Sanders, Sally Forrest, Thomas Mitchell, Howard Duff, James Craig, John Barrymore, Jr., Mae Marsh.

An impressive cast, tight direction by Lang, and a better-than-average screenplay by veteran writer Robinson help to make this movie worth a viewing. The story basically concerns life, extracurricular and otherwise, at a New York newspaper, and the search for a disturbed young killer in which the personnel becomes deeply involved. Not surprisingly there are more than a few romantic liaisons at the paper as well. John Barrymore, Jr., plays the "Lipstick Murderer" who enjoys killing blondes.

WHISPERS IN THE DARK

★★ Paramount, 1993, c, 103 min. Dir and SP: Christopher Crowe. Cast: Annabella Sciorra, Alan Alda, Jamey Sheridan, Anthony LaPaglia, Jill Clayburgh, John Leguizamo, Deborah Unger, Anthony Heald.

Sciorra is a Manhattan psychiatrist with problems of her own, including several off-the-wall patients who may be dangerous—to themselves and to others. When one of them is murdered, Sciorra is shocked to discover that her latest boyfriend (Sheridan) may be the killer. Or was it the deeply disturbed young artist (Leguizamo) who has kinky sexual fantasies? The real mystery is why so many highly capable actors would agree to play key roles in this lurid and preposterous thriller.

WHITE HEAT

★★★☆ Warner Bros., 1949, b/w, 114 min. Dir: Raoul Walsh. SP: Ivan Goff, Ben Roberts, b/o story by Virginia Kellogg. Cast: James Cagney, Virginia Mayo, Edmond O'Brien, Margaret Wycherly, Steve Cochran.

After years of playing mostly law-abiding citizens, and even a few song-and-dance men, Cagney returned to the sort of role he had made famous in the thirties with this blistering crime drama. As vicious gang leader Cody Jarrett, he's not only certifiably insane but also plagued with a giant-sized mother complex. Cagney's audacious performance rivets our attention, never more so than in the prison scene in which he goes berserk after learning of his mother's death. His last line atop an exploding gasoline-storage tank is now part of screen legend.

WHITE LIGHTNING

★★☆ United Artists, 1973, c, 101 min. Dir: Joseph Sargent. SP: William Norton. Cast: Burt Reynolds, Ned Beatty, Jennifer Billingsley, Bo Hopkins, Matt Clark, Louise Latham, Diane Ladd, R. G. Armstrong.

Convicted Arkansas moonshiner Reynolds is let out of prison so that he can help establish evidence against a nasty, corrupt small-town sheriff (Beatty). Reynolds is really out for revenge: years earlier, the sheriff drowned his kid brother. Standard melodrama, with more than its share of car chases. There was a sequel called *Gator* in 1976. Look for the film debut of Laura Dern, Diane Ladd's daughter.

WHITE LINE FEVER

★★★ Columbia, 1975, c, 92 min. Dir: Jonathan Kaplan. SP: Ken Friedman, Jonathan Kaplan. Cast: Jan-Michael Vincent, Kay Lenz, Slim Pickens, L. Q. Jones, Leigh French, Don Porter, Martin Kove.

A better-than-average action movie, with fast pace and believable characters that compensate for the familiar storyline. Vincent stars as a young trucker, recently out of the Air Force, who learns that his business is dominated by a powerful network of corrupt businessmen and politicians in league with hoodlums. In his efforts to stop them, he is blacklisted, nearly killed, and framed on a murder charge. Things really heat up when he organizes a truckers strike. Expert photography helps.

WHITE SANDS

★★ Warner Bros./Morgan Creek, 1992, c, 101 min. Dir: Roger Donaldson. SP: Daniel Pyne. Cast: Willem Dafoe, Mickey Rourke, Mary Elizabeth Mastrantonio, Sam (Samuel L.) Jackson, Mimi Rogers, M. Emmet Walsh, James Rebhorn, Maura Tierney.

Sheriff Dafoe comes upon the dead body of an FBI agent in the New Mexico desert. Was it suicide or murder? To find out, he assumes the dead man's identity, leading him into dangerous territory. He gets involved with, among others, a shady buyer of black market military hardware (Rourke), an FBI man with dubious motives (Jackson), and a thrill-seeking heiress (Mastrantonio). Before long he's trapped in that familiar film noir world of skulduggery and double-dealing. A scenic but tangled and confusing mystery, with little to recommend it.

WHO DONE IT?

★★☆ Universal, 1942, b/w, 75 min. Dir: Erle C. Kenton. SP: Stanley Roberts, Edmund Joseph, John Grant, b/o story by Stanley Roberts. Cast: Bud Abbott, Lou Costello, Patric Knowles, William Bendix, William Gargan, Louise Allbritton, Mary Wickes, Thomas Gomez, Don Porter, Jerome Cowan.

Fans of comedians Abbott and Costello will find some laughs in this hectic mystery-farce. They play aspiring radio writers who pretend to be detectives in order to catch the murderer of a network president. As usual Costello bears the brunt of the old vaudeville routines: coping with an uncooperative drinking fountain, teetering on a high window ledge, and the like. Best: reliable Mary Wickes as a secretary.

WHO FRAMED ROGER RABBIT

★★★☆ Touchstone, 1988, c, 103 min. Dir: Robert

Zemeckis. SP: Jeffrey Price, Peter S. Seaman, b/o novel by Gary K. Wolf. Cast: Bob Hoskins, Christopher Lloyd, Joanna Cassidy, Stubby Kaye, Alan Tilvern, Joel Silver. Voice of Roger Rabbit: Charles Fleischer. Speaking/singing voices of Jessica Rabbit: Kathleen Turner/Amy Irving.

A marvelously imaginative combination of live action and animation, *Who Framed Roger Rabbit* takes the conventions of film noir and sends them spinning giddily in all directions. In 1947 Los Angeles, a seedy detective named Eddie Valiant (Hoskins) tries to prove that cartoon character Roger Rabbit is innocent of murdering the human lover of his sexy wife, Jessica. The plot is routine noir; the real fun comes from the state-of-the-art animation and the flow of visual puns and inside jokes about beloved cartoon characters. Personal favorite: Daffy Duck commenting on Donald Duck: "Does anyone understand what the duck is saying?"

WHO IS KILLING THE GREAT CHEFS OF EUROPE?

★★★ Warner Bros., 1978, c, 112 min. Dir: Ted Kotcheff. SP: Peter Stone, b/o novel by Nan Lyons, Juan Lyons. Cast: Jacqueline Bisset, George Segal, Robert Morley, Jean-Pierre Cassel, Philippe Noiret, Jean Rochefort, Madge Ryan.

Robert Morley spent most of his lifetime stealing films and plays from his fellow actors, and he does it again in this clever, lighthearted comedy mystery. He plays a magazine editor who not only rates restaurant dishes but also eats and enjoys them with matchless gusto. The story revolves around the murder of Europe's foremost chefs, with Bisset as the pastry chef who seems to be next in line. The movie is never sure of whether it wants laughs or suspense, but it's amiable fun.

WHO KILLED MARY WHAT'S'ERNAME?

★★☆ Cannon, 1971, c, 90 min. Dir: Ernie Pintoff. SP: John O'Toole. Cast: Red Buttons, Alice Playten, Sam Waterston, Sylvia Miles, Dick Williams, Conrad Bain, David Doyle, Gilbert Lewis.

Offbeat movie stars comedian Red Buttons as a diabetic, wealthy former boxing champion who sets out to solve the murder of a prostitute named Mary, whom he never knew. His reason: "nobody cares anymore." The list of suspects includes Mary's best friend (Miles), a penniless filmmaker (Waterston), and a genial drunkard (Bain). Nice cast, but not much.

WHO'LL STOP THE RAIN

★★★ United Artists, 1978, c, 126 min. Dir: Karel Reisz. SP: Judith Roscoe, Robert Stone, b/o novel by Robert Stone. Cast: Nick Nolte, Tuesday Weld, Michael Moriarty, Anthony Zerbe, Richard Masur, Ray Sharkey, Charles Haid, David Opatashu, Gail Strickland.

A post-Vietnam mood of disillusion permeates this gloomy but fairly absorbing adaptation of Stone's best-selling novel *Dog Soldiers*. Nolte is an ex-marine who is persuaded by old friend Moriarty to smuggle a cache of heroin from Vietnam into America. Instead Nolte finds himself fleeing with Moriarty's drug-addict wife (Weld) from sinister characters out to kill him and seize the heroin. Motives are not always clear and the movie is depressing to watch, but Nolte gives a forceful performance as a man who wrongly fancies himself as some sort of superman—he reads Nietzsche just for kicks.

WILD AT HEART

★☆ Lava, 1990, c, 127 min. Dir and SP: David Lynch, b/o novel by Barry Gifford. Cast: Nicolas Cage, Laura Dern, Willem Dafoe, J. E. Freeman, Diane Ladd, Crispin Glover, Harry Dean Stanton, Isabella Rossellini.

Unquestionably like no other movie (the half-star is for originality), this David Lynch film is a wrenchingly violent and grotesque concoction that some viewers may find wickedly funny. Sailor Ripley (Cage), an Elvis-acolyte with a snakeskin jacket, flees across the country with his dull-witted girlfriend Lula (Dern). Her ferocious crackpot mother (Ladd) appoints several men to kill Sailor while other grotesque characters become involved. Somehow we are supposed to associate this pretentious claptrap with *The Wizard of Oz*, but don't ask why.

WILD ONE, THE

★★★ Columbia, 1954, b/w, 79 min. Dir: Laslo Benedek. SP: John Paxton, b/o story by Frank Rooney. Cast: Marlon Brando, Mary Murphy, Robert Keith, Lee Marvin, Jay C. Flippen.

First of the motorcycle gang movies, *The Wild*

In Witness *(1987), detective Harrison Ford must protect Amish boy Lukas Haas, who has witnessed a murder.*

One is now notable mostly for Brando's trend-setting performance. He plays Johnny, surly head of the Black Rebels, the marauding band of cyclists that takes over a small California town. Johnny's utter contempt for society and its norms is underminded when he is smitten with the sheriff's daughter (Murphy). Marvin nearly matches Brando with his portrayal of a vicious hood. Based on a real-life incident, the movie is heavy-handed but it retains some crude power.

WINDOW, THE
★★★☆ RKO, 1949, b/w, 73 min. Dir: Ted Tetzlaff. SP: Mel Dinelli, b/o story by Cornell Woolrich. Cast: Bobby Driscoll, Barbara Hale, Arthur Kennedy, Paul Stewart, Ruth Roman.

An unheralded sleeper in its year of release, *The Window* is a small-scale but exciting variation on the theme of the boy who cried wolf. Little Bobby Driscoll, a city boy prone to fabricating stories, sees a murder being committed by a neighboring couple (Stewart and Roman), and of course nobody will

believe him. His life in jeopardy, he must use resourceful measures to elude the pursuing killers. In its modest way the movie works up a considerable amount of suspense, and the climactic chase across the city rooftops and into an abandoned building is genuinely harrowing. Twelve-year-old Driscoll gives a credible performance as the terrified boy.

WISDOM
★ Fox, 1986, c, 109 min. Dir and SP: Emilio Estevez. Cast: Demi Moore, Emilio Estevez, Tom Skerritt, Veronica Cartright, William Allen Young, Richard Minchenberg.

It may not have been the height of wisdom for Estevez to write, direct, and star in this glum little caper film. He plays (yes) a young man named Wisdom who cannot get work because of his police record. Joined by girlfriend Moore, he begins to rob banks, not for their money but to destroy mortgage records and thus help downtrodden American farmers. The idea doesn't work, and neither does the movie.

WITHOUT A TRACE

★★☆ Fox, 1983, c, 120 min. Dir: Stanley R. Jaffe. SP: Beth Gutcheon, b/o her novel. Cast: Kate Nelligan, Judd Hirsch, David Dukes, Stockard Channing, Jacqueline Brookes, Keith McDermott, Kathleen Widdoes.

Nelligan is a good actress, and here she enacts moments of grief and rage with force and conviction. But she is unable to give much momentum to this movie. She plays an anguished mother whose young son suddenly vanishes. The opening sequence is frightening, and the end is predictably heart-warming, but in between the film remains becalmed as a sympathetic cop (Hirsch) searches for the boy and others offer support while the mother agonizes over her plight or searches fiercely for clues. Never dull, but not as good as it might have been.

WITNESS

★★★☆ Paramount, 1987, c, 11 min. Dir: Peter Weir. SP: Earl W. Wallace, William Kelley, b/o story by William Kelley. Cast: Harrison Ford, Kelly McGillis, Josef Sommer, Lukas Haas, Jan Rubes, Alexander Godunov, Danny Glover, Patti Lupone.

This enormously entertaining movie has suspense, romance, and an unusual background. When Amish boy Samuel Lapp (Haas) becomes the sole witness to a murder, his life, and the life of John Book (Ford), the seasoned detective on the case, are in jeopardy. Book hides out in the idyllic Amish community, where he falls for the boy's mother (McGillis). The clash of Amish and city-smart cultures has both harsh and amusing aspects, until the culprits turn up for a shoot-'em-up climax. The mixed ingredients do not always jell, but the film is eminently watchable from first to last. *Witness* won Academy Awards for Best Original Screenplay and Best Editing.

WITNESS FOR THE PROSECUTION

★★★★ United Artists, 1957, b/w, 114 min. Dir: Billy Wilder. SP: Billy Wilder, Harry Kurnitz, b/o story and play by Agatha Christie. Cast: Tyrone Power, Marlene Dietrich, Charles Laughton, Elsa Lanchester, John Williams, Norma Varden, Henry Daniell, Torin Thatcher, Una O'Connor.

A dazzling courtroom drama from director Wilder, by way of Agatha Christie's novel and play, *Witness for the Prosecution* will keep viewers intrigued until the triple-surprise ending. Dapper Leonard Vole (Power) has been accused of murdering a wealthy widow (Varden), who has bequeathed him a fortune in her will. The celebrated barrister Sir Wilfrid Robarts (Laughton) takes his case, expecting the chief witness for the defense to be Vole's German-refugee wife, Christine (Dietrich). But on the stand, Christine swears that their marriage is bigamous and that Leonard confessed his guilt to her. Is she lying, and if so, why? A first-rate cast handles the plot's twists and turns with professional ease and even a few dollops of humor. The movie won six Oscar nominations, including one for Best Picture.

WOMAN IN THE WINDOW, THE

★★★☆ RKO, 1945, b/w, 99 m. Dir: Fritz Lang. SP: Nunnally Johnson, b/o novel by J. H. Wallis. Cast: Edward G. Robinson, Joan Bennett, Dan Duryea, Raymond Massey, Edmond Breon, Bobby (Robert) Blake.

In this gripping melodrama, Robinson sheds his thirties tough-guy image to play a soft-spoken psychology professor who finds himself trapped in a web of murder and deceit. Sexually obsessed with beautiful Bennett, he kills the man who attacked her in a jealous rage. Now he and Bennett are linked forever in a crime they desperately try to cover up. The ingredients for a quintessential film noir are all here, from dark city streets to an alluring and dangerous heroine, and director Lang serves them up piping hot. The only catch is a surprise ending that seriously undermines, without destroying, everything that went before.

WOMAN ON THE RUN

★★★ Universal-International, 1950, b/w, 77 min. Dir: Norman Foster. SP: Alan Campbell, Norman Foster, b/o story by Sylvia Tate. Cast: Ann Sheridan, Dennis O'Keefe, Robert Keith, Ross Elliott, Frank Jenks.

This modest but trimly turned out melodrama finds Ann Sheridan with an agonizing problem: her estranged husband (Elliott) witnessed a gangland killing and now he has disappeared. She desperately wants to find him before the persistent police or, more dangerously, the actual killer (O'Keefe) finds him first. (He's a reporter, pretending to help her.) Sheridan sheds her "Oomph Girl" image to give a credible performance as the terrified lady.

WRONG MAN, THE

★★★ Warner Bros., 1956, b/w, 105 min. Dir: Alfred Hitchcock. SP: Maxwell Anderson, Angus MacPhail, b/o story by Maxwell Anderson. Cast: Henry Fonda, Vera Miles, Anthony Quayle, Harold J. Stone, Nehemiah Persoff.

Hitchcock does a decent job of directing this true story, but it's simply not his sort of film. It concerns a musician named Manny Balestrero (Fonda) who, early in 1953, is accused of having committed several armed robberies. Although he is a hard-working family man with a wife (Miles) and two children, he is identified by several witnesses and brought to trial. The ordeal is so harrowing that his wife suffers a nervous breakdown. Eventually, he is exonerated. Fonda plays a familiar Hitchcock character—the innocent man trapped in a waking nightmare—but the movie's semidocumentary approach does not allow for the director's usual stylistic flourishes, and the result is moderately interesting but drab.

YEAR OF THE DRAGON

★★☆ MGM/UA, 1985, c, 136 min. Dir: Michael Cimino. SP: Oliver Stone, Michael Cimino, b/o novel by Robert Daley. Cast: Mickey Rourke, John Lone, Ariane, Leonard Termo, Ray Barry, Caroline Kava, Eddie Jones, Joey Chin.

Another self-indulgent exercise from Cimino, the director of *The Deer Hunter* and *Heaven's Gate*. Everything in *Year of the Dragon* is excessive: overheated atmosphere, overstated dialogue, overdecorated sets. Mickey Rourke is a police captain and Vietnam veteran who is determined to bring down the businessman

(Lone) who heads a vicious gang in New York City's Chinatown. (Interesting note: Chinatown was recreated on sets built in North Carolina.)

YOUNG DILLINGER

★★ Zimbalist, 1965, b/w, 102 min. Dir: Terry O. Morse. SP: Don Zimbalist, Arthur Hoerl. Cast: Nick Adams, Robert Conrad, Mary Ann Mobley, Victor Buono, Dan Terranova, John Hoyt.

A cheaply made film that purports to tell us about the early years of the notorious thirties gangster John Dillinger, played here with the appropriate snarl by Adams. Familiar figures from old gangster movies, such as Baby Face Nelson and Pretty Boy Floyd, appear as Dillinger's buddies.

YOU ONLY LIVE ONCE

★★★ Walter Wanger-United Artists, 1937, b/w, 86 min. Dir: Fritz Lang. SP: Gene Towne, Graham Baker. Cast: Henry Fonda, Sylvia Sidney, Barton MacLane, Jean Dixon, William Gargan, Jerome Cowan, Margaret Hamilton.

A loose reworking of the Bonnie and Clyde story, this bleak Depression drama has the doom-laden, fatalistic attitude characteristic of many of director Lang's films. Fonda plays an unlucky three-time loser who is returned to prison for a crime he did not commit. Bitter and desperate to be with his loyal wife (Sidney), he escapes from prison, killing a kindly priest (Gargan) in the process. The final consequences are tragic. The familiar Depression theme—a hostile, uncaring society breeds criminals—is overstated here; just about everyone treats poor Fonda with contempt or indifference. Still, *You Only Live Once* has a cumulative power that will keep you interested. Sidney, that quintessential Depression heroine, makes a touching figure as the beleaguered wife.

BillboardBooks

THANK YOU FOR BUYING A BILLBOARD BOOK. IF YOU ENJOYED THIS TITLE, YOU MIGHT WANT TO CHECK OUT OTHER BOOKS IN OUR CATALOG.

THE BIG BOOK OF SHOW BUSINESS AWARDS
by David Sheward
A handy resource guide covering the Oscar, Tony, Emmy, and Grammy awards as well as other major show business honors. Also provided is a wealth of historical information, gossip and trivia relating to the awards, and a gallery of lively photographs. *352 pages. 100 photos. Paperback. $21.95. 0-8230-7630-X*

THE ENCYCLOPEDIA OF DAYTIME TELEVISION
by Wesley Hyatt
The definitive daytime television resource, covering all series airing for three or more weeks on a commercial network between 1947 and 1996, plus 100 nationally syndicated programs. Each entry includes info on when the show began, how long it ran, and who its principal cast members were. *528 pages. 100 photos. $24.95. 0-8230-8315-2.*

THE HOLLYWOOD REPORTER BOOK OF BOX OFFICE HITS
Revised and Enlarged Edition by Susan Sackett
The complete scoop behind the top five motion picture box office successes each year since 1939. Fascinating behind-the-scenes stories and plenty of rare photos make this a must-have for movie fans and trivia buffs alike. *416 pages. 328 photos. Paperback. $21.95. 0-8230-8324-1.*

HOLLYWOOD SINGS
by Susan Sackett
An entertaining history of all songs nominated for the Academy Award each year since 1934. An engaging look at the tunes, the singers who performed them, and the movies in which they appeared. *336 pages. 125 photos. Paperback. $21.95. 0-8230-7623-7.*

PRIME TIME HITS
Television's Most Popular Network Programs by Susan Sackett
An entertaining, informative history of the most popular television series of the last 40 years with a focus on each year's top 10 shows, including vital statistics and fascinating background stories. *368 pages. 150 photos. Paperback. $19.95. 0-8230-8392-6.*

TERROR ON TAPE
by James O'Neill
The ultimate connoisseur's resource guide to horror movies on video. A complete, comprehensive guide to over 2,000 terrifying films from the past 75 years, from mainstream masterpieces to cheesy exploitation flicks, from cult classics to deservedly unknown bombs. *400 pages. 75 photos. Paperback. $16.95. 0-8230-7612-1.*

SCI-FI ON TAPE
by James O'Neill
An extensive, entertaining reference guide to over 1,250 science fiction and fantasy films available on videocassette, from pioneering motion pictures to the latest releases. Each entry includes a story synopsis, review notes, rating, and running time. *240 pages. 75 photos. Paperback. $16.95. 0-8230-7660-1.*

BLACK & WHITE BLUES:
Photographs by Marc Norberg, edited by B. Martin Pedersen
Portraits of 60 of the finest blues musicians of all time, with the artist's personal statement about the blues. A CD-ROM disc is packaged with the hardcover edition. *192 pages. 60 photos. Hardcover (with CD): $69.95. 0-8230-6480-8. Paperback: $45.95. 0-8230-6471-9.*

GRAPHIS MUSIC CDS
edited by B. Martin Pedersen
This wide-ranging international collection from Graphis Publications includes innovative covers, foldouts, inner sleeves, and compact disk surfaces created by graphic designers specializing in cover and packaging design for music CDs. *224 Pages. Over 300 illustrations. Hardcover. $75.95. 0-8230-6470-0.*

These titles should all be available from your neighborhood bookseller. If you don't find a copy on the shelf, books can also be ordered through the store or directly from Watson-Guptill Publications. To order by phone or to request information on any of these titles, please call our toll-free number: 1-800-278-8477. To order by mail, send a check or money order for the cost of the book, with $2.00 postage and handling for one book and $ .50 for each additional book, plus applicable sales tax in the states of CA, DC, IL, OH, MA, NJ, NY, PA, TN, and VA, to:

WATSON-GUPTILL PUBLICATIONS
PO Box 2013
Lakewood, NJ 08701-9913